King Saud al Saud before a portrait of his father at the Saudi Arabian Embassy in Washington when he visited this country as Crown Prince in January and February of 1947.

The Arabian Peninsula

RICHARD H. SANGER

ᘛᘚᘛᘚᘛᘚᘛᘚᘛᘚᘛᘚᘛᘚᘛᘚ

Cornell University Press, Ithaca, New York

PRINTED IN THE UNITED STATES OF AMERICA BY THE

VAIL-BALLOU PRESS, INC., BINGHAMTON, NEW YORK

Introduction

IN HIS remarkable book, *Civilization on Trial*, Professor Arnold J. Toynbee has written, "Future historians will say, I think, that the great event of the twentieth century was the impact of Western civilization upon all the other living societies of the world of that day. They will say of this impact that it was so powerful and so pervasive that it turned the lives of all its victims upside down and inside out." [1]

Nowhere has this "impact of Western civilization" been more striking than in the Arabian Peninsula. From the Red Sea to the Persian Gulf, from the Syrian desert to the Arabian Sea, the timeless heart of the Arab East is stirring; the Arabian Peninsula is beginning to move into the twentieth century. Up to twenty years ago, this great tract of land, larger than India and almost one-third the size of the United States, had been visited by only a few dozen Europeans, most of whom had seen little but its coastal cities. They reported that it was virtually unchanged since the time of the Prophet. Now, after standing still for twelve hundred years, time is on the march again in Arabia. A score of years have seen more changes in some parts of Arabia than have all the centuries since the death of Mohammed.

Many factors contributed to this change, including automobiles, airplanes, radios, and two world wars. But undoubtedly the two most important factors were the unification of most of the peninsula under a single strong ruler and that ruler's consolidation of his kingdom at the

[1] Oxford, 1948, p. 214.

time when the Western world discovered that the sands of Arabia were floating upon oil.

As a result, a pastoral, nomadic, and medieval society which had for centuries kept out almost all but Moslem visitors has begun to open its doors to non-Moslems. Limited first to a few Western geologists and executives, the number has increased year after year in Saudi Arabia, and to a lesser degree in the other countries of the Arabian Peninsula.

How this impact of Western civilization is turning the lives of some of the inhabitants of Arabia upside down is dramatically illustrated in the city of Jidda, Saudi Arabia's diplomatic capital on the Red Sea. The last seven years have seen the city's walls torn down, its main streets paved, its lagoon rimmed by electric lights, fresh water brought down from the hills, a radio station built nearby, a pier run out to deep water in its harbor, a busy, hard-surfaced airport constructed, and a building boom take place.

Planes of the Saudi Arabian Airlines span the country daily, crossing skies untraveled as little as ten years ago. Public utilities are going into Riyadh, King Saud's mud-walled capital in the heart of the Nejd, in whose narrow streets new convertibles and shiny station wagons are literally crowding camels to the walls. On the oil coast, in eastern Saudi Arabia, a standard-gauge railroad runs inland to Riyadh. A large pipe line flows oil to refineries on the Persian Gulf and northwest to the Mediterranean, and Dhahran, the central headquarters of the Arabian American Oil Company's operations, is the first city in the world to be centrally air-cooled. In fact, the Hasa province of Saudi Arabia, in which the oil coast is located and which was without European inhabitants twenty years ago, now contains one of the largest colonies of working Americans outside the territorial limits of the United States.

The impact of Western progress is striking in Saudi Arabia, but the fingers of change are pushing open the doors of half a dozen other Arab states. A town as modern as Phoenix, Arizona, has grown up around the oil company's intricate installations on the pearl-rich island of Bahrein; the tranquil waters of the Persian Gulf off the Sheikhdom of Kuwait are churned by the propellers of barges bringing drilling rigs, prefabricated houses, cold-storage units, and operating tables from a row of cargo steamers anchored not far from the newly constructed dock in the shadow of Kuwait City's mud wall.

Just south of the Sheikhdom of Kuwait, in that curious political anomaly, the Kuwait Neutral Zone, of which King Saud and the Sheikh of Kuwait each have undivided halves, the spring grass, burned by the sun to a tawny gold, is flattened by the footprints of geologists tapping the wadies for water and poking the sand dunes for oil. The bare, sandy ridges of the sheikhdom that comprises the Qatar Peninsula are furrowed by the trucks of drillers, pipe layers, and contractors. The bedouin of the seven tiny sheikhdoms that make up the Trucial Coast, their minds still on camels and raiding parties, look up to see planes circling above the wind-blown landing strip at Sharja. The dapper Sultan of Muscat, drowsing through the noontide in his high-roofed palace above the hot basalt rocks that guard his twin harbors, is anxious for Western help in the development of his country. Autos that were packed by pieces on the backs of camels over the mountain passes from the seaports of the southern coast now bump across the gravel wadies below the mud skyscrapers in the valley of the Hadhramaut, where an airlift brought food to the starving in the spring of 1949. The Crown Colony of Aden, England's Gibraltar at the southern end of the Red Sea, has gone in for town planning, while in the ruin-scattered hinterland of the Western Aden Protectorate, the lead of the Sultan of Lahej in installing electric lights and serving ice-cooled drinks is being followed by other local rulers. Even forbidden Yemen, after sleeping through the centuries behind a protecting mountain range whose lowest passes are over nine thousand feet, has received foreign missions and sent a prince to the United Nations.

Arabia is indeed changing under the impact of Western civilization, and no one who has seen its dust and dirt and poverty, its half-blind children, its women old before their time, and its men struggling to wring a barren living from a dust bowl of sun, sand, and rock, can doubt that on the material side the change is for the better. For some six centuries after Mohammed, this part of the Arab world was an active force. During the next six hundred years the drive died out, to be revived again in the 1930's. If Arabia can assimilate the progressive know-how of the West while retaining her inner calm, then her future will be more a renascence than an echo of her vigorous past.

If the whole world is to benefit, the ever-widening circles of change must prove helpful to more than the distant countries of the Western world, whose engines are drinking deep of Persian Gulf oil. The change must modernize the thinking of the kings, sheikhs, and sultans of Arabia with their air-cooled palaces, Cadillac convertibles, and evergrowing oil royalties. It must bring a broader outlook to the wealthy merchants in their lofty countinghouses by the newly made harbors of the Red Sea and the Persian Gulf, merchants whose trade is shifting overnight from frankincense and harem silks to bulldozers and radios. It must affect the labor and irrigation policies of the great landowners, whose palm groves stretch as far as a camel can walk in a day, and the powerful sheikhs, whose herds of black sheep and flocks of tawny camels cover the wadies in spring.

The change must also help the struggling bedouin, who need new wells to water their scrawny flocks. It must give employment to the beggars in the towns, who in the past have looked to Allah and the King's bounty for a handful of dried dates and a bowl of camel milk and who are now finding employment as unskilled workers in the budding industrial revolution. It must benefit the artisans and handicraft workers, who can make more in a week running a lathe than they could in a month ornamenting sandals. It must enrich the petty merchants, sitting cross-legged in their stalls, whose trade is fast reviving as the earning power of the people rises. It must give direction to the intellectuals, who can replace days of endless talk over black coffee and nights of recounting the past with hours of learning of the present and planning for the future that will make them the teachers, doctors, engineers, and builders of a new Arabia. Above all, it must produce a sense of social consciousness to replace the fast-fading feudal and tribal obligations.

So far, the United States has played the major role in these changes, largely through the initiative and farsightedness of private industry, but it has no monopoly. England, Holland, and France, as well as the neighboring Arab countries of Egypt, Lebanon, Syria, and Iraq, are all helping to alter Arabia, assisting it to exchange its oil, gold, air routes, and pilgrimage revenues for the machinery and techniques of the Western world. Distance from the West, severe climate, deserts, lack of water, and six hundred years of highly localized, fragmented government all contribute to the difficulty of the task. Former President Truman in his Inaugural Address, introducing what has come to be known as Point Four, anticipated United States help in facing this difficulty. Speaking on January 20, 1949, he said:

We must embark on a bold new program for making the benefits of our scientific advances and industrial progress available for the improvement and growth of underdeveloped areas.

More than half the people of the world are living in conditions approaching misery. Their food is inadequate. They are victims of disease. Their economic life is primitive and stagnant. Their poverty is a handicap and a threat both to them and to more prosperous areas.

For the first time in history, humanity possesses the knowledge and the skill to relieve the suffering of these people.

If Western civilization succeeds in helping the Arabs toward a higher standard of living, the pattern of life in this subcontinent where the rich tend to stay unproductively rich and the poor remain too poor, where the sick too often fail to get well and the average man pays a high toll to ignorance, may be reoriented toward a new Arab culture befitting both the past and the new age. A middle class may develop with opportunity to build in the heart of the Near East a bastion against all forces of totalitarianism. This is the challenge of Arabia. It cannot be met in a year or a decade, but if the present pace of change continues, the outward lives of many of the next generation will be very different from those of their fathers. The inner, deeper changes we must wait for our sons' sons to assess.

This book is an attempt to make the average reader aware of the new frontier which has sprung up on the Arabian Peninsula, of the American role in developing it, and of the challenge which it presents to us, to other Western nations, and to the Arabs. This effort to suggest what Arabia is like today, to give sufficient history and background to show why it is that way, and to indicate the various paths down which Arabia may go in the future is not political and it is not all-inclusive. But I have intended to tell enough of the walled cities and bedouin camps, the sandy deserts and barren mountains, the ancient cultures and colorful rulers, and the plain people, so that the reader may better understand the scope, importance, and new-found vitality of the Arabian Peninsula.

RICHARD H. SANGER

Washington, D.C.
December 1953

Contents

	Introduction	v
I	Jidda: Diplomatic Capital and Pilgrim Gateway	1
II	Reopening One of King Solomon's Mines	16
III	The Rise of the House of Saud	27
IV	King Saud al Saud	41
V	Model Farms of Al Kharj	58
VI	The People of the Tent	73
VII	The People of the Palm	89
VIII	Aramco: America's Largest Near East Investment	99
IX	Up and Down the Oil Coast	113
X	British Explorers of the Empty Quarter	125
XI	Bahrein: Islands of Pearls and Petroleum	140
XII	Kuwait: Salem of the Persian Gulf	150
XIII	The Trucial Coast: Pirates and Petty Sheikhdoms	170
XIV	Muscat: Our Oldest Near Eastern Friend	184
XV	The Colony of Aden: England's Arabian Gibraltar	201
XVI	The Aden Protectorates: Lands of Incense and Skyscrapers	213
XVII	Land of the Imam	235
XVIII	Mission to Yemen	253
XIX	Revolt in San'a	272
	Acknowledgments	280
	Bibliography	282
	Index	289

Illustrations

King Saud al Saud before a portrait of his father at the Saudi Arabian Embassy in Washington when he visited this country as Crown Prince in January and February of 1947, *frontispiece*

Following page xvi

1. Sailing dhows landing at Jidda with Moslems on their annual pilgrimage to Mecca
2. Harem balconies in an old section of Jidda

Following page 32

3. Heavily laden camels crossing a paved thoroughfare in Jidda
4. The plant of the Saudi Arabian Mining Syndicate at Mahad Dhahab
5. Pilgrims in Jidda boarding a bus
6. The late King Abdul Aziz ibn Saud
7. Entrance to the palace of the late King at Riyadh

Following page 64

8. Laying the Trans-Arabian Pipe Line
9. Saudi Arab employees riding a Diesel engine of the new Saudi Arabian Railroad
10. Modern agricultural machinery on an Al Kharj district farm
11. Harvesting young onions on a farm in the Al Kharj district

Following page 96

12. Bedouin family serving coffee to an American guest from the oil coast

13. The author in a date garden of Hofuf

14. Bedouin watering their camels at a Saudi Arabian oasis

Following page 128

15. Twilight view of Arabian American Oil Company's stabilizer installation at Dhahran

16. A Saudi Arab plant operator instructing Arabian American Oil Company trainees

17. Awali, a residential section on Bahrein Island

Following page 160

18. Sheikh Sir Salman ibn Hamad al Khalifah, ruler of Bahrein

19. The suq in Kuwait

20. Primitive methods used in lifting water in a palm garden

Following page 192

21. A deep-sea dhow in the port of Kuwait

22. Sixteenth-century Portuguese fort guarding Matrah Harbor in Muscat

23. Skyscrapers of Shibam in the Hadhramaut

Following page 224

24. Aden harbor, with Steamer Point in the distance

25. Colonel William A. Eddy signing the agreement of commerce and friendship with Yemen in the guesthouse in San'a, April 1946

26. The entrance to the Moon Temple at Marib

Following page 256

27. Wood market in the central square in San'a, Yemen

28. A house in the residential section of San'a

MAPS

1. Physical map of the Arabian Peninsula, *page 18*

2. Political map of the Arabian Peninsula, *page 19*

Unless otherwise indicated, all illustrations were supplied by the Arabian American Oil Company or by the author.

The Arabian Peninsula

1. Sailing dhows landing at the Red Sea port of Jidda with Moslems from all over the world on their annual pilgrimage to Mecca. The passengers were picked up from steamships in the harbor.

2. Harem balconies in an old section of Jidda. The parapeted architecture is typical of cities in this part of the Arabian Peninsula.

I

Jidda: Diplomatic Capital
and Pilgrim Gateway

THE plane for Jidda rises slowly in the cool Egyptian dawn, sweeping low over the modern hotels and the ancient mud-washed columns of the temple of Luxor. As it climbs higher, the traveler to Arabia catches a glimpse of two stone statues of Memnon standing tall and lonely in a green field across the Nile. Beyond, the ruins of the City of the Dead drowse in the early-morning sunshine. The winding green ribbon of the Nile Valley narrows behind as the plane bumps and drones above the brown hills and eroded wadies of Egypt's Arabian Desert. For the next hundred miles a camel caravan plodding single file along a desert track may be the only sign of life below. Then the plane strikes the cloud bank that forms where the moist air from the Red Sea hits the dry Egyptian mountains, and the bare summits of the coastal range are blotted from sight.

Soon the plane emerges into the blue sunshine, and the warm waters of the Red Sea, brushed by the northwest breeze, stretch below, crisp with whitecaps. For an hour the flight runs straight into the morning sun, and the plane dodges white clouds that seem to rise from the sea. On the far right the twin peaks of Nugrus and Hamata guard the southeastern corner of Egypt. Gradually they fade into the distance. A faint line appears ahead and sharpens into a series of surf-whitened reefs from which light-green shallows run back to a brown shore line. This is the coast line of Saudi Arabia, the Arabia of the Sauds—the threshold

1

of more than eight hundred thousand square miles of desert, rocky plateaus, palm-filled oases, Moslem shrines, and oil fields.

Just offshore the plane turns, skirting the barren coast stretching eastward to the seven-thousand-foot peak of Mount Radhwa. Below lies the town of Yanbu, a faint white speck on the monotonous coast line. Near this seaport for Medina the Roman general Aelius Gallus, the first well-known European traveler in the Arabian Peninsula, outfitted his expedition to Yemen in 24 B.C.; close by its harbor the Turks turned back in World War I and so lost their British-Arabian campaign.[1]

An hour's flying time from Yanbu, changing pressure on the traveler's eardrums gives notice that the plane is dropping down over Jidda, chief Saudi Arabian seaport, water gate for the Mecca-bound pilgrims, and the diplomatic capital of Saudi Arabia. Passing a group of sand-blown huts occupied by African Negroes and a flat bit of desert which the foreigners of Jidda bravely call the golf course, the plane sweeps over the new compound of the American Embassy. Beyond it rise the red walls of many buildings, including the Saudi Arabian Mining Syndicate headquarters. Then come the Royal Garage and Motor Park, western headquarters of the fleet of trucks with which King Saud is supplanting camels on the main routes of his kingdom. On a bluff ahead the traveler sees a modernistic green stucco house of the sort favored by Egyptian pashas, which was formerly the residence of the United States Ambassador to Saudi Arabia. Beyond lie more houses and the open roadstead of Jidda, where foam-splashed reefs shelter a fleet of native dhows and a growing number of small steamers. The rusty hull of the French liner "Asia," which, loaded with pilgrims from Yemen, piled up on a reef in Jidda harbor and burned one stormy night in 1934, is still visible. According to local recollection of the tragedy, many of the pilgrims on board, moved at the sight of the "Holy Land," believed the fire an act of Allah and knelt in prayer instead of trying to save themselves. Few were saved except those forcibly thrown overboard by a party of English rescuers.

Now the plane banks sharply over the city, showing the traveler rows of closely packed four- and five-story houses, built of white or yellow stucco, some of them leaning at alarming angles from the perpendicular. At last it lands at the modern sand-swept airport a mile east of the town; the Arab steward throws open the door; and the hot, sandy breath of Arabia fills the plane.

Our traveler, accustomed to the sights of Cairo, finds little in Jidda

[1] T. E. Lawrence, *Seven Pillars of Wisdom*, pp. 127, 130.

that is familiar. No trolleys clang through its dusty streets; no movie houses line its thoroughfares; and most of its back lanes are just wide enough for two donkeys to pass under the carved projecting balconies for which the city is justly famous. The relentless Arab sun has cracked the dry plaster of the older buildings, and the balconies themselves are worn smooth, bereft of paint. Often the very walls seem to lean in dejection as their foundations settle slowly into the mud flats of the Red Sea shore. The effect is that of a city which, long slumbering on its feet, has lacked space to lie down and sleep properly.

The dusty lanes of Jidda, sprinkled rarely by a primitive water cart, become quagmires after the cloudbursts that annually break over the city. The sand of the coastal plain lies heavy over the town. It swirls in brown clouds on gusty days and settles quietly on sill, table, and floor when the wind is stilled. Jidda, with its heat, dust, smells, and flies, powerfully rocks the traveler's senses. As he gradually adjusts, the strangeness is dispelled and the dramatic transformation the city is undergoing claims his attention.

Until the middle of 1947, the city of Jidda was surrounded by a high wall of mud and stone, which had kept off attack for generations but which also kept out the refreshing Red Sea breeze that alone could make life bearable there during the summer months. The manner of its passing was as follows:

One day in the late spring of 1947, Mr. English, an American vice-president of the International Bechtel Corporation, a firm which with the Arabian American Oil Company (Aramco) has greatly changed the face of Saudi Arabia, was driving around Jidda with Sheikh Abdullah Suleiman, Minister of Finance for Saudi Arabia. They were discussing a project long dear to Sheikh Abdullah's heart, the construction of a pier in the harbor of Jidda which would enable ocean-going steamers to come alongside.

"Where can we obtain fill?" the Finance Minister asked as the car passed through a gate in the wall of Jidda.

The engineer considered a moment. Then he gestured toward the wall. "There is the sort of material we need."

"Then take the wall down and use it," ordered the Finance Minister.

It remained standing for some time longer, however, and the rumor spread that it was too much for Bechtel. But one day, within twenty-four hours, dynamite charges were set off all along the base, and the whole structure went down like the walls of Jericho, to be flattened by a battery of bulldozers and hauled away in giant trucks. The dirt

3

and rocks that kept Arab, Egyptian, and Portuguese invaders out of Jidda now help travelers to come ashore.

The town of Jidda dates from pre-Mohammedan times, but its history as an important city began in A.D. 648 when the Caliph Othman chose it as the harbor for Mecca. In 1541 a Portuguese squadron made an unsuccessful attack on the town, thus beginning somewhat inauspiciously the long and bizarre history of the city's relations with Europe.

During the nineteenth century the British and French established consulates in the city, and a small number of European merchants took up residence there, although the stricter Moslems objected to this intrusion of unbelievers on the sacred soil of the Hejaz. In 1858 resentment flared up unexpectedly. According to the London *Times* of July 15, 1858, the British cruiser "Cyclops" had been in the harbor of Jidda for a week after bringing the British and French consuls from Suez. Everything appeared calm until the evening of June 15, when some Greek residents of Jidda who swam out to the "Cyclops" reported that a mob of fanatics had forced its way into the British Consulate, sacked the house, torn down the flag, and killed Mr. Page, the British consul. This report was followed by the news that shortly afterward the same mob had killed M. Eveillard, the French consul, and his wife and had wounded his daughter. The next day the crew of the "Cyclops" tried to land, but they were beaten from the pier. Rioting continued for four days until the governor of the Hejaz arrived from Mecca with five hundred Turkish soldiers and restored order. By that time a total of twenty-one Christians had been murdered. When the Turkish authorities refused to take action against the rioters, the "Cyclops" shelled the town until eleven of the culprits were hanged. The crew then landed and, escorted by a body of Turkish infantry, marched to the newly made graves, which can still be seen in the small European cemetery south of the town. Jidda, incidentally, was again captured by the British Navy during World War I as a start in the campaign to push the Turks out of Arabia.

The United States first recognized the Kingdom of Saudi Arabia on May 1, 1931. Bert Fish, the first American Minister who was also Minister to Egypt, presented his credentials on February 4, 1940, but never set up residence in Jidda. It was not until May 1, 1942, that well-trained, Arabic-speaking Foreign Service Officer James S. Moose, Jr., now United States Ambassador to Syria, opened a legation there as chargé d'affaires.

Moose could not reach his post by plane, for though the first commercial plane had flown into Jidda in the late 1930's and British Over-

4

seas Airways started a weekly service the year he arrived, the airport was, at the date of his assignment, a little-used strip of gravel fighting a losing battle against drifting sands. Consequently Moose came down the Red Sea on the S.S. "Talodi" accompanied by Karl S. Twitchell, J. G. Hamilton, and A. L. Wathen, members of the first United States agricultural mission to Saudi Arabia, who were on their way to make a survey of agricultural and water resources. Because there was no hotel at that time, he was given accommodations by the Arabian American Oil Company until he located a chancery, which he used as combined office and living quarters. He had no desks at first and no typewriters for six months. For a long time he used a barrel for filing unclassified documents. He had brought with him a suitcase full of stationery and code material, and as the dial on his safe would not work, he was forced to sleep with his confidential documents under his bed. Communication with the outside world was by monthly steamer or by slow cable service through Port Sudan, and social companionship was largely restricted to approximately forty Christians, including only four women, eight Americans, and about a dozen Europeans. It fell to Moose under these trying conditions to work out the pattern of basic United States–Saudi official relations.

Moose was succeeded in August 1944 by the distinguished soldier and scholar Colonel William A. Eddy, whose fluent command of Arabic, attained during his youth, contributed greatly to the strengthening of United States ties with Saudi Arabia. The most famous incident of his strenuous wartime term of office occurred in January 1945 after he escorted the late King Ibn Saud, members of the royal family, retainers, and provisions, including a small flock of sheep, on board the United States destroyer "Quincy." Although the King had been to Bahrein and Kuwait, this was his first trip out of sight of the Arabian Peninsula. The meeting between President Roosevelt and King Ibn Saud which followed at Great Bitter Lake in the Suez Canal marked the high point in American-Arab friendship.

On July 1, 1946, Colonel Eddy resigned as Minister and was succeeded by J. Rives Childs, a Foreign Service officer and career Minister with a long and brilliant career in Arab countries from Tangier to the Persian Gulf. For more than four years Childs served in Jidda coping with the problems of postwar readjustment and the strains brought about by the Palestine situation. The Saudi Arabian and United States Government signed their first agreement concerning the strategic Dhahran airfield during his tenure of office. On March 18, 1949, he became

5

the first United States Ambassador to Saudi Arabia, which post he held until September 1950. He was replaced by another career officer, experienced and wise in the ways of the Middle East, Raymond A. Hare, who served until mid-1953. The present United States Ambassador to Saudi Arabia is George Wadsworth, a veteran diplomat who has spent a lifetime in the Near East.

Visitors to Jidda during the early postwar years used to be put up at the Hotel Jidda, a wartime innovation fifty yards to the south of the faded yellow chancery. A four-story building, unblessed by fly screens, clean beds, dependable electric lights, or running water, this hostelry housed many of the State Department officials and most of the American businessmen who came to the city before the present hotel was built.

In contrast to this earlier Red Sea hostelry, Beit Aramco, the Arabian American Oil Company's nearby Jidda headquarters, is an excellent example of Jiddawi architecture. It leans hardly at all from the perpendicular and had its origin as the town house of a rich merchant family. No cracks mar its plaster, the shutters of its unbroken windows are freshly painted, and its tiers of brown balconies have a New Orleans flavor about their carved grillwork. Here, the Arabian American Oil Company, chiefly represented in Jidda by Garry Owen, who is in charge of government relations, houses its Jidda staff. The rooms are air cooled, the commissary is well stocked, and the whole atmosphere makes a visit to Beit Aramco on a steaming Jidda morning as refreshing as a trip to the mountains of Lebanon.

A street formerly ran around Jidda just inside the wall. Now that the wall has been razed, the way has been broadened into an outer boulevard which runs from Beit Aramco to the edge of the harbor and then south along the waterfront. On it stands a series of imposing buildings with which the visitor soon becomes familiar. They include the Egyptian, Dutch, Syrian, Iraqi, Lebanese, and French Legations, the Chinese and other Consulates, and the British Embassy.

In the British garden is a wooden bandstand, which was built in World War I under unusual circumstances. According to Lawrence, he and Ronald Storrs, who was in charge of a British political mission to Arabia at that time, were talking one night when the telephone rang and Sherif Hussein in Mecca asked if the Englishmen would not like to listen to a brass band from the Hejaz command of the Turks, one which had been captured near Taif. Storrs and Lawrence replied in the affirmative, listened over the telephone to the band playing in Mecca,

6

and expressed their thanks; whereupon the Sherif announced that the band would be sent to Jidda by forced marches to play for the British in person.[2]

Soon afterward Prince Abdullah, one of the four sons of Sherif Hussein, came to dinner at the British headquarters followed, as usual, by his brilliantly dressed household servants and slaves. Behind them were a group of tired, unshaven men, wearing torn Turkish uniforms and carrying tarnished instruments. They were Hussein's band, just arrived after a hard march from Mecca and forced without a rest to grind out "heartbroken Turkish airs." While they were playing, the Sherif called up from Mecca on his telephone and listened in. On being asked to play something European, the musicians broke into an inappropriate and scarcely recognizable version of "Deutschland über Alles." After dinner the Englishmen sent food to the poor wretches, who begged to be sent back to Turkey; but Prince Abdullah and his father liked the band too well to part with it, and the bandstand was built for its use.

Along the outer boulevard among the legations are the headquarters of the important Western companies doing business in Jidda. These include the American construction firm of International Bechtel, the American Eastern Trading Corporation, and the British company Gellatly Hankey, perhaps the best-known trading firm on the Red Sea. The last not only carries on an extensive import and export business but does banking on the side. By piping water to Jidda from the oasis of Wadi Fatima, some thirty miles to the east, Gellatly Hankey also helped to lessen the shortage of fresh water in Jidda which used to occur when the pilgrims swelled the population from twenty thousand to one hundred thousand or more.

To inaugurate this modern water system, a great celebration was held on November 18, 1947, climaxed by a reception at the fountain outside the north gate of the city where the pipe ended. More than twenty-six thousand people gathered around the tents which sheltered the Finance Minister and his guest of honor, the Crown Prince, now the ruler of Saudi Arabia, members of the royal family, the diplomatic corps, and other notables. In keeping with the modern spirit of the occasion, lengthy speeches were carried by a public address system, but the crowd showed more interest in the six planes of the Saudi Arabian Airlines, which American pilots flew in tight formation back and forth over the city, than it did in the flow of oratory, or the fact that the Crown Prince himself took the first drink from a specially made silver cup.

[2] *Ibid.*, pp. 73–75.

A little south beyond the house of the British Ambassador, the outer boulevard jogs inland, leaving the water-condenser plant, a newly opened auto showroom, and an enormous old mansion called Beit Baghdadi on the waterside. Beit Baghdadi is one of the finest examples of Jidda architecture to be seen. Hand-carved shutters cover its windows; its walls, broken by a series of dilapidated screened balconies, hand-carved and unpainted, impart an air of shabby grandeur handed down from the days when it housed the Turkish Governor. The noted explorer of Arabia, H. St. John B. Philby, once lived in Beit Baghdadi, and it was Aramco's first home in Jidda.

On the land side of this rambling structure, now housing almost fifty families, lies the entrance to the *suq*, or market. As part of Jidda's modernization plan, a large arcade has been built to provide modern shopping space. Dubbed the Amir Faisal Suq, it is not full at present because many of the merchants prefer their time-honored locations in the dirty, noisy, colorful Old Suq. The latter consists of narrow, winding alleys lined with small stores and screened from the burning Arab sun by flimsy awnings of wood and straw matting. Most of the shops are little booths that range in size from that of a money-changer, who sits in an alcove four feet square, to that of a rug merchant, which may be twenty by thirty feet. In one section, the Wall Street of Arabia, bearded money-changers are ready to trade in all the currencies of the world. The British gold sovereign is the highest-priced coin in Jidda, because it is used for hoarding and for large transactions. Whereas the world price for the gold sovereign is about $8.25, the rate in Jidda varies from eleven to twenty dollars, depending on supply and demand. Even gold sovereigns differ in value, the King George coin being worth more than the Edward sovereign and the Edward in turn topping that bearing Queen Victoria's image. This is not, as is sometimes said, because the Arabs object to the sight of an unveiled woman, but because they reason that wear and tear have reduced the metallic content of the older coin.

The standard coin of Saudi Arabia is the riyal, a silver piece worth about twenty-five cents, which is now being minted in England, the United States, and Mexico. The extensive activities of the Arabian American Oil Company, with its huge payroll, has increased the need for riyals tremendously, and at times shipments of newly minted riyals have had to be flown from the United States to prevent financial crises. It is amusing to see these shipments of silver unloaded under heavy guard and then picked up casually by an Arab truck driver and taken without guard to the bank or the Finance Ministry, where they lie about in boxes for weeks quite unwatched.

Another coin frequently seen in Jidda is the Maria Theresa thaler, which was until recently the standard coin of Ethiopia and is still the recognized currency of Yemen. Silver thalers were originally minted in Austria, but they have been counterfeited in most of the Near East. They bring from forty to seventy cents in the Jidda market, depending on the condition of the coin and the volume of recent purchases between Yemen and Ethiopia. No paper money is issued in Saudi Arabia. Some of the Jiddawi money-changers have remarkable collections of old Turkish, Czarist Russian, Indian, and Chinese coins, along with antiquities from Rome, Greece, and the Himyarite civilization of southern Arabia.

Partly because of a strong stand taken by the late King Ibn Saud, a rigid Moslem puritan, against the making of images and paintings, the handicraft seen in Jidda tends to be both crude and uninteresting. Among the best of the items offered the foreigner are wooden sandals with leather bindings, decorated in blue and silver inlay. Jiddawi craftsmen also make bracelets, earrings, and belt buckles out of silver coins. Some rugs are manufactured, but for the most part Saudi Arabian merchants get their rugs from Iran and India. Only small amounts of goat's and camel's hair cloth are made locally, but large stocks of textiles come from the four corners of the earth, Indian products predominating in the cheaper grades and British and American in the more expensive, now in good supply. Japanese textiles, which were important before the last war, are again appearing. The few tourists who come ashore show a preference for Indian brass pots and decorated brass trays.

Unless the European has a blunted sense of smell, he would do well to avoid the stalls of the fish sellers late in the day. In the early morning, however, these vendors offer a splendid variety of fresh Red Sea fish brought by the fishing boats of Jidda and by runners from fishermen in nearby villages. Regardless of the time of day, only those with strong stomachs should frequent the stalls where thin carcasses of sheep, goats, and steers hang quivering with flies. Though such meat and the meager local vegetables may cause "Jidda tummy," health restrictions are constantly being tightened, and their effectiveness was shown by the complete absence of cholera in Saudi Arabia at the time of the severe outbreak in Egypt in the autumn of 1947. At that time all incoming visitors, including the King's sons, were kept in quarantine on an island in the harbor of Jidda for five days before they were allowed to land.

Many of the booths in the suq offer an assortment of dusty junk which might be the leavings of a small farm auction. Keys, crude lanterns, candlesticks, trays beaten out of old tin cans, odd bits of metal, matches, fragments of cloth, and bric-a-brac mingle with charcoal, pots and pans, and tins of kerosene. But the apparent forlornness of the wares does not deter the shoppers. They pack the narrow stalls. Arrogant Jiddawis in spotless white dress, brown-robed bedouin from the desert, and ragged beggars all jostle one another and members of the palace guard wearing Sam Browne belts and scimitars. Ethiopian servants, broad-shouldered and erect, carry the purchases made by their heavily veiled mistresses, who come to shop for their middle-class households in the morning hours and fill the suq with their shrill bargaining.

Beyond the suq, on the main boulevard, stands the modern office building of Jidda's largest commercial firm, the Netherlands Trading Society, locally known as the Dutch Bank. Of the millions of Moslems in the Dutch East Indies, thousands pass through Jidda each year on their way to Mecca. The Dutch Bank has grown prosperous handling their affairs. Another financial house, the Banque de l'Indochine, has also a branch in Jidda, where it is carrying on a very profitable business trading in gold sovereigns.

Jidda has many mosques. Most of these have no minarets because of the puritan tastes of the rulers of Saudi Arabia. A mosque near the bank, however, has not only a minaret, but one which is so far out of plumb as to rival the leaning tower of Pisa.

South of the Dutch Bank stands the former staff house of the American Embassy. From 1945 to 1947 this also accommodated the American Legation clinic, which provided the only modern medical care available in western Saudi Arabia during the war.

The outer boulevard eventually broadens into the Midan Malik Abdul Aziz, the principal square of Jidda, center of all public festivity and receptions and occasionally a place of execution. Here the customhouse stands on the waterside, flanked by the many arches of the quarantine pier and by pilgrim docks that stretch along the waterfront for a considerable distance. Most of the time these docks handle only light coastal traffic from such Saudi ports as Wedj, Yanbu, and Lith, or from Port Sudan, or from Hodeida in Yemen. But for two months each year they present a scene of feverish activity as forty thousand to one hundred and fifty thousand pilgrims flow into Jidda from every corner of the Moslem world. Speaking a score of Arab dialects and a dozen other languages besides and ranging from indigents who work their pilgrimage by begging to wealthy merchants and princes with retinues of half a hundred persons, they swarm into the city like flocks of migrating birds.

Most pilgrims make the trip to Mecca only once in their lifetime; often they save for years before the event and spend heavily on their trip. This makes the pilgrimage big business and, when war or disease do not prevent, six to eight million dollars in various foreign currencies flow into the coffers of King Saud. A few pilgrims struggle along taking a year or two to reach Jidda, but the average Moslem's trip is planned and run for him by an agent, who takes his money and arranges every detail of the passage. Although some pilgrims still come overland by camel and three to four thousand of the richer Moslems fly to Mecca, the bulk of the faithful arrive by boat, spend their five days at the quarantine stations of Tor or Jidda, and then come ashore at the pilgrim docks. Arrival in the Moslem Holy Land is a great emotional experience for the more devout, who fall on their knees and kiss the earth trod by Mohammed. Most of the houses of Jidda take in paying guests during the pilgrimage season, but a substantial number of pilgrims sleep in the streets. During the months when the pilgrim tide is flowing, the Midan Malik is packed night and day with groups of encamped pilgrims. Some sleep on reed beds in open-air "hotels" on the Mecca road outside the city. Most are men, but a certain number of Moslem women go to Mecca each year, and their presence adds to the confusion and mystery of Jidda in pilgrimage time.

From Jidda most of the pilgrims used to make the journey to Mecca on the backs of lumbering camels. In keeping with the modernization of Arabia, however, a fleet of buses now travels a hard-surfaced road from Jidda to Mecca, thus cutting the time of travel from two days to two hours. Loud-speakers have been installed in and around Mecca so that all pilgrims can hear the services. It is interesting to speculate whether, if the pilgrimage becomes too easy, it may lose some of its spiritual value.

No non-Moslem is permitted to go up the Mecca road beyond the stone gateposts some fifteen miles outside Mecca in the hot, black foothills. A few rash souls, among them Sir Richard Burton, have taken grave risks to give us detailed accounts of the fervent religious spirit often witnessed in the last stage of the pilgrimage.

Next to the green quarantine pier on the Jidda waterfront stands the candy-pink Finance Ministry, from which astute Sheikh Abdullah Suleiman, Ibn Saud's right-hand adviser for so long, handled the rapidly

11

growing finances of Saudi Arabia. He spent much of his time in Jidda, although major financial questions like all other important matters in Saudi Arabia have always been decided at the political capital, Riyadh.

In striking contrast to the older buildings in Jidda, there stands at the southern end of the newly paved Midan Malik the whitewashed Ford and Lincoln showroom, repair shop, and office building belonging to the Alireza family. This powerful merchant clan, one of the richest in the Hejaz, amassed a fortune of several million dollars through trading in pearls, harem silks, and frankincense. Now, however, it is concentrating on Fords, Lincolns, and Zenith radios. Arabia's first neon sign lights the showroom façade at night, and a gleaming, new, four-door sedan usually stands behind the big glass windows, surrounded by colored advertisements of station wagons and convertibles, car styles much admired by the Arabs.

One order for trucks placed in the United States by the Alirezas was so large that the firm chartered an entire ship to deliver it to Jidda. Until 1949 there were no docks anywhere on the Red Sea coast of Saudi Arabia where an ocean-going ship could tie up; for this reason the Alirezas have an LST which can push its nose onto the sand and put cars and trucks ashore wherever they are needed. The garage adjoining the showroom is a model of efficiency, and the warehouse is crammed with spare parts, for motor vehicles wear out fast in Saudi Arabia. Much of the modernity is due to Ali, the younger son of the Alireza family, a graduate of the University of California who is married to an American girl and who is a great believer in American ways. Ali would like to devote his time to business, but owing to his knowledge of America he has spent most of his days recently acting as interpreter and adviser to Crown Prince Faisal, Saudi Arabian Foreign Minister and its chief delegate to the United Nations, and is now Minister of State.

The most desirable place to live in the environs of Jidda is on or near the road to the airport or on the relatively high ground to the north of the city. Just as the French colonizers in North Africa left the old Arab cities comparatively untouched and built new suburbs for European residents outside the walls, so the foreign colony and the richer inhabitants of Jidda are moving out of town to the north and east. The roads to this development leave the old city where the Mecca gate once stood and skirt a shallow lagoon in which Arabs are busily filling small dugouts with dark-brown clay to serve as mortar for binding the coral blocks in the new Jidda structures. Already the lagoon is bordered by a string of street lights that illumine the northern extension of the outer

12

boulevard, the site of the new Saudi Arabian Foreign Office building.

The rambling yellow barracks of the Jidda garrison stand on the inland side of the lagoon road, their gate flanked by high-wheeled, saluting cannon. Driving on past rows of new houses, one can see the flat roofs of the King's palace, a building whose chief distinguishing feature is a circular automobile ramp running up to the second story.

Travelers are puzzled by an enclosure to the northeast of the old Mecca gate. Here a wall surrounds a mound some forty feet in length which, according to tradition, is the tomb of Eve. It was once a great tourist attraction, but veneration of such a shrine was distasteful to the strict Wahhabi tenets of Ibn Saud, and the entrance has been sealed. The Jiddawis still insist, however, that the town is called Jidda, or "grandmother" in Arabic, because Eve is buried there.

Whether women had their origin near Jidda or not, the present status of women there has its roots deep in a period prior to Islam. The lives of Jiddawi women are changing, but Islam and ancient custom have combined in a pattern of life so rigid that few women have broken through it to lead anything approaching independent lives. In the center of a square, in front of the former American chancery, there stands a dusty, heavily shuttered structure of stucco and unpainted wood known as the Indigent Women's Home. Here widows, women who have no relatives to take care of them, or women who have proved themselves too difficult to fit into any normal household are cared for through the charity of the local merchants. Normally every woman in Saudi Arabia is under the care of her nearest male relative, a pattern of society laid down by Mohammed, who was deeply disturbed by the low estate in which he found the women of the Hejaz.

Mohammed allowed every good Moslem to have no more than four wives at a time and those only if he could do justice to all of them. The place of women was in theory protected by law, divorce was regulated, and the property rights of women were laid down. His belief that women should not be forced to fend for themselves in the struggle for life persists today.

American men in Jidda never speak to Arab women and seldom see them unveiled, although they know that the women watch them from the lattice-covered balconies found in all Jidda homes. However, the few American women who have been stationed in Jidda, either in the Foreign Service or as wives of American businessmen, are able to transmit an impression of what life is like for the women in the better homes.

Jiddawi women, even wealthy ones, do not fit into the traditional Eng-

13

lish or American picture of harem glamour. Overrich cooking, complete lack of exercise, and unhygienic habits frequently lead to sickness, and a general lack of schooling perpetuates illiteracy. A certain amount of time is spent with their children, but many nurses are available and the load is not taxing. Furthermore, there is the Arab custom of assigning a little boy or girl servant of the same sex and age to every child, assuring each a playmate.

Arab women while away most of the day in talking, eating, and drinking innumerable cups of coffee and glasses of tea. Conversation centers on food, health, children, sex, and clothes. Much of their attention is devoted to dress, and the women of Jidda love spangles and great amounts of costume jewelry.

Even in the harem, however, the impact of the Western world is apparent. Western European clothing, especially evening dress, has found favor with the women of the wealthier families. Some of the larger homes of Jidda now have their own power plants, electric lights, ceiling fans, refrigerators, and, in a few cases, air cooling. A growing network of telephone speeds gossip. The introduction of running water into the city in 1947 has brought modern bathrooms. Most of the richer Jiddawi have American automobiles, and there is a traffic jam at five o'clock each evening as the merchants take their wives and children, previously confined to the harem, for a drive along the wind-swept coastal road north of town.

Many of the important families of Jidda go for the summer to the nearby hill town of Taif, as well as to houses in Mecca, Medina, or even Riyadh, the capital of Saudi Arabia, about five hundred miles in the interior. Thanks to the advent of the Saudi Arabian Airlines travel to and from these cities has become quick and comfortable, and a group of heavily veiled Arab women, surrounded by black servants and numerous children, is to be found on almost every flight. The fact that Cairo, Beirut, and Damascus are five hours or less away by plane has encouraged rich Hejazi women to fly up and see their cousins, a new custom which will broaden their outlook.

For some time it has been the custom among the Europeans to gather regularly at one or another of the legations to view movies. Gradually the number of Saudi Arabs attending has increased until the showings now compete with the radio and the printed word as the principal means by which Saudis are introduced to Western ways. There are no movie theaters, but pictures are shown not only at the embassies and legations, but also at the Jidda airport, at the headquarters of the

Saudi Arabian Mining Syndicate and its mine in the mountains of the Hejaz, at the British military mission in Taif, and at the American-manned agricultural station at Al Kharj. In addition, the Arabian American Oil Company puts on nightly showings in its oil coast towns. The King and the older princes all have their own projectors, and some of them, such as young Prince Nawwaf, have become ardent movie fans.

Some of the larger homes in Jidda and in the other main cities boast motion-picture projectors of their own, and the women are becoming enormously interested in the new diversion. Egyptian films are commonly shown in homes, but a growing number of European, British, and American ones are now reaching Saudi Arabia, where they are passed from house to house and reshown dozens of times. Through them, hundreds of Arab women in the more important families are seeing for themselves the way women look, dress, eat, and behave in the Western world. The result is a new feeling that their daughters should have more education, exercise, and freedom than their mothers have been allowed.

But Arab women will not change overnight. Recently an American woman in Jidda was attending a motion picture at the home of an important government official. It was an Egyptian picture and dragged on until late in the evening. At eleven o'clock a recently installed telephone rang. It was the husband of several of the guests, who asked that one of his wives be sent home to him; it did not matter which one. Four plump and slow-moving ladies promptly got up and left, begging the hostess to allow them to come back the next night to see how the picture ended. King Ibn Saud opened Arabia's door on the Red Sea a little, and his son King Saud is opening it wider, but it takes time for the twentieth century to come in.

II

Reopening One of
King Solomon's Mines

MANY people have talked about modernizing Arabia, but the first American who did anything about it was the businessman and diplomat, Charles R. Crane. Having struck up a personal friendship with the late Imam Yahya of Yemen, Crane decided to help the ruler and put into effect a personal Point Four program under which he gave Yemen over one hundred thousand dollars' worth of roads, bridges, water pumps, and know-how. The know-how came mostly from a young American engineer named Karl S. Twitchell, whom Crane engaged in 1927.

For six years Twitchell worked in mountainous Yemen. At the end of that time, his reputation had spread throughout the entire Arabian Peninsula, and when Crane paid a visit to King Ibn Saud he was asked if Twitchell could come to Saudi Arabia and help with the development of its water resources and other projects. Crane assented to this, and beginning in 1931 Twitchell, often accompanied by his valiant English wife, journeyed up and down Saudi Arabia looking for water, for minerals, and for other exportable products which might yield Saudi Arabia income other than that from the pilgrimage.

In 1932 Twitchell reported to the Finance Minister, Sheikh Abdullah Suleiman, that the geology of the Hejaz and Asir provinces of western Saudi Arabia was such that he felt they might contain mineral wealth, possibly copper, platinum, or lead, and probably silver and gold. Previously, in a journey across Arabia which terminated in the island of

16

Bahrein before the first wildcat well there had reached commercial oil, Twitchell had met Dr. L. P. Dame and his staff at the Dutch Reformed Church Mission. At this meeting one of the women asked him if he had seen the famous gold mines of Arabia. The Bible, she recalled, states that gold is in the land of Havilah and the gold is good (Gen. 2:11, 12). Twitchell, interested, afterward located other allusions to gold in the Bible. Three verses (6:1, 21, 22) from First Kings ran:

> And it came to pass in the four hundred and eightieth year after the children of Israel were come out of the land of Egypt . . . that he [Solomon] began to build the house of the Lord.
> So Solomon overlaid the house within with pure gold: and he made a partition by the chains of gold before the oracle; and he overlaid it with gold.
> And the whole house he overlaid with gold, until he had finished all the house: also the whole altar that was by the oracle he overlaid with gold.

Bible readers had perhaps wondered where this gold came from. The inefficient methods of the early miners lent probability to the theory that it came not from a single mine but from many small diggings. First Kings 9:26–28 said:

> And king Solomon made a navy of ships . . . on the shore of the Red sea, in the land of Edom.
> And Hiram sent in the navy his servants, shipmen that had knowledge of the sea, with the servants of Solomon.
> And they came to Ophir, and fetched from thence gold, four hundred and twenty talents, and brought it to king Solomon.

Where, then, was the land of Ophir? Was it the legendary lost city of Ubar in the heart of the Rub al Khali? Was it in far-off Oman on the coast north of Muscat, or in Zanzibar, or in Ethiopia, or in Yemen?

Twitchell told Sheikh Abdullah he believed that some of King Solomon's gold came from the Hejaz, as many ancient gold mines were reported to be in "the land of Midian," north of Wadi Hamdh, a region described by Sir Richard Burton in his book, *The Gold Mines of Midian*. In order to help the Arab financier identify mineral-bearing rocks, Twitchell wrote him a simple descriptive handbook. The Finance Minister had it translated into Arabic and from that time he rarely traveled in Saudi Arabia without stopping to compare outcroppings of rocks with descriptions in Twitchell's book. When next they met, Sheikh Abdullah told Twitchell of a mountain halfway between Mecca and Medina with conspicuous veins of white rock exposed on its northern

17

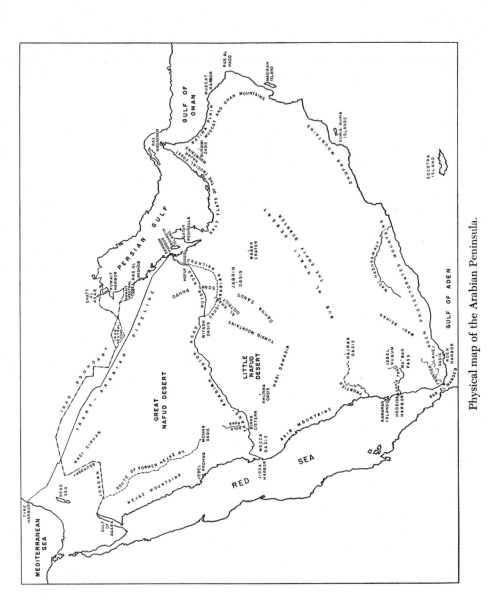

Physical map of the Arabian Peninsula.

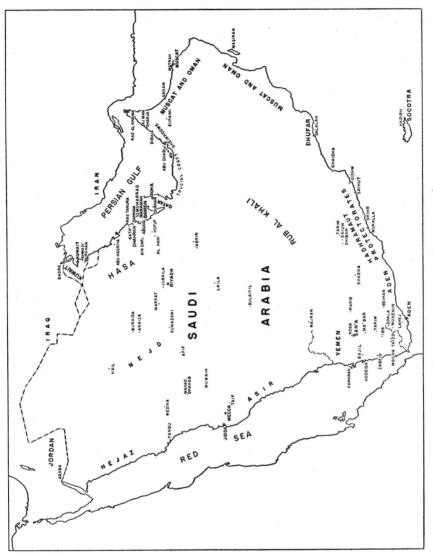

Political map of the Arabian Peninsula.

side, veins that corresponded to Twitchell's description of gold-bearing ore. With transportation arranged by the Finance Minister, the American engineer set out at once for the spot.[1]

Eight days later, after great difficulties, his tired motor caravan came to the mountain called Mahad Dhahab, the "Cradle of Gold." It was indeed a gold deposit and may well have been one of King Solomon's richest mines. Evidence showed that it had been worked in very ancient times, possibly by the Phoenicians, as well as by the Romans, so active in mining in Cyprus, and by others in the days of the Caliph Harun al Rashid about A.D. 800. Armed with a letter of authorization from King Ibn Saud and on a mission to interest foreign capital, Twitchell proceeded to America and then to England. Late in 1934 he finally persuaded a group of investors to form a company called the Saudi Arabian Mining Syndicate. Operations began in the summer of 1939, and the mine is now the largest industrial enterprise in the western part of Arabia.

To get to it from Jidda one should rise early and be off in the cool of the morning. It is well to have at least two cars in the convoy, perhaps a passenger vehicle such as a station wagon, and a truck or command car to carry gas and water, baggage, and the ever-present Saudi Arab guards, veterans of desert warfare, with old, well-oiled rifles slung over their shoulders and bandoleers of cartridges across their chests.

After passing the Sams (Saudi Arabian Mining Syndicate) dock and staff house, the road runs for half an hour across the sandy coastal plain, green in patches with grass and desert thorn. Flocks of black sheep are herded from the road by bedouin shepherd boys, while now and then white-tailed antelope bound ahead across the dusty plain. The highway built by the mining syndicate is one of the best in Saudi Arabia and makes it possible for cars to eat up the 250 miles of sand and gravel in about ten hours' running time.

Some four or five miles out of Jidda the way runs past a well pumped by one of the few windmills in Arabia. It has been used here instead of the traditional camel, wooden wheel, and rope because of the strong Red Sea wind and the unusual presence of water near the surface.

Past the windmill the road leaves the plain and climbs through the barren western foothills of the coastal range. Deserted valleys lie hemmed in by low hills whose rocks have been polished by the sun, wind, and sand into a dark brown "desert varnish." On the crest of a

---

[1] The writer is indebted to K. S. Twitchell for this and other material from his book *Saudi Arabia.*

hill the ruins of a two-hundred-year-old stone fort with six broken towers stand as a reminder that until a generation ago the Turks considered this an important supply line.

A few miles beyond the fort the hills open into a valley. Its barren floor is broken by a dusty date grove and a village of perhaps a hundred houses, built of the trunks and fronds of palm trees. This is the oasis of Asfan, where, after twenty-six days of difficult travel across the wastes of northern Arabia, the caravans from Baghdad join the main pilgrim route from Damascus to Mecca. Here Mohammed, after being driven out of Mecca, found shelter and rest; and from here he began the trip to Medina which marked the beginning of his religious and temporal power, and the starting point of the Mohammedan calendar, our year 622.

The Hejaz is dry today, but rain water once supported a much larger population than now subsists there. Evidences of this are to be seen in the series of low, unmortared stone dams ranging from three to fifteen feet in height on the Medina caravan trail a few miles north of Asfan and in the ruins of almost a dozen large dams, one in the Wadi Leiyah, some twenty miles from the town of Taif. This last is complete except for a hole where the sluice gate once stood. It is made of large cut stones laid in cement and measures six hundred feet long by twenty-six feet wide, rising to a height of fifty feet in the center. None of these large dams show Turkish workmanship, and they probably date back to the thirteenth or fourteeth century. It seems reasonable to assume that they not only checked floods and provided surface reservoirs, but also resulted in underground water storage. Their restoration would be neither difficult nor expensive, and offers a way to increase the land under cultivation and to raise the standard of living of the people of western Arabia.

Four hours out from Jidda the road to the mine climbs in switchbacks to the flat top of an escarpment that marks the western edge of the Arabian plateau. From here for the next fifty miles stretches one of the most desolate areas in the world. Called the Harra, or "burned-over place," it consists of rock left behind long ago when a lava flow cracked into a million pieces. Travelers from central Arabia must cross mile after mile of this black, stony wasteland on their way to Jidda or Mecca. To the Arab traveler on foot or camel, the crossing is unendurable in the heat of the day. Even the shade of a station wagon does not dispel the traveler's feeling that he is one of but few survivors in a stifling atom-bombed world.

At one place the black surface of the Harra is broken by two hills, one of white, the other of black, marble. There, 125 miles out of Jidda, the caravan turns south from the Gold Road to the rocky canyon of Wadi Hamma, where the mining syndicate has a halfway house called Madriga. A patch of fertile soil is hidden there on which, during the early forties, an energetic, gray-haired employee of Sams, O. R. Durham, cleared two half-acre fields and built a few outbuildings and a whitewashed, one-storied house.

Durham was an Englishman past middle age, with a white mustache and goatee, a twinkle in his eye, and a salty wit that made one relax immediately upon entering his simple living room. The walls were hung with Persian rugs, the windows were bright with gay curtains, and piles of books lay everywhere. Through an open window at the rear one could see ducks, chickens, turkeys, and a tame monkey playing about together. Durham served his guests a cool melon from his garden and then complained good-naturedly about what a nuisance he found travelers from the Gold Road. Talk then turned to the needed rain, the speed at which Jidda was changing, and the steady growth of his garden, which was moving into the Harra at a rate of about twenty feet a year.

"After a good meal, rest! After a poor meal, no work! That is my motto," Durham would say with a wink, "so stay awhile and sleep until it gets cooler." But travelers thought of the 130 miles of rough road ahead and reluctantly, since the heat and the good food made them sleepy, said good-bye to the keeper of the rest house, the only non-Arab farmer in that part of Saudi Arabia. Durham has gone to greener pastures now, but the farm still bears his imprint, as does the road which he maintained so well.

Twenty more miles of desolate Harra and a desert track turns east from the main road. It is the trail to Riyadh, capital of Saudi Arabia, four hundred miles away. Soon afterward the black stone table ends abruptly. Here there is a stone reservoir of a type the Arabs call *birka*, one of many built A.D. 810 by Queen Zubeidah, widow of the famous Caliph of Baghdad, Harun al Rashid, for the pilgrims coming from that city to Mecca. The reservoir is now filled to within ten feet of the top with dry, cracked mud but remains in use. To this day bedouin slip off their mangy camels nearby, spread prayer rugs under the thorn trees, and then walk slowly to the same birka that provided water there 1,140 years ago.

Beyond the birka the road crosses a sandy waste dotted with scrawny camel thorn. Graceful, short-horned gazelles dart off the side of the road, and lazy brown and yellow lizards, some as much as three feet long, sun themselves in the dust by the roadside. They are iguanas, a reptile not usually associated with Arabia and called *thubs* by the Arabs. They dart away rapidly when chased by the bedouin, who hunt them because their tails are good eating, possessing a flavor rather like that of frogs' legs. This stretch of countryside is so bare that progress across it is reckoned by "the tree," a solitary acacia about thirty feet tall which has found a moist spot in the gravel of the desert. "The tree" shares honors as a landmark with a little hill familiarly known as Jebel al Chai (tea mountain) because the drivers of the mining syndicate's trucks often stop for tea in the rare shade provided by its huge granite boulders.

The early miners who worked on the Cradle of Gold in King Solomon's time and again in the time of Harun al Rashid must have been short of water, for they apparently relied on the poor wells nearby or on water brought in on the backs of camels. Perhaps they mined only during part of the year, when the spring rains dotted the nearby wadies with pools of water. But the engineers of the Saudi Arabian Mining Syndicate, finding no water at their golden mountain, drilled wells in a wadi thirty-four miles to the west and brought water to Mahad Dhahab through a pipe line. The first signs of the mine from the road are the pumping stations along this pipe line, each surrounded by patches of green garden. Then at last the twin peaks of Mahad Dhahab come into view. Beyond them the bare Arabian landscape is broken by a ninety-foot head frame, a power plant, a crushing unit, and a cyanide plant, together with the auxiliary buildings of a modern mine. On the other side of the valley live the mine workers in orderly rows of whitewashed bungalows spread across the mountainside or circled around a mess hall, a recreation center, and the guesthouse to which the weary traveler repairs.

Wherever an Englishman goes, it is said that he takes with him his tea, his *Illustrated London News,* and a recognizably English state of mind. Wherever the American goes, he takes electric lights, modern plumbing, air cooling if needed, pie à la mode, coffee, and movies. All of these are found and appreciated at the mine. The management staff, thirty in all and mostly Americans, gather after the day's work to eat heartily and joke with one another and any new arrivals. When dinner is over, all move to the recreation center, where those who are not bridge or ping-pong players enjoy out-of-door movies in the cool of the evening.

23

King Saud, like his stern father before him, does not want his poorer subjects exposed to what he considers the unhealthy influence of feature pictures. The newsreels, travelogues, and educational pictures featured at the mine are not taboo, however, and a considerable number of the Arabs who are working in the mine or studying to be engineers turn out for every possible performance. The young among them exhibit especial interest in scenes of American life that show airplanes, motorcars, railroad trains, skyscrapers, and farm machinery; and their comments show that they take what they see seriously. One newsreel depicted American soldiers in Japan uncovering a hoard of gold bars. A ten-year-old boy, squatting on the hillside, was heard to remark that this seemed a much easier way of getting gold than the process used in Arabia.

Mahad Dhahab is 3,250 feet above sea level and seems relatively dry and cool after the humid air of Jidda. Refreshed by sleep and strengthened by an enormous American breakfast, the traveler sets off for a tour of the mine. He is struck immediately by the youth of the skilled Arab employees. If any equipment breaks at Mahad Dhahab, it must be repaired on the spot or else trucked to the coast for shipment all the way to America. The machine shop is therefore one of the most important parts of the whole enterprise. A few American superintendents and technicians excepted, most of the workers there are Arab boys from twelve to eighteen years of age. Some are beginners who learn by standing beside European or older Arab machinists. Others handle the lathes, presses, drills, and complicated machines by themselves. The Diesel power plant that turns the wheels of the largest industrial enterprise in the Hejaz is operated each shift by one American engineer assisted by three intent Saudi Arabs in their twenties who, up to six years ago, had seen nothing more modern than a camel saddle.

Entering the cage one soon drops down through the darkness to a level six hundred feet below the surface, where the air is warm and humid. From the well-lighted shaft and level stations he proceeds to the outlying tunnels, where carbide lamps provide the only illumination and where young Saudis shovel blast-broken rock into one-ton handcars. When the mine went into operation, work stopped often as the Arabs went above ground five times a day to face toward Mecca and pray. Now there are Arabic signs in the tunnels pointing toward Mecca, and the miners bow in prayer three hundred to six hundred feet below the surface of the earth.

After an hour spent tramping through the sticky darkness to the roar of the pneumatic drills, it is a relief to crowd onto the cage and rise again to the blinding Arab sunshine. Nearby is the crushing unit, where the ore from the mine is broken into pebbles and sent on a conveyor belt to a ball mill. There it is mixed with water, ground to powder, and processed. The product thus obtained runs approximately 25 per cent gold, 25 per cent silver, and 50 per cent various impurities. It is packed into steel drums, trucked over the Gold Road to Jidda, and at regular intervals loaded onto lighters and put aboard a steamer bound for a smelter in New Jersey.

The contrast between old and new, which is one of the most striking features of Saudi Arabia today, presents itself again when one calls on the amir or governor of the district. The trip from the mine to his house is more a journey in time than in space. Pneumatic drills and hoists seem far away as one sits cross-legged on the floor of his reception hall and drinks sweet Yemeni coffee, heavily flavored with cardamom. Here Arab etiquette holds: it is impolite to take more or fewer than three of the tiny cups, fewer indicating a dislike for the brew and more suggesting such a state of thirst that the host should have supplied food as well. The coffee server, who is an honored person, pours drinks with great dexterity from a long-spouted bronze coffeepot into handleless china cups, held stacked one above the other in his left hand. When the guest has finished, he signals the coffee pourer by shaking the cup as he returns it. After "first coffee," tea of a delicious Indian variety is served in small glasses, and the guest drinks two of these.

Conversation with the Amir of Mahad Dhahab is strained until a personal bond has been established. Friendship and respect are not easily won from most Saudi Arab officials and their etiquette does not include an obligation to keep the conversational ball rolling. But the Amir is fond of hunting, and presently he tells a story or two indicating that certain game which formerly came to Arabia from Africa no longer does so because of the Suez Canal.

In the midst of this traditional and leisurely household, it is startling to hear the Amir ask how the new generator is working and if the grease for the hoists has arrived. After tea, coffee comes around again, a sign in the ritual of Arab etiquette that the meeting is over and that guests are at liberty to leave.

From the Amir's house one should continue on a two-mile trip to a little valley north of the camp where the perpendicular faces of the large rocks are ornamented with primitive pictures and carvings. A short scramble up canyon sides brings one within good view of a dozen or so rock pictures, mainly of men with bows and arrows hunting long-horned deer, antelope, and sheep, though one excellently preserved panel shows about thirty men around a wounded lion. Mohammed for-bade drawing or making images of people or animals; it therefore seems reasonable that this primitive art predates the middle of the seventh century. Most of the stones on which the drawings are cut have split, and even the cracks are weather-beaten. Many travelers in Arabia, in-cluding Charles Doughty and Lady Blunt, describe similar drawings seen in various visits to northwest Arabia. The local chief of police claims that until recently all the animals in these rock pictures could be found in the mountain fastnesses of the Hejaz, including the lions, but he cannot say who made the drawings. Questions as to who made them and ones similar to them in other places, when they were done, and what light they can throw on pre-Islamic Arabian culture would seem to justify an expedition for their study.

Before leaving Mahad Dhahab the visitor should also drive out to the north side of the mountain a little west of the present minesite and explore the caves, shafts, and holes dug by the primitive men who first mined gold here. Some of these tunnels appear to have run as much as 150 feet into the mountain. The extracted rock was heated over a fire and cooled suddenly by a dash of cold water, this cracking process being repeated until the pieces were small enough to be ground into powder between millstones. Some of these stones may still be seen scat-tered around the ancient diggings, and a few have been taken to Jidda and the United States as garden ornaments. But no tools of this period, either of metal or stone, have been found at the mine. Crude methods in the past led to only partial extraction of the gold, and for the first few years of its operation the mining syndicate simply reworked the large dump of tailings from these earlier days.

When the short twilight falls, the bedouin, squatting around their fires at the edge of the diggings, make one think of King Solomon's miners. Through the fading light, the sunburned hills frame them in a scene unchanged by the passing of thirty centuries. The pungent smell of camel-dung fires, the dates and camel milk that make their meal, the earthy subjects of their conversation, and the impromptu songs they sing about the events of the day, all belong to ages past as much as they belong to the present. Then suddenly, from the gathering darkness, electric lights shine out in the streets of the camp across the valley, and a giant flood lamp at the head of the hoist lights up the dusty metal buildings of the mine. In the machine shop the lights come on and a class in internal combustion motors starts, attended by the sons of the Arabs squatting around the fires.

III

The Rise of the House of Saud

ALTHOUGH well known in the Nejd for centuries, the Saud family first entered on the pages of world history in the mid-eighteenth century.[1] At that time the Moslem reformer, Mohammed ibn Abdul Wahhab, returned from study at Baghdad to urge his coreligionists in Arabia to turn aside from the loose and idolatrous practices which had brought misfortune upon Islam and to live by the word of the Prophet alone. He converted the Amir Ibn Saud, the leader of a branch of the Sauds which for generations had ruled the town of Dariya near Riyadh. Together, Amir Saud and Abdul Wahhab spread the new doctrine of Moslem puritanism among the bedouin and townspeople whose religion had lost its force in meaningless ritualism. In 1803 a later Wahhabi Saud entered Mecca and smashed a multitude of supposedly holy objects that were being worshiped there side by side with the Kaaba.

After Amir Saud's death his son, Abdul Aziz, for whom the present King and his father were named, expanded his authority up to Damascus, and a new generation of teachers denounced the worldly and superficial approach to Islam prevalent throughout the rest of the Moslem world. The growth of Wahhabi influence and power angered the Turkish rulers in Constantinople, who considered themselves the spiritual leaders of Islam. They enlisted the support of the ruler of Egypt, whose son set out to defeat the Wahhabis. He advanced by slow stages and eventu-

[1] For part of the following background information on Ibn Saud, the author is indebted to Kenneth Williams' book, *Ibn Sa'ud.*

27

ally, in 1818, captured the Saudi capital of Dariya, reducing it to its present state of ruin. The Saudi state was broken, and the Sauds returned to Riyadh, where they lived throughout most of the nineteenth century, replaced as the real power in central Arabia by the Rashidi family.

Mohammed ibn Rashid, head of the Rashidis, made the northern desert city of Hail his capital. He accepted Turkish overlordship, expanded his realm, and in 1885 took Riyadh. Later Abdul Rahman, the head of the Saud family, fled into the desert. After a period of wandering he found refuge in the little sheikhdom of Kuwait on the northwestern shore of the Persian Gulf. There he renounced his claim to the throne in favor of his eldest son, Abdul Aziz.

During ten years under the shadow of the Rashidis and ten more as an exile among the tribesmen on the northern edge of the Rub al Khali, Abdul Aziz ibn Saud developed into a leader of men. Forceful and physically strong, he determined to reconquer the homeland of his family. Taking only a few men with him, the young pretender set out from Kuwait in January 1902. After some weeks spent looking for recruits, he came secretly to the edge of Riyadh oasis. There he left about thirty of his men with the instruction, "If no message reaches you, tomorrow haste away; you will know that we are dead." Advancing stealthily, Ibn Saud stationed his brother, Mohammed, with twenty men in a grove near the city. As twilight fell, the pretender and ten faithful companions laid a palm tree log against the wall and climbed into the city. Hurrying across the roofs they came to the governor's house, which they entered in his absence, silencing the terrified residents with threats of death. After enjoying some of the governor's coffee and dates, the little band passed the rest of the night in the house reading the Koran. At dawn the guards opened the gates of the inner fortress of Riyadh. From their vantage point Ibn Saud and his followers saw the governor's horses led out for exercise. They were soon followed by the governor, who, as was his custom, had slept in the fortress. Ibn Saud's men rushed forward and killed him along with some of his bodyguard. The rest of the guard retreated into the fort and tried to shut the gates, but they were stopped by the vigilance of one of Ibn Saud's closest friends, Abdullah ibn Jiluwi, who held the gates open long enough for the attackers to get inside. A short fight ensued and then the garrison surrendered. After seventeen years of exile, a Saudi prince was once more master of Riyadh.

Ibn Saud's success aroused the Turks to action. In the late spring of 1904 eight Turkish battalions with Ibn Rashid and his Shammar tribesmen advanced across the sands of northeastern Arabia. Ibn Saud fell back before them to the neighborhood of Shinana. There the opponents faced each other for three months without doing battle. Then Ibn Rashid's Shammar tribesmen left him to take their cattle north to autumn pastures. The Turks had to follow, harassed by Ibn Saud's cavalry. Young Saud, faced with a last chance to rid himself of the Turks, led a charge into the heart of the Turkish Army. It was a risky maneuver, but the very boldness of his move turned the tide. The Turkish battalions broke and fled, leaving their guns, baggage, and gold for the victors. Within eighteen months Ibn Rashid was dead, and young Saud was master of central Arabia.

Turning his thoughts temporarily from war, Ibn Saud devoted himself next to a series of internal reforms. The first of these was the organization of the Ikhwan movement. At every likely oasis or spring, Ibn Saud established a new village or expanded the existing settlement into an agricultural center. Each center was put under the supervision of a Wahhabi missionary, who, with a series of faithful followers of Ibn Saud known as the Ikhwan or brethren, ran it as a military encampment, farm, and center of Moslem puritanism. More than one hundred of the Ikhwan colonies sprang up and thrived. Ibn Saud found himself with a growing nucleus of loyal and devout followers, not unlike the Janizaries of the Turkish sultans. The result was an end to the raids which for centuries had characterized tribal life in central Arabia.

Strengthened by the Ikhwan, Ibn Saud decided in the spring of 1913 to capture the Hasa, easternmost province of Arabia along the Persian Gulf. In one of the greatest of his forced marches, he led his warriors from a camp near Tuwaiq to the large oasis of Hofuf, covering a five days' journey in a day and a half. Once again he used the trunks of palm trees as scaling ladders and led his men over the walls of the city. The Turkish officials and their families retreated to the central mosque of the town, which Ibn Saud threatened to blow up. The Turks, knowing that Ibn Saud was a man of his word, marched out of Hofuf without firing a shot. Like snow on a roof, Turkish rule melted away, and Ibn Saud's domain extended to the Persian Gulf. Had the Turks realized that the Hasa contained as much oil as there is under the United States, they might have made a greater effort to keep it under their control.

No sooner had Wahhabi power reached the Persian Gulf than the British Empire, acting through the Persian Gulf Administration, established contact with it. With the outbreak of hostilities against the Turks in World War I, the British decided to rally Ibn Saud to their side. Sir Percy Cox, the top British expert on the Persian Gulf and chief political officer of the British Mesopotamian Expeditionary Force, sent Captain Shakespear hurrying to Riyadh. His orders were to line up Ibn Saud against the Rashidis, who stood firm with the Turks on the west flank of the British forces in the Tigris and Euphrates valleys. The captain was successful in his mission to the Wahhabis but while watching the first battle of the war at Jarab was struck down by a stray bullet and finished off by Rashidi knives. Shakespear's death ended Ibn Saud's active role in World War I, for it cut the main British link with the Wahhabi sultan. Thenceforward the Allied war effort in the peninsula was run by the Arab Bureau in Cairo, which had a "Red Sea slant" and backed Ibn Saud's rival, King Hussein of the Hejaz, as the leading contender to drive the Turks out of the peninsula. With Prince Feisal al Hussein, Lawrence of Arabia rode north along the Hejaz Railway into the adventures so familiar to the English-reading public, and Ibn Saud was left to sit out the war in relative quiet.

It is not surprising, therefore, that during the closing years of the war friction increased between Ibn Saud and King Hussein of the Hejaz, who was a very ambitious and inflexible man. In September 1918 King Hussein sent an expedition under his son Abdullah to take the oasis of Khurma from the Wahhabis. This force of some five thousand was ambushed by Ibn Saud in the dark, and less than a hundred survived, among them the Amir Abdullah, who slipped away and eventually became the late King of Jordan. This, incidentally, was the closest that Ibn Saud and Abdullah ibn Hussein came to meeting until their historic conference at Riyadh in June 1948.

Panic ensued at Jidda as people sought to escape before the fanatical Wahhabis fell upon the town. Ibn Saud, however, preferred not to push on to the Red Sea, feeling that the victory of his men had assured him peace on his western frontier and had established him as a force to be reckoned with in the plans of the Arab Bureau in Cairo. Acting on the latter premise, he sent his clever, handsome second son, Faisal, to London. Faisal was only fourteen years of age at that time but, guided by St. John Philby, the new British representative at Kuwait, he made an excellent impression.

King Hussein, unsuccessful in his direct assault, turned to stir up the leaders of the province of Asir, which lies south of the Hejaz on the Red Sea, against Ibn Saud. Asir was in theory an independent state, although actually it then paid allegiance partly to Yemen, partly to the Hejaz, and partly to the Turks. Ibn Saud organized a force of five thousand men under the command of young Faisal, who had recently returned from England. This army made a successful seven-hundred-mile march from Riyadh to the town of Abha in Asir and subjugated the state. Faisal marched back to Riyadh a warrior-hero.

Ibn Saud's next move of expansion was precipitated late in 1920 by the assassination of the strong leader of the Rashidis and the succession of a weak and lazy nephew, Abdullah ibn Mitab. Ibn Saud attacked Abdullah, bringing about his surrender after a short fight. He then took him to Riyadh, where he lived until his death in 1947 in considerable comfort, in company with many other members of the Rashidi clan who were brought to that city after the fall of Hail. Thus did the sands of time run out for the Rashidi amirs, who as rulers of the Shammar tribe had dominated northern Arabia during the nineteenth century.

Ibn Saud's reputation for mercy as well as strength was much enhanced by his treatment of the inhabitants of Hail. Not only did he keep his followers from looting, but he distributed the rice which had been brought along for his own army to the city's hungry. The leaders of Hail expected to be wiped out by the Wahhabi puritans. Instead Ibn Saud called them together and gave them his personal written guarantee of security. As a final gesture he and his oldest son, Saud, each married girls of the Rashidi family. By these acts of statecraft, widely recognized throughout the Arab world, Ibn Saud not only gained the gratitude of the Rashidi family but secured the allegiance of the town of Hail and half of the Shammar tribe as well, the other half of the tribe moving to Iraq.

In March 1924 King Hussein made a last fatal mistake. He had himself proclaimed Caliph of all Islam. The vigorous and puritanical Ibn Saud had never had much use for King Hussein as a king or as a religious leader. The idea that this old and, to Ibn Saud, wicked man should be Caliph of Islam was too much for the Sultan of the Nejd. Ibn Saud promptly issued a proclamation ridiculing King Hussein's claims to the caliphate and calling a meeting of the religious and military leaders of the Nejd. Ibn Saud's venerable father, Abdul Rahman, presided over it and heard the warrior-farmer fanatics of the Ikhwan tell their sultan that they intended to make the pilgrimage to Mecca, which would indicate an acceptance of Hussein's assumption of the caliphate. Here might be rebellion; Ibn Saud rose to meet the crisis. He forbade the pilgrimage as such but told the Ikhwan that they could go and conquer the Hejaz for the true Islamic faith. Mecca and Medina were not to be attacked, but the Hashimites were to be removed from power and the holy places purged.

From the border oases of Khurma and Turaba, the Wahhabi camel corps crossed into the Hejaz in August 1924 and headed for the hill town of Taif, 5,500 feet up in the mountains behind Jidda. King Hussein fled to Mecca and was forced to abdicate in favor of his son Ali. Mecca was then evacuated by the Hashimite forces, and the Wahhabi warriors entered behind them. There was no slaughter or looting, but the puritans from the Nejd, led by Ibn Saud in the robes of a pilgrim, smashed many of the shrines, tombs, and other "sights" which had sprung up in and around the city.

Shortly thereafter King Hussein was taken by the British to Cyprus, where he lived in comfort until his death in 1931. On Christmas Day, 1925, the Sultan of the Nejd entered Jidda, informing the small foreign colony that he brought "peace and justice." With the Rashidis and Hashimites conquered, a single Arabian state stretched from the Persian Gulf to the Red Sea.

In the final act of the drama the religious and political leaders of the Hejaz met in Mecca and decided that, provided he ruled in accordance with the Koran and Sunna, or way of life, and Hadith, or sayings of the Prophet, the Sultan of the Nejd should henceforth be King of the Hejaz. On January 8, 1926, in a simple ceremony at the Great Mosque, the citizens of Mecca swore their allegiance to their new King. Thus did Ibn Saud become a force with which all Moslem countries and many foreign states as well were bound to be concerned.

Upon assuming his new responsibility, King Ibn Saud issued in April 1926 an invitation for a world Moslem conference at Mecca. More than seventy religious leaders attended this gathering and went home to report that a new day had dawned in Arabia. The next year almost two hundred and fifty thousand persons made the pilgrimage—a remarkable revival. Ibn Saud's ambition to purify Mecca and make the pilgrimage safe for all Moslems had been largely realized.

He was now recognized as King by Great Britain and several other European states. These gestures from the west he reciprocated in the autumn of 1926 by sending his second son and ranking diplomat, Amir Faisal, on a courtesy visit to Great Britain, France, and the Netherlands. During this second visit to England, Amir Faisal met King George V, was widely feted, and saw several impressive air shows put on by the RAF. Crossing to the Continent, he was received by Queen Wilhelmina

3. A line of heavily laden camels crossing a paved thoroughfare in Jidda, with modern apartment buildings in the background.

4. The plant of the Saudi Arabian Mining Syndicate at Mahad Dhahab, the site of one of King Solomon's gold mines.

5. Pilgrims in Jidda loading their belongings on a bus for the journey to Mecca.

6. The late King Abdul Aziz ibn Saud, who built the modern kingdom of Saudi Arabia.

7. Entrance to the palace of the late King at Riyadh, capital of Saudi Arabia.

of the Netherlands and the President of the French Republic. He returned to Arabia laden with honors and, now familiar with European civilization, became his father's Foreign Minister.

Shortly after Prince Faisal returned, the British, through their consul at Jidda and the late writer George Antonius, who was attached to the Palestine Government, attempted to work out a new Anglo-Wahhabi treaty. The talks were unsuccessful at first. Ibn Saud broke off the negotiations and returned to Riyadh, where a gathering of religious and tribal leaders elected him King of the Nejd, the area over which he had previously been sultan. Negotiations with the British were then resumed, and in May 1927 the Treaty of Jidda was signed. By this treaty Great Britain recognized the conquests made by Ibn Saud since World War I and his rights as an independent sovereign.

In the summer of 1927 the Ikhwan, the fanatical farmer-warriors whom Ibn Saud had planted in towns throughout the Nejd, were aroused to anger by what they considered to be unjust restrictions of their territory and they began attacking Iraqi border settlements. To deal with this crisis the King called a conference at Riyadh of representatives of all of his tribes. Leaders and wise men came from the Hejaz and Asir, from the Nejd and Hasa, but the rebellious leaders of the Ikhwan did not appear. Once again a ruler who had set up a Praetorian Guard found himself threatened by the war machine he had created.

This Riyadh conference, however, showed Ibn Saud at his best. He led the meeting as King, but he made sure that his rulings were discussed and voted upon. He even asked for a decision on himself, saying, "I want you also to consider whether I am fit for ruling you." The answer came back unanimously, "We have no desire for any king to rule over us except you, O Abdul Aziz."

At this conference an interesting incident occurred which was to have considerable bearing on the modernization of Saudi Arabia. One of the charges brought against Ibn Saud was that he had set up wireless stations and communicated through them, an act that was not specifically approved by the Prophet. After the opposition had been heard, the King got down from this throne and pleaded in his own defense. He pointed out that there was nothing in the Koran or the words of the Prophet against the use of wireless. And he ended by having a section of the Koran repeated over the radio.

"Can anything be bad," he said, "which transmits the words of God?"

The Ulema, or council of religious elders, agreed that he was right

33

and thus sanctioned the King's use of the radio, an essential weapon if he was to pacify the scattered and rebellious tribesmen of the Ikhwan settlements. It was a first step in gaining approval for a program which was to extend to automobiles, electric lights, Diesel pumps, railroads, and airplanes.

Having established his leadership both in politics and in economic affairs, Ibn Saud laid down a policy of peace. It was approved by the conference, but not by the Ikhwan. Ibn Saud made several attempts to settle the dispute peacefully but was rebuffed. It became clear that if his kingdom was to be held together, it must be done by force. Collecting all the available gasoline in the Hejaz, he raced eastward across Arabia in a great motor caravan, the first ever used in central Arabia's many wars. The Ikhwan leaders were pushed back to the Kuwait and Iraq frontier where, on December 2, 1929, they turned and fought near the town of Riqji. Ibn Saud's men were victorious, and this time there was no pardon. Those of the rebels who escaped fled into Iraq and Kuwait, where they surrendered to the authorities. After negotiations with Ibn Saud, who guaranteed them his protection, the rebels returned to Saudi Arabia, where they lived out their days as loosely guarded prisoners of the King. Thus did Abdul Aziz overcome the greatest threat to his authority within his kingdom. After that he was without any real opposition in the heart of the Arabian Peninsula.

The Ikhwan revolt against Ibn Saud had been followed with close attention by the Western powers, which promptly took cognizance of his victory. Late in 1929 the French raised their consulate at Jidda to a legation. In February 1930 Sir Andrew Ryan was appointed first British Minister to Saudi Arabia, and the other states with consulates at Jidda followed suit. The Moslem powers wished to have their representatives located in Mecca, but the King took the position that, since non-Moslems could not go to Mecca, Jidda was the natural diplomatic capital and all representatives of foreign nations should reside there together.

In 1932 Ibn Saud changed the name of his country from the Kingdom of the Hejaz and Nejd to Saudi Arabia, the "Arabia of the Sauds." And to solidify his rule further, he announced in May 1933 that his oldest living son, Amir Saud, Viceroy of the Nejd, was the official heir to the throne. Thus did the sultanate of the Nejd expand to cover an area a quarter of the size of the United States and to become the largest state of the Arabian Peninsula.

With this background in mind, it is easier to understand the unusual

34

organization of the government of Saudi Arabia. The basis of Moslem law is the Sharia, or canon law, which rests on the Koran as revealed by Allah to his Prophet Mohammed. This Sharia is interpreted by a group of wise men, called the Ulema, who live at Mecca and Riyadh and who devote their lives to the study and application of the Koran, the sayings of Mohammed and the commentaries. In most Moslem countries such as Egypt or Syria, modern civil and criminal jurisprudence has in part superseded this ancient religious law. This has not happened in Saudi Arabia, however, and the Sharia, as interpreted by the wise men and administered by the King, is still the supreme law of that country.

When King Ibn Saud conquered the kingdom of the Hejaz, he felt that the primitive organization of government which had held together the tribes of central Arabia from time immemorial was insufficient for the government of the more advanced area where Mecca and Medina are located. As a result, in August 1926 he promulgated a form of constitution known as the "Organic Law for the Kingdom of Hejaz." Although much modified since then, this document is still the basis of organic law for the Hejaz and in theory for the whole Kingdom of Saudi Arabia.[2] At various times since 1926, the question of a constitution for the country as a whole has been considered but none has been adopted, partly because of the varied nature and customs of the population. There is no suffrage in Saudi Arabia. Officials are appointed by the King, his ministers, or in the case of some officials by groups of prominent citizens. Regulations covering the kingdom are promulgated by the central government in Riyadh, which acts in part through the Legislative Assembly. The latter is not unlike the British House of Lords in its earliest form, being made up of tribal and religious leaders. Among the subjects with which it deals are government finance, economic development and concessions, laws and regulations, pilgrimage affairs, and the civil service. This assembly drafts regulations covering the various provinces and at times the kingdom as a whole.

Until 1953, when the Crown Prince was given a form of cabinet, Saudi Arabia had no council of ministers such as is found in most Western states. The nearest approach to this was the Council of Deputies originally set up in 1941 under the presidency of the Viceroy of the Hejaz. In addition to the president, it was made up of the Foreign Minister, the Finance Minister, and the acting president of the Legislative

[2] For much of the material on the government of Saudi Arabia, the author is indebted to the excellent treatise on this subject by Rodger P. Davies.

Assembly. The Council was divided into two sections, the Diwan or staff of the Viceroy (which literally means the place in which the official and his councilors sit to hear complaints and which has incidentally given us the English word "divan") and the Presidency of the Council. Under the Presidency came the Ministries of Foreign Affairs, Finance, Interior, and Military Affairs, the Legislative Assembly, the judicial courts, and the governors of the amirates.

Before 1925 the King handled all contacts with foreign powers himself. Then a Directorship of Foreign Affairs was established, which was raised to the rank of a Ministry the next year, at which time Prince Faisal became Foreign Minister, though all decisions of importance were still referred to the King.

Through his control of the purse strings from 1928 to 1953 the Minister of Finance, Sheikh Abdullah Suleiman, became one of the most powerful men in Saudi Arabia, for the other ministries were to a greater or lesser extent dependent upon him for funds. Sheikh Abdullah had various ups and downs in power, largely because of two real handicaps. These were his close association with some of the largest merchants of the country, who were growing rich too rapidly, and the compounding difficulties inherent in running a country with an income of over $190,000,000 a year by means of an antiquated financial structure almost unchanged since the country was little more than a collection of tribes. Sheikh Abdullah worked hard at his job. He visited the United States several times, traveled extensively, and met many people. But the job had become too big even several years before the death of King Ibn Saud.

A Ministry of State for Developmental Projects was created in April 1947. It had a director-general for developmental projects and divisions for petroleum and minerals, foreign companies, legal affairs, and land, sea, and air communications. But it was dependent on the Finance Ministry for funds.

Until 1944 the Minister of Finance also acted as head of the Agency of Defense, working directly under the supervision of the King. In the autumn of that year, a royal order appointed a Minister of Defense and Inspector-General of Military Affairs. Under Prince Mansour, who headed this Ministry until his death in 1951, the Ministry increased in importance as Saudi Arabia progressed out of the sword and camel era of warfare. The Ministry of Defense included a department of aviation, which supervised the war planes that make up the small Saudi

36

Arabian Air Force, as well as the commercial airplanes owned by the government. The department had jurisdiction over the students at the pilot-training school, which was being run by a British air mission at the hill town of Taif, and at the school for training airport personnel, which the United States Air Force maintained at Dhahran.

The basic fact to remember about the government of Saudi Arabia is that in spite of some modernization all important decisions are made by the King. Organization as yet means little, and personal favor with the King is all important.

This is in general the case with King Saud, but it was completely so with his father. More than any other nation today, Saudi Arabia is the creation of one man, King Abdul Aziz ibn Saud; he was Saudi Arabia, and Saudi Arabia was his shadow.

No one could meet Ibn Saud without recognizing immediately and instinctively that he was a natural leader. He combined shrewdness with integrity and a powerful will with a simple, direct manner. The scope of his knowledge of domestic and world affairs impressed visitors from the outside world. Parties coming to Riyadh often contained experts in different fields, one specialist on finance, another on health conditions, and still another on transportation. To each of these people, the King talked with remarkable understanding.

Ibn Saud's knowledge of affairs extended far beyond the confines of Saudi Arabia. He had four translators constantly at work monitoring foreign-language broadcasts and regularly bringing him news of the world. At times during the most critical days of the last war these monitors reported to him every half-hour, even when he was in camp. Ibn Saud followed the campaigns of World War II with great interest. One of his monitors was an advocate of Allied invasion of Europe through the Balkans, but the King insisted that the best place for attack was in Normandy, and well before D-day he outlined a possible plan of attack which turned out to be quite similar to that actually used. Thus, although the King rarely saw a newspaper, he kept in touch with events throughout the world, discussing them in Riyadh almost as soon as they appeared in the papers of Washington, London, or Moscow.

The most important of the forces that motivated the late King was his deep religious feeling—a sense of closeness to God and a belief that Allah directed his every act. This thinking dominated his life and made him a religious as well as a political leader. He was strict in his observance of all the traditional prayers, fasts, and pilgrimages and

37

appeared to get a never-failing sense of satisfaction from leading his people in prayer. He liked to have one or more persons reading the Koran aloud in his palace at all times.

As a part of his deep religious conviction the King believed that the severe puritanism of the Wahhabi sect was the only true interpretation of the teachings of Mohammed. When he entered Mecca in December 1924, he purged it of many of the practices which had sprung up there, such as eliciting money from pilgrims for visits to all sorts of so-called shrines and holy places. He followed strictly the teachings of the Koran and looked to Islam for guidance regarding justice, the treatment of the poor, and many other aspects of human conduct for which Islamic practice through the years has provided a prescription. This explained his strict opposition to the drinking of alcohol by Moslems. By the same token, he would not pay interest on borrowed money, though he was willing to get around the Koranic injunction against interest by requiring that the sum repaid be in excess of the sum borrowed. He also stood firm against any practice among his people of prostitution, mixed bathing, Western dancing, and the appearance in public of unveiled women.

Next to religion and upholding the Moslem way of life, the King's greatest interest was his family. A good Moslem, he never had more than four wives at a time and was married to his number-one wife most of his life. The second and third wives were considered political; if relations with a tribe could be improved by doing so, he married one of its daughters. Such political wives and the children they have produced did much to cement the bonds of friendship between the King and his former enemies throughout Saudi Arabia.

The number-four wife was usually an "away from home" companion, for Mohammed felt that a man should not be without feminine company when separated from his harem. Many of the more than one hundred women who held this position were his queens only for a night, but they were legitimate wives, and by marriage to the King they gained wealth and lifelong prestige.

American and European women were seldom invited to Riyadh for a visit. One of the earliest was Mrs. L. P. Dame, the wife of a missionary doctor stationed on the Bahrein Islands in the Persian Gulf, who visited the capital in April 1933 with a woman doctor and a nurse.

In addition to missionaries, women who have been to Riyadh include Mrs. Karl Twitchell, Mrs. William Eddy, the Duchess of Athlone, Mrs. Cyril Ousman, Mrs. Kermit Roosevelt, and some of the wives of officials in Aramco. Mrs. Bolton, the energetic Congresswoman from Ohio, in

September 1945 not only visited the harem but was ushered, unveiled, into the audience chamber, the first woman to be so received at Riyadh. She relates that when she thanked Ibn Saud for having set aside one of the most deeply rooted of Arab traditions by receiving her unveiled, he replied, "No tradition is so great or so small that it cannot be set aside to bring about a closer understanding between our two nations."

The King spent a good deal of time with his children and signified his pleasure with them by calling one or another to his side to meet a visitor. In addition to Saud and Faisal, he left several sons with high royal but little official rank, such as the strong-willed and independent Mohammed and Nasir. Younger princes include Khalid, Saad, Fahad, Abdullah, Bandur, Misaid, Abdul Muhsin, Sultan, Mashail, Mitab, Talal, Abdul Majid, Hadhlul, Mashur, Mamduh, Thamir, Sitam, Ahmed, Suleiman, Majid, Fuad, Naif, Nuwwaf, Badr, Turki (the second), Abdur Rahman, and Mishari. None of Ibn Saud's thirty-six sons or of his more than a hundred grandsons has received formal education outside Arabia, and virtually none possesses technical training.

Alongside the King's interest in his religion and family ran a deep concern for his country. Anything which bore on its development, such as a network of roads between main towns or a scheme for making better use of existing underground water, interested him intensely. Against considerable opposition the King insisted on the building of a railroad across the Dahna sands from the Persian Gulf to his capital, a distance of about 350 miles. He pointed out that equally difficult sands have been crossed by railroads in North Africa. He also reminded critics, who said that there were virtually no towns between the oases of Hofuf and Riyadh, that in the American West the towns sprang up along the route of the railroad; they were not there before it. Alongside the railroad line the King planned to drill a series of wells to attract bedouin from the dry plains and thus start towns. This gradual urbanization he was sure would help the bedouin and provide the railroad with traffic. The railroad has now reached the capital, and engineering studies justify the King's support of it, for it has cut the cost of hauling freight to Riyadh sharply.

Three stories illustrating King Ibn Saud's handling of domestic affairs attained wide circulation. The first concerned the case of a woman whose husband was killed when a man fell upon him out of a palm tree. The first judge urged the plaintiff to accept money in settlement, but she insisted that the man who killed her husband should himself be killed. The case was passed on from judge to judge until finally it came to the King as the supreme court of Saudi Arabia. After listening to both sides of the case, the King gave the following judgment: "It is your right under Koranic law to insist on the death of this man. It is only fair, however, that he be killed as he killed. He will therefore be tied under a palm tree and someone will be dropped on him until he is dead. Since you are the person most directly concerned, you will be dropped." The woman decided to take the money.

The second story concerned the King's method of putting down banditry and thieving. According to it, a bedouin arrived at the King's camp and told him that at a well far south on the edge of the Empty Quarter he had found a sack of Yemeni coffee which he wanted to report. "Good," said Ibn Saud. "Give this man three riyals for having passed on this information. Also give him three lashes with a heavy whip." "Why am I being punished?" asked the man. "Since you report the bag was filled with Yemeni coffee, it is clear you must have opened it, and," ruled the monarch, "no one in my kingdom tampers with other's property."

The third story concerned his willingness to reconsider when injustice had been done. When the harem moved, each of Ibn Saud's wives was given a ticket entitling her to a separate plane for her children, relatives, and servants. In the spring of 1949 one of the wives received a ticket for fifteen persons plus baggage, which is very heavy when the harem travels. In order to take more of her relatives with her, she changed the number to read thirty-five. The Saudi official at the airport refused to honor the forged ticket because it would mean dangerously overloading the plane. Thus rebuffed, the wife complained bitterly to the King and aroused him to a fury. Through an aide he sent word to the officer in the newly finished skyroom at Jidda, "Don't leave your chair until my soldiers come to get you." Luckily for the official, one of the King's sons, Mansour, who as Minister of Defense had charge of Saudi aviation, heard what had happened and spirited the official off to Mecca for the night. The next day the incident was thoroughly explained to Ibn Saud, who forgave Mansour and the official and turned his anger against his wife.

One cannot remain long in Saudi Arabia without hearing such tales about the former King. Already they have become legends, passed on from bedouin father to son around the campfires, and from merchant to merchant in the bazaars. King Ibn Saud is dead, but his life and deeds are part of the folklore of the land he unified. No greater monument can any Arab achieve.

IV

King Saud Al Saud

TO APPRECIATE the Sauds and their capital, the visitor should approach Riyadh by camel from Jidda. If the traveler decides against devoting twenty-one days to such a caravan but nevertheless wants to obtain a better idea of western Arabia than can be had by plane, he may compromise by driving overland in a truck equipped with oversized sand tires. The peace which the Sauds have brought to their kingdom permits the foreigner to drive across Arabia safe from molestation, and though the trip is rough, with proper equipment and a soldier or two it is not dangerous. Essential supplies include blankets, a metal brazier, sacks of charcoal, a few cans of food including fruit juice, auto-repair tools, spare tires, tire-repair kit, drinking and radiator water, and a plentiful supply of riyals for gratuities.

The main road from Jidda to the capital runs through Mecca and is, of course, forbidden to non-Moslems. To avoid a rough detour it is best to follow the well-graded road of the Saudi Arabian Mining Syndicate for the first 150 miles. Just before Queen Zubeidah's birka, one leaves the road to the mine and turns east across a smooth gravel plain which floods after heavy rains. If it is dry, twenty miles of comparatively fast going bring one to the main Mecca-Riyadh road, known as "the King's highway." Here a difficulty arises from occasional patches of deep, sugarlike sand, and the traveler soon learns whether or not his car is desert-worthy.

The first town of note is Muwaih, where the Saudi Arabian Government maintains an eighteen-thousand-gallon gasoline pool, small repair shops, and a radio and telegraph station. Beyond the village this trans-Arabian highway, now merely a broadened camel trail, bumps over rough salt and gypsum flats for about twenty-five miles. These give way to sparsely settled country, so dry that gazelles are scarce and not even tamarisk trees can grow. For a hundred miles it is the same; then the motorist approaches Afif, a village of about two hundred Arabs, who live by selling eggs, chickens, and sheep to travelers on the highway. Most motorists stop here to collect gasoline and food. As staying outside the towns is preferable, one drives on to camp for the night by the clean desert roadside.

At length camp is made and a few bedouin appear to ask for water, looking hopefully at the food. The twilight is short, and the cool of the night creeps into the camp as soon as the rocks and sand, ceasing to reflect the sun's rays, relinquish their stored heat. The fire made of charcoal or desert brush dies down shortly after supper, for the Arabs do not waste fuel by building large campfires. Soon the traveler relaxes, curled up in his blanket in a hollow of sand. The night wind whispers in the thorn trees and rustles the clumps of dried grass, while overhead the clear Arabian stars light up "the most beautiful roof in the world."

One is awakened early in the cold upland dawn and served thick Yemeni coffee and hard-boiled eggs from Afif, washed down by a drink of canned fruit juice. From here eastward for a total of 115 miles, the King's highway crosses a series of flat, brown plains to Duwadami, a dual oasis surrounded by low, stony hills where about four thousand inhabitants cultivate date palms and kitchen gardens. A mud-walled fort stands between the two islands of green, well supplied with gasoline and topped by a wireless tower.

Beyond Duwadami the traveler enters the Nejd proper, the central plateau that makes up the Arabian heartland. As late as April a cool breeze blows over plains dotted with yellow flax and wild thyme. Herds of black-headed camels graze contentedly with their young, making the most of that gift to the desert from the few inches of winter rainfall—a carpet of green. To see the Nejd in April with the smoke spiraling from the black tents, to taste the rich camel's milk offered by the herdsmen, and to breathe deeply of the pure, electrifying air—these are true Arabian pleasures.

After forty miles across the rich plain the traveler watches a dot appear on the mirage-swept horizon and sees it expand, to become a band of copper-colored sand. This is the Nafud al Sirr, a protecting arm of sand from the Nafud desert of northern Arabia that shields Ibn Saud's capital.

Most Americans think of Saudi Arabia as a continuous sea of rolling sand, but this is far from accurate. For the most part the kingdom consists of gravel plains and dark rocky hills. In the north, however, lies a great lake of sand, the Nafud, which the English traveler Lady Blunt described as the color of "rhubarb and magnesia," [1] and in the south rolls that vast ocean of sand, the Rub al Khali. The prevailing wind is from the northwest, and the Nafud moves slowly southward into the Rub al Khali along two great rivers of sand. One of these is the Nafud al Sirr, flowing to the west of Riyadh; the other is the Dahna, which throws a barrier of sand dunes between Riyadh and the Persian Gulf. Where the King's highway crosses, the Nafud al Sirr is about fifteen miles in width, a jumble of magnificent copper-red sand dunes that run up to fifty feet in height and progress south at the rate of about thirty feet a year. Most of them are shaped like crescent moons, with their broad backs to the prevailing wind, which has blown away the sand from the underlying gravel in many places. During the hot months or late in the day, motor vehicles must be equipped with sand tires to make a crossing. In any case, it is wisest to travel away from tracks of other vehicles and to maintain speed.

Forty miles beyond the eastern sands of the Nafud al Sirr is Marrat, the largest settlement between Mecca and Riyadh. It is another walled town with a radio tower, a gas station, and several gardens clustered around its walls. Marrat's location is particularly dramatic, for the western horizon is lined by dunes of the Nafud al Sirr, while to the east rises the Tuwaiq escarpment, whose perpendicular cliffs of limestone rest on soft marl aglow with brilliant colors. The way, which leads up the cliffs, is steep, narrow, and rough. Once on top the road winds painfully through sandy wadies. Most trans-Arabian travelers stop in this area for their second night, wrapping themselves tightly in their blankets against the cool night air of the plateau three thousand feet above the Red Sea.

The next morning the truck proceeds in a southeasterly direction for some thirty miles to the town of Jubaila, rebuilt since 1930 around the ruins of a very old Arab settlement. This area is one of the most thickly settled in Saudi Arabia; the plateau is dotted with small villages that have sprung up around wells. At each well, patient donkeys

[1] Lady Anne Blunt, *A Pilgrimage to Nejd*, p. 156.

walk solemnly down an artificial incline, stop, turn, and climb up again, raising the dripping hide buckets and upending them into central irrigation ditches. Vegetables, dates, barley, and wheat grow well here unless checked by an exceptionally dry year or by the visitation of locusts, which black out the sun and devour every leaf in their path.

Beyond Jubaila the pastoral landscape gives way to clay plain. Then green palm trees and enclosed gardens dominated by the brown clay walls of a city signal the approach to Riyadh.

The visitor going to Riyadh by air has quite a different experience from that of the overland traveler. Instead of several days of hard travel, he makes a four-hour flight from the Red Sea to the middle of the Nejd in a Saudi Arabian Airlines or Aramco plane. Such a trip may unfold a magnificent panorama of coast, mountain, plain, and desert, though just as often the ground is blotted out by sand in the air, and the traveler sees nothing but brown haze under the blue Arabian sky.

The air strip where he comes in was at first laid out many miles away from Riyadh on the desert but has been gradually moved to within two miles of the city; its improvement and its progress toward the town are perhaps symbols of the breakdown of Saudi Arabian isolation. The American construction firm International Bechtel has erected stone buildings and turned the rough air strip into a two-runway airport lighted for night use.

Western visitors arriving by plane may be greeted by a Saudi guard of honor. These Arab infantrymen wear greenish European-style uniforms and puttees, and head-coverings of red-checked scarves held on by black silk coils. When there are official greetings, they are usually administered by the chamberlain of the court, who escorts the visitors to a white tent richly carpeted and furnished with arm chairs set around the walls, and there special ceremonial coffee is served. After fifteen minutes of talk about the King's health and the recent journey, the visitors are bundled into one of the royal cars and the motorcade sets off, the cars driving side by side across the flat desert to Riyadh.

No Hollywood director designing an Arabian city could possibly achieve a more fantastic set. Outlined sharply in the clear sunshine of the Nejd plateau rise the sun-baked walls of a sprawling Arab city, once confined within ancient crenelated battlements commanded by fifty-foot towers. Brown mud buildings including the great mosque and the citadel are stacked one against another, four and five stories high. But the town is dominated by the massive whitewashed palace built by Ibn Saud. Designed for defense as well as for a residence, the palace expanded around a series of inner courtyards as the King's family grew. In addition to the King's quarters, and those of his womenfolk, children, and their servants, it contains extensive public rooms, reception halls, audience chambers, and offices. The latter are used frequently by King Saud, who also has his own modern palace nearby.

Visitors to Riyadh are often driven past the city to the Badia Palace, which lies in a wadi about a mile and a half west. The parapet around its roof and inner courtyard is decorated with a crenelated design, typical of Riyadh, resembling rows of half-melted snow men. An oblong, two-story building, always freshly whitewashed, Badia Palace has been modernized for the reception of Western visitors. Some of the windows have glass; most of the rooms have single electric light bulbs hanging from the ceiling and abundant furniture, elaborate in design and showy in execution. Servants are constantly carrying water in dripping sheepskin bags or five-gallon kerosene tins to a tank on the roof which feeds two bathrooms. Servants also tend the fire under a water heater made out of a gasoline drum. In fact, a corps of "personal" servants surrounds the visitor every time he leaves his room. American breakfasts are provided. Plentiful Arabian mutton and rice with the customary side dishes predominate, however, at the noon and evening meals. Fortified by solid fare and relieved to be free of the bouncing truck, the traveler drops off to sleep almost unaware of the constant squeak of the wooden water wheels and the braying of the laboring donkeys.

Even the seasoned traveler feels a sense of excitement when he leaves the Badia Palace for his first meeting with the newly crowned King Saud. The car bumps across the gravelly wadi where the water may rise above the hub caps after the spring rains. Racing along the dusty road toward the walls, the car passes the power station which International Bechtel built in 1948. Entering one of the town's nine gates, it creeps along winding, unpaved streets, freshly swept and crowded with bearded townsmen, bedouin, and barefoot soldiers. Here and there among the throng are women on their way to market or the houses of friends, their faces and figures completely hidden by black robes. The driver blows the car's horn constantly, and people scatter quickly before the noise. But camels, overloaded donkeys, and flocks of black sheep and goats are not auto-conscious and take their time moving out of the way. Sidewalks are nonexistent, and the brown clay walls rise directly from the streets. What windows there are on the outer walls begin at the second story and are guarded by rusty iron bars. Whitewash is expensive; nevertheless many windows and doors are neatly outlined in it

45

or in white clay, as are the eaves and corners of most buildings, while the palaces, mosques, and other important structures are often completely whitewashed.

Europeans have not yet lost their novelty in Riyadh, and their arrival attracts a crowd at the gate of the palace, but the curious are kept from approaching the car by a detachment of khaki-clad King's Guards. Taking the Guards' salute and passing through an inner gate, guests climb a narrow stone stairway to an embellished balcony that encircles a gleaming-white inner courtyard. Adjusting the unfamiliar Arabian robes necessitated by court etiquette, they then proceed in order of rank into the *majlis,* or great reception room, where they face left and form a line across the end of the room farthest from the throne. The hall before them is about one hundred feet long, forty feet wide, and twenty feet high, with walls of smooth blue plaster and a molding of many colors. A row of heavy columns, painted to resemble marble, runs down the center, and along the right-hand wall a number of barred windows let in the bright sunshine and frame squares of the desert beyond the city walls.

As the visitor's eyes become accustomed to the shade of the room, he notices that the walls are lined with straight-armed sofas and formal chairs upholstered in elaborate brocade. In the largest of these, at the far right corner of the room, sits King Saud ibn Abdul Aziz al Saud, the fifty-one-year-old ruler of Saudi Arabia. His complexion is like that of a Spaniard, and the salient feature of his face is a prominent Arab nose. Through smallish dark glasses, penetrating black eyes size up the visitors advancing across the carpeted floor of the majlis. A mustache almost covers his full lips and matches a spot of black hair on his lower lip and his beard. The King rises, gives a firm shake with his large hand, and waves his ranking guest to a seat on his right. Then, usually speaking through an interpreter except to those who understand Arabic, he soon puts his guests at ease.

In spite of his wealth, the King dresses simply, usually wearing an ankle-length *saufrin* rather like a white cotton nightgown under his black or brown *aba,* a robe trimmed with gold braid. On his head he wears a white *ghutra,* held on by *igals* of gold thread, the Arabian sign of royalty. The former King, Ibn Saud, was very fond of red-and-white-checked *ghutras,* and the present ruler wears them occasionally. Although not as large as his illustrious father, King Saud is about six feet two inches in height and weighs well over two hundred pounds. Like his father, he has weak eyes, but he has also inherited Ibn Saud's magnetic smile and a keen sense of humor, which wins him many friends. Although he has not the compelling force of his father or the sharp brilliance of his brother Faisal, he has in recent years developed a poise and self-assurance which, combined with his size and commanding presence, give him a kingly manner.

King Saud was born in Kuwait on the night in January 1902 on which his father climbed over the walls of Riyadh with a small band of followers and reconquered the capital of the Nejd. Actually, he is not the oldest of Ibn Saud's three dozen sons. A brother, Turki, was born a short time before him but died in the influenza epidemic of 1917–1919 when that worldwide plague penetrated even to the heart of Arabia. Although this left Saud the senior prince of the realm, he was not named Crown Prince until May 11, 1933. This was because Arabs feel that succession to a throne should be determined not by seniority but by ability in leadership, suitability of character, and the indefinable characteristic of being lucky. For hundreds of years the death of a great ruler in the Arab world has usually been followed by a "night of long knives," and until recently most of the bedouin and many others in Saudi Arabia felt sure that King Ibn Saud's death would result in a blood bath.

The former King, however, studied his sons from every angle. He noted that the third prince, Mohammed, who was born in 1910, was generous, reckless, and brave, an excellent type to lead a bedouin tribe, but that he lacked the balance and maturity to rule a country one-third the size of the United States. Prince Faisal, the second son, who was born in 1904, was both wise and clever. As Foreign Minister, however, he was forced to spend much of his time abroad, and prolonged stays in the Western world are not the kind of background to endear even a Saudi prince to the strict Wahhabis of Arabia.

In contrast to these two brothers, Saud was neither reckless nor brilliant. But he was built like his father, looked something like him, and thought and acted as a Arabian ruler must to command the loyalty of both bedouin and townsfolk. He was physically strong, a good rider, a good swordsman, and a keen hunter of desert game. In the war against Yemen he commanded the eastern front of the Saudi line and showed himself not only a brave and able general, but a lucky one as well. One of the most religious of the King's sons, Saud was always a leader at prayers and, like his father, enjoyed hearing the Koran read aloud. He had made the pilgrimage to Mecca frequently and had given substantially to various Moslem institutions, particularly for the restoration of mosques.

One of the greatest sources of Amir Saud's strength was his close relations with the bedouin tribes. His youthful exploits in war and on the hunting field had endeared him to the tribal sheikhs, and his father capitalized on this by putting him in charge of tribal affairs. This meant that he got to know the important personalities of the bedouin groups very intimately. In addition, he handled the regular distribution of the subsidies which the King had always given to his tribesmen and personally allotted special sums to tribes whose grazing lands were dried by drought or whose camels were decimated by disease. Thanks to this, Prince Saud had what might be called "grass-roots" political strength among the fighting tribes of central Arabia to an extent not possessed by any of his brothers. It was the combination of these traits and factors, plus proof that he was lucky, that finally convinced King Ibn Saud that Amir Saud should be designated Crown Prince.

King Saud first left Saudi Arabia when he was twenty-four years old to go to Egypt to consult an oculist, who found his eyes weak but not seriously defective. He traveled abroad again in 1935, visiting various European capitals, including London where he stayed for five weeks. He represented Saudi Arabia at King George V's silver jubilee and at the coronation of King George VI. In 1940 he paid a courtesy visit to Italy, and he went to Egypt for an Arab conference in 1946. The foreign trip, however, which appears to have influenced him the most was his tour of the United States in 1947. It had been hoped that King Ibn Saud might come to this country, but the King said it would be more useful if the Crown Prince went in his stead. As a result, Amir Saud and his party of eight left Dhahran the first week of January 1947, being given an unprecedented send-off by a dozen of his brothers, half the officials of Saudi Arabia, and almost all of the American oil workers and their families. The royal plane, the chartered TWA airliner "Gates of Suez," was delayed for two days in Lisbon by bad weather, a period long enough to permit Gulbenkian, the mysterious Armenian who owns 5 per cent of the stock of the Iraq Petroleum Company, to give the Crown Prince his views on the international oil situation.

An impressive reception committee met the Crown Prince at the Washington airport, led by the then Under Secretary of State, Dean Acheson, the military and naval aides of the President, and the Arab diplomatic corps. At noon the next day the Crown Prince paid a courtesy call on President Truman at the White House. Amir Saud gave the Chief Executive a sword in a golden sheath set with jewels, and in return received an autographed picture of the President.

After lunch at Blair House, where the royal party was staying, the Crown Prince drove to Mount Vernon. There he surprised his guide with his knowledge of American history and compared the work of his father, Ibn Saud, in setting up Saudi Arabia with that of the American father of this country. Moving on to the Saudi Arabian Legation (now Embassy), the Crown Prince showed that he could handle an American press conference almost as well as a gathering of bedouin chiefs. In addition to answering questions, the Crown Prince read a prepared statement which he himself had written and which sheds considerable light on his thinking about Saudi Arabia and the United States. It read in part:

The place in the world played by each of our great countries attracts us toward each other. My country is the Holy Land of Islam and the cradle and Ministry of the Arabs. It is the land where Islam, the religion of a great part of the human race, was born, and it is the land toward which the hearts and eyes of many hundreds of millions of Moslems in all parts of the world turn five times daily. It is the land which has given great spiritual light and hope to peoples throughout the world. On the other hand, the United States of America is the champion of democracy. It is the center of industrial and scientific progress and it is the country toward which the hearts of all freedom loving people turn for guidance and inspiration.

The next morning the royal party visited the Capitol, where they were received by Senator Vandenberg, president pro tem of the Senate, and the entire Foreign Relations Committee. The Prince then spent half an hour in the Senate gallery, where he listened with considerable surprise to a violent attack by Senator Lodge of Massachusetts upon the power of the President over military expenditures. It was clearly a new experience for him to hear the head of a state so criticized in public. After more sightseeing the Prince was shown the mass production of paper currency at the Bureau of Printing and Engraving. No paper money is used in Saudi Arabia, and the Crown Prince asked a good many questions about its advantages and disadvantages, particularly the latter.

Another place that interested the Crown Prince was the Government Agricultural Station at Beltsville, Maryland, where Secretary of Agriculture Anderson gave him a personally conducted tour. The Crown Prince, who had several farms of his own including a new one in the Al Kharj district, showed particular interest in several new varieties of fruit being developed for use in a dry country, along with some unusually hardy types of sheep.

The high point of the Crown Prince's stay in Washington was an hour's talk with President Truman and Secretary Byrnes—a frank and friendly discussion of United States–Saudi Arabian relations. Then, after several more days of sightseeing and a variety of official entertainments, including a reception at the Saudi Arabian Legation, where two sheep roasted whole were served on trays smothered in rice, nuts, and rare spices, the Prince and his party left by train for New York.

During the early days of the visit, the Crown Prince's manner had been stiff and strained. As the time went by, however, he adjusted to the pattern of American official hospitality. He joked more and more frequently with his companions and American guides and began to enjoy himself thoroughly. Sitting in the observation compartment of his private car, the Prince was in particularly good form, asking many questions about the farms and factories that flashed by outside the car window. Even before Baltimore had been reached, the Prince said he was more than ever convinced that his father was right in starting to build a railroad across Saudi Arabia.

On reaching Pennsylvania Station, the Prince's car was switched to the Presidential siding. Then, paced by a motorcycle escort whose wailing sirens the Prince referred to as "jinn" or demons, he was hurried to the Empire State Building. The day was clear, and from the 102nd floor the Saudis marveled at the magnificent view of the city of New York spread out below them. The Crown Prince was told that New York was bigger than all the cities of the Near East put together, and that five thousand people worked in some of its skyscrapers.

"There are about that many in my father's palace," the Crown Prince replied.

The sun was setting as the party reached the royal suite on an upper floor of the Waldorf Towers previously occupied by various important visitors from abroad, including Winston Churchill and Queen Wilhelmina of the Netherlands. The Prince stood for a while at the southwest window of the apartment looking down on the rush-hour traffic sweeping up Park Avenue and across to the lights beginning to shine in the towering skyscrapers of the city.

"I thought my brothers were exaggerating when they told me about New York," he said, "but they did not tell me half the truth."

Before the party had been at the Waldorf half an hour the Prince called for his prayer rug, and, while the Christian members of the party withdrew to the hall, he led his Moslem countrymen in evening prayer. Unconfused by the rapid travel of the afternoon and the maze of hotel corridors through which he had come, the Crown Prince turned his face correctly in the direction of Mecca.

The next morning was devoted to writing letters, and the Crown Prince sent his father in Riyadh a detailed description of his official visit to Washington. As he explained later, he wanted to emphasize the friendliness he had found among all ranks of Americans from President Truman to the waiters in the dining car. He also felt he must tell his father of the beauty of Washington, the mile after mile of factories he had seen on the train trip, and the size and orderliness of New York City.

One of the real problems presented by the visits of all Saudi princes to this country is the influx of Levantine salesmen who crowd the princes' outer apartments, loaded down with all manner of "American bargains," which they offer at about three times the articles' normal price. Since the visiting Arabs have no knowledge of American prices, are backed up by virtually limitless funds, and are fascinated by everything they see, from automobiles to ball-point pens, the greatest care is necessary to keep them from squandering their money. Not long before Amir Saud arrived, one of his younger brothers, the twelve-year-old son of the King's favorite wife, turned up at the Waldorf and asked for $15,000 at breakfast the first morning.

"What do you need so much money for?" he was asked.

"We are going to be in New York for three days, aren't we?" the boy replied.

The Crown Prince was wiser. American automobiles and radios were no novelties to him, but he was planning a new palace at Riyadh and wanted to see American kitchen equipment such as electric stoves, refrigerators, and oversized deep-freeze units. When he left the Waldorf he told the Saudi Arabian Minister he had put some unwanted items in his bureau drawer. The Minister went up to the royal apartment and found twenty-one trays of diamond rings.

One of the days the Crown Prince enjoyed the most during his stay in the New York area was spent at Princeton University, where the famous Arabist Dr. Philip K. Hitti acted as his guide. The Prince was surprised at the extent of the University's Arabic library and at the number of students studying that language and Middle Eastern problems. He was told that little study and research had been done in the United States on the Moslem world before 1930, but that that area was now attracting a rapidly increasing number of graduate students interested in foreign affairs.

That evening the Prince was the guest of honor at a banquet at the

Waldorf Astoria given by the Arabian American Oil Company. King Ibn Saud had recently entertained a distinguished group of the oil company officials at a banquet near Dhahran. On that occasion five thousand chickens, twenty-five hundred roast sheep, and the hump of a young camel were spread out on the carpeted floor of the huge banquet tent. The oil men, not to be outdone, arranged a display that was equally impressive in its way. A single table filled the center of the main ballroom of the Waldorf, its surface laid out to represent a New England landscape in wintertime. A river of mirror flowed between snow-covered hills, curving under a covered bridge and skirting an electrically lighted model town. Motor cars were stalled in snowdrifts along a miniature highway, and an electric railroad wound through the winter wonderland, with its various loading and unloading sidings ready to be operated from a control panel located at the Crown Prince's place. When the health of the King was proposed, a Saudi Arabian tune known as the "Prince's Song" was played for the first time in America.

One day the Crown Prince motored down through the canyons of Wall Street, where, in the vaults of the Federal Reserve Bank, far below the city streets, he walked among four billion dollars' worth of gold bars.

"Your wealth is in oil and you keep it underground," said one of his guides. "Our wealth is in gold, and we keep it here."

"And now we are getting up our oil to send to you, and you are taking up your gold to send to us," the Prince replied. "Let us hope that the exchange makes us both happy."

On another occasion the party drove out to Lake Success, where the Amir was received by the Acting Secretary General of the United Nations.

"The Moslem world gets together each year during the pilgrimage to Mecca," said the Prince. "I am delighted to see the place where the representatives of the whole world come each year to make a pilgrimage in the interests of world democracy."

After a busy week in New York, Amir Saud set out as a guest of the Arabian American Oil Company on a tour of the United States. Although he was shown the industrial centers of Pittsburgh, Detroit, and Chicago, the longest part of the trip was spent in Texas, Arizona, and California—warm, dry, and often sandy areas, where conditions were like those to be found in his own country. At the experimental farm of the Texas Agricultural and Mechanical State College he was shown new and simple methods of growing, harvesting, and spinning cotton, of improving the quality of wool, and of developing breeds of cattle

52

adapted to semidesert conditions. He was told that, only a month before, a group of experts in desert farming from this college had been sent by the United States Department of Agriculture to run the experimental farm in the Al Kharj district south of Riyadh. Several days were also spent near Phoenix, Arizona, motoring through once-desert country which had been irrigated and was now green with fields of young lettuce and cauliflower and dotted with groves of orange and lemon trees and date palms. There he met an old American friend, David Rogers, the former head of the Al Kharj farms, who showed him striking examples of how the farmers of the American southwest have conquered the desert.

Still another high point of the trip was a visit to Boulder Dam with its thirty-two million acre-feet of stored water, its giant generating plant, and its system of tunnels and canals that carry water to the homes and industries of southern California more than 240 miles away.

"More than anything else I have seen," the Prince said, "this project shows the greatness of America and the way you Americans have mastered nature for the good of all. In this sort of thing we have much to learn from you.'

During his stay in southern California Amir Saud was pleased to find that some of the architecture there could be traced back to Arabian designs, having come to us via North Africa, Spain, and Mexico.

After touring the citrus experiment station of the University of California, the Crown Prince said, "I never cease to be amazed at the amount of time, money, and effort which you Americans devote to making good crops better. Most people would be happy with what you start with, but you are never satisfied. This drive for something better produces a restlessness that often robs you of life's true goal, which is inner peace."

The Crown Prince enjoyed enormously the morning he spent at the Kellogg Horse Farm near Pomona, California. There, seated in an honor box, the Amir watched as some of the finest Arab stallions in the country were put through their paces in a demonstration of superb horsemanship.

Most education in Saudi Arabia is Koranic and thus not susceptible to basic change. There is, however, a need for vocational schools, and the Crown Prince spent some interesting hours at the San Francisco Trade High School where he saw examples of woodworking, ceramic production, and the teaching of simple mechanical skills. "This school should be transplanted to Saudi Arabia," the Prince told his guides, and in a manner of speaking this did happen, for several trade schools have since been developed by Aramco in Saudi Arabia. In fact, many of the things which the Crown Prince saw in this country have now been introduced into Saudi Arabia at his instigation or with his support. These include deep wells, special methods of irrigation, and some varieties of drought-resistant crops and cattle. The development of piers for ocean-going steamers, hospitals, paved roads, and better facilities for air travel also date in part from his visit. One of the best proofs that King Saud is as farsighted as he is ready to learn can be seen in these modern improvements.

When the six-week visit was over and the Crown Prince boarded the President's plane in Washington for the first leg of the trip back to Arabia, he took with him the Medal of the Legion of Merit for his assistance to the Allied war effort. More important, however, he carried in his heart a warm friendship for America and its people, and in his mind ideas for the modernization of his country, its government, and its economy, which have already proved useful and which will be an important factor in determining the path which his country will follow during his reign.

The six years that elapsed between Amir Saud's visit to America and his succession to the throne of Saudi Arabia on November 9, 1953, were a time of growing responsibility for the Crown Prince. To the outside world Amir Saud was still a rather colorless figure in the shadow of his father, the first among many princes who sat silently along the wall while his father held court in the great majlis in Riyadh or who handled the routine entertainment of visiting dignitaries. Actually, however, under the guidance of the old King Prince Saud was taking over more and more of the work of running the country. For years he had handled the affairs of the King's household and his far-flung property, as well as his relations with the tribes. To this were added certain negotiations with Aramco over the oil concessions, with the American Ambassador over political relations, and with the American commander at the Dhahran airfield over problems affecting that base. Prince Faisal continued as Foreign Minister, but Amir Saud worked with him on some aspects of foreign affairs such as the dispute with the British over Saudi Arabia's boundaries with certain British-protected sheikhdoms of the Persian Gulf.

There were many rumors, during these years, that Crown Prince Saud would never be able to hold together the kingdom his father had built and could not control even his own brothers. But as the Crown Prince showed increasing capabilities in affairs of state, his brothers fell in line. The pattern was set by Prince Faisal as far back as 1948. Coming back that year from the United Nations meeting in New York, the Saudi Arabian Foreign Minister was met at the airport in Riyadh by his older brother. When they drove into town together in an open car, the Crown Prince sat on the back seat while Prince Faisal sat on the floor at his feet. There were those who said that this was but outward show. Events so far, however, have indicated it was more than just that and have proved that the King was right in choosing Saud for his Crown Prince.

In the middle of 1950 Ibn Saud's health began to fail noticeably. At first he gave up working at night, and then he cut the time he spent on official matters down to a few hours in the morning. It was Crown Prince Saud meanwhile who picked up the reins of government as they slipped from the hands of the aging King. At first he was frequently outmaneuvered by the clique of cunning Levantine advisers whom King Ibn Saud had brought in to aid in the running of his ever-expanding government. But the Crown Prince learned with experience, and by the time in September 1953 that the King, who was at Taif, suffered a serious heart attack, Crown Prince Saud had actually been in control of the government for some time. Before his father died he was acting as Commander-in-Chief of the armed forces and as Prime Minister, in addition to his other responsibilities. Through brothers who were friendly to him or through advisers whom he trusted, he was able to dominate those of his brothers who questioned his leadership and to neutralize the machinations of the more unscrupulous advisers who had entrenched themselves in the palace. His position was further strengthened when, on October 9, 1953, a Cabinet of Ministers was set up responsible to him, a move that was really an implementation of a 1932 decree.

King Ibn Saud rallied from his September attack after three days in an oxygen tent, but it was clear that the end was only a matter of months. The Crown Prince kept a firm hand on the army, continued full payments to the tribes, and cemented the ties between himself and the brothers who were friendly to him.

On November 8 the health of the King, who had refused to leave the hill town if he had to go on a stretcher, again took a turn for the worse. Scheduled Saudi Airlines flights were canceled in order to use the planes to carry fifteen of the thirty-six sons, some of the forty-three daughters, and a few of the older grandsons with their retinues to Taif. Several foreign airplanes were chartered to bring home those princes who were abroad. For a few hours it looked as though Ibn Saud's iron constitution would enable him to rally once again, but his eleven old wounds and strenuous seventy-three years of life were too much. At about six o'clock on the morning of November 9, King Ibn Saud was gathered to his fathers. Within an hour of his passing his sons met in the majlis of the palace at Taif, pledged their support to the new King Saud al Saud, and chose Prince Faisal as the new Crown Prince.

As was necessary under local law, the body of the late King was put temporarily underground before sundown that night. The next day it was flown to his beloved city of Riyadh, where he was buried beside his father. During the five days of official mourning many stores were closed, flags flew at half-mast, and voices were hushed in palace and market place. Then, rather to the surprise of many observers, the country gradually returned to normal. According to rumors, there may still be trouble from the tribes or the ambitious princes, but as yet this has not occurred in any serious form. Ibn Saud is dead, Saud al Saud rules in his place, and neither assassination nor rebellion has marked the change. Speaking over the radio soon after Ibn Saud's death, the new King announced that he would carry on the policies of his father, support those who supported him, maintain most of the officials in their former posts, and make no basic changes in Saudi Arabia's foreign policy. In part he said:

In the administration of the country and its affairs, I shall follow the rules of the religion, seeking the powerful help of God. I pledge to adhere to God's generous book and the laws of his Prophet, for which I shall struggle with my sword and tongue, doing my utmost to make my dear people happy and prosperous. I shall work for the country's political, economic, and social progress. I shall watch over the interest of the country and insure the rights of its people, overcoming every obstacle in the way of these interests and striking at every corrupt and shameful manifestation. We shall devote particular attention to our military and national forces. I shall also continue to tighten the Islamic and Arab fraternal bonds with the Islamic and Arab States, and I shall maintain the friendship of the foreign countries, which have enjoyed the kind attention of our departed Monarch. I shall make our dear country occupy its proper place in insuring world peace.

King Saud then granted amnesty to most of the prisoners in the country's jails. He relaxed certain restrictions on foreigners which had been imposed during the declining years of the late King, and indicated that he will continue his father's firm stand against communism.

Since coming to the throne, the King has spent a good deal of time in Jidda, where he received the foreign diplomats and business community, and in Mecca, where he met with the religious leaders of that Moslem shrine. His residence, however, is in Riyadh, where he has been visited by a number of relatives and rulers and friends from other Arab countries. Although he does not show his father's capacity for putting in eighteen-hour working days, King Saud is nevertheless working hard and diligently at his job of running Saudi Arabia. He no longer has time for the long hours he used to spend in his hunting tent, the cool garden of his retreat outside Riyadh, or with his wives and children in his modern palace. But he still enjoys an informal dinner on the roof of the palace, where, as host to one or two foreign visitors, several of his brothers, and a group of court friends, he presides over a dinner cooked by his American chef, which often features more Western than Arabian dishes.

The feeling of tension which he occasionally showed on first becoming King is giving way to an air of calm confidence. Persons who have dined with him recently say that his sense of humor is as keen as ever and that particularly after dinner, when he relaxes with a group of friends in one of the smaller sitting rooms of his air-cooled palace, he shows that he has made the transition from Crown Prince to King successfully.

Thanks to the wisdom of the late King, the present ruler is well trained for his job. He is clearly able to swim in deep political waters if they are calm. Whether he can swim in stormy waters remains to be seen. But students of government, particularly those interested in the early development of modern states, would do well to keep their eyes upon him. Under King Ibn Saud the heart of the Arabian Peninsula changed in a single generation from a late-bronze-age federation of nomadic tribes, warring villages, and independent city-states into a unified kingdom roughly comparable to that of William the Conqueror. It remains to be seen whether the next thirty years will show real political progress in the direction of a constitutional monarchy or a return to fragmented tribal rule. The key to that future is in the hands of King Saud.

V

Model Farms of Al Kharj

IN THE Al Kharj district, 500 dusty miles inland from the Red Sea and 275 miles west of the oil coast, a handful of American experts, surrounded by the rugged and untutored tribesmen of central Saudi Arabia, have made the desert bloom. The work they have done and are doing on model farms in this isolated spot is the spearhead of modern agricultural development in Saudi Arabia, the start of a plan which King Ibn Saud hoped would quadruple the farm produce of his country.

To understand the Al Kharj farms, one must bear in mind the pattern of the central Arabian water supply. Down the center of barren Arabia there stretches a series of hills some four thousand feet in elevation, known as the Tuwaiq Mountains, on which four or five inches of rain fall each year. Running off the eastern foothills of these mountains, the rain water flows underground at a depth of 50 to 800 feet. At the oasis of Hofuf, the largest in Saudi Arabia, the water comes to the surface in some forty springs, one of which alone produces 22,000 gallons of water a minute. Farther east it reaches the Persian Gulf, where some of it bubbles up in a series of fresh-water springs. For years the pearl fishermen of Bahrein Island have replenished their water jugs by diving overboard through the salty water of the Persian Gulf and filling their containers from this underground source.

In the Al Kharj district, the water flowing underground has undermined the surface limestone and opened up a series of pits or large natural wells which look like abandoned stone quarries. The main wells,

Ain Semha and Ain Dhila, are about 300 feet in diameter and approximately 420 feet deep. The average water level in both is about 30 feet below the surface of the desert when the pumps are not running, and the two wells are connected underground, so that pumping in one causes the water level in both to drop proportionately.

Old camel trails leading part way down into these pits and faintly discernible ruins of long-vanished settlements nearby show that in the past the water level was perhaps 25 feet higher than it is at present and that the pits once watered substantial settlements, as did those at Al Aflaj farther to the south. But during the centuries of intertribal warfare and the concomitant disintegration of Arab society prior to the "Pax Ibn Saud," the settlements were abandoned. In 1938, through the initiative of Sheikh Abdullah Suleiman, pumps were installed at one of the largest wells in the Al Kharj district, and a small canal was cut to the best nearby land. The hiring of an Iraqi engineer, the interest of the Finance Minister, and the support of the King should have led to further development and use of this water supply, but results were limited primarily because of the type and quantity of equipment used.

The need for water and for food in fast-growing central Arabia increased. It became so pressing that in 1942 the King appealed to the United States, and President Roosevelt used his emergency fund to finance the first United States agricultural mission to Saudi Arabia. It was an advisory mission headed by Karl Twitchell, with J. G. Hamilton of the Department of Agriculture and A. L. Wathen of the Department of the Interior as the other members. The mission traveled eleven thousand miles, and its report laid the groundwork for most subsequent planning.

Later on, receiving appeals for assistance from the King in getting water to the farms at Bijidiyah in Al Kharj, Aramco brought new and better pumps and set them firmly on the edge of the pits at Ain Dhila. From them a cement-lined canal fifteen kilometers long was dug to the little settlement, where there were eight thousand level acres. This land looked like the rest of the desert to the untrained eye, but experts recognized that it had possibilities if watered.

Development of the farmland at Bijidiyah moved slowly, and the output was so limited that central Arabia still had to import most of its wheat, rice, vegetables, and fodder. When the spread of World War II made it impossible for the government of Saudi Arabia to buy these abroad, a serious food shortage developed and the tribes became restless. Disturbances broke out that threatened the stability of the Arabian Peninsula and might have interfered with the development of Saudi Arabia's oil. The American and British Governments decided that the Saudi Arabs must be fed and that, to save shipping, food production in Arabia should be increased. As a result, a second United States Government agricultural mission was sent to Saudi Arabia in December 1944, under the sponsorship of the Department of State but financed and directed by the Foreign Economic Administration. Working under the direction of David A. Rogers of Arizona, the mission began work to contribute to Saudi Arabia's self-sufficiency in food and to instruct Saudi Arabs in the latest and most effective methods of irrigation and agriculture.[1]

The physical difficulties against which these men struggled were tremendous. Civilization, in the form of the oil camp at Dhahran, was 275 miles east across a desert whose dunes are sometimes a hundred feet high and were then impossible to cross except by camel or by motor vehicles especially equipped with sand tires. The problems of obtaining trucks, cars, and agricultural machinery in wartime United States were bad enough, but they were minor compared to the problem of getting that equipment to the Persian Gulf and then inland to Al Kharj. All fuel had to be trucked across the desert from Dhahran, and at times not only the tractors but the Diesel engines which ran the pumps had to shut down. No suitable housing was available, and for six hot and difficult months the government mission lived cooped up in two small rooms, along with the engineers previously sent out by the oil company.

The group was shut in by the drifting sands and surrounded by a hostile or indifferent population; it wilted in heat that ran to 125 degrees in the shade and was cut off for weeks at a time from contact with the outside world except by radio. Tension mounted, personal eccentricities became irritants, tempers ran short, and only the men's courage and skillful handling by Rogers kept the project going. Work began on the first experimental farm in 1945, with a labor force of thirteen hundred Saudis supplied by the King. Scrawny, hump-backed zebu bulls, directed by twisting their tails, and a few tractors brought in by the mission provided the power. Under the direction of the American experts, the irrigation canals were extended and clear water poured out of the pits onto the thirsty fields.

It seemed as though Nature, long left alone in the remote Arabian

---

[1] For much of the material on this history of the Al Kharj project, the author is indebted to David A. Rogers and K. J. Edwards, former directors.

plateau, had determined to challenge the invaders to the utmost. Just as the Americans were finishing their first sowing, disaster struck in the form of a cloudburst fifty miles to the west in the Tuwaiq foothills. Rushing down a wadi, the flood hit Al Kharj in a roaring brown torrent half a mile wide. When it had passed, there was nothing left of a vital section of the main canal, and the carefully developed network of small canals was completely washed away. Rogers rallied his men, and the end of another month saw the big canal and its branches once more in operation.

An intensive period of planting followed, and the face of the desert turned green with wheat, alfalfa, and vegetables. Suddenly, when all seemed well, locusts appeared. Alighting on the fields, their long wiggling bodies formed a carpet five miles wide and so thick a man could not step without crushing a dozen. For forty-five days the mission fought "the battle of the locusts." They dug ditches, threw up earthen barriers, and laid lines of flaming oil. The Arabs, who enjoy eating locusts, grew tired and complained that it was foolish to go against the will of Allah and destroy food sent from heaven. But the Americans kept on, working eighteen hours a day, until they grew thin and exhausted. In the end they saved only a fraction of the crops already planted. Most of the fields that had been so green were as bare as before the Americans came over the Dahna in their trucks.

But these men who had left their families and traveled halfway around the world on a challenge were not to be permanently stopped. Most of the seeds brought from Arizona had been planted, but they took what was left, supplemented it with new seed bought locally, and replanted. Once again the fields of Al Kharj began to turn green; and in one respect the disaster had proved a blessing in disguise, for the mission found that, when given proper water and care, many local varieties outproduced American seed.

During the war these farms, under the supervision of the Foreign Economic Administration with Middle East headquarters in Cairo, demanded all the energies of the American mission members, who never found time to fill out the many forms required by a government agency; consequently, an administrative officer was sent down from Cairo to help them with their bookkeeping. According to report, he was not a man accustomed to rough travel, and the trip across the sands of the Dahna from Dhahran left him exhausted. The primitive living quarters on the farms undid him further, and the meager fare set on the table for his first dinner was the last straw.

61

"How is the drinking water here?" he asked.

"Much better," joked one of the mission. "We have reduced the camel urine to less than 10 per cent."

The administrative officer left in the morning, and it was a long time before Al Kharj got another.

At first there was resentment in the nearby Arab communities over the intrusion of American unbelievers into the heart of the Moslem world, and the most strenuous efforts on the part of Rogers and his assistants were required to obtain labor. Once recruited, each laborer had to be shown how to perform every elementary operation. These Arabs had never seen a long-handled shovel and tried to cut down those that were given them to the length of their own inefficient tools. Strange as it may seem, the idea of using camel manure for fertilizer had never occurred to them. When Rogers borrowed seventy-five of the King's camels to go about the countryside and collect dried camel dung from native corrals, the drivers shook their heads at the crazy superstitions of the Christians. Only the fact that the King had ordered his men to obey the American farmers in every detail prevented a mutiny. Months later, when the ground which had been fertilized out-yielded untouched soil three and four times, the Arab farmers admitted that there must be something to the practice, and word spread from mouth to mouth about this use of camel dung for something besides fuel.

For centuries the Arabs had worked on the theory that if a little water was good, a lot of water was better. Local foremen often kept the fields flooded, wasting water and hurting the crops. Furthermore, the Arabs felt that the more that could be planted on an acre of land the better and rebelled against the idea of thinning out their groves and fields. The wisdom of limited use of water and the proper spacing of trees and crops in order to allow for maximum growth took repeated demonstrations but has at last been accepted by the Arabs.

In 1945 the King was reminded that the war was over and that, although the United States was most friendly to Saudi Arabia, there was no longer any justification for taxing Americans to finance the Al Kharj project, especially since King Ibn Saud's oil royalties now gave him enough money to continue the work.

"My people need food and they need guidance in better farming methods," Ibn Saud said. "Al Kharj is giving us both. I will take over its financing."

Not long after this, a third American agricultural mission, consisting of President Franklin Stewart Harris of Utah State Agricultural College, Dean R. E. Buchanan of Iowa State College, and Dr. Afif Tannous of the Department of Agriculture, visited the Al Kharj farms. Their findings confirmed the King's belief that in spite of many obstacles real progress was being made.

As a result of the King's interest and of this favorable report, it was decided that the Al Kharj farms should be not only continued but expanded. King Ibn Saud agreed to put up the money and the Arabian American Oil Company to recruit new American personnel to relieve Rogers and his pioneer farmers, who had by then turned the sandy valley of Al Kharj into a series of well-irrigated farms. Rogers and most of his men returned to the United States in 1946, and, when Crown Prince Saud was visiting here in 1947, he spent several days in Arizona with Rogers and his "old Arab hands," seeing American farm methods applied on their home soil. The work on the Al Kharj farms has since been carried on by about two dozen American agricultural experts, at first under the direction of Kenneth J. Edwards, a former county agent from Texas, then under his assistant, and later under Frank Brookshier. Under their care the farms have been expanded to about three thousand acres, and it is possible that up to ten thousand acres more may be eventually brought under cultivation.

The visitor may tour three separate model farms in the Al Kharj district, driving for miles along smooth roads past concrete irrigation ditches whose banks are lined with young tamarisk and eucalyptus trees. On either side, lush green fields of alfalfa stand out against the brown desert like squares on a chess board. Recently, over 900 acres of wheat, 345 of maize, 327 of barley, 278 of alfalfa, 45 of Sudan grass, 28 of millet, 2 of sugar cane, and half an acre of grapes were in production. Trucks or cars on the new railroad leave Al Kharj daily for Riyadh carrying watermelons, tomatoes, carrots, radishes, honeydews, cucumbers, cantaloupes, onions, squash, cabbage, cauliflower, broccoli, eggplant, lettuce, okra, peas, peppers, and turnips, to mention only the more important items. These vegetables were either high-priced or unobtainable in central Arabia until a few years ago. Most of them go to the palace, but more than five thousand people receive food from palace supplies, all of whom are eating better than they ever did before. Furthermore, "what the palace eats today, the town will eat tomorrow," and a taste for new and better foods is spreading throughout the Nejd. So great is the need there for green vegetables that even alfalfa is bought by Riyadh housewives to serve as a vegetable.

63

In addition to the crops mentioned above, a number of new ones have been introduced in Al Kharj. These include high-quality Irish potatoes that have been transplanted from Lebanon and strawberries brought from Beirut. Peanuts were introduced, but the crows went after them almost as fast as they were planted. From Iraq new varieties of pears, pomegranates, figs, apricots, oranges, and tangerines were imported. Various types of desert gourds, whose seeds contain oils that are useful for human food and for industry, have been sent to Al Kharj for trial from the Texas agricultural experiment substation at Chillicothe. Experiments are also being made with various varieties of rice. This is a crop usually associated with wet parts of the world, and the Saudis import a great deal; therefore its production in Arabia would be both helpful and profitable. Recently effort has gone into raising chickens with the idea of bettering the scrawny bird familiar in most of Arabia.

The management of the project has endeavored to improve the living conditions of the farm workers and has set up a food program under which the lower-paid workers on the farms can buy food at a saving of about 25 per cent. A start has also been made on building houses for the higher-paid Arab workers.

One of the serious drawbacks to farming in the Nejd has been the almost complete lack of trees for windbreaks, firewood, or lumber. More than 35,000 trees have been set out throughout Al Kharj as windbreaks, and over 250,000 tamarind and *athel* (tamarisk) trees have been planted in more than eight acres of wood lots. When they mature, the trunks of the athel trees will be used for rafters, substituting for mangrove poles from Africa.

About 10,000 date palms have also been planted in Al Kharj. Although the Arabs have produced dates since time immemorial, new strains and methods developed by the California date growers have been introduced and have increased yields and improved qualities. These methods include careful selection of the stock, the planting of fewer trees per acre, more scientific irrigation, which uses less water than the old Arab methods, and more careful pruning and pollination.

Since 1947 the date crop of Al Kharj has increased fourfold, and the quality is much improved. Some Arabian dates have to be harvested as soon as they mature. They are particularly delicious but require a great deal of labor; therefore the trend is toward dates which stay on the trees and can all be harvested at the same time.

Nursery stock planted on the Al Kharj farms includes 3,000 grape

8. Laying the Trans-Arabian Pipe Line to carry oil from Saudi Arabia to tankers waiting near Sidon on the Mediterranean.

9. Saudi Arab employees riding a Diesel engine of the new Saudi Arabian Railroad in the eastern part of the country.

10. Modern agricultural machinery on an Al Kharj district farm, transforming barren desert into producing fields.

11. Harvesting young onions on a farm in the Al Kharj district of central Saudi Arabia, where American experts are demonstrating modern methods.

cuttings, 2,000 fig cuttings, 2,000 pomegranate trees, 1,000 mulberry trees, and many varieties of citrus. All these items do well if given proper soil and water. Unfortunately, the water available in this part of Arabia contains a high volume of salt, and many acres which have been irrigated for a long time without proper drainage have become unproductive. It has been necessary to start rehabilitating them by improving drainage, plowing deep, adding the proper fertilizers, and planting special crops.

One of the minor problems that the American farm experts in central Arabia have had to overcome has been the rapid growth of Bermuda grass in fields supplied with water. The grass, introduced by the Americans less then five years ago, has already become a pest, choking out less hardy plants such as vegetables and even alfalfa.

In addition to the more than twenty miles of main canals, the workers have made almost five hundred miles of smaller irrigation ditches, as well as many miles of small dams to check the destructive floods that at intervals in the past have wiped out crops in the area. This extensive irrigation demanded more labor to dig ditches and make dams than was available locally. Consequently, machines for this work have been brought in, along with tractors, combines, and commercial fertilizer distributors. In spite of the low cost of labor in Arabia, tests have shown that it is often cheaper to use farm machinery than native manpower. One such test run in the spring of 1949 near Hofuf showed that the cost of plowing and "floating" by machine was 18 riyals ($4.50) an acre. The cost of turning over this land by hand, without even leveling it, would have been at least 35 riyals an acre, plus the price of one meal and tea and coffee for the Arab workers each day. In addition the tractor plowed much more deeply and broke up the clods of earth more smoothly.

The Americans at these farms now live comfortably. Housing facilities, complete with modern plumbing and electric lights, have been expanded to accommodate a limited number of families. Trainees' quarters, laundry and warehouse, office, garage, workshop, battery shop, welding shop, blacksmith shop, tool room, powder magazine, water tank and pump house, and a mosque for the local farm laborers are other new features. The most colorful spot is the Arab Room in the headquarters building, decorated by an expert sent down by the King, with fine rugs, cushions, curtains, and overstuffed chairs from the monarch's summer palace. All important visitors to the farm have been entertained in this impressive "majlis."

Among such visitors should be mentioned Mohammed al Bessan, a landowner who came to Al Kharj several years ago to get a "few American seeds" for his farm at Kissim and became a regular caller; Abdul Karim Sheraif, an influential Arab farmer, who was skeptical of American ways at first but became ready to try out every new idea he saw in successful operation there. Whenever possible, men like these leaders in their communities have been made chairmen of local agricultural committees to demonstrate new techniques of farming to their neighbors.

Amir Abdullah, the late King's uncle, became enthusiastic about modern farming and bought a battery of pumps, a tractor, a threshing machine, and a small ditchdigger, employing a mechanic to keep them running. Amir Saud al Kabir, one of Ibn Saud's brothers-in-law, is also improving his nearby farm, on which he has tried out the American idea of "planting less and harvesting more," after frequent visits to Al Kharj.

Since his visit to the United States, the present King has gone often to Al Kharj and drives around the farms comparing what is being done there with what David Rogers showed him in Arizona. On one such visit he brought with him the Sheikh of Kuwait, who was much impressed but said that he would never be able to convince his friends in Kuwait of the size and variety of the fruits and vegetables grown in Al Kharj. When he left, the Americans filled his plane with huge watermelons, cantaloupes, and honeydew melons. The Sheikh sent back word that his friends were so impressed by these samples that they wanted to have a similar project up in Kuwait.

Saudi Arabian farms average a little larger than the victory gardens that flourished in American cities during the last war. They range in size from a quarter of an acre to five acres, and a fifty-acre farm is considered enormous. Most Arab farms are run by a father and his sons, helped by numerous uncles, cousins, and other relatives. Poor seed and lack of proper cultivation and fertilizer reduce the yield to only five to ten bushels an acre of such crops as wheat or barley. Al Kharj, however, has shown that similar soil can be made to yield up to fifty bushels per acre with modern farm methods. The King has become particularly interested in fertilizer on this account, and he has allowed his own farm in the Al Kharj district to be used to demonstrate the value and use of camel manure and chemicals such as 20 per cent superphosphate. There increases in wheat yields have been substantial. Small areas of land have also been treated with bird guano brought in sacks from the islands of the Persian Gulf. This fertilizer is inexpensive even when it has to be transported by camel, and now that the railway from the Gulf goes through Al Kharj use of it may become widespread.

The originator of the project and one of the first visitors to the Al Kharj farms was Sheikh Abdullah Suleiman. Among other things he encouraged the establishment of a weather station and follows reports of rainfall and temperature changes with interest. This weather station, incidentally, reported a temperature of 21 degrees at Al Kharj in January 1949, a frost that killed over fifty acres of tomatoes and nearly all the other vegetables except onions and carrots.

In spite of the support of Sheikh Abdullah and certain other prominent Saudis, the work being done by the American farm experts in Al Kharj was severely criticized until six years ago. Attacks came, on the one hand, from fanatical Wahhabis who objected to having nonbelievers living on the sacred soil of the Nejd and, on the other, from ordinary Arab farmers who thought that the methods that had been good enough for their fathers were good enough for them. To counteract opposition, the Finance Minister persuaded King Ibn Saud to make another visit to Al Kharj during the summer of 1947, accompanied by more than two thousand of his most important relatives and officials.

Before the King's arrival, every room in his rambling palace a few miles from the headquarters of the farms was sprayed with DDT, and all pools of stagnant water were treated with crude oil. For the first time in their lives the Arabian court found themselves free of flies and mosquitoes. The Crown Prince was so impressed that he ordered all his palaces treated in a similar manner, and the rapidly growing use of DDT in Saudi Arab households may be traced in part to this occasion.

For the King's visit the Americans leveled two landing strips, one near the palace and one near the farm headquarters. Two special ramps were made so that the monarch could walk easily out of his plane to the ground, devices which pleased him so much that he promptly rewarded the mechanic who made them.

While the King was there, ordinary affairs in Al Kharj stopped completely, and the place became a cross between an American state fair and Versailles when Marie Antoinette was "farming." During the fourteen days of the visit the usually quiet roads of the farm were packed with automobiles. The biggest group always accompanied the King, who traveled in an old Pierce Arrow phaeton that he liked because of its large windows and ample headroom. With him were several of the older princes. Following close behind was a string of shiny new cars filled with relatives, ministers of state, and armed guards. There was nothing on the farm that the King did not see, although visitors riding in the rear cars saw little except the dust, which swirled about the cavalcade as it moved and hung in the still air as it stopped. When the King was not driving about the farm, the main cavalcade split into two or three groups, which raced about and produced indescribable traffic jams when they met.

This sudden influx of visitors created innumerable problems for the American hosts. It was necessary to keep the water trucks running night and day to supply the needs of the thirsty Arabs, who drank deeply of the good Al Kharj water, which they said was far better than that of Riyadh. Some of the visiting Saudis were introduced to ice water for the first time, and the demand became so heavy that the farm ran out of ice. A constant stream of requests for repairs to palace cars swamped the limited facilities of the farm garage and overawed the native mechanics, who, having been trained to repair broken-down trucks, suddenly found themselves under the hoods of new Cadillac limousines and Chrysler convertibles. About one o'clock one night Edwards was awakened by a loud banging on his door. It was a representative of the King's household in a high state of excitement because the refrigerator sent down from Riyadh for the King had broken down. Replacing this was a tough assignment in the middle of the desert. After trying unsuccessfully to get through to Dhahran by radio, Edwards solved the problem by giving up one of his own. The King saw the refrigerator being delivered at the palace early the next morning and rewarded his representative, although he probably suspected whence the machine had come.

More serious than these requests for personal service were the requests from junior members of the royal family or officials for tractors, trucks, mowers, cultivators, donkeys, and hand tools for their own farms. The depredations of the locusts were as nothing compared to the damage which the project would have suffered had these requests been filled from the stock of movable equipment. In desperation Edwards announced that nothing would be given out except on orders from the King, who promptly ruled that what was there should stay there. The requests ended abruptly.

Many women of the King's household, including some of his wives, daughters, and their ladies-in-waiting and servants, joined the court entourage. They were all delighted at this chance for a vacation in the country and, though heavily veiled, enjoyed the refreshing greenness of the landscape and small expeditions to pick grapes, cantaloupes, or other fruits and vegetables. The King said he was glad to have the women of his court enjoy Al Kharj because nowhere else in Saudi Arabia could they learn so much about new foods.

The climax of the visit was a feast of melons, which was held at the farm headquarters. Ibn Saud, his sons, and his chief ministers sat in the Arab Room, where they were served coffee and huge trays of ripe melons. Squatting in outer rooms and other buildings of the farm and spreading about on the grass like a camping army were hundreds of courtiers and attendants who ate melons by the truckload.

The King seemed in a particularly jovial mood that day, joking with Edwards about the merits of American versus Arabian melons and suggesting that it was high time that Edwards settled down and got married. But when he left, he said in all seriousness, "This is what my people need. If there were enough farms like this in Saudi Arabia, the bedouin would stop their wandering and settle down in green pastures. There must be not one but many such farms stretching from the Red Sea to the Persian Gulf. It is up to you to get them started. No one in Saudi Arabia can doubt that you are doing great things. If there is anything you want, let me know."

Graciously, he shook hands all around, climbed into his old Pierce Arrow, and drove off across the acres of watermelon rinds until his cavalcade, heading for the nearest air strip, was lost in a cloud of dust. Arabs love to refer to events as "days," and the "day of the Feast of Melons" is the greatest in Al Kharj history. Largely as a result of the favorable impression that the project made at that time upon the King and his ministers, Edwards was able, with the help of sixteen more agricultural experts, to establish four smaller farms in different parts of Saudi Arabia, one at the oasis of Qatif, one at Hofuf, one at the mountain town of Taif in the Hejaz, and one as an expansion of the Haddi farm, originally started by Sheikh Abdullah Suleiman in the fertile Wadi Fatima which supplies Jidda with water.

The selection of sites for these new farms stirred up much local interest. At Hofuf, for instance, the powerful Amir Saud ibn Jaluwi appointed a committee of twelve landowners to help the Americans locate the new farms and to supply information about soil and water conditions. The visitors were asked time and again such questions as, "Why have these farms not had children before?" "Will their produce be available for all?" and, "Can these new methods of farming be used by the poor as well as the rich?"

Instead of aiming at large-scale production, as the Al Kharj project has done, these four new centers were to emphasize research, demonstration, and education. In a speech in the House of Representatives on February 4, 1948, Representative Teague of Texas anticipated their contribution when he said:

In the beginning, work at the centers will concern various types of field crops and vegetables and will include all phases of the soil-improvement program. Work with livestock and poultry will be done as soon as the crop operations are well underway. With the entire approval of the Arab farmer committees, special emphasis will be given to setting up a phase of the work similar to the 4-H program for boys in the United States.

Experimentation and demonstration in crops will include the use of better seeds, fertilizers, insecticides and fungicides. Extensive introduction of new crops of all kinds will be made. Improvement of soil fertility will receive major attention, and drainage in the Hofuf and Qatif areas will be of great importance. Within due time it is hoped that these centers will become the sources of supplies of good seeds for all the farmers, as well as the distributing point of improved livestock. Tractors for rice and wheat threshing services will be provided to a certain extent. It may be necessary that Government programs supplying fertilizers and insecticides and other farm supplies to the farmers at reasonable cost be instituted for a while until the farmers can handle the purchase of these supplies themselves.

Though the program is extensive and can scarcely be evaluated yet, the experience of Abdullah ibn Ismael is an example of the spread of American know-how and initiative among the poorer Arabs. In 1946 this man had no land and lived by doing odd jobs on other men's farms. After working in Al Kharj for a while, he determined to get a farm of his own. He went to the Finance Minister, who let him have a small piece of unused land. On it he and his family dug a well and struck a good supply of sweet water. He was able to buy a used Ford engine on credit, and, as a demonstration project, the American expert from Al Kharj helped him rig up a used pump. As a further demonstration the Americans sent over a tractor, plowed his land, and furnished Abdullah with some seed and a little fertilizer. The result has been a small but profitable farm which supports Abdullah and his family and has enabled him to pay off his debts. Word of Abdullah ibn Ismael's success has spread among the landless Arabs of the Nejd, and his example is being followed by other poor but ambitious farmers.

Rogers, Edwards, Brookshier, and their men have done much in Al Kharj, but it is not correct to assume that through their efforts any large section of Arabia has, or can, become a Garden of Eden. Apart from the fact that the water is dangerously saline, that the rain, when it comes, usually comes in floods, that winter frosts are sometimes killing and summer droughts common, there are various other problems still unsolved.

One of these is the prevalence of thievery. Recently it was calculated that at least 10 per cent of the crops disappeared through this means. Once a mechanic threatened to quit because all his tools were stolen from the running board of the truck on which he was working while his head was under the hood. The theft of gasoline presented special problems; one truck used up to ninety gallons of gasoline a day until a padlock on the gas tank "improved its carburetor adjustment." Because the movable parts were stolen night after night from the same machine, Edwards finally built a compound surrounded by a six-foot barbed-wire fence; the only gate was then guarded night and day. This cut thefts to a minimum while machines were in the compound. But the problem of thievery continued. Custom and law decree in Saudi Arabia that thievery shall be punished by the cutting off of a hand, but Americans regard this punishment as horribly severe and are unlikely to turn an Arab, impelled by these new and powerful temptations to steal, over to such grim justice.

Another problem confronting the project is its dependence on Aramco for items ranging from fuel oil to monkey wrenches. In Arabia to produce oil and not vegetables, the oil company believes that the most satisfactory administration for the farms would be a fully developed Saudi Arabian Ministry of Agriculture, and the aid it has given has been with that end in view. The completion of the railroad from the Persian Gulf through Al Kharj to Riyadh and the increased responsibility recently assumed by the Ministry of Agriculture have helped, and further improvement will come as farm machinery becomes available through regular commercial channels. But supplies will not be readily available until farming in the fertile parts of Saudi Arabia is much more developed.

Just as basic a problem is the distribution of all the produce of the farms to the King. This is understandable, but a wider distribution would benefit Saudi Arabian farming as a whole. It may be possible to maintain some farms for the royal family and use the rest for demonstration. The other agricultural stations set up at various places throughout Saudi Arabia were intended to be such demonstration projects; but the fact that some Saudi officials do not see a distinction between their own and public property makes it extremely difficult to extend the benefits of these farms beyond official circles.

Each passing harvest, however, sees more crops produced, and the choicest crop, knowledge of modern farming techniques, finds an ever-wider Arabian market. Little by little a few dozen Americans at one of the world's most isolated model farms are helping to establish, among Arabs from the Persian Gulf to the Red Sea, farming habits that give promise of a new life for the bedouin.

VI

The People of the Tent

THE Al Kharj farms south of Riyadh are less than three hundred miles from the oil coast of the Persian Gulf. But they are not miles to be undertaken lightly, or without benefit of sand tires, extra water, and gasoline. Thus provisioned, trucks leave the neat buildings and green, fertile squares of these model farms in a cloud of dust and bump eastward across flat, barren plains rimmed with low hills. Their big tires move steadily along the desert track, and even though it is not midsummer the temperature may be 120 degrees in the shade. At least once every hour engine radiators must be refilled, and at every halt the moist bags of drinking water, hung on the outside of the trucks, will be opened.

In some places the gravelly brown plains are so smooth that a motor caravan can hit better than forty miles an hour, but most of the time the speed is less than half that. Leaving the Al Kharj valley, the road winds over three low escarpments and then takes off straight across a stony plain. The red sun climbs in the cloudless sky, and the little whirlwinds of dust, which the Arabs call *jinn*, chase each other across the flat, occasionally hitting the truck with a blast of sand. Mirages come and go, smooth blue lakes that fade as the motor reaches the "water's" edge.

A low red peak appears ahead, followed by another and another, until they stretch in an unbroken line across the eastern horizon. At first the traveler dismisses them as mirages, but as the miles pass they attach themselves to his surroundings. They are the dunes of the Dahna,

73

the eastern "river" of copper-colored sand which connects the Nafud desert of northern Arabia with the even larger desert of the Rub al Khali in the south. The Dahna sands run for almost fourteen hundred miles and vary in width from twelve to one hundred miles. Sometimes they divide to become rivulets, but principally they form a concentrated line of sand dunes ranging from forty to a hundred feet in height, born of disintegrating sandstone in northern Arabia, and moving southward from ten to thirty feet a year under the impact of the prevailing wind. They are crescent shaped, with their backs to the wind, and often wear a plume of sand flowing from their summits.

The trail from Al Kharj to the oasis of Hofuf crosses the Dahna sands at one of their narrowest points. But, like rivers, the dunes of the Dahna make up in depth for what they lack in width and demand the utmost of man, beast, or motor that tries to cross them. Until the development by Aramco of oversize sand tires, these dunes were considered uncrossable by motorcar without the assistance of several dozen Saudis to act as pushers. If the crossing cannot be undertaken in the cool of the morning, the air pressure in overheated tires must be reduced and motors properly cooled before one leaves the gravel of the plain.

Standing on top of an open truck crossing the Dahna is like riding in a launch over the huge red waves of a motionless sea. At the bottom of each dune one sees nothing but orange-red sand rising on all sides to the blue sky. Gathering speed across the flat hollow, the truck races up the soft side of the next hill of sand to the relatively hard crest. There, high above the trough, one looks out across wave after wave of these gigantic dunes, molded by the north wind. Again like the waves of the sea, every fortieth dune is likely to be larger than its neighbors, a miniature mountain with a faint cloud of sand hiding the peak. The Dahna is a magnificent sight at all times, but to see it at its best one should camp in the dunes and watch the sun rise. Then the coloring grows more startling as the quick Arabian dawn augments the reds and yellows and drives the long morning shadows into retreat.

Trucks crossing the Dahna follow a well-churned path, but when the wind freshens, the tracks are soon wiped out and the traveler feels that his vehicle "is the first that ever burst into this silent sea." Minus tracks, the drivers steer by compass and in some places by markers like spar buoys, driven at intervals into the tops of the highest dunes.

The going is so hard that even desert-worthy trucks stop every fifteen minutes to cool their motors and prevent the vapor lock that comes when the engine gets so overheated that the fuel vaporizes in the gas line before it reaches the carburetor.

Almost as majestic as sunrise in the Dahna is the sight of a camel caravan plodding across the great red dunes. The lean Arab riders, with their headgear wrapped over their faces to keep out the wind and sand, seem part of the camels rather than passengers on the rolling ships of the desert. Without the camel primitive men could never have crossed the deserts of Arabia. In fact, without the camel he probably could not have lived in central Arabia at all, for that animal supplies not only transportation but food, drink, clothing, medicines, and even beauty aids.

The camels of Arabia are of the one-hump variety. Among the more easily recognized ones on the peninsula are the bad-tempered black, which are used mostly for carrying freight, the reddish-brown *Omaniya,* which come from the region of Oman and have great speed but not much endurance, and the fawn-colored *Hurrah,* which are a cross between an Omaniya and the camel of the northern Nejd. These are not as fast as the Omaniya but have much greater staying power.

The camel is such an indispensable part of the life of every bedouin that it is not surprising that wealth is reckoned by the number of camels a man owns. The huge soft feet of this beast of burden permit it to travel fully loaded, with two hundred pounds on either side, where no other animal can move. It likes to travel at about two miles an hour, stretching down its long neck to nibble on the desert shrubs. It is thus unnecessary to stop for feeding. Although camels prefer to drink daily, three days without water does them no harm. In an emergency they can go as long as five days without water, using the liquid which they have stored and consequently making possible crossings of waterless desert which could not otherwise be undertaken. On long, dry marches they are sometimes forcibly fed with a little water through the nose, a process known as snuffing.

Next to furnishing transport to the Arab, a role which is decreasing with the growth of trucking, the camel's greatest usefulness is as a dairy animal. Camel's milk is the staple food of the bedouin. In spite of the fact that it contains no fat and cannot be used for making butter, the milk can be curdled into a cheese which is highly prized. In cases of emergency, a camel can be made to vomit, bringing up a fluid from its stomach which has saved the life of many a lost bedouin.

Almost every part of the camel is eaten by the Arabs. An old and scrawny camel makes tough chewing, but the hump of a young camel is quite palatable and is likely to be on the tent floor at every important Arab banquet. Later the uneaten fat, which fills part of the hump, can be rendered for additional uses. The fanciest camel dish, reserved for very ceremonial occasions, is roast camel stuffed with roast sheep, stuffed with roast fowl, stuffed with boiled eggs, stuffed with rice.

The chief fuel of the nomads is camel dung, and in many places a good part of the bedouin's income is derived from collecting camel dung in camel's-hair bags and selling it to the nearby villages to be burned in place of wood. In the spring the Kuwait Neutral Zone is dotted with such bags, waiting to be taken north to the treeless sheikhdom of Kuwait. Even camel urine is highly regarded by the bedouin. It is used as a shampoo for both men and women and is said to kill all parasites in the hair and leave a "pleasant" odor of desert herbs. Newborn babies are anointed with camel urine, and fresh urine is used by the Arabs to warm their hands on cold mornings.

Bedouin employ camel's wool to make clothing and sometimes to weave into tents, although black goat's hair is more widely used for this purpose. From the camel's hide are made sandals, belts, and water bags. Along with the donkey, the camel is the irrigation pump and tractor of Arabia; wherever there are wells, camels draw water, and in farming areas such as the Nejd or the Tihama of Yemen they pull the primitive plows and drags. If a bedouin warrior is killed in war, his favorite camel is often killed with him and the skin used to wrap the slain man's body for burial, thus completing the cycle of camel usefulness from birth to grave.

Although it has been said that the camel's domesticity is "the tameness of stupidity," camels defend themselves well when attacked by wolves or stray dogs, for, being double-jointed, they can kick both forward and backward. A fondness for camels may be an acquired taste, for most Westerners find them slow, stupid, obstinate, lazy, and dirty. On the other hand, Carl Raswan, who lived among the bedouin, wrote of them in *The Black Tents of Arabia* as follows: "I learnt to appreciate in all their significance the noises peculiar to a camel; to realise that in the loud diapason of its stomach rumblings and in the gurglings of its throat there lies a meaning too deep for words. Even its full-throated belching is an expression of its lordly thoughts." [1]

Arab history is full of stories about camels who were famous for great speed or endurance, about camels whose instinct for water saved their

[1] Pages 52–53.

master's lives, and about deep friendships between bedouin and their camels. Many a tribal war has been fought over camels and many a murder committed for them. The most famous of all Arabian camels was Al Kaswa, Mohammed's favorite mount, who showed supernatural powers in guiding Mohammed. Once she refused to lead his caravan into an ambush, and on the occasion of his entry into Medina in 622 the Prophet allowed her to determine where he would live by announcing that he would stay in the house in front of which she knelt down.

In view of the many uses of the camel, it is not surprising that the breeding and selling of these beasts occupy the time of numerous tribes. There are many famous camel markets, of which the city of Buraida in the northern Nejd used to be the largest. During the 1920's as many as fifteen thousand camels were sold in Buraida every year. But railroad, trucks, and planes are gradually supplanting the camel and pushing it from the main trade routes. Twenty-five years ago King Ibn Saud traveled only by camel, but now the King has a fleet of automobiles, as well as his planes. Four thousand camels are still used in the trade between the capital city of Riyadh, the date-rich oasis of Hofuf, and the Persian Gulf, but more and more desert-worthy trucks are crossing the Dahna, and the cars of the railroad displace most of the camels on this haul.

Compared with the camel, the horse is a newcomer in the Arabian Peninsula, probably coming there from Egypt about the time of Christ. Once established, it flourished in the healthy climate of central Arabia and, shut off from contamination by inferior breeds, developed the characteristics of speed, liveliness, good nature, and stamina which have made Arabian stallions famous throughout history. The best of the Arabian horses come from the Nejd, where the high limestone content of the water produces strong bones and the antimony in the soil gives a blue-black coloring to the skin.

Mohammed was fond of horses, and several of his stallions took part in and won races. Racing is still one of the most popular sports on the peninsula, and a visit with the Arabs is complete only if it includes a horse race. During the last century the stables of the Rashidi family at Hail were the best in Arabia, but now King Saud's horses at Riyadh are the finest.

Historically, the Arabs who swept across North Africa in the eighth century rode Arabian horses into Spain. From there the breed spread into Europe, and, when William the Conqueror landed in England in 1066, many of the horses he brought with him had Spanish ancestors.

During the Crusades, a caliph gave King Henry I of England two Arabian stallions. Under Queen Elizabeth several Arabian horses were imported into England for breeding, and still later, in the reign of James I, Arabian horses were brought there for racing purposes. According to strict terminology, however, a horse is not a Thoroughbred unless its entire ancestry on the male side can be traced directly back to one of three Arabian stallions which made the long sea voyage to England in the early 1700's.[2] These were Byerly Turk, Darly Arabian, and Godophin Arabian. As early as 1771 it became evident to racing fans in England that Thoroughbred horses were faster than pure Arabian horses, although other qualities made the pure Arabian stock more desirable in Arabia. Until recently, the Arabs would not allow any horses but stallions to leave their country, all mares being reserved for breeding purposes.

The traveler who expects to see Arabs racing over the desert on horseback is headed for disappointment, for the horse is generally much less useful and more expensive than the donkey or the camel and therefore far less prevalent. He requires special food, he cannot go long distances without water, and his speed is greatly cut down in sandy or mountainous areas. For these reasons, the limited horse population centers mostly around stables belonging to the King, his sons, and the biggest landowners. In 1953 a pack camel cost 300 riyals in parts of Saudi Arabia, a donkey 1,000, and a horse 3,000 or more.

Like youth in the West, Saudi youth takes to the new and different, and the princes of Riyadh spend as much time arguing the relative merits of Cadillacs and Chryslers as they do those of the horses of Riyadh and Hail. In Arab warfare the horse is beginning to take second place. Lawrence of Arabia set the style in World War I with his Rolls Royces. Before Ibn Saud stamped out the practice of intertribal raids, fighting tribes such as the Ruwala were using touring cars rather than Arab horses to move their war parties. The spearhead of the column with which Prince Faisal routed part of the Yemeni Army in 1931 was made up of lightly armored automobiles, and King Saud is turning more and more to motor-borne infantry as the heart of his army.

Little "big game" in the African sense can be found in Arabia today. Probably the simple reasons are the peninsula-wide scarcity of food and water and bedouin hunting prowess. Before the Suez Canal was cut through, occasional lions were reported in the mountains of the Hejaz, and early lion hunts are shown in some of the rock paintings

[2] Cecil G. Trew, *From 'Dawn' to 'Eclipse': The Story of the Horse*, p. 127.

such as those near Mahad Dhahab. Panthers and leopards are the largest game animals found today, and even these are rare except in isolated mountain districts. Perhaps the most exciting creature to hunt is the rarely seen ostrich, which, though it looks ungainly, can run faster than a horse for a short distance.

Venomous snakes are relatively rare, and the largest reptiles are the sun-loving iguanas. Hyenas, wolves, foxes, and hares are found separately or in small bands. Snow-white rim gazelles, with several other species of the gazelle family, roam the desert in herds, and one of the sports of the foreign colony at Jidda is gazelle hunting in a jeep. If the jeep is not old at the start of the hunt, it is sure to be at the end, and several accidents have occurred because motorized hunters have become so excited that they upset their jeeps or shot each other.

Quite a number of Arab sheikhs train falcons for hunting. This is a slow and difficult task requiring the full time of one or more men. Because of the intense heat in the summer, hawking is carried on mostly from November to March. Two types of falcons are used: sakers, which are noted for their sharp eyesight, and peregrines, which are most in demand because they are believed to be quicker and braver than sakers.[3]

Most of the peregrines are caught on the salt flats and coastal islands of the Persian Gulf. Two falconers go to a place where peregrines have been seen, taking with them a live pigeon as bait. They tie a string to the pigeon's leg, fasten a stone to the other end, and throw the stone and pigeon into the air until the peregrine is attracted. The falcon swoops down, kills the little bird, but is unable to carry it off because of the stone; it is then caught while eating the pigeon.

The first step in training the falcon is to seal its eyes by passing a thread through the eyelids; later a hood is substituted for the thread. The training takes two to three weeks, during which the falconer carries the bird about with him, feeding it himself and letting it sleep close beside him. As soon as the bird begins to trust its master and answers to its name, the falconer starts teaching the bird to retrieve, using a lure made of bustard wings tied together. At first the falcon is always kept on the end of a string, but as it becomes more attached to its master this is dispensed with. A trained peregrine is worth from fifty to sixty riyals, but famous falcons sometimes bring three times as much.

The usual prey for a falcon is rabbits, curlews, and bustards, with the latter the most popular. Once the bustard has been sighted, the

[3] Wilfred Thesiger, "Desert Border Lands of Oman," *Geographical Journal,* October–December 1950.

falcon is unhooded and tossed into the air by its master. Peregrines are much faster than bustards, and when overtaken the bustards settle down on the ground. An exciting fight then takes place, but the big birds are no match for the sharp beak and claws of the falcon, which can kill as many as seven or eight bustards a day.

Beyond the rolling sands of the Dahna and in the valleys to the east, bedouin encampments remind the traveler that, though there has never been a real census, it is estimated that about one-third of Arabia's population is nomadic, descended from early tribes who have been pushed out of fertile and well-watered areas. Some of these tribes came originally from Yemen, possibly at the time of the breaking of the great dam of Marib in the fifth century A.D. Gradually adapting themselves to life under arid conditions, they learned to graze their herds upon the grass that for a few months lines the wadies of the desert and then to move on, following the rains to other parts of the peninsula.

The bedouin of Saudi Arabia are the spring from which other groups in the population have revitalized themselves periodically through the centuries.[4] These nomads divide the Arabs into four main groupings. At the top come the Badia, bedouin who live exclusively in black hair tents. They spend nine months of the year in the heart of the desert, raise camels as their only livestock, marry only among themselves, and look down on the rest of the world. The aristocrats of this group are the Sharif tribes who are pure in blood descent from the patriarchs and Ishmel and Qahtan. It was Qahtan's son Yarab, they believe, who gave his name to Arabia and the Arabs.

The leading Sharif bedouin tribes of the peninsula include the Anizah, Shammar, Harb, Mutair, Ajman, Dhafir, Murra, Qahtan, Duwasir, Manasir, Qawasim, and Hawaitat. Also Badia, but not of pure blood and therefore not Sharif, are the Awazim, the Rashaida, the Hutaim, and the Sulubba, considered to be the lowest of all real bedouin and thought to be descendants of Christian Crusaders.

Somewhat inferior in manner of living, in the opinion of the true bedouin, but akin to them in blood are the Arabdar, or seminomads, who have lost caste because they live part of the year in towns such as Kuwait. Some of the Arabdar are of good Sharif stock and so may intermarry with their true bedouin cousins. But the real men of the desert consider them to be soft and decadent, although they like to stay

---

[4] Much of the information that follows comes from conversations with Col. H. R. P. Dickson, who spent more than sixteen years among the bedouin of Iraq, Kuwait, and Saudi Arabia, and from his classic work, *The Arab of the Desert.*

with Arabdar relatives on the rare occasions when they come to town to trade.

The third group of desert dwellers are the Hukra, or shepherds, who look after the sheep of the important tribes and of the city dwellers. They are "inferior" because their sheep cannot range as far as camels do, so their movements are more restricted than those of the true bedouin who take the whole desert for their winter home.

At the bottom of the bedouin world come the Hadbar, persons who live in permanent houses of mud or stone and are therefore despised by the true bedouin, though their merchants provide many items that are necessary to the desert dwellers.

Leadership in bedouin society is in the hands of the paramount sheikh of each tribe. Such a leader must come from a particular family but need not necessarily be the oldest son. He must be the son or cousin of the old sheikh who has the greatest combination of courage, leadership, and luck, or *hadh*. Without luck no number of other virtues can benefit the tribe. Lastly he must be generous to all his followers.

Each tribe has its own home wells, about which it camps in the hot summer months from June into early October. Then with the coming of the first rains it is off, roaming about its *dirah* or special part of the desert. The dirah of a typical bedouin tribe is about 125 miles east and west and 200 miles north and south. In dry years tribes are forced to move into the territory of friendly neighbors, and the need for such overlapping of grazing areas is one of the reasons why the bedouin tribes are bound together in loose confederations, such as the Ajman-Murra-Najran and the Dhafir-Shammar-Awazim alliances. The fact that a tribe may be in more than one confederation gives added cohesiveness to the social structure of the desert. In addition to forced journeys to find grazing in dry years, members of a tribe may cross the dirah of other members of the same confederation when need be, such as during the annual trip to market.

The Anizah, who pass their summers in Syria and Iraq and winter in northern Arabia in and around the Nafud, are one of the most important tribes. They pitch their tents of black goat's hair in a circle when the party is small; if the tents are numerous, however, they are laid out in rows. Even the richest Anizah families live all in one tent, unless there are two wives who cannot get along with each other, and then a smaller tent is set up nearby. Polygamy, however, is a luxury and not often found among the bedouin, though divorce is common.

Until recently the Anizah were active in tribal wars, and blood feuds

81

still persist. Like many of the bedouin, they will not attack at night for fear that the women's quarters might be entered during the melée. No bedouin men, women, or children are taken captives in raids, for booty is the only objective. Slaves, when found, count as booty.

One of the best-known subdivisions of the Anizah is the Ruwala, part of whom are to be found in Saudi Arabia and Iraq, though most are in Syria. Until a few years ago the Ruwala were usually at war, for they love the excitement of raiding and war gave them a chance to show off their bravery, endurance, and guile. As a consequence, few Ruwala men have lived to a ripe old age, four-fifths of them dying in battle or of disease before reaching forty. When the Ruwala bury their dead, the body is lowered into a shallow grave and covered with sand. Gunpowder is then strewn over it to frighten away hyenas. They have no permanent graveyards, but they believe in a spiritual world peopled in part by jinn who lurk in rocky places. The evil eye is universally feared among the Ruwala, and they look with distrust upon persons who have blue eyes or who lack the two front upper teeth. In contrast to their fear of such "unpleasant" characters is their veneration of certain men and women who, they claim, can heal the sick and see and know hidden things.

Like those of most bedouin, the tents of the Ruwala are made from coarse black cloth woven of goat's hair or sheep's wool, or both. Their floors are covered with carpets over which are laid quilts filled with cotton. Pillows stuffed with wool or camel's hair are placed around the edges of the tent. Both men and women wear their hair long, and most of the women are tattooed extensively on their faces and bodies.

One of the Arabian tribes about which the outside world has heard a great deal is the Harb, whose territory centers in the Hejaz. Because of their proximity to the Red Sea, some have intermarried with Negroes and thus have lost so much caste with other tribes that the pure bedouin will not intermarry with them. As a result, the western Harb do not belong to any group or confederacy of tribes but are a sort of outlaw band. They used to live by raiding the caravans going from Damascus to Medina, Jidda, and Mecca. The building of the Hejaz railroad just before World War I, however, was a serious blow to these warriors, for they could not raid the trains. The Harb fought on the side of the Turks in the war, and after the railroad's destruction by Lawrence began once again to prey upon the pilgrims. After giving them repeated warnings, Ibn Saud lost patience and turned his fierce Ikhwan warriors upon them, with the result that comparatively few members of the Harb tribe are alive today. In many encampments only one person was left to spread word of the defeat.

A much more important tribe than the Harb is the Shammar, whose leaders, the Rashidis, dominated central Arabia throughout much of the nineteenth century. Combining bedouin with city life, the Shammar center around the town of Hail but range far to the north into Syria and Iraq. The last of the great Shammar chiefs was Abdul Aziz ibn Miteb, who ruled until 1906. He was a heroic man, much admired by his friends and feared by his enemies. One night in 1906, while inspecting his troops in preparation for a battle with Ibn Saud, Ibn Miteb lost his way, mistook Ibn Saud's tent for his own, and was killed. The Shammar fought with the Turks against Ibn Saud and the British in World War I, but their leadership went from bad to worse, and they finally surrendered to Ibn Saud in November 1921.

The northeast corner of Saudi Arabia, near Kuwait, is the home of the Mutair tribe, a proud and warlike people who gave the late King Ibn Saud a great deal of trouble during his conquest of Arabia. In spite of this record, a large percentage of the Ikhwan, or warlike puritans whom Ibn Saud used as the nucleus of his agricultural settlements, came from the Mutair. Many Ikhwan leaders are still suspicious of the West's penetration of Arabia, but gone is the militant spirit Rihani ascribes to them in his *The Maker of Modern Arabia*—"And the Ikhwan, the roving, ravening Bedu of yesterday, the militant Wahhabis of today, are the white terror of Arabia."

Allied with the Mutair in their struggle against Ibn Saud were their southern neighbors, the Ajman, who had come originally from Yemen but who, by the end of the nineteenth century, grazed their flocks from Kuwait to the northern fringes of the Empty Quarter. Although treacherous with outsiders, the Ajman are brave fighters, and they defeated Ibn Saud several times and killed his brother Saad before he finally conquered them.

Coming out of the sandy wilderness of the Dahna into the strip of gravel and grassland between the river of sand and the low coastal hills, the traveler is likely to run across the tracks of the extensive herds of black sheep and brown camels of the Manasir tribe, who range from the Trucial Oman to the plains north of Abqaiq. During the latter half of the nineteenth century the Manasir were one of the most warlike tribes in Arabia and accumulated much wealth from plundering their neighbors. Even now one finds circular towers of refuge about twenty-five feet in height, which were built by the shepherds for protection against the Manasir. Inside Saudi Arabia the Manasir live peacefully, but as late as 1948 they were at war with Abu Dhabi, one of the sheikh-doms of the Trucial Coast, a venture which they claimed was far safer and more profitable than the fight to the north against the Israeli.

The bedouin are cold to strangers unless the latter are traveling with a member of their tribe or federation. If this is the case and a blood relationship between the tribesmen and the guide can be established, hostility changes to warmth, and the traveler is urged to dismount among the black tents. The women and younger children hurry into their end of the tent. An extra covering of rugs is then spread on the ground, a polished brass bowl, partly filled with coffee beans, is brought out, and soon the clear air resounds to the musical pounding of the pestle. Summoned by this rhythmic coffee "bell," men and boys hurry over from the nearby tents to form a circle in front of the head man and his guests. Soon the aromatic smell of coffee fills the tent. The sheikh's coffee pourer picks up a long-spouted metal pitcher and a stack of little handleless china cups, and the visitor is welcomed in true Arab style.

The bedouin always urge a traveler to stay and rest after his coffee, and the man with time to spare will do well to accept their invitation and settle down comfortably against a camel saddle. Then a column of smoke rises from a nearby tent, and a start is made on the three-hour task of preparing a meal fit for visitors. Boys, the smallest of them com-pletely undressed, escape from the women's quarters at the other end of the tent and shyly take up their places at the outside of the circle, while around the edges of the cloth dividing the tent the traveler glimpses the dark eyes of women peering through the holes in their veils.

The tribesmen talk of rain and grass, of the state of their sheep and camels, and of fighting. In return, the traveler is expected to bring news of the King, the oil company, and the far-off world of Bahrein, Jidda, or Cairo. The bedouin are full of quaint, grave questions such as whether a jeep gets tired, how one breathes in a plane, and how long it would take to move everyone present to Riyadh by airplane. Among the Arabs of the cities compliments are tossed back and forth in a kind of conversational game. Tell a city Arab that you look forward to see-ing him in Washington and he will wax eloquent on the pleasures of that meeting. Tell a bedouin the same thing, and he will say, "Why talk of it? Everyone knows I will never go to Washington." And the subject changes, while the group around the camel-dung fire scowls as if to say, "Why waste time on such talk?"

84

As the burning sun slips down through the cloudless sky to the horizon, the flap of the tent is raised to catch the evening breeze for the bedouin tent is well designed for desert life. It is made of coarse black or brown cloth, woven from goats' hair or sheeps' wool. The average bedouin's tent is about twenty-five feet long and is made up of four to six strips of cloth, supported by two poles. A sheikh, however, will have a four- or six-pole tent, up to seventy-five feet long. A bigger tent than this would not be practical while on migration. A tent usually has as many ropes per side as it has poles.

Bedouin tents are separated into two or three compartments by brightly decorated curtains that extend beyond the tent top on the side on which the tent is open. The decorations of these wall hangings vary from tribe to tribe, and the women who weave them are very proud of their workmanship. Undecorated strips of material for the bigger tents are now being made in towns that lie near the grazing areas of the bedouin.

In all these tents the furnishings are of the simplest and most utilitarian. The men's side contains a carpet or two, several small mattresses to sit on, at least one camel saddle, some cushions, and a few rifles. Around the small hole in the sand that serves as a fireplace are placed the three long-nosed pots necessary to make good coffee and the coffee roaster, that looks like a long-handled spoon. Nearby are the coffee cups in a brass case, the pestle and mortar used for crushing the beans, and the incense burner.

The coffee beans, the cardamom seed to flavor the drink, the firewood and the camel manure fuel, and the drinking water are kept on the women's side of the tent until needed. Also in the women's quarters are found small rugs, older mattresses, the cooking utensils, stores of food such as rice, dates, sugar, and flour, the saddle bags, and extra clothes, quilts, and equipment for spinning cloth. The women's quarters are traditionally at the western end of the tent, which is oriented to catch the prevailing breeze in hot weather and to get the maximum shelter from sand dunes or other obstacles during cold spells. Hunting dogs are allowed in the women's quarters, but watch dogs, of which there are many, must remain outside at all times. Closeness to water and grazing areas, of course, receives first consideration in tent location. Tents are usually moved every week or two, both for sanitary reasons and to give the animals new grass.

Nature has endowed the Saudi Arabian desert with scarcely enough resources to sustain the bedouin, and they will consume almost anything edible that they can find. The women are the cooks, except for coffee making, and are responsible for keeping the tents supplied with water, though herdsmen bring it in from a distance if there are no wells nearby. When water runs short, the bedouin use sand for washing. During the cooler months, from October to February, they may go without water for as long as three days.

The small consumption of water, however, is balanced by a high consumption of camel's milk. A female camel will produce between one and seven liters a day, and the milk is either drunk warm or else poured into a leather bag and allowed to sour, making a very popular drink which sits well on the stomach in the hot climate. Largely because the supply of milk varies directly with the amount of pasturage, the nomads keep their flocks moving in search of the new forage which springs up after the desert rains.

Dates are a staple among the oasis dwellers of Arabia and among those of the bedouin who are able to procure them. They may be eaten for breakfast, lunch, and supper. Some of the bedouin have their own date groves in deserted oases to which they go twice a year, once to help pollinate and once to harvest.

Rich households use bread frequently, but among two-thirds of the bedouin families bread is not baked all year around, and some women bake it only once or twice during their lives, on important feasts celebrating a birth, marriage, or victory in war. Although sometimes made into heavy loaves, the dough is generally spread thin in a large round pancake, which also serves as a plate, pusher, fork, and napkin. Most of the bread cooked in the summer is unleavened, but during the cold weather yeast is added to the dough in the evening, and the loaf is baked the next day. Instead of actually making bread, most of the bedouin add salt and water to the flour and boil the mixture into a thick paste, which forms the main part of the evening meal. Because wheat is too expensive in Arabia for the poor bedouin, they use flour made from sorghum, durrah, maize, or millet, costing about half as much. A bitter flour made from sesame seeds, kneaded with *ghee* (butter made from the tail of the fat-tailed Arabian sheep) and water and boiled to make a porridge, adds variety to the diet.

Rice is another food immensely popular with the Arabs. Imported, it comes under the heading of luxuries for the bedouin and forms only a small part of their food. Other minor items of bedouin diet are *basise*, a thin gruel for children made of grape honey and wheat flour; *madruse*, a paste of dates boiled with flour and ghee; and *humeja,* which is bread boiled in milk and covered with camel's suet.

There is no more striking example of man's ability to make the most out of misfortune than the bedouin fondness for locusts. Not many crops are grown in Arabia, but what there are suffer seriously from locust invasions. The struggles of the American experts at Al Kharj with locusts have already been mentioned, and anyone who has traveled widely in Arabia has seen parts of the sky darkened by these flying pests. To stamp them out, the British have for several years maintained a locust mission in Arabia with headquarters just outside Jidda. Equipped with desert-worthy trucks, its personnel range from Kuwait to Yemen and from Aqaba to Oman. Compared to the members of these locust brigades, who have covered thousands of miles of territory previously unseen, most of the other Europeans in Saudi Arabia can be said to have seen only the edges of the country.

One of the problems faced by the locust mission is that the bedouin enjoy eating the locusts and therefore object to their extermination. When a swarm of locusts lands near a bedouin encampment, the whole tribe will go out to kill and collect as many as it can. The dead locusts are then dried in the sun, after which they may be ground into powder for use as flour or strung on long threads to be eaten like shrimp. Taken raw, they taste like insipid cabbage. Once the wings and legs have been pulled off and the husk roasted and dipped in salt, locusts taste much like tender spinach.

When the Arabian American Oil Company first employed bedouin, it was surprised to find that they tired easily and could not put in an eight-hour day. After eating the company's meat for six months, however, the workers became noticeably stronger. Under existing conditions the bedouin eat virtually no beef, for the grass in most of Arabia is too sparse to support cattle. Furthermore, sheep, goats, and camels are too valuable to the bedouin to be slaughtered except on ceremonial occasions. Gazelle and *thub* meat are excellent roasted, and the bedouin eat other game including wolves, foxes, weasels, hyenas, hedgehogs, field rats, and kangaroo mice when they can get them. In addition, those who range near the Persian Gulf or the Red Sea rely heavily on fish in fresh, dried, or salted form, with cod, mackerel, rockfish, and sardines predominating.

Even so, the tribesman's diet is simple and rather monotonous. Breakfast for most bedouin is merely a handful of dates. Lunch, eaten shortly before noon, consists of a drink of camel's milk and food left over from the night before. The main meal, supper, is eaten shortly after sunset and is composed of as many of the items mentioned above as are available. Eating is done in shifts: first the older men and their guests, then the younger men, and later the women and children. A single platter is usually set on the carpet, or, if the meal is sufficiently important, it is surrounded with auxiliary dishes. At a nod from the host everyone starts scooping with his right hand. Except in the company of outsiders, the bedouin allow conversation to cease while they eat. The majority of them are hungry most of the time, and when a meal is spread before them they waste no time in consuming it. The fact that the average Westerner sees them only on festive occasions, when they of course overeat, gives him the impression that bedouin are hearty eaters. On the contrary, when the bedouin repeat "health and good digestion," rise to clean their fingers on the side of the tent, and step outside to brush their teeth with a stick, they are usually far from full.

The bedouin's "sociable cup" is not hard liquor, which the Koran forbids, but coffee, prepared and served by the men with great ceremony. The beans are first roasted, then ground into a fine powder to which water is added. Next the mixture is boiled and poured into a third pot containing a little cardamom. Sometimes a pinch of saffron and even a little ginger are added, and the mixture is boiled once more. Finally, the brew is served up in a manner which suggests the bedouin's natural hospitality and dignity, and many are the tales, lusty, humorous, and wise, with which the bedouin fill the evenings over these pungent cups.

Life is hard for the bedouin, and its very hardness makes them scornful of all who do not live as difficult a life. Ill-fed and ill-clothed, they are too proud to work, though not too proud to accept large-scale gifts from a ruler like King Ibn Saud, the present King Saud, or the Sheikh of Kuwait. When there is no strong central authority, they gain wealth by raiding other bedouin to whom they are not allied, or better still, townsfolk or farmers who they feel are beneath contempt, and probably provided by Allah for just such a purpose.

The quality the bedouin hold most important is *sharaf*, or pride, a combination of self-esteem and patriotism. Second is *arltr*, or family honor, which relates particularly to womenfolk. Third comes hospitality and courtesy to those accepted into the family circle. Around these three virtues the bedouin build their lives.

VII

The People of the Palm

ON ITS eastern side, the Dahna has spilled over, scattering irregular patches of red sand across the stony plateau. For two hours the travelers' truck rumbles across this area, bringing them at last to the water tower, stucco buildings, tents, and trailers of Al Hani, refueling and repair post on the road to the oil coast. During the war the Arabian American Oil Company drilled a water well at Al Hani for camels, and later this serviced the trucks which carried supplies to Riyadh from Hofuf. Already, a little town populated by former bedouin has sprung up around it. At Al Hani travelers climb down from their truck and introduce themselves at the station. Soon after, they are eating steak and apple pie, washed down with coffee or CocaCola, and listening to stories of midnight repairs on Saudi trucks and of the drop in the number of camels being watered at the well. Where, the men wonder, will the camel caravans and the trucks find freight to haul now the Damman-Riyadh railroad is in operation?

Darkness falls as the meal progresses, and the drowsy tinkling of camel bells suggests a night's rest. But the cool of the evening is a good time to drive, and the travelers reluctantly bid good-bye, board the truck, and head east under the desert stars. At times, now that the motor will not heat up, the car speeds at forty miles an hour, and the passengers, exhilarated by the cool night air, hold tight to keep from being thrown out as it bumps across the flat ground and rolling hills.

About an hour's drive from Al Hani, the glow of a flare appears on the horizon, marking the position of Abqaiq, a major oil field now in

89

production. The noxious gas found in solution with the oil is separated from it nearby and piped to the edge of town, where it burns in forty-foot pillars of flame that can be seen eighty miles away. As the oil wells spread westward, more and more of these perpetually brilliant beacons light the way of the desert traveler to the towns of a new frontier.

The tires remain solid, and the car, avoiding a flock of sheep grazing on the desert track, speeds for two hours more to the walled fort that guards the western entrance to Hofuf. Here, in this largest of the Arabian oases, about a hundred thousand Saudis live amid date gardens clustered around a series of fresh-water springs. On the outskirts of the city, a pair of Arab soldiers climb on the running boards and may pilot the truck through the dark to the gate of the palace of Ibn Saud's Finance Minister, Sheikh Abdullah Suleiman. They thump with their rifle butts on the massive, hand-carved wooden door until they arouse the gatekeeper, who in turn awakens a dozen tired porters and the bustling keeper of this guesthouse. Owing to the narrowness of the gate, the travelers follow the porters on foot along an imposing avenue banked with oleander bushes fifteen feet high. By the time the party has reached the doorway, the dark interior of the moonlit palace is aflicker with the lanterns of a small army of retainers.

A broad outside stairway leads to the second floor, where the baggage is stowed in a long hall filled with beds. The travelers wash in a basin held by a servant and continue up the outside stairway to the flat roof, where they sink down on soft carpets for an hour of coffee and talk with some official. The stars hang close overhead, and the night wind speaks to the palm trees of the palace garden. From all sides comes the high-pitched squeak of the water wheels as patient camels or donkeys toil through the night, while close at hand rises the most luxurious sound in Arabia, the gurgle of running water.

It is not long before weariness overtakes the travelers. But Arab hospitality does not permit sleep before the host has offered dinner. Protesting tiredly, they descend from the cool of the roof to the hot central hall of the palace. At the door stand three servants, one holding a basin into which another pours water, while the third provides a towel to dry the visitors' hands. Beyond the three, a white tablecloth some twenty feet long and eight feet wide is spread upon the carpeted floor. The visitors take their places and sit cross-legged on cushions. Before them are yard-long platters, each holding a roast lamb which oozes gravy onto a pile of rice. Around the platters lie plates of peas, beans, potatoes, tomatoes, durrah, rice, curry, and chicken, so numerous that they com-

90

pletely cover the white cloth. There is no cutlery; one eats with the right hand, breaking thin rounds of bread and dipping them into the food which has all been cooked in ghee.

Every dinner has about ten side dishes, plus plates of Hofuf dates and other fruits. Obviously, only a fraction of the food set out can be eaten by the visitors and the small group of Arabs who dine with them. In Arabia, however, one need have no worry that food will be wasted. Hardly have the guests arisen, washed again at the portable basin, and started for the roof than their places are taken by additional Arabs. When these have finished, the remaining food is taken to the quarters of the women and children; then it is made available to the house servants and finally to the outdoor servants and slaves. Thus a single meal for visitors provides food for a household that may number fifty or more. The Arab host wastes no time guessing what his visitors will like; he puts everything possible on the table. Soon after this filling meal, the travelers stretch out on the roof and fall asleep.

The cry of the muezzin reminds the faithful that prayer is better than sleep, and soon the quick Arab dawn lights up the tops of whitewashed houses and turns brown mud walls to gold. A breakfast of fried eggs, tomatoes, rice, dates, and coffee follows on the floor of the dining hall; then the travelers set out along crowded dusty streets to the palace of the stern and silent Amir of the Hasa, Saud ibn Jaluwi.

About twenty of the fiercest looking warriors anywhere in Arabia sit cross-legged on the floor just inside the entrance to his majlis. Bristling with swords and daggers ornamented with gold, they stare coldly at the Westerners, who walk past to shake hands with the fifty-year-old Amir. The ruler himself is a man of medium height with a black beard, a large nose, and cold, stern eyes. Until recently he was acutely cross-eyed. During a visit to India, however, his eyes were straightened, and the change improved his appearance, aided his vision, and made him more prone to relax in the presence of foreigners. Until his death in 1930, the Amir's father, Abdullah, was Ibn Saud's closest friend, having proved his loyalty in January 1902 when he and a handful of trusted warriors climbed over the wall of Riyadh with the young Saud, captured the city, and started Abdul Aziz on the road that made him the lord of Arabia.

Amir Saud ibn Jaluwi has never been garrulous. He speaks in a scarcely audible voice, and when he is feeling unwell, he seems barely able to utter laconic replies to the visitor's thanks and polite inquiries. At such times talking with the tough warrior under the inscrutable stares

91

of his trusted fighting men may be quite an ordeal. But when he is feel-ing well, the Amir is a memorable companion. Conversation ranges from the possibility of applying American rain-making experiments in Hasa to discussions of the nature of justice, which the ruler has a reputa-tion for meting out in strict accordance with Islamic law. Amir Saud ibn Jaluwi has been called the most feared man in Arabia. Certain it is that Hasa province is now safe enough for a truck driver to spend the night in the desert alone; thirty years ago he would have run a grave risk, even accompanied by a band of armed men. One cannot contem-plate without a shiver what it would be like to appear before the Amir as a prisoner. But as a friend one receives a greeting in the highest tradition of Arab hospitality. Once an American friend of the Amir who had failed to visit him in several months was gently rebuked by the pro-vincial ruler, who said with a twinkle in his eye, "If you do not come to see me more often, I shall have to send a car and kidnap your wife to Hofuf. Surely then you will come."

Until recently, when the silent Amir of Hofuf wanted refreshments for his guests, he would mutter the word "coffee" into his beard. Immediately thereafter, the group of warriors at the far end of the room would all shout out "coffee," and the cry would be repeated all the way down to the fires below. By this time even the bravest visitor was alarmed. But customs are beginning to change in Hofuf, and now the Amir, a little self-consciously, reaches out and pushes an electric buzzer beside his chair to summon the coffee pourer.

Following the call at the palace, the visitor embarks on an escorted tour of the town of Hofuf and the series of smaller oases around some forty natural springs. The largest spring, Ain al Haql, pours out more than 22,000 gallons of cool, pure water a minute. Another of the larger springs contains a walled portion where ladies may bathe, while a third has a rest house equipped with a ramp built up to it for the use of the King. Several of the pools boast a deep-blue coloring not unlike that of the Morning Glory Pool in Yellowstone National Park. Standing beside one of these, it is possible to watch an Arab jump straight down into its dark mouth and then see him propelled up and half out of the water by the power of the flow. Most of the springs have networks of canals leading from them to nearby date groves, vegetable gardens, orchards, and small fields of grain. Here and there are clusters of adobe houses plastered with mud or white limestone, while between them run walled lanes filled with an endless procession of hennaed donkeys, bearing loads of palm sticks and alfalfa to the city or the busy new railroad station.

Returning to the city proper, one passes through a narrow gate guarded by Saudi soldiers, for Hofuf is still a well-garrisoned fortress city. Inside, one observes the central market square where camels are tethered on their knees, the open and the covered suq where visitors buy Arab coffeepots in all sizes, the guarded gate into the Amir's inner city, and the thousands of ordinary dwellings stacked against each other like brown paper packages.

Most Hofuf houses are one or two stories in height, with windows facing on the courtyard rather than the street. Mangrove poles from East Africa provide the rafters for the larger homes, and palm trunks do for smaller buildings. As families grow and if land is available, new courtyards are added; otherwise new rooms are built on the flat roofs, with outside stairways leading to them. The most interesting exterior architectural features are carved doors, shutters, and latticed balconies through which the women may look out unobserved. Inside, the emphasis is on colonnades and courtyards, often paved in striking arabesque designs.

Because of the thick walls and few windows, the houses remain cool in contrast to the hot streets. Instead of tables and chairs, one finds low divans running around the walls, with brightly colored cushions behind them. Floors, when they are covered at all, are thickly overlaid with carpets, many of which come from Iran. Candles and gasoline-pressure or kerosene lamps provide light for all but the rich. Bathrooms are small, bare chambers, furnished only with large jars of water and slots cut into the floor to let water run out into the street or down the front of the building. The flat roofs play an important part in family life. They are used as dining rooms and bedrooms on hot nights and serve as all-purpose rooms during the cool weather. Although the streets are dirty, the interiors of the houses are carefully swept and cleaned. But even frequent spraying with DDT cannot completely eliminate the swarms of flies in the daytime and the mosquitoes and gnats at night.

Arab households are traditionally large and include the husband, from one to four wives, their children, and a collection of uncles, aunts, sisters, cousins, servants, and slaves. The sexes are segregated on different floors or in different parts of the same floor, and each wife is allowed a room or suite of rooms. Usually there is a central kitchen,

93

although in the larger houses each wife may have one of her own. Should there be more than one wife, the husband is expected to divide his time equally, spending successive nights with each of his different wives. If the wives get on well together, they may all join with the husband in a dinner party in the rooms of the wife whose turn it is to entertain, leaving promptly after supper while he spends the night with the hostess. In the poorer households, the wife cooks and serves the meals for her family unit, but in the rich homes servants or slaves usually do so.

In the Arabian Peninsula the word harem (more accurately transliterated hareem) does not connote dancing girls in diaphanous trousers; it simply refers to the women of the household. There is no mixing of the sexes outside the family group except in the case of elderly women, who may be seen by persons outside their families. Children go about freely until they are ten; then the boys join the men and the girls stay with the older women. Women must obtain their husband's permission before leaving the house; they remain veiled so long as they are in public and scarcely ever unveil except in their own homes. Their main outside diversion is shopping, though sometimes they will go for a walk with friends or attend a tea party.[1]

Under this rigid system the young city people are never together; therefore the parents select husbands and wives for their children. A girl may catch a glimpse of her prospective husband through a lattice balcony, but he has to depend upon descriptions of his future bride given him by his mother and sisters. It is interesting to note, however, that in arranged marriages of this sort the couple often fall in love afterward. Divorce is accepted as natural if a marriage does not work out, though it is not so frequent as in America. A divorced woman usually goes back to her mother, and her husband contributes to her support.

During the cooler hours of the day the main streets of Hofuf are crowded from wall to wall, for there are no sidewalks. In the areas around the big market place, motor cars slow down to the pace of the camel caravans, heavily loaded donkeys, and crowds of shoppers and idlers on foot. In the outlying areas, the narrow dusty lanes between the brown mud walls that shut in each date grove are traversed by black-robed women going to the wells and by boys driving donkeys to market, to the fields or to water.

---

[1] The author is indebted to Miss Mary Van Pelt's remarks and article in the *Middle East Journal* (January 1950) for some of the background material on family life in Arabia.

When the call of the muezzin echoes from the mosques, the Arabs stop what they are doing and, without self-consciousness, bow together in prayer. Both bedouin and townsfolk are deeply religious, but the latter are likely to be theologians as well, steeped in both the practical and the theoretical side of the Moslem faith. To understand the town Arabs, therefore, one must consider at least briefly the teachings of Mohammed.

The Prophet was born in A.D. 570 at Mecca and died at Medina some sixty-two years later. His contribution was not so much a new religious concept as a new pattern of life. At the time of his birth, Arab society was virtually without moral precept or guidance. Mohammed conscientiously set out to correct what he thought were the worst features of that society. For example, he ended the practice of female infanticide, which before that time had been left to the judgment of the father. Through his teachings, the position of women greatly improved, as the number of wives was limited to four at a time and divorce was regularized. Mohammed laid down laws for what he considered the proper treatment of orphans, slaves, prisoners, and animals. He forbade bearing false witness, worshiping idols, or speaking ill of chaste women. Because the main drink of the Arabs then was a potent beverage made from the heart of palms, which quickly reduced the user to a state of belligerent stupidity and led to many quarrels and sometimes to bloodshed, Mohammed forbade the use of intoxicating liquors. He also felt that the practice of gambling had weakened Arab society in his day and prohibited it too.

In the eyes of true Moslems, the Koran is the word of God, or Allah, which was transmitted through the Angel Gabriel to Mohammed and then recited by him to the faithful. During Mohammed's lifetime his sayings were memorized by his followers. Then, as those who knew the holy words began to pass away, the messages were written down and finally put together in an official text in the year A.D. 651. The Koran is not only the Holy Book of Islam, the source of jurisprudence, and the basis for all Islamic science and culture, but it is the textbook used by most Moslems in learning to read; thus it standardizes written Arabic throughout the entire world. Some of Mohammed's teachings deal in detail with habits of daily life. For example, his followers are forbidden to eat the meat of animals which have not been freshly killed by a Moslem. By the emphasis on prayer, which makes Moslems the world over stop what they are doing and pray at sunrise, noon, midafternoon, sunset, and bedtime, Mohammed and his followers from that time to this have expressed their philosophy that life and religion are inseparable.

Many of the Old Testament figures, such as Adam, Abraham, Joseph, Moses, David, Solomon, Jonah, and Job appear also in the Koran. But Zachariah, John the Baptist, Jesus, and Mary are the only New Testament figures who receive more than passing mention. Jesus is revered by all pious Moslems as a prophet second only to Mohammed. Furthermore, the Koran states that Jesus was sinless and born of a virgin, two attributes not claimed for Mohammed. One passage in Surah 21, Verse 105, of the Koran is apparently a direct quotation from Psalm 37:9, and other passages in the Koran are sufficiently similar to parts of the Bible to suggest that Mohammed was influenced in some degree by the teachings of Christ.

The duties of a Moslem are built around the five Pillars of Islam. The first of these is the profession of faith: "There is but one God, and Mohammed is his apostle." The second is frequent daily prayer, which is largely supplication. The Fatiha, which might be called the Moslem's Lord's Prayer, is repeated by some Moslems as many as twenty times a day. The most important prayer of the week occurs at noon on Friday, a public ceremony which must be observed by all Moslems. Mohammed emphasized the necessity for this gathering, and the need for the pilgrimage to Mecca, in order to bring Moslems together and weld them into a single community.

The third Pillar of the Moslem faith is the giving of alms. This started as a voluntary act, became obligatory for a while, and in most parts of the Arab world today has again become voluntary. The fourth Pillar is fasting in the month of Ramadan, the month during which the Koran was first revealed to Mohammed and the battle of Badr was won. During this month the true believer can eat no food and swallow no drink from dawn until sunset, unless he is ill or on a journey. Apparently fasting was not practiced widely in pagan Arabia before the time of Mohammed, and it seems probable that he learned of the benefits of fasting from the Christians or the Jews, or both.

Making the pilgrimage to Mecca is the fifth Pillar of Islam. Every true Moslem tries to do this once during his lifetime. If he goes at a certain time of the year, it is called the Great Pilgrimage or Hajj; during the rest of the year, it is known as the Lesser Pilgrimage or Umrah. Special ceremonies peculiar to the pilgrimage include striking down the devil with stones in the Valley of Mina, sacrificing a sheep or camel there, entering into the prescribed holy places wearing a seamless gar-

12. Bedouin family serving coffee to an American guest from the oil coast.

13. The author in a date garden in Hofuf, the largest oasis in Saudi Arabia.

14. Bedouin watering their camels at a Saudi Arabian oasis. (Photo by Carl Twitchell.)

ment, walking seven times around the Kaaba, and devoting oneself to prayer.

In addition to Saudis, anywhere from forty thousand to more than one hundred and fifty thousand devout pilgrims come each year from as far away as Morocco on the west and the Philippines in the east to make the pilgrimage. The Hajj has been responsible for giving some three hundred million Moslems throughout the world a community of outlook which has been a source of great strength throughout the ages. It is more than a religious rite; it is the town meeting of the Moslem world.

Around these Pillars of Islam the townsfolk of Arabia have built their lives, in a pattern that is reminiscent of life in New England under the Puritan Fathers. Following noon prayers, when the still heat of the day has settled upon the oasis, it is pleasant to join a group of Arab men in a summer house in the heart of a date grove. There one lies back against silken pillows or oriental rugs and enjoys the deep, cool shade. A white sheet is spread, and barefoot servants set out bowls of tomatoes, pomegranates, oranges, and many varieties of dates. In such a setting the peace of Arabia enters one's soul. The bustling, dirty cities of the Near East, the hot sand-swept spaces of the desert through which the bedouin move constantly in their search for green pastures, the Western world of alarm clocks, telephones, and rush-hour crowds, all seem far away. The leaves of the tall palm trees rustle in the faint breeze that ripples across the oasis. The high-pitched squeak of water wheels and the cooing of doves form a refrain to which the water in the canals improvises an obligato. In a pastoral mood, the Arabs talk of the good life in Hofuf, of date palms, and of dates.

The date palm is one of the oldest cultivated plants. For many centuries it has been the custom to detach the suckers, or shoots which grow out from the trunk of the female tree, and to plant them in the sandy soil. By the second year after such transplanting the shoots are sturdy young trees, and by the eighth year they are bearing fruit. At thirteen they reach maturity, and the average life of a tree is a century.[2]

To grow properly and to produce a copious and succulent crop of dates, the parent tree requires two special conditions: "Its head must be in the sun, its feet in water." Rain is not needed, but wind helps the palm by exercising and combing it. The female palm trees bear the

[2] See George Green's article, "The Date," in the *Home Geographic Monthly*, April 1932.

fruit, but nature has provided no efficient means for their self-fertilization. Consequently, in each date orchard a few male trees are grown, and when early spring arrives the grower transfers the pollen from the male tree to the stamens of the female tree and thus fertilizes his grove. The dates grow in clusters, which develop into bunches weighing twenty to twenty-five pounds. In August the date is soft, sweet, and most delicious. But dates in this condition cannot be shipped any distance, for they would soon ferment. Therefore some dates for local use are picked at this stage, but most are left on the trees until September, when they become much more solid. The mature date is 58 per cent sugar and because of this is easily preserved.

More than seventy varieties of dates are grown in Arabia. Most of them are eaten locally, though some are baled and sent to India and other neighboring countries. The Arabs have given the date over five hundred names, among them being "Mother of Perfume," "Red Sugar," and "Daughter of Sever." One outstanding variety of dates found in Hofuf is fondly called "Khalas," which, freely translated, means "quintessence." This has a rich amber color and a ruddy, semitransparent look; it is esteemed by all who have eaten it.

It is almost impossible to overestimate the importance of the date in the life of the Arab. In many places, such as in Hofuf, it is the staff of life and the staple of commerce. Mohammed is said to have told his followers: "Honor the date tree, for she is your mother." More human life can be supported per acre by date culture than by any other crop that can be raised in Arabia. The by-products of the date are probably as valuable as the fruit itself. From it the Arabs make a viscous syrup, date pits are ground up and fed to cattle, the fronds are woven into mats, and the fiber is used for making rope. The trunks of the palms serve as house beams. The pistils of the date blossom contain a curly fiber which is used as a sponge. It is not surprising that the oasis dwellers call themselves "the people of the palm."

VIII

Aramco: America's Largest
Near East Investment

ONE day, just after the turn of the century, an Australian financier named William Knox D'Arcy had lunch with a friend who remarked that automobiles would soon be widely used and would require quantities of oil. According to the story, D'Arcy was so impressed by this observation that he began to look around for promising oil properties. His business manager, H. E. Nicholas, ran across a Persian named Kitabishi who had obtained a concession from the Persian Government for certain oil seepages in Iran which had attracted attention since ancient times. Nicholas worked out a deal with him, and in May 1901 D'Arcy secured from Mozaffar ed Din Shah a sixty-year concession to prospect in all but the five northern provinces of Iran. For seven years the first exploration company labored to find oil in commercial quantities. At last, in 1908, a gusher came in at Masjid-I-Suleiman. Soon after, the newly formed Anglo-Persian Oil Company supplanted the earlier company, and British operation of the great Iranian fields began.

As world demands for oil increased, the struggle for Persian Gulf oil grew fiercer. An American, Admiral Chester, obtained certain short-lived concessions in the Turkish domains. British and German interests also secured concessions in Iraq. Then, as a result of World War I, the Germans were forced out of the area, and French and American firms took up interests in what is now the British-dominated Iraq Petroleum Company.

99

The oil fields of both Iran and Iraq proved to be rich. In consequence, oil men seeking new fields turned to the western shore of the Gulf. An oil pioneer, gentleman farmer, army officer, and trader named Major Frank Holmes, having obtained promises of concessions from the Sheikh of Bahrein and from Ibn Saud, who had recently conquered the Hasa, offered these concessions to the Anglo-Persian, now Anglo-Iranian, Oil Company. In April 1926, however, the geologists of that company unwisely advised their principals that the chances of finding oil in the Bahrein Islands and eastern Arabia did not justify taking up options. Nevertheless, Major Holmes and other entrepreneurs succeeded in interesting the Standard Oil Company of California which, on December 28, 1926, organized the Bahrein Petroleum Company, Ltd. Staffed by experts from the Standard Oil Company of California, the Bahrein Petroleum Company lost no time in sinking a well at a site recommended by Fred A. Davies, now chairman of the board of the Arabian American Oil Company, and the well produced oil in commercial quantities. Others followed, and it became apparent that Bahrein lay above an oil-rich structure. The Texas Company was then brought into the organization as an equal partner because of its marketing facilities.

Work on Bahrein was hard and hot, and it is said that sometimes in the evenings Davies, the company's manager, E. A. Skinner, Bert Miller, and Krug Henry would sit on the highest hill on the island to catch what little breeze stirred over the still waters of the Persian Gulf. Through field glasses they looked west to where the flat, sandy coast line of the Arabian Peninsula broke into a series of low hills. One particular *jebel*, or hill, back of the village of Dammam, caught their fancy. From a distance it looked just like the structure of Bahrein Island. If Bahrein has oil, they thought, the mainland must have it also. Little was known about Arabia, and no real exploration for oil had ever been attempted there, but Davies told the directors of the Standard Oil Company of California that it could not afford to overlook the oil possibilities of Saudi Arabia.

The company approached Major Holmes, and later St. John Philby, the British Arabist, with an idea of obtaining a concession from the King. In the fall of 1932 the American engineer Karl ·Twitchell, who had been in Saudi Arabia looking for water and gold and was on good terms with the King, entered the negotiations at the latter's request. Twitchell and Lloyd Hamilton, an American oil man, proceeded to Jidda during February 1933, and when they arrived they found representatives of the Iraq Petroleum Company staying in the same build-

100

ing. Ibn Saud weighed all the factors and decided that he wanted Americans as partners because he liked the idea of tying his economy to a country as large, as powerful, as distant, as skilled in the techniques of oil production, and as little interested in imperialism as the United States.

Just as the deal was about to be closed, the United States went off the gold standard and stopped the export of gold. After much discussion, the terms of the royalties to be paid Ibn Saud were set at "four gold shillings per ton or its equivalent in dollars or pounds sterling," a wording which has complicated the company's financial life not a little. The concession runs for sixty-six years. It originally covered 281,000 square miles, extending in a great half-moon down the east coast of Saudi Arabia, including the Rub al Khali in the south, and continuing as far west as the borders of Yemen, thus omitting the old rocks of the "Arabian shield." Ibn Saud ratified the document, and it became effective July 14, 1933. In 1939 the area was expanded to cover approximately 440,000 square miles. In 1948 Standard of New Jersey and the Socony–Vacuum Oil Company were admitted in order to provide funds for a trans-Arabian pipe line which would bring Persian Gulf oil to the Mediterranean.

It took time to organize the advance exploration parties for entry into virtually unknown Saudi Arabia, but in September 1933 the first group, including Krug Henry, Bert Miller as chief geologist, and Karl Twitchell as guide, landed on the mainland. Crossing from Bahrein by launch, the group went ashore at the small Arab settlement of Jubail, some ninety miles north of Dhahran. There, in a rented mud house, the geologists set up their army cots and a small portable desk; a handful of Saudi Arabs were hired; and the Arabian-American adventure was begun.

The first field work was done on Dammam Dome; then parties started inland by truck and camel. Over gravel or rock the cars rolled easily, but when they crossed drifting sand the wheels dug in and stopped. Special tires had to be obtained, their size based on the relation between the size of a camel's foot and his weight. As the first sand tires proved inadequate, Aramco experimented and developed better designs. Now motor vehicles travel with little difficulty across the sands of Arabia.

Oil exploration continued throughout the winter of 1933–1934, three field parties of two men each exploring inland as far as the oasis of Hofuf. All supplies for the operation except dates, mutton, and camel's

101

milk had to be brought over by small boats from Bahrein. Drinking water, the greatest problem, came ashore in drums until a water well could be drilled. But despite supply and other complications, the oil company had begun to get the lay of the land by mid-1934.

The first nongeological group came ashore in December of that year to look for the best site for a pier. At first the little fishing village of Dammam was selected, but it was soon noted that an easier landing could be made at a still smaller town called Al Khobar, a few miles to the south. Consequently the pier was built there. Now four piers adequately serve Saudi Arabia's east coast: the seven-mile, dry-cargo pier at Dammam, the oil-loading pier at Ras Tanura, and two small-craft piers, one at Al Khobar and the other at Ras al Mish'ab.

On December 26, 1934, another group landed at Al Khobar and pitched a camp several miles inland, where the macadam road from the airport now meets the Khobar-Dhahran thoroughfare. This camp, so situated because of nearby water, consisted of four tents. The first was the bedroom and kitchen of the Chinese cook; the second served as a dining room, the third as a sleeping tent, and the fourth as office and storage space. The first problem which a member of the party, who is now an Aramco vice-president, had to deal with involved two turkeys that had been brought from Bahrein for New Year's dinner. These birds were much admired by the Saudis, and when they disappeared on December 30 suspicion fell on a newly hired Arab. A search party, however, revealed that a dog had killed the birds, stuffed himself, and then fallen down the well. Sadly disappointed, the party fished the dog out of the well and sat down to a New Year's dinner out of cans.

As early as conditions permitted, a rough road was built four miles inland from Al Khobar to the site of the first oil well, now known as Dhahran. There the first permanent living quarters and office buildings were set up. Meanwhile, exploration continued, though shifting sands on the surface made it hard to spot likely formations. The first well was started on April 30, 1935, and showed signs of oil in August of that year. In December drilling got down to the zone at which oil was found on Bahrein, but here only a little oil and lots of sweet gas appeared. Well after well was drilled, none of them showing oil in commercial quantities. There was short-lived excitement when, in 1936, a well brought in a heavy flow of oil, then petered out. By the end of 1937 millions of dollars had been spent and a lot of energy consumed, but eastern Saudi Arabia still looked more like a sand pile than an oil field. Something new had to be tried. On Bahrein Island a well had

102

been run down through the oil-producing zone to 4,600 feet, but little resulted from the experiment except gas. As a last resort the reduced and discouraged staff at Dhahran decided to run a deep test in Saudi Arabia. If it failed, there was good reason to think the whole enterprise should be abandoned. Well number seven was deepened, and in March 1938 oil was struck in volume.

Overnight the picture changed. Men and money began to pour into the oil coast. New wells were sunk, old ones were drilled deeper, and a pipe line was built from Dhahran to the little port of Al Khobar, where storage tanks were erected. In September 1938 the first oil was shipped to Bahrein Island, and a month later the company officially declared its discovery of oil in commercial quantities. In accordance with the terms of the concession the government of Saudi Arabia received an initial payment of fifty thousand gold pounds.

In May 1939 King Ibn Saud, who was staying in a tent city built especially for him, drove to Ras Tanura accompanied by four hundred automobiles filled with followers. In an impressive ceremony he turned the valve and started the oil flowing through a submarine line into the Standard of California tanker "El Segundo" tied to the new pier. At last Saudi Arabian oil was directly available for the tankers of the world.

Continued exploration indicated further rich possibilities. Seismographs and gravity meters, brought into use in 1938, led to the discovery of a field at Abu Hadriya, north of Dhahran, and to one under the high sand dunes at Abqaiq, forty miles to the west. Everything pointed to a period of rapid development.

Then in September 1939 World War II broke out, and the normal trade of the world stopped. Men and supplies could no longer be sent directly to Arabia but had to go around Africa or across the Pacific. One September night in 1940 Bahrein and Dhahran were bombed in one of the real surprise attacks of the war. Coming all the way from the Island of Rhodes, about half a dozen long-range Italian bombers reached the oil coast completely undetected. The raiders bombed and broke one oil line but damaged little else and caused no deaths or injuries. From Dhahran they apparently flew westward over the Rub al Khali to Asmara, Eritrea. Some may have been forced down in unexplored territory, for bedouin have since reported several planes in the sands south of the Trucial Coast.

The war greatly slowed up geological work, drilling, and construction on the oil coast. Nevertheless, 12,000 barrels of oil went from the mainland to Bahrein Island daily. Many oil company workers returned to the United States via the Pacific, getting through just before the war encompassed that area. American women and children were evacuated; the last groups left by ship and British plane to Karachi and Bombay, for Aramco had no planes of its own at that time, and no army planes were available.

The future of the Aramco concession looked anything but hopeful. Revolt in Iraq underscored the instability of parts of the Arab world; General Rommel was on the move in North Africa, threatening to break through to the Nile Valley at any time. In consequence, top Aramco officials drew up complete evacuation plans. By the end of 1942 the American population of the oil coast had dropped to ninety-two workers, most of them maintenance men.

Then Rommel was stopped in the Mediterranean, and an expanding United States war machine, hungry for oil, turned to Saudi Arabia. There was talk that Secretary of the Interior Ickes favored government purchase of all or part of Aramco; at any rate he put forward a suggestion that a government-financed or government-owned pipe line be constructed from Dhahran to the Mediterranean. Meantime, workers began to return to the field, and production again increased.

A 3,000-barrel-a-day refinery had been completed by Aramco in 1939, but it soon became clear that a larger refinery would be needed in Saudi Arabia. Therefore, working under pressure, Aramco and the construction firm of International Bechtel succeeded in completing, in nine months, a 50,000-barrel-a-day oil refinery on the sand spit at Ras Tanura. Despite loss through enemy action of one cargo ship carrying vital supplies, the Ras Tanura refinery began operations in September 1945. Almost from the start, it produced an output much in excess of its scheduled 50,000 barrels and now runs at a rate of over 130,000 barrels a day.

The oil coast towns, principally Dhahran, Ras Tanura, and Abqaiq, are comfortable, bustling, and modern. Laid out much like American towns except for the bilingual traffic signs and the gated compounds, they contain central, air-cooled dining halls, theaters, hobby rooms, and recreation areas. Each town has a swimming pool, tennis courts, and bowling alleys. Hundreds of comfortable bungalows equipped with electricity, modern plumbing, efficient kitchens, and air cooling now house American and other workers. Thanks to central heating and air cooling, Americans sleep, eat, and work almost entirely in a temperate climate, though actual temperature during the Arabian summer may be 120 degrees in the shade, and during the winter near freezing.

104

The average yearly rainfall is three and a half inches, most of it coming during two or three winter days. Fortunately, the fresh water deep under Dhahran is sufficient to supply the community. Many energetic householders have planted jasmine, oleander, and Kenya grass around their bungalows, and in the early spring bougainvillaea and summer shrubs and flowers brighten the tawny landscape with their Persian-carpet colors.

A point system determines who shall occupy the houses, for Aramco has been unable to keep up with housing needs. Air-cooled bunkhouses accommodate the lower-paid employees, who cannot expect to take their families out with them before they have completed a twenty-four-month tour of duty. Meantime, Aramco continues to struggle with the problem of housing. Swedish portable houses and native fieldstone apartments have recently been erected to ease the situation.

By 1954 there were thirty-seven hundred American employees in Saudi Arabia, over five hundred wives and four hundred children. With but few exceptions, the wives have adjusted well to their air-cooled bungalows, their Bahreini, Adenese, Yemeni, or Indian servants, and the close-knit community life on the oil coast. They have busied themselves with clubs, parties, relief work, singing groups, and flower shows, and have started a generation of healthy American children on Arabian soil.

At Dhahran and Ras Tanura the pioneering phase is past. Large new motion-picture theaters, taxi service, bus and telephone systems, four-engine-airplane service to the United States, and increased shopping facilities in the nearby towns of Dammam and Al Khobar signal a more abundant life. At the air field near Dhahran a modest hotel, owned by the Saudi Arabian Government, offers accommodations for transients, and a new travel service assists them on their way.

In their nonworking hours, Americans sometimes undertake excursions to Hofuf to see Arab life there; also popular are shopping tours to Al Khobar and Dammam; and occasionally a trip by boat to Bahrein yields an opportunity to buy pearls, Persian rugs, and sandals, as well as to see the prehistoric burial mounds and the old Portuguese fort. For most Americans, however, the language barrier, the differences in religion and social customs, and the fear of local diseases make friendship with the Arabs hard to establish and difficult to maintain. There is every reason to believe that in time Arabs and Americans will develop a larger experience in common and that their cultural differences will diminish. At present, the Americans, with notable exceptions, live on what amounts to an American island in an Arab sea. With the completion of the causeway and pier, Dammam is growing into a normal city in contrast to company towns like Dhahran. The development of a more cosmopolitan center will encourage settlement of educated Arabs from other parts of the Moslem world, who now find it difficult to fit in either with the self-sufficient American community or with the uneducated local population.

Learning about the Arabs and their country has thus far been a diversion for only a few Americans. Others have turned to fishing, which is excellent on the Gulf; hunting, which invites a few on week-end expeditions into the interior; and horseback riding, which flourishes as a sport despite the charge of forty dollars a month to board a horse. Softball and football games, golf tournaments on a sandy course with oiled "greens," and boxing and wrestling matches all draw crowds. Informal parties are frequently held at home, while picnics on the dunes of Half Moon Bay, together with occasional dinners at the Italian camp, provide a change of atmosphere and menu.

All Americans on the twenty-four-month tour of duty receive fourteen days' regional leave with full pay, which they may take in Cairo, Beirut, Teheran, Asmara, or some other Near Eastern city. In addition, they earn two months' paid vacation in the United States every two years. Wages range from $250 a month for file clerks to over $800 a month for executives, and a high percentage of income can be saved because there is little to spend it on in Saudi Arabia.

Aramco has been careful in screening its workers. A few who arrive dislike everything about Arabia and soon leave or become troublesome and have to be sent home. But a high percentage have signed more than one two-year contract, and many are becoming permanent residents. This is not surprising, for pay is good, and the oil region of Saudi Arabia is similar in appearance and climate to parts of east Texas and Oklahoma. In order to train new employees for the specialized problems of duty in Saudi Arabia, Aramco in 1948 opened an indoctrination school near New York. This was moved to Sidon, Lebanon, in 1951. The intensive course includes training in colloquial Arabic and in principles of job instruction, as well as background information on the oil industry, on Aramco, and on Saudi Arabian history, geography, customs, and laws.

Before the advent of Aramco, the Hasa province was an empty desert. The great date gardens, which once ran along the western shore of the Persian Gulf from Kuwait to Muscat, had been drying up for centuries, and only a few remnants of them were visible, as at Qatif, where the palm gardens still fight a losing battle with the advancing sand. The inhabitants of the few small villages in the area had little enough to eat themselves. The company, therefore, had to feed its men from other sources. During the war years, when shipping was difficult, it planted vegetable gardens and kept chickens and herds of cows. As shipping became available, much of this program was abandoned as uneconomical. At present, Aramco operates a commissary on a scale large enough to supply the army of a small European state. Cargo ships leave the United States regularly, bringing frozen meat and packaged goods to the commissary. All the executives and many others eat food prepared in their own bungalows. The rest of the American workers are assured of clean and hearty American fare, served in a dining hall equipped with every available device for the sanitary and rapid preparation and service of food.

In addition to Americans, Aramco employs about twelve hundred Italians, most of whom came from Eritrea. First brought in during the war, they supply such skills as carpentry, stone masonry, and master plumbing. King Ibn Saud laid down the principle that, except for Americans, no foreigners should have better treatment than his subjects. The Italians were consequently in a difficult position as they were not part of the American community but at the same time had almost nothing in common with the local Arabs. An additional hardship arose from the fact that they were not yet allowed to bring their wives to Saudi Arabia. To meet the problem, Aramco built intermediate camps, complete with air conditioning and swimming pools, at Dhahran, Abqaiq, and Ras Tanura where occupancy is on a salary basis. There the Italians live with some eight hundred skilled Palestinian refugees who were recruited in Lebanon.

Apart from the Americans and Italians, the Aramco labor force is made up of almost fourteen thousand Arabs. The majority of them are Saudis, but some are from Iraq, Bahrein, Aden, and other countries, making a total of twenty different nationalities. Collecting a labor force for as complicated an operation as producing, transporting, and refining oil, when local labor is untrained and limited in numbers, has been one of Aramco's most difficult problems.

The company has from the beginning tried to employ as many Saudi Arabian workmen as possible. Through the years, a large number of them have developed skills. Some drive trucks, buses, road scrapers, and bulldozers; others run gas stations and work in the repair shops.

In the production field, drilling crews are now frequently composed of Saudi Arabs, many of whom have worked together for as long as ten years. Under skilled American direction they have set records in fast drilling, despite difficult conditions. Some of Aramco's Saudi employees have developed into skilled lathe and milling-machine operators, electric-motor repairmen, gas-engine mechanics, linemen, pipe-line fitters, and welders. They excel in the craft of masonry, which has been handed down to them for many generations. Some of the more energetic among them have become buildings contractors, supervising their own crews of workers.

The company gives medals to employees of long service and has honored a substantial number of ten-year and some fifteen-year Arab men. Ahmed Rashid, who has worked for the company since December 1933, has one son at the American University at Beirut and a nephew, whom he is sponsoring, at the University of Pennsylvania.

When Aramco began its operations nineteen years ago, the wage rate for unskilled workers was half a riyal, or twelve cents a day. The starting rate is now 3 riyals a day and increases to a top of 15 for those on a daily-rate schedule. Monthly rates of pay run from 90 to 1,500 riyals. Good rations are issued at very low cost, and housing, fuel, and light are provided free to all bachelor employees.

In December 1947 the company started a thrift benefit plan under which the employee contributes 5 or 10 per cent of his salary and the company adds a bonus, so that an employee who leaves the firm after fifteen years or more receives a bonus of 100 per cent of his savings. At first this plan ran into opposition because it was thought to violate the Moslem law regarding interest, but it is now gaining acceptance.

Aramco now supplies excellent medical and surgical care free to all Americans and to its other employees on the oil coast with over one year of continuous service. At the end of 1953 there were more than one hundred Americans working in the medical department, including dentists, nurses, and doctors specializing in surgery, obstetrics, internal medicine, and eye, ear, nose, and throat diseases. In addition there were Indian and Italian doctors and an Italian dentist. In one month the treatment and hospital care provided for employees and their families have involved more than 25,938 out-patient calls and 797 hospitalizations. This is not surprising when one considers that the life expectancy in Saudi Arabia is about thirty-three years, that tuberculosis is common, that typhoid and smallpox are endemic, that 70 per cent of the population has trachoma, and that at least 40 per cent suffers from syphilis. From the company's point of view, malaria was a particularly difficult problem, for almost 98 per cent of the people suffered from it in oases like Qatif. The company has carried on an extensive campaign with insecticides in the coastal towns, and the incidence of malaria among its employees has been reduced to negligible proportions. A sixty-five-bed Arab hospital, modern in every detail, was completed in 1948 at Dhahran and has since been expanded.

In order to operate its oil business, Aramco has built three complete American villages and several smaller camps in eastern Arabia and has trained and given regular employment to more than twelve thousand Saudi Arabs. Through the nature and magnitude of its operations, it has affected both the world oil picture and the relationship between America and the Arab world. If the results of the mutually advantageous partnership have sometimes fallen short of the goals set, the reasons are to be found, on the one hand, in the policies of the parent American oil companies, who have failed to assess the full implications of running an oil business in this new setting and, on the other, in the policies of the Saudi Arabian Government, which imperfectly appreciates the complexities of the world oil business in general and the tremendous technical difficulties involved in producing and marketing Saudi Arabian oil in particular.

One of the technical problems faced by Aramco has been that of Arab housing.[1] Aramco offers all its bachelor employees free housing, but as of 1951, sixteen years after the company began its operations, about 50 per cent of the Saudi workers were still living in temporary quarters. Well aware of this unsatisfactory situation, company management then pushed ahead with the building of permanent stone or brick dormitories which furnish free water, light, gas for cooking, sewage facilities, and fans. Unmarried Arab workers become eligible for these improved accommodations on a seniority and pay basis. At the beginning Aramco took the position that housing for married Arab workers was not its responsibility. As a result, squalid and unsanitary settlements sprang up near the permanent bachelor quarters. Early in 1949, however, the company set up a committee to study the problem of housing for Arabs with families. Some students of the situation have come to the conclusion that the company should obtain government approval to act as a town planner for nearby Arab settlements, laying

[1] For much of the information on labor conditions in eastern Saudi Arabia, the author is indebted to William J. Handley, Labor Attaché, American Embassy, Cairo, Egypt.

109

out suitably planned subdivisions, complete with all public utilities. Married Arabs working for the company could be invited to build houses there with money put up by Aramco, one-half to be repaid over a ten-year period. Probably the establishment of some such scheme is the only way to erect properly planned towns, fit neighbors to the modern American communities on the oil coast.

Apart from a strike that tied up production in the late autumn of 1953, Aramco's relations with the Saudi Arabian Government and with its Arab workers have been good. The company must adjust, however, to the modernization of Arabia. Conditions which seemed excellent to the young Saudi of 1935 appear inadequate to the modern Saudi, particularly one who has traveled outside Arabia for training. So far the company has seen remarkable success in turning illiterate bedouin into craftsmen of varying degrees of skill. But the great need in Saudi Arabia is for primary education. Conscious of this, Aramco, through its director of training, Roy Lebkicher, and its chief of liaison with schools, Harry Snyder, is progressing carefully in the formation and execution of an educational program which should have far-reaching effects in Saudi Arabia. As the former American Ambassador to Saudi Arabia, Rives Childs, pointed out, the program will be a real test of Ibn Saud's thesis that his people can absorb the technical skills of the Western world without harm to their religious and cultural ideas.

The management of Aramco faces the challenge in this thesis day by day. Arab workers, no matter what their jobs, must be allowed to pray five times a day and to attend the weekly prayer on Friday at the mosque. No intoxicating liquor of any sort can be sold or made available to them. Non-Moslem men can have no contact whatsoever with Arab women. The education of the workers' children must be along Koranic lines, with the study of English and technical skills as secondary subjects. Workers must be encouraged to give to the poor, make the pilgrimage, and otherwise live up to the best tenets of the Moslem faith.

King Ibn Saud kept a watchful eye on all this by communication with local officials and even by personal trips to the oil coast. After each such visit he expressed himself as well satisfied, not only with the gains Aramco has made in increasing oil production, but also with the progress seen in giving better working and living conditions to his subjects.

Oil production now equals almost 850,000 barrels a day, and the goal of a million barrels a day is possible. Up to the end of 1950, Ibn Saud received four gold shillings a ton, or about thirty-three cents a barrel. In December of that year, however, a new contract was negotiated, known as the Jidda Agreement. Under its terms the government receives up to one-half the company's net operating receipts. This increases the government's royalties to well over forty cents a barrel, and means that, at present levels of production, the King's oil income is almost $200,000,000 a year.

This constitutes 90 per cent of his total income and makes him one of the world's richest men. But it must be remembered that his finances and the finances of his country are one and the same. That total income not only has to suffice for himself, the royal family, and his household of five thousand, but has to run the government of Saudi Arabia, to pay subsidies to many of the tribes, and to take care of the needy, for whom under Moslem law he is directly responsible. Lastly, and in the long run most important, it is out of royalties that King Saud modernizes his country and brings the concepts and conveniences of the modern world to his five million subjects.

The average Saudi Arab working for Aramco starts his life as a bedouin living in the black tents of his forefathers and roaming the desert to the west of Dhahran. His first contact with the Americans is probably with a field party which has penetrated to the part of the desert where his tribe grazes its flocks. Puzzled by the automobiles, trucks, air-cooled trailers, and other equipment which he sees for the first time, he asks questions of Arabs who work for the company. From them he learns of the possibility of having limitless water, plentiful food, and a regular salary with which to buy more things for himself and his family than he previously thought possible for any but the sheikh of his tribe. As a result, he moves east and pitches his tent within sight of the jebel at Dhahran. Here he spends a few days getting used to the roar of traffic by day and the flares by night. He talks to fellow tribesmen who are already workers and goes with them to the Arab camp. Then one day he enters the employment office, is interviewed, fingerprinted, and numbered, and begins to work digging a ditch, carrying stones, or loading a truck.

The regularity and supervision may be too much for him, and he may pack off again. But after the first few paydays have brought him clothes, pots and pans, and a new dress for his wife, he probably moves his tent into the "unrestricted" Arab camp.

Months pass, and he is accepted as a regular Aramco worker. He moves again, this time into one of the rows of *barasti*, or palm houses, found in the old company camp. Here there is running water readily accessible, and he begins to learn the rudiments of modern sanitation.

111

Before long he gets a small raise in pay. He talks to his friends and realizes that, if he were more skillful, he could make still more money. When his foreman picks him out as a possible assistant driver, he agrees to take a course in truck driving. In another year he is at the wheel of one of Aramco's lighter trucks, still wearing his native headgear but dressed in a khaki shirt and long khaki trousers. By now, if he is a bachelor or if his family lives elsewhere, he has moved into a room in one of the newly completed brick or stone barracks, where he has electricity, running water, and ample cooking facilities. If he is married, his wife, who lives in a nearby village, has probably been to the company hospital, where the world of modern medicine opened before her, and his eldest son is attending the first year of the Aramco school. Already the boy speaks more English than his father and is full of plans of one day becoming an accountant in the office of the company.

Sometimes in the gathering twilight he and his son sit with other fellow workers on the concrete porch in front of the barracks. They look across the green shrubs and flowers just beginning to take hold at the entrance to their building and over the roof of the million-riyal Arab hospital. Beyond the well-oiled road which runs to the airport, a promontory of Jebel Dhahran sticks out toward the Persian Gulf. Under the rimrock are a series of caves inhabited by bedouin who have not yet taken the plunge into the twentieth century. Their long-haired figures stand out in sharp silhouette against the evening fires. There is no water up there, little food, no regular pay, no medical attention, no school, and little chance to buy even the necessities of bedouin life. The worker and his son are only across the road, to be sure, but they have journeyed into a new era.

IX

Up and Down the Oil Coast

THE eastern coast of Saudi Arabia is almost barren of verdure except for the large Hofuf oasis and the groves around Qatif. For years its population of nomadic tribesmen, fishermen, date growers, and petty shopkeepers eked out the meagerest sort of existence. Meanwhile the blowing sand engulfed more and more of the cultivable land. During the last twenty years, however, much has been done to break this deadly cycle. Desultory trade between a handful of crumbling villages and neighboring Persian Gulf ports has grown into a flourishing Gulf-wide business, with American customers on the one hand and an expanding group of salaried Arabs and middle-class traders on the other. The once-quiet towns on the coastal flats are booming. For some distance inland the dunes and gravel plains, which a few years ago recorded only the footprints of infrequent caravans and the unmistakable traces of bedouin encampments, are crisscrossed with motor and railroad tracks, telephone wires, and pipe lines. Oil drums used as markers and road signs in English and Arabic give new character to the landscape in the daytime, while giant gas flares light up the landscape at night. Every month sees new white buildings in the established American-developed towns of Dhahran, Ras Tanura, and Abqaiq, as well as in the frontier settlements of Ain Dar and Uthmaniyah.

Because it is over three thousand miles by sea from Suez to Ras Tanura, more and more travelers are coming to eastern Saudi Arabia by air. Dhahran lies approximately halfway between Cairo and Karachi, about thirteen hundred miles distant from each. It is thus a natural air center, and as many as a thousand planes have landed there in a single month. In this number are included planes of the Saudi Arabian Airlines, which uses Dhahran as its eastern terminus; Trans World Airways; and the Royal Dutch Airlines, KLM. In addition, many military planes and planes operated by Aramco's aviation division, which carries on the largest noncommercial air operation outside the United States, use the airport regularly. In Aramco's fleet are two luxurious DC-6B's which shuttle between New York and Dhahran carrying company personnel and supplies, while additional Convairs, DC-3's, and Navions facilitate company business in the field.

Construction of the strategic Dhahran airfield was begun during World War II to create a stopping place for flights supplying American troops in India and Southeast Asia. The war ended before the field was completed, and in the national interest the Department of State and the Air Force went to Congress for appropriations to finish the job. With two seven-thousand-foot runways and hangar and repair facilities, the airport is now the best in the Persian Gulf area.

According to the terms of the formal airport agreement between the United States and the former King Ibn Saud, the Saudi Arabs are being taught to operate the field. To this end, a training mission of American officers and men is instructing a hand-picked group of Arabs in maintenance, in the study of weather conditions, and in the workings of the control tower. The best men graduated from this course proceed to the United States for advanced training.

Proof that such instruction was not at first adequate to prepare the Arab for practical problems at the field may be found in the story of a Saudi student who was taking the weather course when one of the princes was due to fly from Riyadh to Dhahran. On this particular day a driving sandstorm swept down from the north, reducing visibility to zero. The young Saudi weatherman, however, drafted a wire to be sent to the pilot of the prince's plane reporting that the weather at Dhahran was "clear, ceiling unlimited." To the amazed American officer who intercepted this message, the Saudi explained, "I didn't want to tell the prince that anything was wrong at Dhahran. It is his country after all, and he might have been offended."

The Dhahran airfield has been the scene of many colorful arrivals and departures. In 1947 when Crown Prince Saud enplaned for the United States, dignitaries came from all over Saudi Arabia to bid him good-bye, surging out onto the cement runways in such numbers that the police had to be called before the plane could take off. In March 1949 the first nonstop, round-the-world flight was refueled from the Dhahran airfield. This flight was one of the most carefully guarded secrets of postwar aviation, with King Ibn Saud the only Arab informed of it in advance.

Although operations at Dhahran airfield are on a businesslike basis, royal permission must still be obtained before a plane can take off from the capital city of Riyadh. Until recently, if a member of the royal family or an important government official booked passage on a Saudi air liner, the plane might wait there all day in the burning sun until he finished his packing, said good-bye to his family, took his siesta, and drove out to the airfield for coffee with such of his followers and friends as wished to see him off. Now that there are special planes set aside for the use of the royal family, the delays have become much less frequent. Incidents such as the following are now things of the past. On one of its earliest trips the air line received a reservation for twenty persons to be picked up at Riyadh and taken to the hill town of Taif. Landing at the capital, the pilot was surprised to see twenty men and an equal number of women waiting to board the plane. "What about these women?" he asked. The Saudi sheikh looked suddenly alarmed. "Must we count them too?" he inquired.

In spite of sandstorms and the necessity for stopping frequently at gravel-surfaced air strips, the American pilots have given this line a wonderful safety record, and the steady increase in traffic justified its purchase of five four-motored planes in the summer of 1952.

While air traffic within Arabia is increasing year by year, the season of the great pilgrimage to Mecca, the Hajj, is the time of greatest activity for the Saudi Arabian Airlines. Many special flights are then made to Cairo, Beirut, Damascus, and Baghdad. In 1952 the government of Saudi Arabia removed the head tax which applied to those making the Hajj, and an unprecedented demand for air travel to Saudi Arabia from all over the East left several thousand pilgrims stranded at the airport in Beirut. It became clear that there would not be enough commercial space available and that the pilgrims would not be in Mecca in time for that year's celebration. Consequently, a group of Moslem leaders asked the help of the American Ambassador to Lebanon, Harold Minor. He telegraphed the State Department, where the interested officials at once saw the importance of helping these stranded pilgrims to reach their goal. Ambassador Minor's first cable reached Washington late on a Friday afternoon. By midnight Saturday the sleeping commander of the American air base in Tripoli, Libya, was awakened with orders to set up an airlift from Beirut to Jidda, which is as near Mecca as non-Moslems can go. By six o'clock Sunday morning the first plane had left North Africa for Beirut, and by eight o'clock on Monday morning, every-hour-on-the-hour service had been started out of Beirut. Before the airlift was over, seventy-four flights had been made along the eight-hundred-mile route to Jidda, and more than thirty-seven hundred Hajjis were taken by modern magic carpet to this religious gathering of the Moslem world.

Up until 1946 trips in eastern Arabia that were too short for airplanes involved a constant battle with desert sands and graveled plains. Now, however, an asphalt plant has been started at Ras Tanura, and there is a growing network of hard-surfaced roads connecting the main centers of the oil coast. Such a road runs from the airfield, past the large enclosure of the American consul general and his staff on a hill above the airport, to Dhahran. Thence it winds southwestward over salt flats and dunes to where the fast-growing town of Abqaiq lies, over one of the largest oil fields in the world. The American-built settlements on the oil coast all look substantially alike with their well-oiled streets and rows of carefully laid out bungalows, surrounded by fences or low walls and occasionally by oleanders and frequently watered patches of green. Apart from its huge sand dunes, Abqaiq is noted for having the largest flares in the Near East and some of the area's most productive oil wells. The average take is over 12,000 barrels a day, in contrast to the American average of less than twelve. With such a supply of oil available, it is not surprising that Aramco's production was over 36,000,000 tons of crude oil in 1951 and topped 40,000,000 tons in 1953. Aramco is continuing its exploration to the west and south of Dhahran. Drilling in 1951 was concentrated in the Ain Dar and Abu Hadriya areas, where eighteen wells were completed. Another important structure has been located at Haradh, more than a hundred miles south of Ain Dar, continuing the line of rich fields heading toward the Rub al Khali.

Some of the oil from Abqaiq and Dhahran passes along the world's longest underseas pipe line to the island of Bahrein, where it is put through the refinery before shipping. Most of it, however, goes through a much shorter underseas pipe line across Tarut Bay to the sand spit of Ras Tanura. Here the 50,000-barrel-a-day refinery, which International Bechtel built so hurriedly during World War II, has been expanded to handle more than twice that amount. The rest of the crude

oil reaching Ras Tanura is sent to a tank farm at the end of the promontory, and part of it is pumped into tankers tied up at the company
piers. Although these docks handle four large tankers at a time, filling each in eight hours, it is not unusual to see a dozen tankers lying
offshore waiting their turn to come alongside. Like Dhahran and
Abqaiq, Ras Tanura is undergoing a tremendous growth. In addition
to the refinery proper, it includes an excellent machine shop, a well-
equipped recreation center, and a pleasant residential area, part of
which stretches along the sandy white beach. Crews of the tankers
used to dread coming into port at Ras Tanura. Now Aramco has opened
a club on a strip of good beach near the loading pier, and there approximately one hundred sailors may be accommodated for recreation
each day. It is damper at Ras Tanura than at Dhahran or the inland
oil towns, but Ras Tanura has fewer sand storms, a breeze off the Gulf,
and such good sea bathing that many of the Americans assigned there
consider it the most pleasant of the Aramco towns.

Except for the oil piers at Ras Tanura, which are always crowded
with tankers, up to five years ago no place along the whole of the
Persian Gulf west coast could berth anything larger than a dhow. In
view of the rapidly increasing imports of Saudi Arabia, a pier for ocean-
going cargo ships was clearly necessary, and the fishing village of Dammam, whose minarets and rapidly growing buildings can be seen from
Ras Tanura across Tarut Bay in the direction of Dhahran, was selected as Saudi Arabia's door on the Persian Gulf. Work began there in
1948 on a fill running out into the Gulf across the reefs and shallows of
the bay. On this, a causeway five miles long was constructed, and beyond it for one and three-quarters miles a trestle now runs to a 750-foot
steel pier. Water has thus been reached deep enough at low tide to
accommodate almost any seagoing merchant vessel. As a result, Dammam has burst into activity. Wealthy Saudi Arabs have staked out lots
and are putting up homes, office buildings, and warehouses in and
around the town. An electric-power plant has been constructed in Dammam by the Al Khobar Power Company, an independently financed
utility which began operations in June 1952 as the first commercial
electric-power producer in the area. It seems likely that within ten years
Dammam will have a population of twenty-five thousand and will be
the most important commercial center in eastern Arabia.

An additional reason for this rapid growth is Dammam's location at
the eastern terminus of the Saudi Arabian railroad. In the days before
World War I, the Turks laid the Hejaz Railway from Damascus to

Medina for the dual purpose of helping pilgrims on their way to Mecca and consolidating Turkish control in the Hejaz. This railway was destroyed by Lawrence of Arabia in a series of raids so successful that the Hejaz Railway of today is nothing but a roadbed, with a few twisted rails and an occasional car lying burned and overturned beside it.

In the winter of 1945 Ibn Saud held his famous talk with President Roosevelt on the cruiser "Quincy," and the American President asked him how many miles of railroad there were in Saudi Arabia. To this the King had to reply that, although there had been several hundred miles of railroad, none of it was workable at present. This conversation started the King thinking about the need for a railroad in his country, and his thoughts were much stimulated by his visit to Egypt in 1946, when for the first time he rode on a train.

In 1947 he instructed his Minister in Washington to inquire about the possibility of a United States Government loan to finance a railroad from the Persian Gulf to Riyadh. The route and its possibilities underwent study, and traffic from Dammam through Dhahran to Abqaiq seemed to indicate a real need for a railroad. An extension of such a line to the oasis of Hofuf, with its one hundred thousand inhabitants and one million date trees, also appeared to be profitable. The remaining miles from Hofuf to Riyadh were estimated as useful but not lucrative, and construction along this route was felt to be more a political than an economic matter.

Consequently, the United States Government informed the Arab King that it preferred to lend him money on improvements such as harbors, roads, public utilities, and hospitals, and suggested that he finance the railroad through private sources. The King went ahead on this basis, and time is proving that he was not foolish in doing so. The main line runs 357 miles westward from the seaport of Dammam to the walled capital of Riyadh. It began operation officially on March 1, 1949, but was not finished till October 1951, when the present King drove a gilded spike into place near Riyadh. Already it is handling more passengers and cargo than was expected, and runs a passenger and two freight trains a day in each direction. A surprisingly large commuter traffic has developed, and self-propelled Diesel cars are proving very popular. Third-class passengers travel on flatcars equipped with wooden seats and present a picturesque appearance as they jolt across the sand with robes streaming in the wind. At first the rest of the passenger accommodations were in prefabricated bodies placed on flatcars, but in 1951 a shipload of passenger cars was received from America, making rail travel more comfortable as well as faster than with the earlier primitive equipment.

The Arab desire to bargain over fares made trouble at first. But the railroad's main problem is sand. In some places this is kept off the track by slat fences like the snow fences used in the United States. Construction of the line through the Abqaiq sands presented unusual difficulties. Dunes there rise to more than fifty feet and move constantly southward. By placing the track on the highest of them, filling in the hollows between, and spraying the dune surfaces with oil, the railroad men have encouraged the sand to blow over the track instead of settling on it. Much of the line required rock ballast, which can be partially cleared of sand by blowers attached to each locomotive. Another unusual problem was the finding of communications equipment which would not be put out of operation by sandstorms.

The line is standard gauge, all single track, with eighty-pound rails. Most of the stations are still very simple, offering the minimum protection from sun and sand. The railroad and port facilities of Dammam will soon have a total of fifteen thousand employees. An extensive program is under way to train Saudi Arabs in railroad operation and maintenance in order that they may take over as many jobs as possible from the Americans. The extension of the line westward to the Red Sea is under study.

It is two generations since the railroads pushed across the western deserts of the United States. Americans from Aramco, watching the Saudi Arabian Government railroad creep across the sands, seemed mindful of the parallel between this and the early American transcontinental crossings. Past the crowded marshaling yards at Dhahran, over mile after mile of gravel plain, hot sand dunes, and wind-eroded mesas, American visitors rode by hand car to the cluster of battered tents that formed the advance camp of the railbuilders. One could sense an atmosphere of excitement at the railhead. This was the kind of pioneering that Americans understood. As one oil man remarked, "I was born too late to see the Union Pacific go across, but this surely gives you the feel of it."

The discovery of oil in Saudi Arabia posed the problem of lifting it cheaply to the Mediterranean. The three-thousand-mile sea haul around the peninsula is long and expensive, and the Suez Canal toll of twenty-two cents a barrel is prohibitively high if the oil is to sell competitively in the European market. An answer to the problem has been found in the trans-Arabian pipe line, running across eleven hundred miles of

119

comparatively flat and isolated country from the Persian Gulf to the Mediterranean Sea. The Trans-Arabian Pipe Line Company, known as Tapline for short, was organized in 1945.[1] At the time it was started, no steel mill in the world had the equipment to roll the necessary thirty-inch pipe, and Aramco had to help the Consolidated Steel Corporation retool for the job. (The "Big-Inch," until Tapline the world's largest-diameter line, is only twenty-six inches in diameter.) The cost of moving eleven hundred miles of large pipe across twelve-thousand miles of ocean was so great that all sorts of money-saving devices were considered. One enterprising company announced itself ready to fasten the pipe together into two-hundred-foot lengths, seal up the ends, make floats out of the sections, and tow them like log rafts to the Persian Gulf. Another suggestion involved shipping the steel plates to the Near East and rolling them into pipe out there. Because there was no mill available in or around the Near East, it was argued that the cheapest way to obtain a plant for this operation would be to buy a small aircraft carrier from the United States Naval Reserve, install the pipe-rolling machinery on its deck, and use its tremendous power plant to operate the floating factory. This would have had the extra advantage of enabling the company to make half the pipe on the Mediterranean and the other half on the Persian Gulf.

It was finally decided to send the pipe to the Near East by regular cargo steamer, with one half of it, thirty inches in diameter, nested inside the other half, thirty-one inches in diameter. Even under this arrangement the shipping contract for the pipe was the largest single peacetime overseas commercial shipment ever made, involving a freighter a week for two years.

After careful study of the possible outlets, experts chose the shore near Sidon in Lebanon as the pipe line's western terminus. A portion of the line was built from there, but a still larger portion was laid from the Persian Gulf.

Off-loading such vast quantities of thirty-foot sections of pipe on the eastern coast of Saudi Arabia presented difficulties, for the only piers on the coast, those at Ras Tanura, were busy day and night loading tankers. A promontory called Ras al Mish'ab at the northern end of the Saudi Arabian coast, just south of the Kuwait Neutral Zone, was therefore chosen for conversion. Here ocean ships could come to within two miles of the coast. At the edge of deep water the engineers of the

---

[1] Burton E. Hull, president of the Trans-Arabian Pipe Line Company, "Tapline Presents Great Organization Problem," *Oil Forum*, November 1948.

International Bechtel Corporation engaged by Tapline built a small island. Between it and the mainland they set up a device known in the logging industry as a "sky hook," really a sort of aerial cable freight car. From a series of eighty-foot supports shaped like the letter "A," a pair of heavy cables was suspended, bearing hooks that could pick up the giant sections of pipe and swing them from the ship to the shore in a couple of minutes. Once ashore the sections of pipe were placed on a roller conveyor which moved them to a welding machine, especially developed to permit two men to complete the welding of two sections in a matter of minutes. Three sections were then welded into a unit, which was moved by conveyor and mechanically loaded into huge Kenworth trucks, each handling five such ninety-foot units. The trucks, which cost $35,000 apiece, were so big that a man's head came only to the middle of the radiator. Equipped with enormous, specially designed balloon tires, they were capable of traversing stretches of sandy desert where an ordinary automobile would sink to its hubs in the first fifteen feet. Ras al Mish'ab had its own radio station, which it used to keep in touch with these monsters of the desert.

Visitors have noted that at the pipe line shop at Ras al Mish'ab Saudi Arabs did a high proportion of the work, including unloading the sky hook, moving the pipe along the roller conveyor, secondary welding, and loading the great trucks. Arabs also played a vital part in the transformation of Ras al Mish'ab promontory. In July 1947 only sandpipers and an occasional Arab fisherman or herder inhabited the barren sand spit. One year later Ras al Mish'ab was an established community, complete with modern hospital and recreation center.

The laying of the pipe line presented many unusual problems. Save for one small river, no permanent bodies of water existed within miles of its route. In the absence of landmarks and maps, sextants often had to be used to determine the positions of field parties.

The vast amount of construction equipment vital to the operation included ditch-digging machines, 150 fifty-ton truck tractors, 500 trailers, 4 sixty-passenger buses, 10 sixty-passenger trailers, 80 refrigerator trucks, and over 500 other vehicles, all especially designed for desert travel.

Until recently Aramco's frontier has moved westward. In 1949, however, this trend was partially reversed when the Saudi Arabian Government agreed to extend the Aramco concession to cover the Saudi Arabian areas of the Persian Gulf. For several decades geologists have surmised that the rich oil deposits that lie along the shores of the Gulf extended under its waters. The last few years have seen great progress

121

in the technique of underwater drilling. In the Gulf of Mexico rigs are now operating successfully in 100 and 150 feet of ocean, and it is expected that these depths will eventually be doubled. Except for a deep channel near the eastern shore, most of the Persian Gulf is less than 300 feet in depth and much of it is under 150 feet. In addition, the western part of the Gulf is sprinkled with small islands, reefs, and shoals, so that a large part of the Gulf can today be drilled for oil.

In September 1945 the United States Government proclaimed its jurisdiction and control over the natural resources of the sea bed and subsoil of its continental shelf, running out to the 100-fathom or 600-foot line. Because the Persian Gulf is so shallow, the littoral states cannot be said to have continental shelves; the whole Gulf is nothing but a continental depression. The problem of who, if anybody, had jurisdiction and control over the oil under the Persian Gulf was, therefore, a most difficult one.

In 1948 the Government of Saudi Arabia asked the United States Government for guidance in solving this problem, and some months later was referred to President Truman's proclamation on the American continental shelf and given some suggestions on how to apply the principles contained in that document to the Persian Gulf. On May 31, 1949, therefore, the Government of Saudi Arabia issued a proclamation in Arabic and English claiming jurisdiction and control over the resources of sea bed and subsoil underlying the waters of its Persian Gulf coast.

The following week the Sheikh of Kuwait and the Sheikh of Qatar met with the Sheikh of Bahrein. Under the guidance of the British Political Resident at Bahrein, who has charge of the foreign affairs of these sheikhdoms, comparable proclamations were issued, followed not long after by similar pronouncements from the sheikhs of the Trucial Coast with whom the British are also in special treaty relationship.

Although these proclamations established principles, they did not establish frontiers, the exact delimitation of underwater boundaries being purposely left for later consultation between the countries involved. But the results of these proclamations are already apparent. Ownership markers are sprouting on shoals and islands, and radio direction beacons have been set up to assist surveyors and seismograph crews in their prospecting. The first successful offshore well in the Persian Gulf was brought in by Aramco early in 1951. New problems and new opportunities are opening for the Arab sailors, fishermen, and pearl divers who have for so long carried on their operations in the tranquil waters of the Gulf. Before long the lateen sails of many of the Arab dhows that now move about the Gulf may be replaced by the stationary spires of oil derricks.

The boundary problems raised by oil structures are in no sense limited to the sea bed, and the last few years have seen disputes between Saudi Arabia and several of the sheikhdoms of the Persian Gulf. To the inhabitants of the little countries of Abu Dhabi and Buraimi it has heretofore made no sense to fix boundaries beyond saying, "In wet years we graze to Wadi A, but when it is dry we may have to go as far north as Wadi B." Unfortunately one cannot locate the ownership of oil wells by such casual reckoning. Until the boundaries of Saudi Arabia are specifically located on the map rather than based on grazing range of tribes that pay taxes to King Saud, there will be frequent disputes, growing pains which this pastoral area must suffer for coming too rapidly into the oil age.

If it were not for oil, no one but a bedouin would want to live on the Qatar Peninsula, for the approximately four thousand square miles of this flat thumb of land are unusually barren even for Arabia. The average rainfall is a little over four inches a year. In the summer the weather combines the humidity of the Gulf with the burning heat of the desert. The few Qataris make a poor living by pearling and fishing in the shallow, reef-filled waters along their coasts and by grazing their animals on the sparse fodder available in this rocky and inhospitable region. Ruins of several settlements scattered about the peninsula show that it once had a larger population than the present twenty thousand Arabs. Doha, however, the east-coast port and capital of Qatar, has been for some time a simple, leisurely Arab town, only partially protected from sandstorms and bedouin raids by a crumbling wall and several old forts.

Here the Sheikh of Qatar lives. His forebears were signers of the truce that ended piracy in the Gulf, and like his neighbors, the sheikhs of the Trucial Coast and of Bahrein, he has chosen to place his foreign affairs in the hands of the British. The Sheikh, whose avocation is hunting, hopes for the day when his oil royalties will increase and registers an understandable interest in his little land's boundary disputes with Bahrein and Saudi Arabia.

On the west coast of the peninsula of Qatar, opposite Doha, is the Dukhan oil field and camp of Petroleum Development Qatar, a subsidiary of the Iraq Petroleum Corporation. Like the latter, the firm is owned 23.75 per cent by the Near East Development Company, an American concern which is jointly owned by the Standard Oil Company of New Jersey and Socony–Vacuum Oil Company. The Sheikh of Qatar granted the concession May 17, 1935, after oil had been found on Bahrein. It was discovered in the Dukhan field four years later, and three wells were drilled but plugged as a defensive measure during World War II. Operations began again in 1947, and unofficial estimates now place the reserves of the Dukhan field at over a billion barrels. Both British and Americans are working in the development of this field, along with Qataris and bedouin. A tank farm and a small refinery have been built near the camp. Shipments of oil started in 1949.

The prospect of oil has already upset the peace of Qatar. In July 1949 Abdullah ibn Qasim al Thani, who had been the ruling chief since he succeeded his 104-year-old father in 1913, received a down payment for the concession rights to some of the submerged areas lying off Qatar. When he refused to share this money with his relatives, a serious split developed within the ranks of the royal family. During August of that year the dispute became first a demonstration against the Sheikh and his backers and finally a small shooting war. The British Political Agent in charge of Qatari affairs thereupon intervened, and on August 20 Sheikh Abdullah abdicated in favor of his son, Ali, thus bringing to an end the first revolution in the Arabian Peninsula to be caused by oil.

X

British Explorers of
the Empty Quarter

NO STORY of the Arabian Penin-
sula is complete without reference to the brilliant and dangerous journeys of three British explorers. The dash across the Rub al Khali, or
Empty Quarter, made in 1931 by Bertram Thomas, along with Philby's
marches in the northwestern part of that desert the next year and
Thesiger's crossings in 1946–1948 marked the end of the great feats of
exploration in Arabia. T. E. Lawrence wrote, in his foreword to Thomas'
fine book, *Arabia Felix*:

> Few men are able to close an epoch. We cannot know the first man who
> walked the inviolate earth for newness' sake; but Thomas is the last; and he
> did his journey in the antique way, by pain of his camel's legs, single-handed,
> at his own time and expense. He might have flown an airplane, sat in a car
> or rolled over in a tank. Instead he snatched, at the twenty-third hour, feet's
> last victory and set us free. . . . All honour to Thomas.[1]

Bertram Thomas was a British official in the Persian Gulf service, who
served as Minister of the Council of the state of Muscat. While there
during the late 1920's he fell under the spell of the unknown desert
which covers southern Arabia for a distance of four hundred miles
north and south and eight hundred miles east and west. Instead of taking his leaves in the cool Indian hills, he began spending his summers
at Muscat and traveling in southern Arabia during the winter, the only

[1] *Arabia Felix*, p. xix.

time when it was possible to move in the terrific heat of the desert. In the winter of 1927–1928 he made a six-hundred-mile camel journey along the southern coast of Oman to Dhufar. Two winters later he explored the country north of Dhufar to the edge of the Rub al Khali, which had never been crossed by a European up to that time.

Thus he was admirably equipped through experience when, in October 1930, he arrived at Dhufar. Long weeks passed as the Englishman secretly worked to persuade friendly bedouin to organize a caravan of fast camels. Just as it seemed that Thomas would have to return by boat to Muscat, a party of ragged bedouin and their riding camels came down from the north, prepared to take him across the desert. The rations consisted of flour, dates, rice, and butter, with the very barest of other supplies. To save weight, not even a tent was taken along.[2]

From Dhufar the route led north across the coastal plain and through the grassy foothills of the Qara Mountains, passing strange caves and water holes on the way. In the wadies beyond he noted men and women collecting the sap of the frankincense tree for export to the temples of the East, just as they had done for three thousand years. In this area also he found a series of pre-Arabic inscriptions on long lines of stones that he believed to be graves, or possibly connected with the star worship of the ancient Sabaeans.

Progress was slow, for whenever there was good pasture the caravan stopped to gain strength for the barren miles ahead. The bedouin usually shared food and water among themselves, but each tried to get the best fodder for his camel. Gradually the wadies became drier, and the hills gave way to rolling plain. For the next hundred miles the route lay across a political no man's land, and the party was in constant danger of attack by raiders. The five daily prayers were now reduced to three, although, as they rode along, the bedouin would sometimes burst out into prayer.

Thomas writes that, as they came to the edge of the sand just beyond the Wadi Mitam, the Arabs suddenly pointed to the ground, which was marked by a series of well-worn camel tracks about a hundred yards across. These caravan tracks were undoubtedly very old but had been preserved by the waterless nature of the area. According to his guides, this was the road to Ubar, a once-great city on the north-south caravan route across eastern Arabia, which was now buried beneath the sand. One of his men said that he had been in this part of Arabia as a boy and had seen strange stones notched at the edge, along with

[2] Most of the material on Bertram Thomas' trip is based on his book, *Arabia Felix*.

126

potsherds of red and yellow, and various other objects that suggested previous habitation.

Thomas was in no position to investigate. He felt, however, that it was quite possible that the footprints were part of a caravan route running from the frankincense country to the Persian Gulf and might well have led to a city or cities on that trail. If the Yemeni city of Marib is the greatest archaeological prize in Arabia, the solution of the riddle of the lost city of Ubar is its most intriguing mystery.

Beyond these footprints the country continued to become dryer, with flat stretches of gypsum. The gravel plain then gave way to mountainous sand dunes, and for the first time Thomas heard a "low droning on a musical note" like the "siren of a moderate-sized steamship." It was the sound of the singing sands, a phenomenon noted by other explorers in high dunes, but Thomas had no time to study it further.

That night he had a Christmas dinner of thin soup and one of the few tins of baked beans he had brought with him for special occasions. By now the camels from Dhufar were tired, and their humps were small, so the meeting with the next relay was most welcome, and the bedouin rubbed noses cordially with their friends. The Englishman was introduced to Sheikh Hamad ibn Hadi of the great Murra tribe, who was to be his next guide. Thomas ordered three bowls of dates to be served with the coffee, paid off his first relay party, and sent them back while he proceeded with only twenty men across the Dakaka sands.

A week later the party reached the well of Shanna, which Thomas estimated to be 330 miles in a direct line from his goal of Doha on the Qatar Peninsula. There the party was reduced to thirteen picked men, thirteen fast camels, and five pack camels that carried rations for thirty days. Only one of the men, a Murra tribesman from Qatar, had crossed the sands that year.

On the third day they passed the last human habitation, two small tents that belonged to a Murra. The owner of one was sick, and even in that remote spot the women remained veiled. The Murra are the most primitive of all the tribes of Arabia. They are not Moslems, but pagans—long-haired, lean men with cunning faces and wild eyes who live like animals on the border line of starvation. Their food consists of dates, which are carefully rationed, camel's milk, and occasionally meat (gazelle) or sometimes the jabru rat and tough desert lizards. Their greatest delicacy is camel's liver, rubbed in salt and eaten full of blood. They have no villages but roam continuously, seeking fodder

127

for their camels. They conduct raids suddenly out of their desert fastness, killing, plundering, and attacking caravans, and then withdraw quickly into their waterless wastes where no one would dare to follow. They have been known to raid as far south as the Hadhramaut, a distance of four hundred miles.

They roam with great confidence over territory where bedouin of the north would hesitate to go. Their tracking instinct is remarkable, an ability which has been built up through the centuries. "They can tell the spoor of a white camel from a black one, the footprint of a virgin from that of a wife, and a warrior from that of a youth." [3]

The Arabs have a saying that a Murra Arab taken on a three days' journey blindfolded, and at the end of that time compelled to bury a *rupee* in the sand by night in the midst of a trackless desert, can return ten years later and get his *rupee* with no difficulty.

From here on, the water at the wells was so bad that Thomas gave up drinking it and relied instead on camel's milk. By now the danger from raiders had passed somewhat, but the heat was increasing, and Thomas' strength began to sag. For relaxation he enjoyed the evenings around the campfires, when the bedouin told long tales of raids and sudden death in the desert. One of his men said he had grazed sheep in this desolate area only four years before, showing how the rainfall varied and why the bedouin were so secretive about their grazing grounds. In spite of the dryness the party ran across a sand-colored fox and the gigantic nest of an eagle whose eggs the bedouin would not touch. They also found sand rats, wildcats, and wolves, with many varieties of lizards among the dry *hadh,* or desert sagebrush.

After nine more days of hard travel the small caravan reached a region of white sand known as Samam, where the water was sweet and the wells extremely deep, going down as far as ninety feet. The fast of Ramadan began on the next night, to be greeted with rifle shots and cries of "Glory to God." Although Thomas' companions had a right to put off fasting in the daytime because they were on the march, no Moslem did so, a tribute to the strength of their religious convictions.

The next important water hole, Farhaja, was surrounded by camel tracks, and they circled to avoid conflict with possible enemies. The night temperature fell to 40 degrees, and the Arabs shivered as they rode but would not cry out in order not to affront Allah, the all-knowing, who had sent the cold. When a sandstorm swept down suddenly, the temperature fell to 30 degrees. The sand got into Thomas' movie camera,

[3] Gerald De Gaury, *Arabia Phoenix,* p. 70.

15. Twilight view of Arabian American Oil Company's stabilizer installation at Dhahran. American-type snow fences control drifting sands.

16. A Saudi Arab plant operator instructing Arabian American Oil Company trainees in the operation of a gas-oil separator plant.

17. Awali, the Bahrein Petroleum Company's residential section on Bahrein Island. (Photo of California Texas Oil Co., Ltd.)

and it was too cold and sandy to make notes. Happily, the next day brought them out of the Samam to the water hole of Banajan, a stone-lined well, where they rested after eighteen days of forced marches through the worst of the desert.

Thomas' guides told him that the desert tribes with the largest number of camels, either milk or riding, were the Murra, the Manasir, and the Manshil. Until about 1910 there were constant feuds between these groups, but warfare was now restricted, due to the long shadow of King Ibn Saud and his much-feared governor of Hofuf, Abdullah ibn Jaluwi. All three tribes pay the King of Saudi Arabia nominal tribute in the form of a camel a year. The influence of Riyadh, however, does not extend to the southern part of the desert, and the tribes there, such as the Sa'ar who can muster almost two thousand rifles, are a law unto themselves.

Beyond Banajan the route lay through Wahhabi territory, and the horizon was constantly scanned for signs of these fierce puritans who would not take kindly to the idea of an unbeliever moving across their land. Luckily they had gone north for the fast of Ramadan, and the party moved ahead unmolested, guided by the Murra tribesman from Qatar. He was their worst guide, and on occasion was so afraid of giving away the secret of his tribe's water holes that he failed to lead them to water or firewood. He did, however, take them to some salt flats and a lake seven miles long with a broad border of white salt, its edges lined with dead locusts. This marked the base of the Qatar Peninsula, an area so low-lying that, until recently, Qatar was an island. Spirits rose as camels and herdsmen were sighted. The next morning the party's thirsty camels seemed to recognize the water song sung by their riders as, coming over a rise of ground, they saw ahead of them the bare walls of the fort at Doha. Thomas had won his battle over the sands, and for the first time in history the Rub al Khali desert had been crossed by a European.

It is surprising how often great achievements go in pairs. Many a scientist works half his life on a project, and another man beats him to the discovery by a few months. Scott reached the South Pole, to find that Shackleton had been there only a few weeks before; and Bertram Thomas, when he crossed the Rub al Khali, completed a project on which his fellow countryman, St. John Philby, had worked for years. As Philby wrote in the introduction to *The Empty Quarter*:

For fifteen years my life has been dominated by a single obsession. Faithfully, fanatically, and relentlessly . . . I have stalked the quarry which now,

129

in these pages, lies before the reader—dissected, belabelled and described.
I have not, perhaps, accomplished all that I planned to do, but I have done
enough to set my soul at rest, released from its long bondage. Nor, again, have
I been alone, or even first, in the field. The honours of priority have gone to
another that outwent me in the race; and Bertram Thomas deservedly wears
the laurels of a pioneer.

On January 11, 1932, approximately eleven months after Bertram
Thomas crossed the Rub al Khali from south to north, Philby set out
to cross it from north to south.[4] His party started from Qatar and headed
southwest toward the Jabrin oasis. The group consisted of nineteen
men; four from the Murra tribe of the great southern desert, two from
the Manasir, two from the Buhaih, a section of the Murra, and three
from the Ajman tribe. In addition, he had with him a chief of transport,
a camel boy, a coffee maker, and a cook. His thirty-two camels, all but
one females of the Umaniya breed, were specially bred for the sands.
Traveling with heavier loads than did Thomas, they took supplies for
three months, chiefly dates and rice.

Occasional groups of bedouin were passed, prompting Philby to
write of the beauty of their formal greetings to one another. Halfway
to Jabrin the party crossed the channel of the Wadi Sahba, one of the
great ancient rivers of Arabia, now long-since dry. This wadi can be
traced for over five hundred miles, from its start in the highlands of
the Nejd until it empties into the Persian Gulf, east of the Qatar Peninsula.

The party stayed three days in the deserted oasis of Jabrin, the last
abandoned outpost of civilization north of the Empty Quarter. Jabrin
was once famous in Arab song and story as a flourishing town, and there
is reason to believe that a thousand years ago an arm of the Persian
Gulf may have extended as far inland as this area. The oasis still contains many palm trees, the ruins of several dozen houses, and some
small forts, along with *kanats*, or subterranean aqueducts of the type
introduced into Arabia long ago by the Persians. Some years before
a group of Ikhwan warrior farmers, at Ibn Saud's direction, had tried
to repopulate it. As had been the case with previous settlers, many
of them died of fever, and the rest gave up the attempt. In 1949 Aramco
sent experts to Jabrin to spread DDT and make the oasis habitable again.

---

[4] Much of the following description of Philby's great exploration of the northwestern section of the Rub al Khali is taken from his excellent book, *The Empty
Quarter.*

On the outskirts of Jabrin the explorers dined with the last human being the party was to see for fifty-three days, a bedouin of the Murra tribe and his wife and two young children. Not far from the oasis the fragments of an ostrich egg were found in the desert, although ostriches are said to have been extinct in that part of Arabia for many years.

Philby's first objective was Maqainama, which was rumored to be a ruined settlement of some size, but which turned out to be nothing more than a desert well. There Philby found an ancient bronze arrowhead. The well itself was 170 feet deep, however, which suggested that it was dug by engineers more advanced than the bedouin who now use it. Such wells were covered with sticks and skins to keep them from filling with drifting sand, and the replacing of this covering was a desert ritual carefully observed by all men of good will.

Turning east the party passed one of the few cemeteries encountered on the whole trip, for the drifting sand covers graves. Near it Philby picked up what his men assured him was a "walking stone." The bedouin said that these stones move rapidly at times because of "something inside them." It is more likely that they move as the sand under them blows away and starts them rolling before the wind, but the question of why some stones move and others do not would seem to justify further study.

An example of how much like a back yard the vast desert is to the bedouin was shown at a well called Numaila, which the party reached soon thereafter. One of the Murra guides had been to this well as a child and remembered hiding his toys there. Going straight to the place, he dug up twenty or more of the small, flat, clay disks with holes through the center which the bedouin children use to play a game called *darraj*, or wheels.

The bedouin told Philby that this part of the desert had been getting drier for the past eight years. A dozen years before, they said, the rolling plain was the home of many *oryxes*, the king of desert game. It is a large, graceful deer with long, pointed horns sweeping back two-thirds of the way to its tail. The party came across the remains of a bull oryx that had died of starvation long before but, because of the desolation of the area, had not been eaten by ravens or jackals.

Like Bertram Thomas and everyone else who has become interested in the Rub al Khali, Philby had been intrigued by the stories of a forgotten city, lost somewhere in its sands. He found that hardly any of his bedouin companions knew of the legend, and only two of them con-

131

nected it with a specific place in the desert. One of these, Ali ibn Jahman, a Murra tribesman and his chief guide, knew a song that ran in part as follows:

> From Qariya strikes the sun upon the town:
> Blame not the guide that vainly seeks it now,
> Since the Destroying Power laid it low,
> Sparing nor cotton smock nor silken gown.[5]

This legendary city, variously called Ubar, Obar, or Wabar, was one of the goals of Philby's trip, and he was delighted to find that Ali could take him to the ruins of this city which had been destroyed by Allah. At last they came to a rise where Ali said they were approaching the ruin, and Philby wrote:

> I reached the summit and in that moment fathomed the legend of Wabar. I looked down not upon the ruins of an ancient city but into the mouth of a volcano, whose twin craters, half filled with drifted sand, lay side by side surrounded by slag and lava outpoured from the bowels of the earth. That at any rate was the impression that flashed through my mind in that moment. . . . So that was Wabar! A volcano in the desert! . . . One could scarcely have imagined a more sensational solution of the riddle of the Great Sands.[6]

It appears that some of the bedouin base the legend of a lost city in the Rub al Khali on these two sand-filled craters surrounded by high walls of slag, which, from a distance, look like man-made castles and which they call Wabar. But the many legends in Arab literature about this lost city must be based on more than craters. The tracks leading to what Bertram Thomas' guides told him was the ruined city of Ubar were some two hundred miles to the southeast of these craters, while in the summer of 1944 an Aramco exploration party in the western part of the desert located the ruins of still another deserted city. It seems likely, therefore, that there is more than one "Wabar," and that the mystery of the lost city of the Rub al Khali is still not completely solved.

From Wabar, Philby made a short side trip east to a point where he crossed the trail of "the Christian" (Bertram Thomas), south of the well of Farhaja. A year had passed, but his Murra trackers said there could be no mistaking the marks left by Thomas' party in the sands.

A few marches farther south, at a well called Naifa in the hollow of huge sand dunes, "the great amphitheater began to boom and drone with a sound not unlike that of a siren or perhaps an airplane engine—quite a musical, pleasing, rhythmic sound of astonishing depth."[7]

[5] *Ibid.*, p. 157.   [6] *Ibid.*, p. 165.   [7] *Ibid.*, p. 204.

It was the sound of the singing sands that Bertram Thomas had come upon the year before. Philby made experiments and found that by going to the top of a sand dune and pushing the thick soft sand from the summit down the steep side of the dune, he could produce a loud rumbling or grating which lasted from two to three minutes, while the sand traveled fifty or sixty feet. The next morning Philby tried again but was unable to get music from the sand; so it would seem that there is some connection between the temperature and humidity of the sand, the direction in which the wind is blowing and the curious sound. The shape of the dune may also play a part, the booming sound being a transmuted echoing of the grating noise made by the moving sand. In any case, the singing sands are one of the most eerie phenomena to be met with in Arabia and are well worth more investigation.

The farthest south reached by Philby was the well at Shanna. It had been dug in the winter of 1929–1930 by Philby's chief guide, Ali ibn Jahman, to provide water for a large body of his followers who had gathered in that area with their tents and cattle. The Murra usually winter far north, but because of the war going on at that time between Ibn Saud and the Ikhwan, part of the tribe decided to keep away from the fighting by remaining in the desert. Sheikh Ali chose what looked to him to be a likely hollow in the desert sand, and after digging down fifty-five feet struck the best water in all the neighborhood. So strained are the relations between bedouin groups in this part of the desert that it is considered bad manners to remain at such a well for more than twenty-four hours. Philby, however, stayed there for two days, resting and preparing for a dash west across the waterless central part of the Rub al Khali to the Tuwaiq hills south of Riyadh. Thomas had camped at Shanna the year before, where he had killed and eaten one of his camels and prepared himself for his final plunge north, 333 miles to Qatar. Thus, Shanna was a jumping-off place for both explorers, the last campsite on the edge of the waterless and unexplored southwestern Rub al Khali.

Actually Philby had hoped to go farther south, but his men rebelled at the thought of longer wandering. They reported that another party, possibly a group of raiders, had been sighted and that it was dangerous to remain in the area. Philby wanted to look over the Ramlat al Shuait, which Bertram Thomas believed was the site of the lost city of Wabar, and was convinced that the alarm was an incident manufactured by his guides; but he was unable to control his bedouin and so had to give up the thought of continuing to the south.

Philby's last objective was a march of exploration west, across the waterless northwest section of the Rub al Khali, where the bedouin rarely go and where there are no known wells and no grazing. Hunting parties from wells such as Shanna had penetrated a short distance into this area looking for oryxes or rim gazelles, and occasional hunters had gone into it from the Wadi Dawasir, the southern tip of the Tuwaiq hills, but it had never been crossed before. In preparation for this march, the thirty-two waterskins were patched, greased, and filled from the well, loads were redivided, and food was selected that would require no water for cooking. Then the camels were brought in for a final watering, but unfortunately they had drunk only two days before and so would not take their fill, a situation that was to have serious results a few days later.

The route west lay over long, parallel sand ridges. At one point they crossed an old river bed dotted with thousands of fresh-water shells, which Philby believed to be the lower reaches of an ancient stream that started in the mountains of Asir and Yemen. Desert larks sang, and butterflies flitted about as they entered an area of great reddish sand dunes, some of which rose five hundred feet into the air. On several occasions they came upon the tracks of oryxes, but saw none. Then the wind fell, and the heat increased until it was like marching into a furnace. The rolling dunes became absolutely bare, and the sand produced countless mirages. After good rains some of the hardy bedouin hunters had come into this region, living on camel's milk and the meat that they killed. But there had been no rain for seven or eight years, and everything was bare. The dry hadh shrubs were half buried in sand, and the hardy *abel*, the longest-lived of the desert plants, lay dead, its blackened roots spread above the hot sand.

After they had gone 140 miles, the men again rebelled. Two-thirds of the journey to the wells at Sulaiyil remained to be done, and the baggage camels were wilting fast, some of them already lying on the ground in a state of collapse. Much water would have to be used to revive them, water that must be saved if the party was to reach its objective. So again, against his will, Philby agreed to turn back and head for the nearest known water, the well at Naifa, where the party had stopped on its way south. The camels that were the worst off were given water from leather tubs. The others were given a "snuffing" by pouring a kettleful of water up their nostrils to cool head and brain on the way to the stomach. It is painful at the time, but it revives a dry and tired camel.

The march back was slow and difficult; the supply of camel milk was

134

almost gone, and even the tea ran out. At last, by a forced march of forty-five miles, they reached Naifa, where Philby drank three bowls of water, the best he had ever tasted in his life. Only when he had finished did he remember that the water from the well of Naifa was foul and briny. During most of the trip he had drunk only tea and camel's milk, a routine that kept him in excellent health.

The party recuperated for several days at Naifa and then split. The baggage camels went north to Riyadh, along the line of wells leading to Jabrin, while Philby and eight of the braver Arabs on the strongest and fastest of the camels prepared to try again to cross the western Rub al Khali to the wells at Sulaiyil. Shortly before they started, a violent rain squall burst upon the camp, lasting four hours and flattening all the tents. Such a rainstorm in the desert is a fantastic sight. Of it Philby wrote:

Great black clouds of sand raced before the gale along the summits around us like squadrons of Valkyries, while from the higher dune-tops streamed as it were dark pennants in the wind and the desert floor was swept as by driving snow, sheet after sheet of white sand, like successive waves of a cavalry charge. It was a spectacle never to be forgotten, that desert in stormy mood with the roll of distant thunder and the blinding flashes that rent the lowering clouds.[8]

When order was restored in the camp, the supplies were divided, the waterskins refilled, and the final marches westward begun. This time the going was much faster, for they were traveling light, even without a tent. Several of the bedouin swore not to drink milk on the trip, as did Philby. One hundred and seventy miles were covered during the first five days, but two hundred miles lay ahead, and a night march was necessary, about which Philby wrote, "I was struck by the curious incandescent effect produced by the conditions of night-marching in this sand country. The dark silhouettes of our camels seemed to be surrounded by vague halos of light, and one could see bushes in the outlines of the dunes with astonishing clearness." This light has been mentioned by other travelers in Arabia and may be due to the exceptional clarity of the air when it is not filled with blowing sand.

The country crossed on the night march was an absolutely flat plain, and Philby speculated sadly that someday the area would undoubtedly be visited by motor parties in search of gazelles and oryxes. His foreboding was, in truth, foresight; motorcars and trucks from Dhahran have

[8] *Ibid.*, p. 297.

driven across these plains from Jabrin at a pace that sometimes touched fifty miles an hour.

This was the most dangerous point of the whole trip, with no water nearer than 190 miles in any direction. An accident, such as a broken leg or an attack of sickness, would have been fatal. In the middle of the desert the party came across the tracks of a female camel and her calf, and the bedouin surmised that they were booty captured by some raiding party, which had strayed away from the rest of the caravan. So "small" is the world of the desert that Philby later learned that this was correct and that the cow and calf had actually returned across this waste to their lawful owner.

The heat increased daily, and the Murra said that it might have been twenty years since there had been rain in those parts. The party found the fragments of an ostrich egg which the bedouin estimated had hatched out at that same spot some fifty years before. Only the oldest of their tribe had seen ostriches alive.

The worst stretch of all was the flat gravel plain of Abu Bahr. Starting very early, the party marched all day, while the sun blazed down ever hotter, and the Arabs dozed in their saddles. Philby finally stopped at two and drank a bowl of tepid brown water, but the caravan pushed on across the never-ending gravel plain. There was a short halt for prayer at sunset, and then they marched forward again, dazed by the heat and the marching. The Arabs talked dully of finding firewood for coffee, but Philby thought only of sleep. At last, shortly after nine o'clock, the Arabs gave up the idea of crossing the Abu Bahr in a single march. The camels kneeled down, having covered more than seventy miles during twenty-one hours of marching. After a bowl of water and a lump of dates, Philby ate one of his two tins of peaches and then lay down to sleep, knowing that the worst of the crossing was behind them.

Leaving the Abu Bahr plain early the next day, they came to the southern extremity of the belt of dunes called the Dahna, well known to all travelers going between Dhahran and Riyadh, and the rolling sands were a pleasant change after the terrible flatness of the plain. Here the camels were snuffed again, and the party continued up the dry bed of the Wadi Dawasir. At last in the distance they saw the low blue outline of the Tuwaiq Mountains. "Verily, Tuwaiq is our father," said one of the bedouin, "and tomorrow, maybe, if God wills, we may look again on the faces of men." [9]

The second morning brought them to a little round watchtower, the

[9] *Ibid.*, pp. 348–349.

first building they had seen since leaving Jabrin. Not far beyond there was a movement in the bushes, and the bedouin grabbed their guns, but it turned out to be seven women from Sulaiyil who were herding sheep. The villagers could not believe that Philby had come across the desert, for no one had ever done so before. Beyond were the wells of Latwa, where the camels were watered after 575 dry desert miles. The water was good, but the camels drank sparingly for they were too thirsty. The dry heart of the Rub al Khali had been laid bare by one of the most rugged trips in Arabian history.

Last but not least of the modern explorers of the Rub al Khali is Wilfred Thesiger, an Englishman who began his career of exploration in the Danakil desert and the Tibesti Mountains of Africa and who made a name for himself by his exploits in and around Abyssinia in World War II. After the war he served with the Middle East antilocust unit in Arabia, traveling in many out-of-the-way areas.

Fascinated by the great southern desert, Thesiger left the locust mission and began a series of travels around and across the Rub al Khali. In the winter of 1945–1946 he traveled along much of the southern border of this unexplored area. The next winter saw his caravan go northward from Dhufar to Liwa, a group of fifty-two settlements near the Trucial Coast southwest of Abu Dhabi. From there he went east to the foothills of the mountains of Oman and south again to the Arabian Sea, the whole central part of the trip being through unexplored country.

Perhaps his most striking expedition was the trip he made the next year, across the western Rub al Khali from the valley of the Hadhramaut to the oasis of Sulaiyil, at the southern end of the Tuwaiq Mountains in central Saudi Arabia.[10]

Bertram Thomas and Philby were in no sense loaded down with equipment, but Thesiger traveled the lightest of all. He had made his crossing of the eastern Rub al Khali with four bedouin and only one spare camel. This time, however, aware of the four hundred waterless miles to the outpost well at Hassi, he carried more food and fourteen waterskins.

Thesiger's little party left Manwakh, the last well on the route, on January 6, 1948, and pushed northward across flat gravel steppes, which soon gave way to sand. The wind was bitter cold, but the travelers welcomed it for it obliterated their tracks and made them safe from pursuit. The region was known for its many raiding parties, and his guides told long tales of alarms and attacks. The riders pushed their

[10] This account is taken from Thesiger's article, "A Farther Journey Across the Empty Quarter," *Geographical Journal*, June 1949.

newly purchased camels hard. Rising at dawn, they had a handful of dates and a cup of black, cardamom-flavored coffee. As soon as the sun rose above the sands, the day's march would begin, with the camels tied head to tail in two groups, one of three and the other of four. The men walked, at first, to keep warm. Then as the sun climbed higher, they would untie their mounts and climb into the saddle, to ride without stopping until evening. The long hot hours were marked by occasional talk or songs from the Arabs. The waterskins, which had been bought at Mukalla on the Hadhramaut seacoast, leaked badly, and the men were rationed to a pint of water a day. The party almost always marched until after dark, when they groped for firewood and baked cakes of wheat flour an inch thick, which they dipped into a little ghee before eating. It is doubtful if any other modern European traveler in Arabia has lived as long as Thesiger on such Spartan fare.

Day followed day of featureless plains or long, parallel sand dunes. They saw a good many oryxes, some rim gazelles, and the fresh tracks of a pelican, a strange bird to find in such a place. About two-thirds of the way to Sulaiyil they came to the mountainous sand dunes of Ranlat Bani Maaradh, some of them over four hundred feet in height. Here they saw the tracks of wolves. Much more alarming, however, were fresh camel tracks. Two of the party went ahead as scouts. Special watches were kept at sunset and dawn, and the men slept fitfully, with their rifles always ready at hand.

On January 18 they came out of the great sands and camped in a dried watercourse some thirty miles from the ruins of the city of Qariya. This was also the supposed location of the Bahr al Safi, a legendary quicksand which the bedouin with Thesiger had heard of but could not locate, so that the explorer thought it unlikely such quicksands exist in the western Rub al Khali. During the following two days, they went along the line of the Aradh, which is an extension of the Tuwaiq Mountains south of Sulaiyil. On the east these hills rise gently from the sands, but they terminate on the west in an escarpment, or cliff, some nine hundred feet high, at the point west of Sulaiyil where the Wadi Dawasir breaks through the range.

At last, on January 21, Thesiger and his Arabs came suddenly on a party of eight traveling from Sulaiyil to the southwestern city of Najran. The meeting was tense but without incident, and soon the thirsty camels were crouching beside the shallow well among the stony hills of Hassi, where one small house marks the southern limit of central Arabian civili-

138

zation. The western Rub al Khali had been crossed; the last big blank in the map of Arabia was filled in.

Stirred by the news of Thesiger's dramatic arrival at Sulaiyil, Philby motored down from Riyadh to the well at Hassi and then proceeded southwest to Qariya, which Thesiger had reported but not seen.[11] The actual discoverers of the site had been an Aramco survey party, which had spent some time in the area and had found inscriptions beautifully carved in Sabaean script. Other inscriptions found by Philby, numerous scattered mounds, ruins of mud forts, and walls with fragments of pottery led him to estimate the date of this settlement around the second century B.C. The ruins were widespread, some of them fortified buildings and others tombs. The rough but passable motor track from Riyadh to Najran now passes through Qariya, and there is good reason to hope that a thorough scientific exploration of the site will not be long delayed.

In the winter of 1948–1949 Thesiger made still another journey in southern Arabia, but the days of camel-and-dried-dates exploration in the Empty Quarter are virtually over. Aramco's planes have made several flights over the heart of the desert on their way to and from Aden. The Rub al Khali is now being explored by parties of geologists, who travel by car and desert-worthy trucks and think nothing of covering a hundred miles in a day. They sleep in air-cooled trailers at their base camps and receive water and fresh food by airplane. Plans are being made to locate a series of air strips through the heart of the desert for use in emergencies. Thus, even the Empty Quarter, the least-known and most inaccessible part of the Arabian Peninsula, is being opened up. Its rolling stones, singing sands, deserted oases, and lost cities will not remain mysterious much longer.

[11] St. John Philby, "Two Notes from Central Arabia—The Qariya Ruin Field," *Geographical Journal,* June 1949.

XI

Bahrein: Islands of
Pearls and Petroleum

WHEN a shamal blows from the north and the air is brown with flying sand, oil men in Dhahran can scarcely see across the street. But on clear days they may look eastward from the jebel across the sands to the little white port of Al Khobar and beyond to the reef-studded waters of the Persian Gulf, faintly blurred at the horizon twenty miles away. The blur is the island of Bahrein which, along with Muharraq, Sitrah, and several less populated islands, comprises the sheikhdom of that name. Largest of the islands, Bahrein is about thirty miles long and ten miles wide, rising only a few hundred feet above the sea at its highest point. Its chief city is Manama, seat of the government, Arab port, and principal trading center of the islands. Bahrein causeway joins Manama to crescent-shaped Muharraq, traditional pearling port and site of the RAF field used by British and American forces during the war.

Bahrein's humidity provides contrast with the climate of the Hasa, but it makes the islands' slightly lower temperatures seem illusory. Little water flows except on the northern end of the main island, where fresh springs from the same source as those of the Hasa nourish extensive date gardens. Submarine springs north of the islands have long provided fresh water to passing dhows. Bahreinis secure it by diving overboard from their canoes and capturing the bubbling fresh water in goatskin containers.

Nearly seventy thousand Arabs live in the Bahrein Islands. More

140

than half of them are Sunni Moslems residing largely in the towns of Manama and Muharraq, while about a quarter are Shia' Moslems living in approximately a hundred villages scattered throughout the archipelago. Small numbers of Pakistanis, Indians, Persians, Jews, and East Africans make up the rest of the population. Tradition says the original inhabitants came from Yemen via the Arabian mainland.

In any event, it seems certain that the Bahrein Islands have been important in the politics, commerce, and trade of the Gulf from earliest times. An Assyrian inscription of 2872 B.C. refers to an island believed to be Bahrein. The Roman writer Strabo, who was born 63 B.C. wrote: "On sailing further . . . there are other Islands, Tyrus and Aradus, which have temples resembling those of the Phoenicians. The inhabitants of these islands (if we are to believe them) say that the Islands and cities bearing the same name as those of the Phoenicians are their own colonies." The Roman geographer, Pliny, knew Bahrein as Tylos, famous for the "vast number of its pearls."

The most interesting historical relics to be found on the islands are some fifty thousand burial mounds or tumuli, the largest of which are described by P. B. Cornwall as fifty yards across and over eighty feet in height. The few which have been opened are much alike. Their entrances face west, and they contain, as a rule, two chambers, one above the other, both formed of large blocks of hewn stone covered with rough plaster. Wood, of which there is little on Bahrein today, has been used in their construction. The mounds contain the bones of men and animals, together with such artifacts as golden amulets, bronze hair ornaments, ivory boxes, painted ostrich shells, and broken earthenware vessels. Much of the pottery is made of red clay, though none exists on Bahrein now. Some experts feel that Bahrein was a burial island to which bodies were brought from the mainland. Others believe that the tumuli marked the graves of important leaders of a Phoenician colony on the islands. Still another hypothesis has it that the Phoenicians came from Bahrein originally. In any case, the period of these tombs is generally placed at 1500–3000 B.C. They are thus linked with the late Bronze Age and may also be linked with somewhat similar mounds on the Saudi Arabian mainland. The gravel plain outside Manama, dotted with thousands of these tumuli, is a strange and solemn place. Further scientific exploration and study of them presents a challenge to Near Eastern archaeologists, and the solution of their origin should shed light on this little-known problem of history.

From the days of the Romans until the sixteenth century, Bahrein

141

was a battleground between the Arabs and the Persians. Soon after 1507 a fleet of foreign craft appeared off the coast of the archipelago. From them, white-skinned men armed with new weapons poured ashore to take over the islands. For the next century Bahrein was an outpost of the Portuguese Empire, one of a series of garrisons established to shut off Persian Gulf trade between India and Turkey.

But the Portuguese could not hold out against the Persians, and in 1622 they had to surrender Bahrein to a Persian general. For the next 150 years the Persian flag flew over Bahrein, giving rise to the present Iranian claim to that island. Then, in 1783, Arabs from the town of Zubarah on the west side of the Qatar Peninsula, just south of the islands, arose and slaughtered the Persians on Bahrein. The town of Zubarah has sunk back into the mud from which it was built, but the Qatari Arabs have ruled Bahrein virtually ever since their victory.

Lacking more reliable sources of revenue, Bahreini rulers, like those of certain neighboring sheikhdoms, became experts in piracy, gun-running, and the slave trade. On January 8, 1820, however, the joint rulers of Bahrein, Sheikhs Suleiman and Abdullah ibn Ahmed, watched heavily armed British ships sink their largest man-of-war, an action which led to the signing of a general treaty between Great Britain and Bahrein, "for the cessation of plunder and piracy by land and sea." The arrival of the British marked the end of the freebooting piracy which had plagued the Gulf states' relations with each other and the West, but it did not mark the end of local rivalries, and several times during the next hundred years the British had to "protect" Bahrein.

The present status of the islands was summarized in a statement made in the House of Commons on April 18, 1934, by Sir Batton Eyres-Monssell, First Lord of the Admiralty. Bahrein, the statement explains, is not British territory. The Sheikh of Bahrein is an independent ruler in special treaty relationship with His Majesty's Government.

For the last century the British have controlled the Persian Gulf through a Political Resident, until recently a member of the Indian Civil Service. British "protection" of the sheikhdoms of the Persian Gulf has been much criticized and much praised. In view of the backwardness of these areas and the shortsighted policies of most of their rulers, the system seems to have done far more good than harm. Constant feuds between local rulers have been stopped and the seas made safe for commerce. Local agricultural methods and the health of the population have been greatly improved, and ruler and subjects alike have

142

received enough Western education to make them optimistic of their own and Bahrein's future.

Until the spring of 1946 the Resident lived at Bushire, Iran. He now resides on Bahrein, where eleven years earlier the British Navy set up its Persian Gulf headquarters. Under the Political Resident, the affairs of the individual sheikhdoms are the immediate concern of the several Political Agents. Most of these men have been capable British officials, with considerable knowledge of Arabic language and culture, who have run the foreign affairs of the various sheikhdoms in the best interests of both the British Empire and local inhabitants. Outstanding among the British officials concerned with the welfare and development of Bahrein is Sir Charles D. Belgrave, K.B.E., adviser to the government for more than twenty-five years and influential in picking British technical advisers, who brought western know-how to Bahrein long before Mr. Truman mentioned Point Four.

From time immemorial Bahrein has been the center of the pearl industry of the Near East, a carefully regulated and specialized trade which once gave Bahrein the highest per capita income in the world.[1] Pearling there centers around the *nakhoda*, or boat captain, often a former diver with a wide knowledge of the pearl banks. The nakhoda may or may not be the owner of the pearling ship, but he is its master and purser. If the vessel is his, he receives one-fifth of the season's catch after all expenses are deducted. While the ship is at sea, he occupies a cot of rope net stretched on a wooden frame from the starboard poop rail. There, on a folded blanket, he sleeps at night and sits cross-legged in the daytime, keeping an eye on his divers, on the ship's crew, and on the strong wooden chest in which he keeps the pearls.

Most Bahrein pearling vessels are dhows of sixty to one hundred feet in length with a single large sail. On each side are usually six square-bladed oars for use in calms. Four or five men work each of them, singing a lusty, deep-throated chant as the oars move in unison.

During the early forties Bahrein sent out some 300 pearling vessels to the banks each year. Qatar and the Trucial Coast each sent out about 200; Kuwait, 100; and Saudi Arabia, 50. A typical pearler has a complement of about sixty-five, including twenty-five divers, twenty-five pullers to help the divers up and down, some sailors, a cook, four unpaid cook's apprentices, a navigator, and a nakhoda. This unusually

---

[1] For a portion of the following information on pearling, the author is indebted to Parker T. Hart, one-time American Consul General at Dhahran.

large crew permits the divers to go down in relays, but it means that crewmen swarm all over the boat in the daytime and sleep at night wedged side by side under the oars.

The pullers are husky Negroes whose forebears were brought as slaves from Africa. As a day's pearling begins, the pullers form a single line reaching half the length of the ship; and chanting and yelling to the accompaniment of a growl like a dozen bass viols, sounded by the deeper-voiced members of the crew, they weigh anchor.

The elite of the ship's company are the divers, who divide among themselves three-fifths of the season's receipts after the ship's expenses and the nakhoda's share have been deducted. Dressed only in a loin-cloth and equipped with a nose clip and a weighted line, each diver daily makes about eighty dives of up to two minutes each. These range from fifty to ninety feet, beyond which depth oysters are rarely found. Although sharks, barracuda, and the terrible pressure of the depths at which they work all take their toll, the divers are a proud and lean clan, and many of them live to a ripe old age. During the season they eat very lightly, for deep dives cannot be made on a full stomach. Breakfast consists of a few dates and coffee; lunch is a gourd of water; and supper may be freshly caught fish, a little rice, and tea.

About two hours after sunrise the first team of twelve divers goes overboard. They rest for a moment on loops of rope hanging from the oars. Each puller then secures a heavy rope from his diver. This has a stone weighing about thirty pounds fastened to it and an adjacent loop in which the diver places his foot. Another smaller line ends in a basket for oysters, and this the diver fastens to his waist. Almost simultaneously the divers put one foot in the loops of the weighted lines, take a deep breath, put on their nose clips, and drop out of sight through the blue waters of the Gulf. If the bottom is more than fifty feet down, the divers cannot be seen from the ship, but their eyes are specially adapted and even without goggles good divers can see as far down as eighty feet.

As soon as the diver has reached the bottom, he takes his foot from the loop in the weighted line, which is hauled in by the puller. For the next minute and a half the diver swims around in the murky darkness of the Gulf bottom, tearing oysters from their beds and putting them into the basket at his waist. Tough as his hands are, he wears leather finger guards to protect them from sharp shells. When he can hold his breath no longer, he pulls on his basket line, loosens the basket from his waist, and comes rapidly to the surface.

144

Divers cover considerable distances while they are on the bed of the Gulf and often come up far from where they went down. They swim to the ship, then regain their breath while hanging on to the rope. Meanwhile the pullers have hauled up the baskets and emptied the shells into a gunny sack. After a rest of three or four minutes, the divers go down again, and on completing ten dives all twelve of them climb on board for a forty-minute rest while their places are taken by another team.

Each day's catch is opened at sunrise the following morning to allow time for the oysters to die. About one out of eleven oysters contains a pearl, usually small, irregular-shaped, and of little value. All pearls, good or bad, are handed over to the nakhoda, who cleans them, ties them up in a little red rag, and locks them in his wooden chest, to which only he has the key. A day's catch for a whole vessel usually contains only one or two good pearls.

The pearling season lasts for four months and ten days, and the *jalboots* and *booms*, as the small and large pearling vessels are called, stay out about a month at a time. The value of the average season's catch of a pearling ship in 1944 was 20,000 rupees, of which the nakhoda probably received 4,000; each diver, 250; and each puller, 180. The Bahrein Government levies no taxes on the import or export of natural pearls, and the importation of artificial or cultivated pearls is strictly forbidden. In addition, pearlers may not come in from outside the Gulf, and diving equipment and machinery, together with the whole process of culturing and producing artificial pearls, have been locally banned.

As soon as the season is over, the nakhoda sells the catch of his vessel to one of Bahrein's pearl merchants. Big pearls are usually matched on Bahrein Island, but the best boring, stringing, and mounting is done in India or France. Pearls were formerly shipped by fast sailing dhows or Persian Gulf steamers, but today for the most part they go by registered air mail.

The pearl merchants are traditionally the most important tradesmen of Bahrein. A visit to one of them usually means climbing to a darkened upper room, where one is invited to sit on cushions and drink tea as the merchant's helper unlocks an iron chest or rusty old safe and takes out a small hand balance and metal sieve for matching pearls. Badly shaped and poorly colored pearls are brought out first. In comparison to these, average ones look good indeed, and the inexperienced shopper may be tempted to buy before, at last, the merchant orders a secret drawer in the chest opened and takes from it an array of really fine pearls.

145

The last twenty years have witnessed a great slump in the Bahrein pearl industry. In 1930 the value of Bahrein's pearl catch as paid to divers and nakhodas was about 2,125,000 rupees. By 1932 this had dropped to a little over 1,200,000 rupees, and by 1940 it was down to 500,000 rupees. Though the trend has veered upward at times since then, it has never approached the 1930 mark. The initial slump was due in part to the world depression of the early 1930's and in part to the swing in fashion away from gems and jewelry and toward automobiles and mink coats. More important than these causes, however, was the development by the Japanese of cultured pearls. The Japanese found out how to open an oyster and place a speck of grit inside, thus spurring the oyster to secrete a "natural" pearl. Such pearls are generally more perfect in appearance, larger, and more uniform than those found in nature. Furthermore, they need be only one-third as costly. One important pearl dealer of Bahrein has estimated that the production of such pearls has cut the profit on the natural product by 85 to 90 per cent and has driven large numbers of discriminating customers away by robbing the natural product of much of its distinction.

In spite of the efforts which the British have made to help the lot of the pearl divers, pearling in the Gulf is a hard life. Now it appears more than ever to be a career without a future. Few people are willing to pay two thousand dollars for a strand of natural pearls when a string of cultured pearls, which only an expert can identify, costs seven hundred dollars, and a passable string of imitation pearls the same size costs twenty dollars. The closeness with which a good cultured pearl approaches the appearance of a natural pearl is shown by the fact that every year a certain number of cultured pearls are smuggled onto the pearling vessels of Bahrein and sold to the merchants as part of the natural catch. There will always be a limited market for the best Bahrein pearls, but the days when three-quarters of the wealth of the island came from pearls are past.

Because pearling, the traditional source of Bahrein's wealth, has fallen on evil days, various efforts have been made to find other sources of income. One of these is the raising of fine white donkeys, an animal much prized by the local Arabs. However, competition from the donkeys raised in the oases of the Hasa has cut down the profits on these colorful animals. There is some working of leather, metals, and wood products, but output is limited by the number of artisans, the small supply of raw materials, and the undeveloped state of the market. Enough fresh water is now available to permit the growing of oranges and lemons,

melons, figs and dates, and some vegetables. But most of these are consumed locally. Lastly, the Bahreinis have achieved some expansion of
their boatbuilding, boat-repairing, and sailmaking industries, in spite
of strong competition from the master boatbuilders of Kuwait.

Unable to compete in production, Bahrein has been reasonably successful in trade. The suq there is stocked with brightly colored leather
sandals, straw hats, and bags. There are rugs from the Gulf and Iran,
textiles from all over the Arab world and India, ceremonial daggers,
inlaid furniture, ornate silver bracelets, long-drop earrings, and, of
course, pearls, pearl shells, and mother-of-pearl ornaments.

Even in its trade Bahrein has run into difficulties in recent years
through competition with Saudi Arabia. The Dhahran airport is much
better than the one on the islands; a high head tax on persons leaving
Saudi Arabia to shop in Bahrein has been instituted to protect the
Saudi merchants; and since the completion of the deep-water pier on
the mainland at Dammam much trade has by-passed Bahrein. Most of
the cotton goods, foodstuffs, lumber, hardware, and other products destined for eastern Arabia now land at this pier, instead of being unloaded
at Bahrein and repacked for shipment to the coast by small dhow.

But no amount of planning or independent enterprise could have
improved conditions materially on Bahrein had it not been for the discovery of oil. In 1910 geologists of the British Indian Survey found a
seepage of oil on Bahrein Island. Twenty years later American geologists made surveys, as a result of which the Standard Oil Company
of California became interested in a concession granted to an English
group in 1925. Its interest led to the formation of the Bahrein Petroleum
Company, Ltd., (Bapco), which set up a camp and started drilling
in 1931. On May 31, 1932, the first well producing oil in commercial
quantities came in. Drilling was pushed fast; tanks were built; a submarine loading line was laid; and in December 1934 the first crude
oil from the island left in tankers and entered the world market. In
the same month the Sheikh of Bahrein granted a mining lease (due to
expire in 1999) covering approximately a hundred thousand acres in
his present and any future domains. In 1940 the lease was extended to
include territorial waters.

There are at present about seventy producing wells on the island. The
oil field lies near the center of Bahrein, south of the little village of
Awali, and the depth of the producing wells ranges from 2,008 to 4,700
feet. In contrast with Saudi Arabia, where the supply of oil is virtually
limitless, production on Bahrein is held at about 30,000 barrels a day,

147

and even this figure must be maintained by taking natural gas from deep wells and injecting it into the main producing horizons to balance oil withdrawal and water invasion, so that pressure is maintained at approximately the original level.

A refinery started in 1936 has been expanded until it now handles 155,000 barrels a day. Most of this comes to Bahrein from the mainland of Saudi Arabia through the world's longest underwater pipe lines. Approximately seventy tankers a month call at Bahrein for cargoes of finished products. All told, more than $75,000,000 has been invested in the Bahrein Islands by Bapco's parent concerns, the Texas Company and Standard Oil of California.

The company's policy is to employ as high a percentage of Bahreinis as possible. At the beginning of 1951 the employees, numbering slightly over six thousand, were divided as follows: 76.5 per cent Bahreinis, 12 per cent British Indians and Iraqis, and 11.5 per cent Americans, British, Canadians, South Africans, and Europeans. A comprehensive program of training is under way that will result in increased employment of Arabs in high-salaried jobs. In 1952 the percentage of Bahreini employees had risen to 78, and nearly all this number had received specialized training of one sort or another.

From the beginning officials of Bapco have realized the importance of developing educational and social projects for the benefit of the workers. In putting these into effect they have worked closely with the Sheikh of Bahrein and his British advisers. New roads and bridges seam the islands. New village water wells and control of malaria, once a serious menace to health in the islands, have made a vast difference in village life. The company has encouraged local businessmen, including a series of Arab contractors. These have carried on an extensive building program on the islands. Local employees of the company can live in houses of their own choosing at reasonable cost. In addition, Bapco has provided free bachelor housing for Bahreini employees in masonry dormitories in which electricity and other utilities are supplied free of charge. Most of the local employees, however, prefer to live in the nearby villages and are transported back and forth by company bus. In addition to teaching the workers sanitation and hygiene, Bapco has provided recreational facilities for those Bahreinis living in company quarters and has helped organize clubhouses in the Arab villages.

Although costs have risen, the wages of Bapco employees have more than doubled in recent years and are considerably higher than the average wages in the islands. In addition, the company provides health and severance benefits and a thrift-fund savings plan. There is a good sixty-seven-bed hospital at Awali.

Thanks to the wisdom of the British advisers and to the Sheikh of Bahrein, Sir Salman al Khalifah, royalties have been quite fairly and usefully administered. Approximately one-third has gone to the Sheikh to be spent by him and his family for their personal needs and charities. One third is invested so that Bahrein will have wealth to fall back upon when oil production ends. And one-third is used for the operation and modernization of the islands. Under this arrangement, the harbors have been improved, roads have been paved, many of the streets of the main towns have been lighted, a proper sewage system has been organized, the supply of fresh water has been greatly increased, and a series of schools at all levels through the equivalent of technical high school has been established. Because of these state schools, Bapco does not operate company schools but concentrates on conducting training courses and sponsoring scholarships. The government owns and operates a hospital and municipal dispensaries as well as a mental hospital. It has also participated with Bapco in agricultural development programs, very important for the islanders. Modern agricultural methods are being taught to the more enterprising farmers. They are helped in the drilling of wells and the proper utilization of water and are given new varieties of seed at cost.

Because of the combination of a forward-looking ruler, able British advisers, and an efficient and modern-minded oil company, the population of Bahrein archipelago faces a busy future. Although its size and limited resources prevent Bahrein from again becoming an important business and trading center, wise expenditure and investment of its oil revenues and wages have already brought the highest standard of living in Bahrein's history and given it an enviable position among the sheikhdoms of the Persian Gulf.

XII

Kuwait: Salem of the Persian Gulf

AT THE northwest corner of the
Persian Gulf, about eighty miles due south of Basra and sixty miles
from the mouth of Shatt al Arab, lies the Sheikhdom of Kuwait, a city
of a hundred thousand inhabitants, separated from six thousand square
miles of desert hinterland by a wall of clay. The name Kuwait, probably a diminutive form of *kut*, or fort, may originally have applied to
a Portuguese castle, remnant of the sixteenth century. But the town itself dates only from the eighteenth century, when members of the
Utubi tribe, wanderers over the arid lowlands, saw in the splendid
natural harbor promise of prosperity from the sea and trade. Part of
Kuwait's population remained nomadic, and even now about a quarter
still remains so, but the German traveler Carsten Niebuhr noted that as
early as 1760 Kuwait had come to sustain itself primarily on pearling,
trading, and fishing, with a fleet of eight hundred ships in use at that
time. During this and the succeeding century its native vessels, designed
for ocean travel, carried the bulk of the trade between India, East
Africa, and Red Sea ports and northeastern Arabia. Out of Kuwait went
sheep, wool, hides, skins, dates, and Arabian horses in exchange for piece
goods, sugar, tea, and rice. Sizable pearling and fishing fleets were busy
in season, and the building of dhows became an industry in itself.

When in 1776 the Persians captured Basra, Kuwait became the chief
outlet on the Gulf for Mesopotamia, but only for a brief interval. A
present-day colony of a thousand Persians in Kuwait survive as a reminder of this period.

150

In those days, British commerce on the upper Persian Gulf was carried on through a series of trading posts, or "factories." One of these was located at Basra, but difficulty with the officials dominating the city led the British to move the "factory" to Kuwait in 1793. In 1821 the British political officer for that part of the Gulf moved from Basra to the island of Failaka, in the mouth of Kuwait harbor. In spite of growing British influence, Kuwait went under Turkish suzerainty in 1829, and rivalry between the two powers for position in the sheikhdom was not resolved until the Turkish defeat in World War I.

In 1850 British General F. R. Chesney recommended Kuwait as the terminus of a projected Euphrates valley railway, a recommendation echoed by the Russians and finally by the Germans in 1901 with their proposal to make Kuwait the terminus of the Berlin to Baghdad railway. However, by this time Great Britain had a treaty of friendship with Sheikh Mubarak ibn Sabah. In 1898 Turkey had threatened to occupy Kuwait but found itself confronted with a strong British protest. Russia at this same time began to manifest interest in the Gulf. Fearful of both these powers, Sheikh Mubarak in January 1899 entered into closer treaty relations with Great Britian, promising not to let or otherwise cede any part of this territory to any government or subjects of governments other than Great Britain, and to receive no representatives of other foreign powers without British authorization. Great Britain on her part agreed to give Kuwait a financial subsidy and to supply its army with enough arms and ammunition to beat off the threatening Rashidis. From 1904 on, the British Political Agent, as adviser to the Sheikh on foreign affairs, maintained a strong position in Kuwait. During World War I British troops were stationed in the sheikhdom as part of the blockade of the Turks and a link in the security system for what the British now regarded as an area of special interest to them. In recent years there has been no serious threat from the north to the status quo in Kuwait.

Sheikh Mubarak, a close friend of King Saud's grandfather, granted the Sauds asylum when the Rashidis drove them from Riyadh. He also joined the older Saud in an unsuccessful effort to recapture the city in 1901. King Ibn Saud went from Kuwait to make the successful attack on Riyadh in 1902 that started him on his rise to power.

In spite of Mubarak's friendship for the Sauds, Kuwait's relations with Ibn Saud's Ikhwan deteriorated to such an extent during the rule of Mubarak's son Salim that only the action of British Air Force planes prevented Kuwait from falling to the Wahhabis in 1919. An additional series of border skirmishes in 1927–1928 proved inconclusive. Meantime, the Kuwaitis rebuilt their clay wall, twelve feet high and two miles long reinforced by five large and fifty-seven small towers; and a new sheikh, Ahmed al Jabir al Sabah, began a rule characterized by reasonableness and good will.

In December 1922 Ibn Saud, then Sultan of the Nejd, met at Oqair, just below present-day Dhahran on the coast, with Sir Percy Cox, British High Commissioner of Mesopotamia; Sadik Bey, representative of the government of Iraq; Major Moore, British Political Agent at Kuwait; and Colonel Dickson, liaison officer at Bahrein Island, for the purpose of settling boundaries on the peninsula.

The talks continued for days in the big tent of Ibn Saud, in Sir Percy Cox's quarters, in public, in private, at innumerable feasts of rice and mutton, and over tepid drinks. Since time immemorial the peninsula had been without frontiers marked on maps, its boundaries set by the seasonal wanderings of its tribes as they moved with the rains. Jacob, the Queen of Sheba, Abu Bakr, and the Turks had all accepted this principle. Now there were to be trades and countertrades, and little by little the southern borders of Iraq and the northern borders of the sultanate of the Nejd would stretch from well to well and wadi to wadi in a definable line.

But east and south of Kuwait neither tradition nor science could draw a proper frontier. Two parcels of land, each roughly fifty miles square, defied classification. In the heat of summer they were empty. At times Ibn Saud's bedouin peopled them; at times the tribes from Iraq had possession; and again, when the quick spring rains covered the rolling prairie with a thin carpet of green, the wells of Arqshadf and Wafra gave water to both Saudis and Kuwaitis, while Samah refreshed the camels of Iraqis and Nejdis alike. Who could say to whom these territories belonged? It was Sir Percy Cox who suggested that the best plan would be to set up two zones over whose undivided halves the ruler of the Nejd and the rulers of Kuwait and Iraq respectively would hold sway. Some day, perhaps in forty years, specific ownership might be decided, but until then these two bits of territory could defy the specific markings of the twentieth century. So two diamond-shaped tracts of land known as the Kuwait and the Iraq Neutral Zones were set up. The governments involved agreed not to fortify these areas and to allow their tribesmen free access to the wells therein. Rights to any subsurface resources such as oil were divided equally between the government of the Nejd on the one hand and the governments of Iraq and Kuwait on the other, though no mention was made of subsea rights. Thus did the Neutral Zones come into being.

Kuwait's foreign contacts have not been restricted to her immediate neighbors. As a virtually free port and a dhow-building center, Kuwait has both welcomed and sent to sea many an adventurous traveler to far lands. The port boasts over a hundred ocean-going dhows, ranging in size from seventy-five to three hundred tons, and the waterfront is one great shipyard, from the British residency in the east to the American hospital in the west.[1]

The story goes that once the keel of a Kuwait dhow has been laid, it is watched night and day by as many as twenty men to make sure that no barren woman jumps across it, for the Kuwaitis are convinced that if one should do so she would surely have a child. And because Allah is just, if He gives life to a baby He must take away a life in exchange. Everyone in Kuwait knows that if the watchers are lax, either one of the carpenters will die before the ship hits the water or the captain will be killed on the first trip. Since the most important thing to the women of Kuwait is having children and many of them are barren, it requires constant watching to keep the newly laid keels uncrossed. This war between the sexes is no joking matter along the Kuwait waterfront, and the carpenters work furiously until they build the sides of a dhow high enough to deter the most energetic woman.

The captain, or nakhoda, of a dhow usually comes from a prominent family in Kuwait. The sons of a nakhoda often go to sea at the age of six and captain their own dhows when they are eighteen, but they never serve as sailors, for that would be beneath their dignity.

Kuwait has no wood of its own; consequently its ships are built of lumber from India. The ribs and knees are made of naturally curved timber, while the mast and planking are of hard Malabar teak. Kuwait dhows are waterproofed with fish oil, which makes them smell abominable when they are first built and worse as year follows year. Although fairly effective against the sea water, the oil is not able to keep off evil jinn, which must be held at a safe distance by building a wall of coral rock and mud between the new vessel and the water. When the ship is finished, this wall is knocked down with great ceremony, and the dhow is launched. Then the sailors themselves sew the sails, rig the vessel, ship the rudder, and fit out the ropes and cables. Such items

---

[1] Much of the following information on Arab shipping is taken from Alan Villiers' *Sons of Sinbad,* and from his article, "Arab Dhow Trade," *Middle East Journal,* October 1948.

as compasses, binnacles, anchors, and wheels are almost always second-hand, having come years before from a Bombay junk yard.

In the past the traditional Persian Gulf craft was the *baggala,* a two-masted ship with a graceful curved bow and an elaborately carved, five-window stern, copied from the Portuguese caravels that sailed the Gulf in the sixteenth century. It was expensive to build, and its place has been largely taken by a two-masted craft known as a *boom.* Booms are double-enders with straight stemposts which stick up like an elevated bowsprit. A smaller craft seen mostly on the pearling banks is the *jalboot,* which has a straight up-and-down bow and a transom stern not unlike the old English naval jolly boat, which undoubtedly gave it its name. The high-sterned *sambuk* so often seen in the Red Sea is almost never built in Kuwait.

The deep-sea dhows of Kuwait are rarely built without the nakhoda's going into debt to one of the town's merchants, a debt which is seldom paid off. The sailors in turn are usually in debt to the nakhodas. In fact, if a sailor does not contract debts himself, he probably inherits them and spends many years of his life working off the debts of a spendthrift father. Great indeed is the social and economic gulf between the proud nakhoda, with his house and wives in Kuwait and his share in one or more dhows, and the debt-ridden sailor, whose home ashore is likely to be a bench in a cheap coffeeshop and whose only possessions are a small chest and the clothes he stands in.

During the hot summer months the deep-sea dhows are hauled on the beach at Kuwait and stand propped up by mangrove poles, their decks protected from the blazing sun by canopies of palm leaves. The nakhodas pass the nights of the summer season with their wives and children and lounge away the hot days in coffeeshops with their friends. Meanwhile the sailors, waging their eternal struggle against debt, are out on the pearling banks. The heat breaks in late September, and the pearlers come back to town, most of them little better off financially for their summer's work. Then the waterfront hums with activity as the deep-sea fleet prepares for another season. Sailors sing as they sew new sails; carpenters hammer feverishly; and the air is full of the smell of tallow and lime and fish oil and the thump of Indian drums. Day by day the heat lessens, and the bazaar is more and more crowded with nakhodas fitting out their ships and with sailors spending half their advance pay on trinkets to be smuggled into the suqs of Lamu, Mombasa, and Zanzibar. One by one the big ships cast off and slip out of the harbor, lightly rigged for the short run up the Shatt al Arab.

154

Many of them meet again at Fao at the mouth of the Basra River, where the ripe yellow dates hang thick among the palm fronds. There, waiting to pick up their date cargo, they lie side by side with carved baggalas from Sur, kotias from Bombay, and sambuks from Aden and Yemen, while the muddy river tugs at their sides.

The size of an Arab dhow is measured by the number of packages of dates it can carry. Two thousand packages is about average, for the Arabs do not like boats that are so big they flood the market where they unload, and the regular crew is one sailor for every one hundred packages. The reason why steamers cannot compete with dhows in certain forms of trade is that these Arab ships act as warehouses as well as means of transportation. If the market for dates in a harbor is glutted, a nakhoda thinks nothing of waiting two or three weeks for the price to rise before unloading his cargo.

After the parched and waterless sands of Kuwait, the Basra River seems like heaven to the Arab sailors, with its miles of green date gardens and its ever-flowing stream of fresh water. All too soon the last package of dates is stowed, the last trinket is bought and locked in the chest in which every sailor keeps his few worldly possessions, and the dhows cast off and slip silently downstream into the Persian Gulf.

The autumn days are all alike in the Gulf, with clear skies and the monsoon blowing steadily from the northeast, and life on the dhows soon falls into a strict routine. Each ship has its muezzin, who calls the faithful to prayer five times a day. When the first streaks of dawn light the eastern sky, he mounts the capstan and breaks the silence with an earsplitting reminder that prayer is better than sleep. Rising slowly from the open decks where they have slept, the sailors wash their hands, faces, and feet in sea water, place their robes or head-dresses on the deck—for they are not rich enough to afford prayer rugs —face toward Mecca, and begin the rhythm of Moslem prayer. God is real to them, and they pray unhurriedly, except for the cook who keeps one eye on the crude firebox. After prayer all hands sit down to the same breakfast of bread and sweet tea drunk from little glasses kept under the helmsman's seat. The younger sailors pour for the older hands, and the meal is over in less than five minutes. Afterward the ship is bailed, for Arab dhows are not as watertight as they might be. Almost no cleaning is done at sea, but the crew is rarely idle and spends long hours making rope or sewing the sails. The men are divided into watches, but this proves unimportant because all hands are needed to trim the big sails or to do any other heavy job. Dhows generally have no ship's clock, no one keeps track of the day of the month, and the Moslem sabbath, or Friday, goes by unnoticed.

About the middle of the morning boiled rice and dried fish are served and eaten in complete quiet, for the seagoing Arabs, like the bedouin, consider their meals too important to be spoiled by talk. The nakhoda, his mate, and one or two more prominent passengers eat on the poop, while the sailors spread their mats wherever they wish. Afterward the crew smoke their water pipes and then drop off to sleep in the shadow of the mainsail. The noon prayer ends this siesta, and then it is time for more ropemaking. In midafternoon there are individual prayers, and the muezzin sounds out a fourth call as the sun dips into the sea. This is followed by supper—more rice and ghee, perhaps a bit of fish, and sometimes Indian corn and peppers. After supper each sailor comes aft and politely wishes the nakhoda good evening. With the work of the day done, the water pipes are lighted with an ember from the cook's fire, and peace falls upon the ship, which sails trustingly through the night without running lights.

Although some of the Kuwait date dhows run directly to Aden or the East African harbors, most of them stop at one or more of the little towns along the southern coast of Arabia to pick up passengers. The height of every nakhoda's ambition is to find such a sizable group of Arabs who are looking for work in East Africa that he can pile them aboard his dhow until there is not a yard of deck space left empty. If not lucky enough to get a large group, the nakhoda can usually count on rounding up a few passengers en route from the Hadhramaut to work in the plantations of East Africa.

Once the deck is loaded with men and boys, long black bundles are passed up from hand to hand and carried down into the small, unlighted, evil-smelling afterhold. These are the women passengers, who will sit in the half darkness for one to four weeks, forbidden to come on deck for a breath of fresh air even at night. Conditions are bad enough on the crowded and unsanitary decks, but the deck passage of the most seasick bedouin youth is luxury compared to what the women have to endure below decks where the temperature often runs above 120 degrees. It is a rare voyage that does not see one of the black bundles dropped overboard or carried ashore dead.

Passengers from Mukalla to Africa usually pay eight rupees for the trip if they feed themselves. The cost is nine rupees with food and twelve for women. No berths are provided except the deck, and as many as 180 persons are often squeezed into an area seventy feet long and twenty-six feet across.

From the Hadhramaut the dhows sail past Aden to ports like Haifun in Italian Somaliland, where half the passengers are smuggled ashore, some dates are sold, and weeks pass while the nakhoda and his crew smuggle trinkets from their chests to the merchants in the native suq.

Haifun, incidentally, is mentioned in the first book on Arab shipping, the *Periplus of the Erythraean Sea*, which is believed to have been written about A.D. 60. In those days it was called Opone and was famous for cinnamon, tortoise shells, and "slaves of the better sort." Then as now the Arab dhows were recorded as bringing in "the products of their own places; wheat, rice, clarified butter, sesame oil, cotton, cloth, and girdles, and honey from the reed called *sacchari*." [2] The girdles or belts are now made in Japan, and the honey is Japanese sugar, but the ships, their sailors, and the manner of trading are unchanged since the time of Christ.

Once they reach the African coast, the dhows progress at an even more leisurely pace than they set between Arabian ports. A certain amount of legitimate business is done. The dates taken on in Iraq are gradually sold off and the other declared cargoes, such as Persian rugs, bolts of cloth, and bags of sugar, bought in the markets of Kuwait and Aden, are disposed of. But the real business of the captain and the crew is smuggling. It is the captain's opportunity for "big profits," and the pay of the sailors is so little that they must make money by smuggling in order to live. Everyone winks at their activities except the customs officials, who carry on a constant but ineffectual struggle to stop illicit trade. Sometimes the Somalis come out at night in their little fishing boats and quietly slip a bale of cotton cloth under a pile of fish as they pass. More often the Arabs take their goods ashore themselves. It is quite a sight to watch a thin sailor fatten out as he dresses, putting on three or four money belts, a series of girdles stuffed with diluted perfume, and six or eight robes. When it comes to dealing in large operations like the illicit loading of an Arab dhow with salt from the foreign port, the local administrators seem to have more luck, and many an Arab nakhoda has been forced to go about from ship to ship to collect funds from his fellow captains to pay the fine that has been levied against him.

The biggest profits from smuggling used to be made in slaves, healthy

[2] Schoff's translation of the *Periplus*.

bucks from the Congo or coffee-colored virgins from Assab, but the British Navy's slave patrol has nearly put a stop to this. Most of the slaves that do get into the Arabian Peninsula are brought not to the Gulf but across the Red Sea at night in the holds of fast dhows that land in Yemen or Asir.

Smuggling arms, a profitable branch of Arab sea trade, is also largely a thing of the past. Until World War I that trade enriched Muscat and the bedouin of the Hasa, but here also the British Navy intervened, and the movement of guns is now by half-dozens rather than by ship-loads.

From Haifun the dhows run south down the Benadir coast of Somaliland, with Mogadishu the next port of call. Here more of the passengers go ashore legally and others drift off over the side in the dark of the moon, while the smuggling goes on as usual. Many illicit goods are sold on credit, and it often takes several years for the smuggler to collect. The nakhodas do not actually take items ashore themselves but designate a trusted member of their crew as second mate and chief smuggler for the vessel.

The next port is Lamu, an island off the coast of Kenya, where the big white houses of the Europeans have spacious verandas and red roofs, and the lanes of the Arab town, some too narrow for a laden donkey, are crowded with busy Arabs. The suq in Lamu is relatively unspoiled, and the careful shopper can pick up fine examples of Damascus steel, Indian woodwork, and Persian pottery, along with American gold dollars left over from the calls of the Yankee clipper ships. Nearby are the Patta and Manda Islands, formerly one of the greatest slave-trading centers on the east coast of Africa. The slaves are gone now and Lamu has to content itself with selling coconuts, beef, and mangrove poles from the nearby islands. These mangrove poles may become the beams of an Arabian house, for most of the houses on the peninsula are supported by mangrove poles from Lamu or from the Rufigi delta. More of the passengers disembark at Lamu, and the smuggling of cloth and cheap perfume continues, along with boxes of cigarettes from Aden that go ashore hidden under a surface covering of dates.

Then comes the town of Mombasa on an island in a deep gulf. This bay has one arm for steamers and another for the Arab sailing craft that come sweeping up to the native anchorage with their drums beating and their sailors chanting thousand-year-old sea songs, while the crews of other Kuwait ships cheer as the newcomers arrive. Many Arabs have settled here, and they dominate the harborside trade of Mombasa. Those that are successful become night watchmen, coffee sellers, and finally shopkeepers, sitting happily in the shade of their own shops dispensing a few mangoes, little baskets of rice, and odds and ends that look as though they had been cast off by a passing seagull. Once an Arab has a store in Mombasa, he sends for his brother or some other male relative to take over for a year while he goes home, and thus eventually the little shop, whose total goods may not be worth more than twenty-five dollars, enables all the male members of the family to travel to Africa in rotation.

The last of the passengers from Arabia usually go ashore here. Then the decks are cleaned for the first time in months and the ship's company celebrates by having a dance. Everyone dresses in his cleanest robe. A new goatskin is stretched over the Indian drum, warmed, and tightened, a musician turns up from somewhere with a guitar, and the sailors dance and sing all night under the dark canopy of the sail and the bright awning of the stars. The nakhodas dance with other nakhodas, the chief smugglers dance with chief smugglers, and the sailors dance with each other. Hour after hour they shuffle across brightly colored carpets that have been spread on the decks, in time to the rhythm of the drums that keeps getting faster and faster until the dancers have to stop moving their feet and stand with their bodies shaking. Suddenly the music stops, the dancers jump high in the air, turn about, and sit down laughing. As the night wears on, cups of fruit juice are passed, bright red, unsanitary, and refreshing, along with little glasses of over-sweet tea and a sticky yellow sweetmeat made of oil of sesame and honey that the Arabs call *halwa*. Each dance is usually followed by bursts of song, sometimes done in chorus, sometimes solo. The tunes are handed down from generation to generation, but the words are changed to describe the adventures of each voyage. At last the sun rises. Without any formality the dance comes to an end, the visitors go off to their various ships, and the crews start work for the day as fresh as if they had spent the night in sleep.

The goal of the Kuwaiti sailor is Zanzibar, a pleasant, low, and heavily wooded island dotted with golden beaches and rich with history. For Zanzibar has long been a turnabout point for the Arabs, the Indians, the Malayans, and the Chinese. According to the Arabs, who talk about it as though it had just happened, the Portuguese mariner Vasco da Gama was able to make his way from Zanzibar to India only with the help of the famous Arab pilot Ibn Majid, who was probably a native of the Hasa. Today deep-sea navigation is virtually a lost art among the nakhodas of Arabia, though for hundreds of years they led the world in mathematics and navigation and thought nothing of sailing their dhows direct to Singapore, Malaya, and the China coast. They now sail from headland to headland. The Westerners and their steamers have come, and blue-water voyages are not the challenge they used to be.

It is a fine sight to see a Kuwaiti dhow foaming up the Zanzibar channel with her drums beating, the white-clad sailors singing on the foredeck, and a special red flag flying in the breeze. The drum beating and singing grows louder, as though the nakhoda and his crew were unaware that the ship was bearing down on the dhows already at anchor at a full eight knots an hour. Kuwaiti nakhodas pride themselves on the showmanship with which they come into Zanzibar. Only at the last minute do they call out their orders; then the huge lateen sails come crashing down, and the ship coasts toward her moorings. Half the sailors jump overboard, still dressed in their clean white robes, and swim to nearby vessels, pulling mooring lines behind them. In less time than it takes to tell it, the ropes are made fast, the sails are shipshape, and the dhow is at anchor, while the crews of the other Kuwaiti craft cheer in greeting.

At Zanzibar the last of the Iraqi dates are sold, except for a few fourthrate bundles, now smelling to high heaven, which have been brought along for sale to the primitive natives in the Rufigi River delta. Zanzibar is the heaven of all Arab sailors, and even the Kuwaitis agree that the suq, with its abundance of meats, vegetables, fresh fish, and tropical fruits, is worth coming a long way to see. There are acres of small stalls filled with mangoes, melons, rich halwa, brightly colored clothing, ornate sandals, and daggers. To the Kuwaiti sailors, however, the girls of Zanzibar are even more attractive than the wares of the market place. There the usual shipboard dances are abandoned and all hands spend their evenings ashore. After working in the morning, sleeping through the hot noontimes, and trading a little in the afternoon from the never-ending supply of contraband goods which they hide in their chests, the Kuwaiti seamen drift ashore by twos and threes in the cool of the evening and do not return until time for the dawn prayer. The strictness of Arabia is far away, and the sailors, when they do think of the Koran, think of Mohammed's words about a "traveling wife."

In preparation for the long sail back to Kuwait, most of the dhows are hauled out and scraped. This used to be done at Zanzibar, but

160

18. Sheikh Sir Salman ibn Hamad al Khalifah, the forward-looking ruler of Bahrein. (Photo of California Texas Oil Co., Ltd.)

19. The suq in Kuwait.

20. Primitive methods used in lifting water in a palm garden. (Photo of Gulf Oil Corporation.)

prices have risen there; consequently many of the Kuwaiti vessels go down the coast to the little islands farther south, where they are pulled out on a sandspit, demasted, and propped up with poles. There, to the accompaniment of much singing, the bottom of the boat is scraped, rotten planks are replaced, and openings are recalked. Camel tallow, which has been brought from Kuwait in old kerosene tins, is heated over a wood fire on the beach and mixed with lime, which the sailors dab on the bottom with their bare hands. After three days of this treatment any but the oldest dhow is shipshape again and ready for the voyage home.

The most common return cargo is mangrove poles. The cheapest place to buy them is the hot, rainy, malarial delta of the Rufigi River, which pours down from the mountains of Tanganyika to enter the Indian Ocean through a dozen mud-filled mouths. The waters of the Rufigi are filled with crocodiles. The mud of the banks is full of leeches and ticks, and the air is heavy with rain and mosquitoes. It is not surprising, therefore, that most of the nakhodas stay at Zanzibar and send their mates to the river. Pushing upstream past the burned-out hulk of the German cruiser "Konigsberg," sunk by the British in World War I, the Kuwaiti mates recruit a gang of Swahili laborers, tie up to the bank, and start cutting poles. The work is slow, almost everyone comes down with malaria, and the strongest sailors are crippled with rheumatism. But little by little the big holds fill up with mangrove poles, some of them bought officially, others smuggled on board at night. At last the ship is loaded. The crew and the Swahilis join in a final prayer, and the dhow sloshes slowly downstream through the ceaseless rain to the Indian Ocean. There, suddenly, the rain ends. The sun shines again. The sky and the water become blue, and the Arab sailors take on new life as though coming out from the mouth of hell.

Back in Zanzibar life is more restrained, as the Kuwaitis stock up on toys for their children, cigarette lighters for their friends, shawls for their wives, and endless bottles of homemade lemon juice, which can be sold in the suq of Kuwait, where it is used in making lemon ice. In addition to lumber, the home cargo of the dhows consists of coconuts, coconut oil, cloves, and vermicelli, along with highly perfumed soap.

By now the monsoon wind has turned around. It blows steadily day after day toward Kuwait. On the way home the dhows coast along within sight of the shore of Africa, which makes navigation easier and is safer in case the overloaded vessels go down in a squall. Ten or twenty Arab sailing ships move up the coast together, racing merrily along while the nakhodas and their important passengers visit from dhow to dhow and swap stories of their adventures in Zanzibar. Often the ships sail so close that the crews pray together at sunset or dawn and sing back and forth to each other. After the swamps of the Rufigi and the heat of the Benadir coast, the salt breeze of the Indian Ocean brings new zest to the Arab sailors, and they call out with renewed vigor when the wind changes and they have to trim the huge weather-beaten sails.

Sometimes on the way home the Kuwaiti dhows put in at Aden or the ports of the Hadhramaut, but usually they keep well away from the pirate-infested southern coast of Arabia until they have rounded Ras al Hadd. Then they beat up the Gulf of Oman and into the port of Matrah, a fishing village nestled below the sharp, rocky mountains of Oman and guarded by two dilapidated Portuguese forts. A little coffeeshop by the beach near the fish market acts as a sort of club for Kuwaiti nakhodas. There the mariners of the deep-sea dhows rendez-vous, drink cup after cup of cardamom-flavored coffee, and talk of African bazaars and the exciting nights in Zanzibar—but most of all of Kuwait, its beach and its harbor, and of their families. The hubble-bubble pipes gurgle through the long, hot noons, but with the cool of the evening the ship captains get down to business. Matrah and the adjacent town of Muscat were once great shipping centers, but few dhows are registered there now, and the trade is in the hands of the Suris and the big dhows from Bahrein and Kuwait. The few mangrove poles needed for building in Muscat and the nearby villages are sold at Matrah, but the nakhodas need not linger long. It is more profitable to hurry north to Bahrein, where the agents of the King of Saudi Arabia and of the Sheikh are waiting to pay top prices for good mangrove poles.

With the lumber over the sides, the dhows leap forward as if they know that home is near, and the captains race them under full sail through the treacherous pearl banks until the lookouts cry "Ras Zor," and the shout of "Kuwait" runs through the ship. The great flag of Kuwait is unfurled, accompanied sometimes by a flag showing a British Overseas Airways Corporation (BOAC) flying boat. The latter flag is run up to the masthead as a sign of modernity. The skins of the drum are warmed, the sailors change into white robes and blue headdresses, and the nakhodas bathe in sea water, shave, splash on some perfume, and prepare for a triumphal homecoming. Ahead, the minaret of the Kuwait mosque rises out of the desert haze. Drums beating and songs echoing across the placid waters of the pale-green bay, the big dhows glide up to their final anchorage. The sails come down, the last of the cargo goes ashore, and the six-thousand-mile voyage is done.

Traditionally, the nakhodas are rowed in state to their white homes along the waterfront, the crew slips ashore for a few days of rest before signing up for a summer with the pearling fleet, and the dhows are propped up on the sands of the beach under their awnings of palm fronds for a few months of well-earned rest. The sweltering heat of the Persian Gulf summer shuts down. Not until the breath of the monsoon ruffles the water will the big dhows again set off for Haifun, Lamu, Zanzibar, and the swamps of the Rufigi.

The gross profit from a typical ten-month voyage is around 10,000 rupees. Once direct costs have been subtracted, about 4,000 rupees are left for the owners of the ship, and 4,000 rupees for division between the nakhoda and his crew. The average Kuwaiti sailor feels that Allah has been good to him if he nets 150 rupees (50 dollars) for his nine months of tugging at ropes in the scorching sun and sleeping, drenched with dew, curled up on a coil of rope. Most of this money may go for debts, but the sailor does not worry. Allah has shown him the world and brought him safely home again.

Strong as the traditions are which bind Kuwait to the sea and free trade, boatbuilding and pearling have nevertheless fallen off since the discovery of oil in Kuwait and the new industry's absorption of one-tenth of the sheikhdom's labor.

As early as 1929 the Gulf Oil Corporation retired from the Near East Development Corporation and, consequently unhampered by the terms of the famous Red-Line Agreement, tried to get an oil concession in Kuwait. It found the way barred, however, by the insistence of the Sheikh's British advisers on the "nationality clause" in the Kuwait-British agreement. This in effect stated that only British oil companies could obtain concessions in Kuwait. After prolonged negotiations and with some help from the Department of State, a compromise was worked out, and the Kuwait Oil Company, Ltd., a British corporation, was formed in December 1934. It is owned half by Gulf Oil Company and half by the Anglo–Iranian Oil Company, with an exclusive seventy-five-year concession for the sheikhdom's six thousand square miles.

The first wildcat well was started in May 1936 but abandoned the next April at a depth of 7,950 feet. The second test well discovered the huge Burghan field and was completed in May 1938 at 3,692 feet. This Burghan field remains the largest known pool of oil. In contrast to the proven oil reserves of the entire United States, estimated at about twenty-four billion barrels, Burghan field is thought to contain twelve billion barrels. Since the population of Kuwait, though increasing, is not yet two hundred thousand, the sheikhdom sits atop petroleum resources that give it the greatest national wealth per capita in the world.

Nine wells were sunk by July 1942, when developments in World War II caused the British Government to order the suspension of drilling in Kuwait. Work was not resumed until June 1945. A year later the first tanker, the S.S. "British Fusalier," departed from the port of Mina al Ahmadi with a load of Kuwait crude.

Gulf has supplied most of the top executives, the drillers, and much of the equipment. As many as eight cargo ships at a time have lain offshore in Kuwait Bay or have been tied to the long steel pier at Mina al Ahmadi disgorging a constant stream of steel pipe, building material, tractors, and all types of material and equipment.

In Saudi Arabia, Aramco's policy has been to put road building last. The thinking of the Kuwait Oil Company, however, has been along different lines, and the result has been a network of smooth blacktop roads spreading out from Kuwait down to the nearby airport and southward to the construction camp of Magwa and the great oil field of Burghan. On a hill east of Burghan stands a tank farm, the big aluminum-painted containers glistening through the desert haze. Nearby rises the employee town of Ahmadi, a modern city of paved streets, public utilities, extensive machine shops, and rows of attractive, air-cooled bungalows.

The Kuwait Oil Company's worst problem has been lack of fresh water. Over a period of years the company has drilled many wells and developed a supply of brackish water fit for industrial use and for livestock. Some fresh water has to be brought by tanker from the Shatt al Arab, but a new condenser plant with a capacity of 500,000 gallons a day has solved the drinking-water problem and helped in other needs, although it does not provide enough to expand the gardens of the sheikhdom. A real solution to the problem would be a large pipe line or small canal from the lower reaches of Shatt al Arab. Several privately financed companies are trying to get the concession for such a project. Part of this water could be purified for household purposes, while the rest could go to irrigate the dry but comparatively fertile prairie north of the bay, thus supplying food to the growing town.

A problem almost as difficult as that of water has been that of food, most of which has had to be imported from Iraq, England, India, Australia, and even the United States. In order to bring in fresh vegetables, arrangements were worked out in January 1949 for convoys of trucks to drive across the desert from Damascus. The route followed by the first convoy was some 2,200 kilometers in length, long stretches of which had never been crossed by motor vehicles before. The first convoy's arrival naturally produced great excitement in Kuwait. Cheering crowds surrounded the trucks, and the Sheikh staged a festival in honor of the drivers. People danced in the streets and many made speeches about those who brought the vegetables of Syria so quickly to Kuwait. Now, however, food comes to Kuwait from Lebanon and Syria in a few hours by airplane.

The winds of change are also blowing across the million-acre Kuwaiti–Saudi Arabian Neutral Zone, just south of Kuwait proper. During the first twenty-five years after it was delineated, this gently rolling area of desert, semidesert, and salt flat, fifty miles long and forty miles wide, was virtually unvisited by Europeans. Not long after the end of World War II, however, the Sheikh of Kuwait let it be known that he was ready to grant an oil concession covering his undivided half of this Neutral Zone. Just to the north lay the fabulous and proven Burghan field of the Kuwait Oil Company, while not far to the southwest the Arabian American Oil Company had tapped a rich field at Abu Hadriya, so there was every reason to think that the Neutral Zone was also underlaid with oil. Oilmen and their representatives from many nations came to the palace of Sheikh Ahmad al Jabir al Sabah. Englishmen, Frenchmen, Dutchmen, and Americans bid and outbid each other in a battle for the first important oil concession to be granted in the Near East in more than a decade. At last on July 6, 1948, Ralph K. Davies, former deputy petroleum administrator under President Roosevelt, announced in London that a new firm of which he was president, the American Independent Oil Company, had come out on top. The terms of the successful bid were not disclosed, but it was rumored that they included a down payment of over seven million dollars, a guarantee to begin drilling in 1949, a fixed annual rental, a promise of oil royalties of about thirty-five cents a barrel, plus a bonus payment.

Before the American Independent Oil Company could begin operations, it was desirable that a concession be granted for the Saudi Arabian undivided half of the Zone. The Arabian American Oil Company had decided not to exercise its option there. As a result, King Ibn Saud threw his half open for bids, and a seven-cornered battle developed, the concession finally going to the Pacific Western Oil Company in March 1949. This firm is a holding company owned by independent oil men and controlled by J. P. Getty and T. A. J. Dockweiler. It has interests in the Skelly Oil and Tidewater Oil Companies. The terms of the concession for the Zone are believed to have included a ten-million-dollar down payment and a royalty of fifty-five cents per barrel, the highest yet granted in the Near East.

In the meantime the American Independent Oil Company began operations. Its first shipload of engineers, surveyors, and drillers arrived in Kuwait harbor in December 1948, and a fully equipped geological group reached the Neutral Zone early in 1949 to make an extensive survey. This was completed by late spring, and drilling began with the coming of cooler weather.

American Independent and Pacific Western worked out an agreement and started prospecting in the Neutral Zone, completing the exploration work already done and drilling a sufficient number of wells to test the property. A converted LST was anchored off the shores of the Neutral Zone to provide living quarters for the exploration parties and drilling crews. At first, dry hole followed dry hole and Aminoil's most publicized act at the time was not its drilling but the gift to the Sheikh of Kuwait of an air-cooled, ocean-going yacht furnished with an ornate throne room, a sheep pen on the top deck, and a kitchen equipped to roast three whole sheep at one time. In March 1953, however, the fifth well struck oil in what seems to be good quality and quantity.

The real problem in Kuwait proper is not extracting oil from the fields, which are shallow and accessible, but helping the Sheikh of Kuwait and his advisers make the best possible use of the wealth which this oil is bringing them. The little sheikhdom, which had almost no settled population outside the town of Kuwait, relied on boatbuilding, pearl fishing, trade with Saudi Arabia and Iraq, and smuggling, but all of these activities were in such a state of depression that even the Sheikh was in debt when oil began flowing.

Oil royalties have now not only driven away the spectre of poverty but they have nearly satisfied the personal wants of the Sheikh's family in terms of palaces, automobiles, air-cooling equipment, and yachts. Intensive thought is now being given to both town and national planning. Ahmadi is growing up as a modern and orderly town. A new hospital, new schools, the rebuilding of the customhouses, and the widening and straightening of an avenue from the Sheikh's palace to the main square in the center of Kuwait are noteworthy improvements. Work progresses slowly, and buildings often have to be changed before they can be used. A small beginning has been made by taking down some of the old buildings and cutting straight streets through the winding lanes of the old town. Modernization may be brought about, however, as the French have shown in North Africa and the Saudis are beginning to prove at Jidda, by leaving the old town pretty much as it is and building a new Kuwait outside the walls. Such a suburb, properly laid out with broad paved streets and parks and well supplied with water, would give the relatives of the Sheikh, the rich merchants, and the rapidly increasing foreign population a first-class residential "garden suburb."

Thanks to the funds that are now available, education in Kuwait is progressing well. Twelve new schools are planned which, like those now in operation, will be staffed by Egyptian teachers and will teach the Egyptian curriculum. Even now Kuwaiti boys can secure secondary education, and the girls can go through elementary grades. In lieu of a college in Kuwait, the government of Kuwait supports a hostel in Cairo known as Kuwait House, where about seventy-five students receive higher education each year. Thus far, Kuwait and Bahrein are well ahead of the rest of the peninsula in education.

The provision of fresh water and better housing should be followed by further improvements in medicine. In the past the chief medical care available to the Kuwaiti was at the hospital of the Reformed Church in America, which first established a station in Kuwait in 1903. A plague attributed to the missionaries broke out soon after, and they were asked by the grandfather of the present Sheikh to leave Kuwait. But in 1908 the ruler of Kuwait became sick, recovering only after being treated by Dr. Bennet, the missionary in charge of the American Hospital at Basra. The Sheikh, to show his gratitude, gave land for a hospital to be established by the missionaries in Kuwait. Dr. Mylray of the Basra Mission came down, and the present men's hospital was completed in 1912. A chapel and three houses were added, and the treatment of women was begun under Dr. E. E. Calverly, who organized a separate hospital while her husband taught the young men to read and write in his bookshop.

As of early 1950 there were three American doctors at Kuwait. The number of converts to Christianity has been few, and the main activity of the mission has been medical. In one year 62,000 dispensary patients were handled. Three hundred major operations and 384 minor operations were performed; 20,000 injections were given in the men's hospital; the women's hospital handled about half as many patients. Considerable expansion of facilities is under way as the mission's relations with the Sheikh and with the oil company are encouragingly good.

The sheikhdom would reap benefits from further extension of its road system to include a paved highway running north from Kuwait to Basra and south across the Neutral Zone to the pipe line port of Ras al Mish'ab in Saudi Arabia. Study should likewise be given to the possibility of linking Kuwait to Basra by railroad, thus tying it in with the Iraq railway network. More urgent, however, is the establishment at Kuwait of a first-class international airport. The rapidly growing needs of the local community, the American Independent Oil Company, and the Pacific Western Oil Company are producing heavy traffic. To handle some of this, the Kuwait Oil Company has built a new airport for four-motored planes about eight miles from the town of Kuwait. Whether Kuwait should follow the lead of Saudi Arabia and set up its own air line is questionable.

It will be difficult to prevent a lopsided economy, too heavily dependent on oil, from growing up in Kuwait. In addition to a reasonable development of truck gardening, and expansion of the sheikhdom's sheep, camel, and donkey population, various simple and basic industries should be encouraged. These might include textile manufacture with Indian or Egyptian cotton and the making of cement, glassware, pottery, and carbon black. It would not take much guidance greatly to improve the quality of Kuwait dhows and to make it possible for their builders to turn out low-priced but high-quality sailing vessels which would be sold all over the Indian Ocean.

During June 1938 the Sheikh of Kuwait set up a Legislative and a Consultative Council.[3] The former was to be elective and to play the role of a parliament. On being established, the Legislative Council almost immediately split into factions, one faction favoring the annexation of the sheikhdom to Iraq and another favoring autonomy under the Sheikh. The so-called "young Kuwaiti" group, which leaned toward Iraq, gained control of the council. When affairs reached an impasse in December 1938, the council was dissolved and new elections were held.

The newly elected council turned out to be very little different from the old one. It drew up a draft of a proposed constitution, which would have loosened the ties between Kuwait and Great Britain and would have diverted a considerable amount of the country's revenues from the Sheikh to the public good.

The political situation grew more and more difficult until March 1939, when the council was again dissolved and its members imprisoned.

[3] From a memorandum by Dr. Herbert J. Liebesny, January 14, 1949.

Rioting broke out and had to be put down by the troops of the Sheikh with some loss of life. Rejecting the draft constitution proposed by the Legislative Council, the Sheikh drew up a new constitution which reaffirmed Kuwait's ties with Great Britain. This new constitution also set up a limited Legislative Council but stated that its decisions were not enforceable until after they were approved by the Sheikh. This Council was to be composed of twenty members elected by the people, but the Sheikh had power to fill vacancies up to half the membership.

Although this constitution is reportedly still in effect, no Legislative Council has met since 1939. Instead the Sheikh has an Advisory Council of eight members, which he appoints but whose advice he is not bound to follow. Thus, the move to change the pattern of Kuwaiti government came to nothing, and the young Kuwaitis, now somewhat older and wiser, had to wait for the death of the old Sheikh before they could witness changes; then they secured several reforms, at least in the economic field.

The new Sheikh, fifty-six-year-old Abdullah ibn Salim al Sabah, who came to the throne in February 1950, lives more conservatively than did his predecessor and first cousin, Sir Ahmed al Jabir al Sabah. He has sold the big yacht to the Regent of Iraq and moved into a smallish palace, where he enjoys his family, a few cars, and his friends. Much of his energy goes toward making Kuwait the "most modern state in the Near East." With royalties of about $165,000,000 a year he may, if his purpose holds, transform a poor sheikhdom into the Middle East's first prosperous welfare state.

Sir Olaf Caroe in his book, *Wells of Power,* stresses the need for international co-operation in the defense of the Middle East, in the distribution and organization of the region's labor, and in the maximum utilization of the profits from its great resource, oil.[4] If Kuwait, whose problems are, relative to those of other states in the area, simple ones, could devote part of its wealth to the development of the area as a whole, it would prove its statesmanship and create hope in the minds of those who feel a strong Middle East must be a prosperous Middle East.

[4] Page 144.

XIII

The Trucial Coast:

Pirates and Petty Sheikhdoms

IT IS an axiom in southern Arabia that the more barren the coast, the more piratical the inhabitants. This was true in Roman times when Pliny wrote: "At the present day voyages are made from Egypt and Arabia every year: and companies of archers are carried on board the vessels as those seas are greatly infested with pirates." Some twelve hundred years later the Venetian traveler, Marco Polo, described cordons of ships which Arab pirates stretched across the sea at the mouth of the Persian Gulf so that no merchant could run between them without being attacked.

The British East India Company had trouble with the pirates of Oman from the start of its activities, losing some of its largest ships in running battles with fast-sailing Arab dhows. As trade with India expanded, piracy in and around Oman became so profitable that unscrupulous Europeans and Americans began to muscle in on the racket. In 1695 five pirate ships flying English colors were reported in Arab waters. Vessels were outfitted as far away as New York for the Persian Gulf pirate trade. The famous buccaneer Captain Kidd did not overlook this opportunity, but the competition from the Arabs was too tough and before long he returned to his old hunting grounds on the Spanish Main.

Thanks to their favorable location which gave them access to the Persian Gulf, the Gulf of Oman, and the Indian Ocean, the pirates of Oman were the most successful of the Arab buccaneers. To the east they ranged as far as the coast of India, to the north they penetrated almost to Basra, and in the west they conquered the island of Zanzibar.

Typical of them was Rahmah ibn Jabir, one of the most dreaded villains of the Persian Gulf in the early nineteenth century. He grew up as a sailor but at an early age joined the Sultan of Muscat in an attack against Bahrein. This was so successful that he next helped the Egyptians in a war against the Arabs of the mainland. As a reward for his victories he was given the little coastal town of Dammam, near Dhahran, now the site of a new deep-water pier and the eastern terminus of the Saudi Arabian railroad. Using Dammam as his base, he organized a fleet of six large dhows and a host of smaller craft, and for a while he and his two thousand followers dominated the waters of the Persian Gulf. After sowing terror far and wide, the often-wounded Jabir met a superior force and blew up his own ship rather than be captured.[1]

During the eighteenth and early nineteenth centuries the stronghold of Omani piracy was the barren coastal plain between the peninsula of Qatar on the west and the promontory of Ras al Masandam on the east. This strip of coast was then nominally part of Oman, which in turn was nominally under the Sultan of Muscat; actually, however, the local sheikhs were either independent or paid tribute to the Wahhabi rulers of central Arabia. The inhabitants were known as Jawasmis, from the name of an important tribe of this area.

As the amount of British shipping increased, so did the attacks of these pirates. The Jawasmis became Wahhabis in 1800; every few months after that saw some British vessel captured or forced to flee for its life. The British authorities in India, however, wished to trade with the Arabs and maintained a policy of compromise and softness toward the pirates. Possibly as a result of this leniency the pirates became bolder and attacked two cruisers of the East India Company, one of them the powerful twenty-four-gun "Mornington." Again the British authorities in Bombay did not retaliate. When the little British ship "Fury" with only six guns beat off a pirate attack, her commander was actually censured by Bombay.

Late in 1808 the Jawasmis captured the large British merchant ship "Minerva" after a long running fight and killed all but two of her crew. The only lady passenger, Mrs. Taylor, was not mistreated but was held until a large ransom was paid. The pirates mounted twenty guns on the "Minerva" and used her as the flagship of their fleet, which was

[1] J. S. Buckingham, *Travels in Assyria, Media and Persia.*

171

made up of sixty ocean dhows and eight hundred small craft and manned by almost twenty thousand men. Finally, however, to rid the Persian Gulf of these marauders, the British sent a fleet from Bombay in September 1809. The Jawasmi pirates were fierce fighters with knife and scimitar, but they were no match for British gunnery. Their stronghold of Ras al Khaima was captured and burned, along with the ships in its harbor, including the ill-fated "Minerva." The other towns along the Jawasmi coast were destroyed, and the British sailors returned to Bombay convinced that the pirate menace was a thing of the past.

The Jawasmis, however, had merely retreated inland, and they soon had new dhows scouring the Persian Gulf for luckless merchantmen. Only the fastest and best-armed trading vessels were safe from these pirates, whose well-gunned ships moved easily in the lightest winds and who swarmed over an enemy vessel in such numbers that the crew had no chance of survival. By early 1818, ships were captured as far east as the coast of India and west to the waters off Aden. But in that year Ibrahim Pasha of Egypt overthrew the Wahhabis of central Arabia. When the pirates lost the support of these fanatics, the British decided it was their chance to strike. They lined up the Sultan of Muscat as an ally and sent the bulk of their Indian Ocean squadron to help him. While the British ships fired from the sea, the four thousand troops of the Sultan attacked the pirates from the rear. After six days of hard fighting the rebuilt stronghold of Ras al Khaima fell and was soon followed by the other towns of the Pirate Coast.

The local sheikhs were forced to sign a general treaty of peace with the British in January 1820, under which the Jawasmis agreed not to engage in piracy against outsiders, although they were allowed to fight each other as much as they wished by land and by sea. This loophole led to a renewal of piracy, and in 1835 the British organized a maritime truce under which the sheikhs of the Pirate Coast agreed not to carry on any hostilities at sea during six months of each year. The local pearl and fishing trades prospered so greatly under this arrangement that the truce was renewed repeatedly. Then, in 1853 a Treaty of Peace in Perpetuity was signed between the British and the Jawasmi pirate sheikhs, whose coast has ever since been known as the Coast of the Truce, or the Trucial Coast.

These truces were in general effective, but it was the coming of steamships that finally put an end to large-scale piracy in the Persian Gulf. They were not at the mercy of wind and tide, and the Arabs soon realized the uselessness of charging these ironclads with their vulnerable wooden dhows. Thus by 1880 piracy had lost its popularity among the Jawasmis, although it was too much to expect that so appealing an activity would cease entirely. In 1905 a British merchant vessel was attacked by pirates in the Persian Gulf, and as late as 1944 a large Arab dhow carrying food to Dibai on the Trucial Coast was captured by them. Today the men of the Trucial Coast view piracy with disfavor tempered by nostalgia.

In 1892 the Trucial sheikhs signed agreements promising not to enter into treaty relationships with any power other than the British. This treaty was expanded in 1911 to cover pearl concessions, and in 1922 a clause was added under which the local sheikhs undertook to consult the British Resident regarding any further concessions asked for by other powers.

Anyone who has visited the Trucial Oman understands why the Jawasmis took to piracy, for the eighty thousand inhabitants of the six sheikhdoms comprising the coast are probably the poorest in Arabia. These sheikhdoms, with an area of about six thousand square miles, lie along a sandy coast which is broken only by occasional mud flats and salt creeks. Rainfall averages only about five inches a year, and summer temperatures run over 110 degrees in the shade, with the humidity in the high nineties much of the time.

A marsh called Sabkha Matti forms the undefined western boundary of the Trucial Oman. The land between it and the town of Abu Dhabi, a distance of 150 miles, is a desolate waste marked by a few ranges of low hills. The region is characterized by salty or sandy soil which can support only coarse vegetation and a few oryxes, hares, and gazelles. It is without a single permanent house and is visited only by a few bedouin of the Manasir, Beni Yas, Murra, Beni Hajir, and Duwasir tribes.

Offshore lie a series of small islands, reefs, and large shoals. One of these islands is Dalma, about three miles long, which is a rendezvous for pearl fishermen and merchants who trade with them during the pearl season; small amounts of iron ore and crystal have been found there. Farther east is the somewhat larger island of Seer Beni Yas, off the promontory of Ras Baraka. From this point the coast swings northward slightly for some forty-five miles to the entrance of Khor al Batin Channel. This lagoon, which is five miles wide and runs along the shore for almost fifty miles, is screened from the Gulf by low dunes, thus affording an ideal refuge for the nineteenth-century pirates and twentieth-century smugglers.

The towns of the Trucial Coast are tied together by a road that is little more than a desert track. In 1931 when a sheikh of the Manasir tribe went from Abu Dhabi to Mecca in a Ford car, his trip was considered a great achievement. The number of cars using the road has increased greatly the last few years, and desert-worthy trucks now move about even without benefit of roads.

Eastward from Khor al Batin the shore curves to Ras Kantor, much cut up by creeks along the way. So intricate is the network of streams and channels along this part of the Gulf that it was not surveyed until 1824. Then Captain Brucks of H.M.S. "Psyche" sent out a series of small boats strongly armed and guarded by the nephew of the ruler of Abu Dhabi, who accompanied the survey and gave it much-needed protection.

The townsfolk of the Trucial Coast are a mixture of Arab blood with Baluchi, Persian, Hindu, and a high percentage of Negro. In the interior live about ten thousand bedouin, the largest number belonging to the Beni Qitab tribe, who graze their flocks on the short-lived desert grass in the spring and spend the hot summer months camped around the few permanent wells.

The inhabitants of the Arabian Peninsula may be divided into men of the desert, men of the mountains, and men of the sea. Like the Kuwaitis and Bahreinis, the men of the Trucial Coast towns are seafarers at heart, building small dhows which they use for fishing, pearling, and trading all over the Gulf.

The second richest pearl beds in the Gulf are to be found off the Trucial Coast and they are still worked during the summer by small craft from the local sheikhdoms. Bedouin from the interior round out the crews of these ships. The management of the fishing fleet and the marketing of its pearls are largely controlled by Hindu and Khoja merchants, who own most of the pearling boats, advance supplies at exorbitant prices to the captain and crews, and formerly made a great percentage of profit out of the catch. Like all the pearl fishermen of the Persian Gulf, however, those of the Trucial Coast have been hard hit by the fall in price of natural pearls. The skeikhs of the Trucial Coast collect taxes on the boats and on the men employed in the pearl trade and, though the take is small, everything helps in so poor an area.

The methods used are the same as those of the Bahrein fishermen, but most of the boats are smaller and the equipment even more primitive than that seen farther north. The pearlers stay out in the Gulf for many days at a time, putting ashore occasionally on the small islands off the Trucial Coast to expose the oysters to the sun until they have rotted away; then the pearls are gathered from the empty shells. Merchants from the towns of the Trucial Coast set up "branch stores" on some of the larger islands during the pearling season, and anyone who is willing to put up with the scorching heat of the summer sun in the Gulf will enjoy the colorful spectacle of these island rendezvous. The pearl fishermen are great storytellers. Squatting over their evening coffee they claim that shark and swordfish are relatively harmless but admit they are scared of sawfish.

Coming along the coast from Qatar, the first town one reaches is Abu Dhabi, built on an island formed by channels that flow out of the lagoon. Compared to Bahrein or Kuwait the towns of the Trucial Coast are far from impressive and Abu Dhabi is no exception. A few of its better houses are made of stone, but for the most part they are constructed of dried mud or palm fronds. Water is so scarce and so brackish that there is little cultivation beyond a few vegetable gardens, a palm grove, and a field or two of grain fighting a losing battle against the sand and dryness.

Similarly, the markets of the Trucial Coast do not compare with those of Bahrein or Kuwait. But the Persian shopkeepers in the suq at Abu Dhabi carry a wide variety of goods in their little stores. Among the items to be found are cloth, cloaks, head cloths, dates, grain, coffee, tea, sugar, spices, sweetmeats, cartridge belts, daggers and saddlebags. In general, Persians are not popular with the bedouin, perhaps because they drive too hard bargains, but they are an important segment of economic life in the towns there.

The bedouin of this part of the coast like Abu Dhabi as a camping ground, and Sheikh Shakbut ibn Sultan counts on their support in his intermittent wars with Sheikh Said ibn Maktum, the ruler of the sheikhdom to the east. Sheikh ibn Sultan lives in a building which is large for Abu Dhabi but would not be impressive elsewhere. In true Arab style, however, he keeps open house for the townsfolk, the bedouin, and such foreign visitors as may call upon him. In addition to the palace there is a mud fort at Abu Dhabi, a low-walled structure with a few rusty cannon (some of which may go back to Portuguese times) lying half buried in the sands around it. The guesthouse of the Sheikh commands a good view of the harbor, which is usually full of small coastal dhows trading in dates, grain, dried fish, and bales of cloth, plus a

175

traffic in water from rock pools on the nearby islands. Because there is no pasture around the town, mangrove leaves have to be imported as fodder for the donkeys and thin cattle.

The harbor is also used by fishermen who cast their nets from dugout canoes. The most-prized fish are seacows, which are captured in the Bazam Channel to the west of the town. Their meat is a delicacy in Abu Dhabi, and the skins are used to make sandals. The pearling fleet of Abu Dhabi was once one of the best along the Coast, but the trade has fallen off in recent years to the dismay not only of the boat-owners but of the bedouin who signed on as part-time sailors in the pearling boats. Although sail is still king, many of the larger dhows going from Abu Dhabi up the coast to Bahrein and beyond now have auxiliary engines, which are invaluable for use against the prevailing north winds or calm stretches.

Politics on the Trucial Coast these days are influenced by the bad feeling between Sheikh ibn Sultan of Abu Dhabi and Sheikh ibn Maktum of Dibai, the largest town on the Coast, which lies about eighty miles to the east. The British stopped actual warfare between these two areas in 1947, but the feeling is still strong and occasionally flares up in the interior, where the tribesmen often adopt the politics of the coastal sheikhs. Dibai is the rendezvous of the Beni Yas tribe. It boasts quite a number of coral-rock houses with square ventilation towers rising from their roofs. Most of the houses, however, are shacks made of palm fronds. The large suqs on each side of a creek have dark and narrow streets roofed over with mats to keep off the blazing sun. The market places of Dibai are the crossroads of the area, and the streets are crowded with Persian merchants, Arab townsmen, Negro servants or slaves, Persian sailors and traders, Arab fishermen and pearlers, and bedouin who have come to town to purchase a six months' supply of necessities. There is also a sheltered lagoon used as a home port by coastal traders and a sadly depleted pearling fleet. Most of the Dibai shore line is a flat and barren waste traversed by small creeks and with little vegetation beyond coarse grass, clumps of mangroves, and an occasional small garden or palm grove around a well. In fact this stretch of coast is so flat that the little hill of Jebel Ali is the chief landmark. A long reef running parallel to the shore has been the grave-yard of many vessels, including the British East India Company's sloop "Elphinstone," which struck there in 1837.

The flying boat base at Dibai provided the Trucial Coast with one of its main contacts with the outside world and a substantial source of needed revenue. Considerable airplane traffic put down there during World War II, and BOAC seaplanes enroute to India stopped to refuel and to leave mail and passengers at the narrow creek beside the town. A trim launch took passengers across the peaceful waters of the creek to a rest house where they sipped coffee and exchanged gossip while their plane was being readied.

The chief merchants in Dibai, who made their money on pearls and harem silks, live in big low houses, half hidden behind high white walls. Although no oil has yet been found, one of the largest houses, with a long façade decorated with brightly painted columns, belongs to the representative of Petroleum Concessions, Limited. Up to quite recently this man was Basil Lermitte, probably the best-known and best-liked foreigner on the Trucial Coast. He was reported to know more about the local tribes than any other European and was on terms of equality with all the important sheikhs, among whom he had spent more than twenty years. He thought nothing of carrying thousands of rupees into the least-known parts of the country in order to pay concession fees. Lermitte regularly wore Arab dress, knew the local dialects, and was a sort of Lawrence of Arabia of the Trucial Coast. One reason he got along so well with the Arabs was his ability to sit with them in their tents for hours without speaking. As the Arabs say, he had "an understanding silence."

Most of the resident BOAC staff did not live at Dibai. Once the transient plane was airborne, they got into station wagons for a nine-mile race across the flat desert to the fort in the neighboring sheikhdom of Sharja where they lived. Sharja boasts a sizable date grove and a theatrical-looking fort, topped by a battery of powerful lights which can illuminate the desert far enough to discourage surprise attacks by bedouin night raiders. The fort goes back to pirate days of the nineteenth century, but the British have renovated it, and the quarters of the top officials contained teakwood furniture from India and were well supplied with British magazines and cool drinks. Teak is also widely used in the Sharja shipyards for the building of pearling and fishing vessels.

Nearby are the quarters of the RAF and the building used by the United States Air Transport Command in World War II. Although the Sharja air strip is excellent in dry weather, even the limited rains of the Trucial Coast winter turn it into a sea of mud, and the steadily declining air traffic does not justify the cost of a hard surface. Because the range of modern airplanes is increasing, more and more planes fly

177

over Sharja, and the march of air progress has limited its use to emergency landings only.

In Sharja, facing the Gulf, is the residence of the British political officer. This has been the home of a series of experienced British civil servants, who advise the Sheikh on all his foreign affairs and many of his domestic problems as well. A quarter of a mile beyond is the fort of Sheikh Saqr ibn Sultan al Qasim, built by the Portuguese in the sixteenth century and still ornamented by cannon captured by his piratical forefathers from European ships. Sheikh Saqr is a young man of dignified and pleasing appearance. He succeeded his father who died in early 1951.

Like all Arab rulers he enjoys entertaining male guests at banquets. Sitting cross-legged around a white cloth spread on rugs, the guests work their way slowly through trays of boiled rice surmounted by roasted sheep and surrounded by dozens of plates piled high with vegetables. The Sheikh starts the meal by pulling off a piece of mutton from the nearest sheep with his bare hands and passing it to the honored guest. Next to the Sheikh's health, the recent rainfall if any, and oil, the main topic is Sharja's fast dwindling place in world aviation. Visitors depart promptly after coffee, their hair and beards well perfumed by the fragrant smoke of burning frankincense, which is passed to them just before they leave.

The paramount sheikhs of the Trucial Coast, such as Sheikh Saqr ibn Sultan, are appointed from the chief local family. All the land in Sharja belongs to the Sheikh. He levies all taxes, collects commissions on what business is done, and in addition receives a rental for the airfield and a landing fee for each craft that comes in. Even so he is not rich, and it is not surprising that he likes to speculate on the possibility that there is oil under his sheikhdom.

In the narrow streets of Sharja the most interesting architectural features are carved doors made of unvarnished teak and studded with brass knobs. The bazaar is not too spoiled by oil drillers ready to pay top prices for poor merchandise. Its little shaded stalls are bright with colored scarves, Persian rugs, curved daggers, and ornate bowls made out of kerosene cans. Some of the silver rings are particularly interesting, having been beaten out of silver coins and decorated with agate, jasper, jade, and other semiprecious stones. Drab, veiled figures of women wrapped in black slip silently by, but the men, clothed in robes of every color of the rainbow, stop to bargain or to pass idle hours in the little coffeeshops, sipping coffee and listening to monotonous Arab songs played on ancient phonographs.

From the point of view of the Westerner, the pleasantest thing at Sharja is the smooth beach near a small suburb called Hera. The white sands of this beach are sprinkled with shells of every conceivable color and shape, while the water, which is too shallow for sharks, is ideal for surf riding and swimming. If Sharja ever becomes an oil center, Hera will be its Riviera.

Five miles north and east of Sharja is the town of Ajman, capital of ten square miles of desert and a deep creek. The town itself is carefully laid out with paved streets and white houses surrounded by ponds and gardens. Close by rises one of the finest pirate forts on the Trucial Coast, complete with buttresses and towers of brown sandstone. Its walls are still pocked with bullet holes and surmounted by ancient cannon, some of which go back to the early Portuguese ships of the sixteenth century.

Rashid ibn Humeid, the Sheikh of Ajman, is a good-looking man in his late thirties, tall, light skinned, and blue eyed. He is a great hunter, and the palace is decorated with the horns of beautiful gazelles he has shot. His chief interest is his stud of Arab horses, most of which came from King Ibn Saud's stables at Riyadh. The four dozen stallions and mares roam at will in the courtyard of the fort during the daytime and are sheltered at night under a shed built along the inner walls. Like most Arabs, the Ajmanis do not use halters but fasten their horses by their hind legs. Sheikh Rashid's stud averages about fourteen hands in height, with full haunches, broad heads, little ears, and small noses. Their manes and tails are worn long, and most of them are white or light gray in color. They are very gentle and obey the knee and voice of a rider whom they know. Because water and fodder are both very scarce, these are almost the only horses to be found on the Trucial Coast.

A few miles east of Ajman is the little fly-infested settlement of Al Hamriya, the Red Town, so called from the color of its five-towered fort. About thirteen miles beyond is the sheikhdom and town of Umm al Qaiwain, as dreary a sand-blown collection of water towers, huts, and adobe houses as exists in Arabia. With piracy prohibited, pearling in a depression, and the time-honored and manly sport of feuding with the neighboring sheikhdoms reduced to a minimum by the British, the inhabitants depend for a living on fishing, which is sometimes good, and farming, which is always poor.

From Umm al Qaiwain the desert track runs up the coast along a flat plain, "rich" in mirages, which the Arabs say are caused by a thin layer of salt and silica on the surface of the ground. For short periods in the spring the plain becomes green and even boasts a few flowers.

The capital of this part of the Trucial Coast is the town of Ras al Khaima, which means "promontory of the tent." The Persians occupied it until 1744, when they were driven out after a fierce fight. It is now the headquarters of the once-dreaded Jawasmi tribe, whose ruler is Sheikh Saqr ibn Muhammad. Like all towns in this part of Arabia, it has a small fort to keep out raiders from the desert. But in contrast to most of the other hamlets, it has a good supply of fresh water, and the fishing is particularly fine in the lagoon behind the town.

Beyond Ras al Khaima is the small port of Rams with a diminutive date grove. Twelve miles farther east is the little settlement of Shuam, which marks the end of the Trucial Coast. Although the inhabitants of Shuam make their living by fishing, they have their homes over a mile from the sea in a ravine full of palm trees and blessed with sixteen wells. On the beach near the town is a mound sixty feet high called Al Sanaim, meaning "the Idol." This was probably a site of pre-Islamic worship, and the mound might be worth excavating. The Persian-looking tomb of a Moslem holy man, Sheikh Zoahair, a battered structure of coral stone, stands nearby. In the wetter hollows are carefully irrigated vegetable gardens, and figs, melons, and pomegranates grow in spots.

As one drives eastward from Ras al Khaima, the foothills of the Shamailiya Mountains come down closer to the sea, while the eight-thousand-foot peaks of the main Hajar range of Oman can be seen faintly in the distance, masses of black basalt and red sandstone piled up against the pale-blue sky. During the cool months of the year these foothills are pleasant to live in and the bedouin camp there in numbers. Then for a few weeks the dry beds of the wadies run with water, and the spring rains draw a cloak of thin green grass across the upland meadows.

These mountains are inhabited by tribes who are among the least-known and most primitive peoples of Arabia. They speak a dialect of Arabic found nowhere else, and some authorities believe them to be descendants of the original inhabitants of the peninsula; the Arabs say they are the descendants of Sinbad the Sailor. Many of them still live in caves or else dig pits which they roof over with acacia logs and earth, making a dark but comparatively cool dwelling. Although basically shepherds, at some seasons of the year "the more civilized" of them come down to the coast, where they fish and even work in the date gardens. Their ruler is Sheikh Hasan ibn Muhammad, who in 1930 refused permission to a British survey party to land on Ras al Masandam. When the British carried on a "humane bombardment," calculated to terrify rather than to kill the inhabitants, a small boat came alongside the H.M.S. "Lupin," and Sheikh Hasan himself came aboard to surrender.[2]

The bedouin of the interior of the Trucial Coast are a law unto themselves, hostile to foreigners and Christians and suspicious of both the Sultan of Muscat and the sheikhs of the Coast. There are many blood feuds still extant among these tribesmen, and so great is their love of fighting that they will often hire out as soldiers of fortune to one or another of the Trucial sheikhs who compete for their support by gifts and comparatively lavish hospitality. Under these circumstances the interior of the Coast is in a perpetual state of tension, alarm, or even actual warfare, and travelers have to go heavily armed as a protection against banditry. A notorious outlaw, Duailan, called the "Cat," was killed six years ago after committing many robberies and murders.

One of the more important age-old feuds is that between the Yaman and Nizar tribes, a struggle which has disrupted the Oman area for years. Such major feuds mean more to the tribesmen than wealth, and as a result they have tried to prevent European exploration of the Trucial Coast hinterlands in the belief that the Westerners would put a stop to the feuds. Although conditions are now slightly more settled, the Manasir tribe was attacked in January 1948 by a feuding party from Dibai and lost fifty-two men.

Personal danger on the Trucial Coast is not confined to the inner fastnesses of the Shamailiya Mountains. In contrast to Saudi Arabia, where Ibn Saud has put an end to intertribal wars, raids still occur. The attacks are usually made during the quarter-moon, which gives enough light to see but not enough to be seen. The bedouin robbers study their objective carefully and swoop down just before dawn, often making a clean getaway before their raid is discovered. So bold are these raiders that in 1944 bedouin entered the RAF and American camps at Sharja, and the raid was not discovered until the medical officer was awakened by a bedouin trying to steal the blanket off his bed. Once they have collected blankets, cooking utensils, rugs, jewelry, or even human captives, who are held for ransom or sold as slaves, the robbers slip off into

[2] Bertram Thomas, *Alarms and Excursions in Arabia*, pp. 240–254.

181

the hinterland of the desert, which is outside the jurisdiction of any of the coastal sheikhs.

The oasis of Buraimi is a favorite hangout of these raiders and is also known for its slave market. Recent reports quote Arab boys selling there for 2,000 rupees, Arab girls for 1,500 rupees, and Negroes at 1,000 rupees. Stern justice is meted out to robbers and slave snatchers if they are caught—"justice" which may include whipping, branding, or the cutting off of a hand or foot or both. But the raids continue and will do so until the area is dominated by a single strong ruler, or until the development of oil, gold, tin, or other natural resources lifts it out of its depressed state.

Buraimi came into world prominence in late 1952 and 1953 when its neighbors clashed with Saudi Arabia over the location of the border. The British backed Abu Dhabi and Muscat against the Saudis, and the resulting friction brought out once again the necessity for delimiting boundaries on the peninsula in this oil age.

In addition to raids by robber bands, the various sheikhdoms of the Trucial Coast still carry on occasional wars among themselves. One of these occurred in 1940 between Sharja and Dibai, growing out of the intrigues of one of the wives of Sheikh Said ibn Maktum of Dibai. Cannon fire was exchanged between the forts of the two sheikhs, and such balls as failed to find their mark were retrieved from the desert under cover of night to be shot over again. When the fort at Dibai was attacked, Husa Umm Rashid, the wife who had started the trouble, personally led the defense. After the first man was wounded, the British political agent stopped the fighting and mediated a peaceful settlement.

A struggle of similar proportions occurred in the spring of 1948 between the inhabitants of Ajman and the Manasir tribes when the Ajmanis objected to where the Manasir were pasturing their flocks. Once again the British agent settled the dispute. Apart from incidents of personal bravery, the history of these "wars" is utterly boring, and their only result is to keep down the size of the population, stifle trade, and destroy productive gardens. They are modern examples of the feuds which comprised what the Arabs refer to as the "Days of the Arabs" in the "Times of Ignorance" before Mohammed; such feuds show how little some parts of Arabia have changed in the last twelve hundred years.

Decade by decade the Trucial Coast is drying up. If the inhabitants are to expect anything other than a slow decline in their already low standard of living, three possibilities lie before them: the discovery and development of oil; a rebirth of their shipping industry, directed not at piracy but at trade; or the resettlement of most of the population in some part of the Arab world better supplied with water. Otherwise they will continue to present the sad spectacle of a basically seafaring people who can no longer make an adequate living from the sea and whose land is drying up under their feet. Luckily for the people of these sheikhdoms, the first of these possibilities has materialized with the discovery of oil near Abu Dhabi.

XIV

Muscat: Our Oldest
Near Eastern Friend

OUR oldest treaty with an Arab
state is with the Sultan of Morocco and was signed in 1787. The second
oldest is with the Sultan of Muscat, a small sultanate at the southeastern corner of Arabia. It was signed in 1833, and since then the Sultanate
of Muscat and Oman has changed hardly at all.

The treaty was due in part to the ablest, most powerful, and most
famous of all Muscati sultans, Said ibn Sultan, who ruled over Muscat
and the island of Zanzibar during the early nineteenth century. During
his youth Muscat had been governed by his uncle as regent. When his
uncle refused to resign and instead plotted the young man's death,
the alert Ibn Sultan requested an audience and promptly stabbed the
ruler. The regent, although wounded, was well enough to escape from
the palace, and the young prince was told by his friends that his work
was only half done. Leaping on his horse, he overtook his uncle and
pinned him to the ground with a spear. After coming to the throne in
1807, Said consolidated his power and became rich and greatly respected. His navy consisted of seventy-five ships carrying from four to
fifty-six guns each, manned by officers educated in India. He even gave
a ship of the line to the government of Great Britain, an act which
showed remarkable confidence, since Britain at that time was mistress
of the seven seas. When Said ibn Sultan made the pilgrimage to Mecca
in the year 1824 in his flagship, the fifty-gun frigate "Liverpool," the

184

Turkish Government gave him an official welcome, and his entire stay in the Hejaz was a personal triumph.

Sailors and pirates from Muscat had long wielded partial control over the east African coast. Said ibn Sultan established a base on the island of Zanzibar, which up to then had been little more than a mud flat. There he built a palace and introduced the cultivation of cloves, which soon became the staple product of the island. He set up a widespread system of commercial agents, who ranged from central Africa, where Livingstone met them at the Great Lakes, to Calcutta, Persia, the Dutch Indies, and even China.

Thanks to this organization, he became very rich. The great treasure which he amassed was supposedly hidden either in Zanzibar or in Muscat, but when he died in September 1856 on the frigate "Victoria," the secret of its location went with him. On his deathbed he continually called for Colonel Hammarton, the British consul at Zanzibar, and it is believed he may have wished to tell that official the hiding place of his wealth, but he died before the colonel arrived at his bedside. It is a fact, however, that he left sixty thousand crowns to each of his twenty-four sons and twenty-nine thousand crowns to each of his twelve daughters. The only known picture of him is in the Peabody Museum at Salem, the American port most active in trade with Zanzibar, and shows a short man with an overlarge head, enormous eyes, and white mustache and beard.

Sultan Said signed the treaty of 1833 with the United States largely because a New England trader by the name of Edmund Roberts had lost money in Zanzibar. This energetic Yankee merchant borrowed enough cash in 1827 to charter the brig "Mary Ann" and sail her to the island of Zanzibar. There his hopes of making money were dashed by the fact that the government had a strict monopoly on trade, and citizens of countries that did not have treaties with the government were at a great disadvantage. Roberts was not a man to be stopped easily, and he protested in person to Said ibn Sultan. As a result of these talks, Roberts became a good friend of the Sultan, who suggested to him that his business would be much improved by closer relations between the United States and Muscat. Captain Roberts returned to America, where he persuaded the Secretary of the Navy Levi Woodbury to appoint him confidential agent to open negotiations.[1] In March 1832 Roberts sailed from Boston in the United States sloop of war

[1] Edmund Roberts, *Embassy to the Eastern Courts of Kochin-China, Siam, and Muscat in the Sloop of War "Peacock" during the Years 1832, 1833, 1834.*

"Peacock" armed with authority "to meet, confer, treat, and negotiate with His Highness Syeede Syede ibn Sultan, the Imaum of Muscat."

After various adventures, diplomatic and otherwise, the "Peacock" with the American emissary on board arrived on the evening of September 18, 1833, at the hot, rock-bound harbor or cove of Muscat, where she anchored under the ruins of the Portuguese forts on the black, sun-baked cliffs. Roberts reported that a boat was sent ashore to tell the Sultan of his arrival and returned "laden with abundance of exquisite grapes of four different kinds, ripe dates, just plucked from the trees, and strung together like large golden beads, refreshening to the taste and by no means too luscious or cloying to the appetite." [2] The boat also brought a message from the Sultan congratulating the Americans on their safe arrival and expressing the Sultan's gratitude that, for the first time, an American warship had visited his port.

Edmund Roberts noted that the town of Muscat had about twelve thousand inhabitants with five thousand more living nearby. He mentioned seeing weavers of fine checked cloth for turbans, as well as blacksmiths, coppersmiths, ropemakers, carpenters, and sandal makers. The New England sea captain was particularly struck with the suq where perfumed Arab dandies shopped for well-oiled slaves, cashmere shawls, rhinoceros-hide shields, and silver-hilted daggers.[3]

He commented on the number of small fish that abounded in the cove of Muscat and the prowess of the native divers who, he reported, could remain under water for more than two minutes. A humorous touch was provided by his description of a whale known as Muscat Tom, which had been a daily visitor to the harbor for more than twenty years and which had rid the place of sharks. Muscat Tom's only absence from the cove occurred when he disappeared for a few days and then returned with a lady whale, who proved a "helpmate unto him" in clearing the harbor of pests.[4]

After eating sweets and drinking some cardamom-flavored coffee at the palace, Roberts presented a letter from the President and made a speech about closer relations with Muscat. The Sultan thereupon agreed to give American vessels and their crews most-favored-nation treatment and to sign a treaty of commerce and friendship with the United States. One of the most interesting features of this treaty was Article 5, which read:

If any vessel of the United States shall suffer shipwreck on any part of the Sultan's domains the persons escaping the wreck shall be taken care of and

[2] *Ibid.*, p. 352.   [3] *Ibid.*, pp. 354–355.   [4] *Ibid.*, p. 356.

hospitably entertained at the expense of the Sultan until they shall find an opportunity to be returned to their country—for the Sultan never receives any remuneration whatever for rendering succor to the distressed and the property saved from such wreck shall be carefully preserved and delivered to the owner or the Consul of the U.S. or to any authorized agent.

The Sultan visited the "Peacock" on August 4 with much pomp and ceremony. When, three days later, she sailed from Muscat, Roberts took with him his copy of the treaty and a letter to President Andrew Jackson full of cordial and affectionate greetings from the Sultan.

The treaty thus secured was ratified by the United States Senate in June 1834, but Robert's adventures in Muscat were not over, for he was commissioned to exchange the ratification. Once again setting sail in the good ship "Peacock," he touched at Zanzibar and then headed for Muscat.[5] All went smoothly until the six-hundred-ton man-of-war piled up on the coral reefs off the island of Masirah, which lies only a few miles off the southern coast of Oman. Three piratical-looking sailing dhows promptly appeared, crowded to the gunwales with armed men. Seizing their pikes and cutlasses, the crew of the "Peacock" hid behind the bulwark, except for a few sailors who ostentatiously sharpened their swords. When, after consultation, some of the Arabs scrambled aboard, all the American sailors leapt to their feet waving their weapons in a demonstration. After announcing that they were subjects of the Sultan of Muscat and would take the message of ratification to him for a thousand dollars, the visitors slipped overboard and swam away.

The next day the ship's cutter, with Roberts on board, went to Muscat to ask assistance of the Sultan. Every effort was made to get the "Peacock" off the reefs before she was broken up by the sea or before the various pirate craft closed in on her. By frequent shots with their "long toms," the crew of the "Peacock" were able to keep the pirates at a distance while they lightened the ship and at last towed her off the reefs. Setting all sails, they outdistanced the Arabs and, after doubling the promontory of Ras al Hadd, they met a small Arab dhow with Roberts on board, coming back to rescue them. No sooner had the "Peacock" anchored in Muscat Cove than the decks were crowded with Muscati visitors who told the Americans that, although many vessels had been caught on the reefs of Masirah Island, the "Peacock" was the only one ever known to have gotten off. The Sultan received the ratified treaty with pleasure, and in accordance with the treaty offered to replace the

[5] This second trip is described in detail in *A Voyage around the World* by W. S. Ruschenberger, ship's doctor of the "Peacock."

supplies that had been lost in the shipwreck, including the eleven guns that had been thrown overboard to lighten the ship.

Soon afterward the officers of the "Peacock" dined with the Sultan, who, following local custom, withdrew after entering the banquet hall in order that his guests might relax and enjoy the repast. According to Dr. Ruschenberger, the ship's doctor, the meal was sufficient for two hundred Englishmen.

After this the "Peacock" stayed a few days longer in Muscat, giving the doctor a good chance to observe the local customs. According to a Muscati informant:

Women spend their whole time in perfuming, dressing, and decorating themselves. . . . A gentleman's wife must have at least four Cashmere shawls, a green, a blue, a red, and a white; then she must have a ruby or a diamond ring for every toe as well as for every finger. . . . Our law allows us four wives, and as many concubines as one pleases; and it is necessary to have some as servants to your wife. For that reason, every gentleman has three or four Circassian or Abyssinian slaves, who soon become as jealous as the wife herself.[6]

On the morning of October 10, 1834, Captain Roberts and his fellow Americans took leave of the hospitable Sultan. They refused the horses which he offered but gave him a map of the United States, an American flag, a book of American poems, and a number of cut-glass lamps. So successful was Roberts in his stimulation of American trade with the sultanate that, whereas only one American ship was reported to have anchored in Muscat harbor in the seven years preceding the treaty, no less than nine American vessels called there in the first year after it was signed.

The first American to take up residence in what is now Muscat and Oman was the cabin boy of the American merchantman "Essex." This vessel had been captured by pirates from the Yemeni port of Mocha, and the whole crew was killed except for one ten-year-old boy, who was kept by the pirate chief. The next year this pirate, Mohammed Akil by name, conquered the province of Dhufar on the southern coast of Arabia, just west of Oman. According to an Englishman who traveled in Dhufar about 1836, the cabin boy had become a Moslem and lived with his wife and family in the town of Salalah.

As the nineteenth century progressed and fewer Yankee clippers sailed the seas, American trade with Muscat declined. Our prestige

[6] *Ibid.*, p. 73.

waned and there came a time when the American consul and the American flag were not treated with proper respect in Muscat, a fact which caused President Fillmore to write a letter to the Sultan in May 1851. This epistle is so different from modern diplomatic notes, and so in keeping with the spirit of those years when a youthful United States was beginning to grow strong and, in a naïve and leisurely way, was interesting itself in the far corners of the earth, that it is quoted here:

To our Great and Good Friend,
  His Majesty Seyed Syeed Bin,
    Sultan of Muscat and its Dependencies.
  I hope your health is good. I pray that your days may be many, and that your reign may continue to be peaceful, prosperous, and glorious and that your shadow may never be less.
  One of my predecessors, Mr. James Knox Polk, received several letters from you. You often inquired about his health. I am sorry to tell you that he no longer is an inhabitant of the earth. The last President was General Zachary Taylor, about whose great battles and victories in Mexico you often talked with Consul Charles Ward. My heart sinks within me when I tell you that he too has joined the ranks of the Immortals. . . .
  The Treaty between our countries is now the Supreme Law of the Land. I cannot change it without the consent of the Great Council of the Nation, the Senate of the United States. Your vessels can visit all the ports of the United States on the same terms as our own. They may enter our numerous harbors in the Atlantic, the Gulf of Mexico, or those of our new State of California on the Pacific, where the quartz rocks of the mountains are filled with gold, and the rivers flow over golden beds, and the sands of the ocean Shore Sparkle with the richest ore.
  From the region of ice which bounds the United States on the North to the flowery land of the orange on the South, is a journey of one hundred days, and from the Eastern Shores, which receive the first beams of the rising Sun, to those on the West, where rest his Setting rays is one hundred and fifty days journey, and this immense country is not a sandy waste, but filled with populous cities, traversed by mighty rivers, and crowned with lofty mountains. By railroads or in Steamboats, the citizens of this immense country pass from one place to another with inconceivable rapidity. From the Seat of Government at Washington I send my commands in a few minutes by the Lightning Telegraph, to all parts of the United States, and they are obeyed.
  I speak of these things not for the sake of boasting; but in the Spirit of Friendship and Peace, and that you may know that all parts of this country are open to you and your Ships and your people for the purposes of Commerce and Trade. I shall welcome in all our ports the Ships which bear your

189

flag. Our vessels may visit all the ports in your dominions. This right is secured by Treaty; and the faith of the Treaty must be observed. Great and
Good Prince: How can you think it just that while we open so many hundred
ports to you, you would wish to confine us to a single port, or prevent our
Ships from going to all parts of your dominions. Great and Good Friend, this
cannot be. Free trade everywhere is desirable, for so can the various produc-
tions of different countries best be distributed throughout the world. I hope
the traffic of our country with yours is mutually beneficial. I hope it will continue and increase. . . .

Your Good Friend

MILLARD FILLMORE

PRESIDENT OF THE UNITED STATES OF AMERICA.

President Fillmore's requests were complied with, the former American
position in Muscat was restored, and trade increased slightly.

Sultan Said died in 1856 and his two oldest sons quarreled over the
succession. The case was submitted for decision to Lord Canning, who
was then Viceroy of India. He decided in 1861 that the island of Zanzibar should be independent of Muscat and that one son should take
Zanzibar and the other Muscat. The next year the British guaranteed
the independence of Muscat.

The most important development in American-Muscat relations during the last years of the nineteenth century was the setting up of a
branch of the American-Arabian mission of the Dutch Reformed
Church at Muscat. The Reverend Peter J. Zwemer, who had joined the
mission at Basra, visited Muscat in 1893.[7] The reports that he sent
back on the possibilities for missionary work were so glowing that he
was allowed to set up a third station of the American-Arabian mission
in that city. The work had a slow start, for tribal wars made travel
difficult and in February 1895 the town of Muscat was captured by the
bedouin. Over two hundred lives were lost, the mission house and the
shop where religious literature was sold were looted, and Peter Zwemer
was forced to take refuge behind the strong walls of the British Consulate. Conditions were quieter next year, and the missionaries and their
converts traveled widely in Muscat and Oman. One of these visited
the Trucial Coast and actually sold a hundred Bibles, or portions
thereof, a remarkable example of salesmanship in a Moslem country.

Not long after this, eighteen Negro boys who had been rescued from
a sinking dhow were placed in the care of Reverend Peter Zwemer,

---

[7] Much of the background on American missionary activity in Muscat has been
obtained from the Reverend S. M. Zwemer's book, *Arabia: The Cradle of Islam.*

who started a school for them. In addition, he obtained a small hand printing press and put out the first Christian tract ever printed in Arabia: *Mohammed or Christ, on Whom Do You Rely?* When the heat and fevers of Muscat proved too much for Dr. Zwemer, he returned to America in 1898 and was "called to his reward." As the Reverend H. M. Cobb, secretary of the mission, wrote of him, "When one considers all that he endured, the wonder is not that he died, but that he lived as long as he did."

The climate of Muscat seems to be especially hard on missionaries. The Rev. Dr. Zwemer's place at Muscat was taken by the Reverend F. J. Barny. After a few months he came down with typhoid and had to be sent to India, being succeeded by the Reverend George E. Stone. But although he was only twenty-nine years of age, the heat of Muscat overcame him, and he died of sunstroke at the coastal town of Barka in June 1899. In spite of setbacks, the American mission continued its work under Dr. Dirk Dykstra, a man of iron constitution. The number of converts was small, but the school proved helpful and the clinic rendered invaluable service.

In May 1913 Homer Brett, who was then the American consul at Muscat, came to the conclusion that American trade and the missionaries could continue in Muscat without the help of a consular officer.

He wrote in an unclassified dispatch to the State Department:

So far as I am able to discover, the total result of six years of effort along trade promotion lines by my predecessors and myself has been the selling of two motor boats and two small pumps, none of which, owing to the mechanical ignorance of the natives, gave satisfactory service. . . .

The only American citizens resident in Oman are missionaries. They are in no way in need of protection, for the same organization safely and successfully operates in Bahrein and Kuwait, where they are without access to a consular officer.

There has not been an American vessel in Muscat harbor since the year 1897, and previous to that there was not one after 1855. There never has been but one case tried in the consular court, and that was many years ago and for a trivial misdemeanor. The only real work consists of certifying some 30 or 40 invoices of dates each year, and this could be done as well and much more cheaply by a consular agent.

From the personal point of view of the consul, Muscat is not a bad post. The European community is small but pleasant, the cost of living is not unduly high, the climate, though bad, is not unendurable, but it is respectfully submitted that two years of practically enforced idleness is not good training for one beginning a consular career.

The wheels of government ground slowly, and it was almost two years before a telegram reached Muscat closing the consulate. Meanwhile, World War I broke out, and the Germans aided the Imam, who ruled in the mountains of the interior, against the Sultan and his British allies, who kept a garrison of seven hundred men at Muscat. The troops of the Imam attacked the city but were beaten off in a bloody engagement which saved the city but was otherwise inconclusive. The end of World War I found the country divided between the Imam in the mountains and the coastal government at Muscat under Sultan Said Sultan, a younger ruler who bore the same name as his illustrious ancestor. In recent years the Imam has been overshadowed by Sheikh Suleiman ibn Taimur, the paramount sheikh of Oman, but authority remains divided between the men of the mountains and the men of the sea.

In November 1923 John Randolph, the American consul at Baghdad, paid a courtesy call on the Sultan of Muscat, after which another ten years of United States–Muscati relations slipped by uneventfully. Then, in order to celebrate the centenary of the United States–Muscat treaty, which Roberts had obtained, and to strengthen the ties of friendship between the United States and Muscat, a special diplomatic mission was sent out in March 1934, headed by the Arabist, Paul Knabenshue, American resident Minister at Baghdad. He was accompanied by his son, Dennis, and James S. Moose, Jr., secretary of the United States Legation there.

Leaving Basra, the party proceeded by slow steamer to the island of Bahrein, just then coming into prominence as a producer of oil. Sailing south again at a pace that seems most leisurely when compared with the airborne speed of most modern missions to Arabia, they crossed the Gulf to Bandar Abbas, where the tropical waters were full of jellyfish by day and phosphorus by night. Twenty-four hours later the steamer dropped anchor in the shadow of the Portuguese forts that dominate the harbor of Muscat, near steep and rocky cliffs painted with the names, written in English, of ships that had called there.

The mission [8] must have felt that they were re-enacting the Roberts mission, as once again a boatload of fruit came out to the ship, along with a welcome from the Sultan. A tour of the town showed that it had not grown since Roberts watched its coppersmiths and sandal makers,

[8] Some of the material on the Knabenshue mission has been taken from the article, "A Mission to Muscat," by Dennis Knabenshue, in the *Foreign Service Journal*, August 1934.

21. A deep-sea dhow in the port of Kuwait. (Photo of Gulf Oil Corporation.)

22. Sixteenth-century Portuguese fort guarding Matrah harbor in Muscat. (Photo by Harold T. Green.)

23. Skyscrapers of Shibam in the Hadhramaut. (Photo by the Expedition of the American Foundation for the Study of Man.)

but had actually lost in size. The slave market was no longer near the landing place, but it still existed in the interior of the country in spite of British restrictions. Inquiry among the missionaries showed also that the position of women had changed little since Dr. Ruschenberger looked into the matter through an "Arab gentleman with whom he became acquainted."

When twenty-four-year-old Sultan Said ibn Taimur al Busaid, who had succeeded to the throne two years before, received the Americans at the door of his palace and took them to the high, narrow throne-room, the ceremonies were almost identical with those that had greeted Edmund Roberts. A rich paste was served first, so sticky that it had to be followed by rose water and towels. Next came cups of cardamom-flavored coffee, followed immediately by pungent incense. Once the servants had left the room, the American Minister and the Sultan exchanged speeches of welcome. The Americans found the ruler receptive to their overtures and interested in better relations and more trade. That evening the Sultan gave a Muscati palace dinner on the floor of his banquet hall. There were no knives and forks, but the visitors and Muscati did ample justice to the huge platters of sheep, roasted whole, as well as to endless plates of rice, chicken, vegetables, cakes an inch thick, mangoes, and grapes that would have been "sufficient for two hundred Englishmen." At the end of the meal, servants brought water and towels to the Sultan and Minister Knabenshue, but the other guests kept their greasy hands in front of them until they had adjourned to an anteroom, where they too were met by numerous servants with brass vases full of water, soap, and towels. Like other Arabs, the Muscati feel that talk should be carried on before and not after dinner, so the incense was soon passed, and the Americans filed out into the warm night air.

The next afternoon Minister Knabenshue opened the new hospital of the American mission at a colorful, flag-decked ceremony attended by Prince Said Hammed as representative of the Sultan, a large number of other princes and Muscati officials, and the foreign colony, which numbered less than a dozen. The completion of this hospital was a great triumph for the Reverend Dirk Dykstra, who had served in Muscat for forty years.

Struggling to get permission to build a hospital, the Rev. Dr. Dykstra had been forced by lack of money to act as his own architect, contractor, and builder, studying house construction with reinforced concrete in order to put up the building. Even then there was no money

193

left over for plumbing, but luckily that most generous of the American friends in Arabia, Charles R. Crane, unexpectedly came to the help of the missionary and gave a complete set of modern plumbing to the hospital, thereby making it the most livable building in Muscat.

Four years later a letter addressed by the Sultan of Muscat to President Roosevelt and dated March 20, 1937, informed the President of the Sultan's desire to return the visit of Minister Knabenshue to Muscat by a trip to the United States. Roosevelt promptly invited the Sultan to be his guest in Washington. The Sultan traveled by way of India and the Far East, reaching San Francisco on February 19, accompanied by his uncle, Al Busaid, his aide, and secretary. On March 3, 1938, Sultan Said and his party, all in native dress, arrived in Washington, where they were formally received at the Union Station by Secretary of State Cordell Hull. For the first time in America the national anthem of Muscat was played by the United States Army Band. After short speeches of welcome, the Sultan was escorted to his hotel by a troop of cavalry. An observer well acquainted with the Sultan described him as "small, very neat, dresses nattily, is carefully groomed, uses very good and precise English, is retiring, super polite, offers others the precedence in entering or leaving a room or car, and appears somewhat shy."

The following day the Sultan lunched with President Roosevelt at the White House, viewed the sights of Washington, and was the guest of Secretary Hull at a state dinner in the evening. He next visited the Washington Navy Yard, which interested him because of the seafaring history of Muscat. After lunch with Colonel Wainwright, commanding officer of Fort Myer, he was the guest of honor at an exhibition cavalry drill and that night attended a dinner given for him by Under Secretary of State Sumner Welles. His visit to Washington wound up with a cruise down the Potomac to Mount Vernon on board the Secretary of the Navy's yacht "Sequoia." He sailed from New York on the "Queen Mary" on March 23, leaving behind him much good will, a letter of thanks to President Roosevelt, and a present of a gold dagger.

During World War II the United States found itself faced with the necessity of developing an air route to India that did not follow the Mediterranean. This meant crossing Africa below the bulge and continuing via Aden. In order to take care of emergency stops on the long hop from that British seaport to Karachi, arrangements were worked out with the Sultan of Muscat and Oman to permit the setting up of air strips near the town of Salalah, at the western tip of the Dhufar province of Oman, and on Masirah Island off southern Oman. Once the war was over, however, the American need for these air strips ended. Most of the equipment was removed, and it was decided to sell the rest to the Sultan of Muscat. Thus, in April 1946, eleven years after the visit of Minister Knabenshue, Muscat was again visited by an American Foreign Service officer when Consul Parker T. Hart, who had recently opened the consulate at Dhahran, flew down to Muscat for a short visit, accompanied by Commander I. L. Herring, USNR, of the Foreign Liquidation Commission in Cairo.[9]

Flying down from Dhahran, the plane refuelled at Sharja on the Trucial Coast. From there it continued south over the steep four-thousand-foot peaks of northern Oman, a virtual no man's land over which neither the sheikhs of the Trucial Coast, the Imam of the Oman, nor the Sultan of Muscat exercised much control. Although most of the lands bordering the Persian Gulf have been extensively explored and in some cases widely developed by Europeans, the Arabian side of the narrow entrance to the Gulf is hardly better known now by the Western world than it was three thousand years ago. And this in spite of the fact that the Sultanate of Muscat and Oman is really the "cork in the Persian Gulf bottle" and one of the most strategically located areas in the world.

The sultanate covers about eighty-two thousand square miles, an area slightly larger than that of its companion country, Yemen, which occupies a similar position at the southwest corner of the peninsula. Its population of less than a million, however, is only about one-fifth that of Yemen. Because of its eight hundred miles of coast, the bare and jagged mountains that cover much of the interior, the impassable desert that forms its western boundaries, and the hostility of its people to non-Moslems, the sultanate is a little-explored corner of Arabia.

Beyond the mountains the travelers looked down on the Omani coastal plain, which is known as the Batina, along which stretches one of the largest palm groves in the world. Although the interior of Muscat and Oman has less than four inches of rainfall a year, there is enough rain on the Batina to encourage intensive cultivation of date palms, the growing of wheat and many kinds of fruit, and the raising of cattle and poultry. The villages are a melting pot of nationalities: Arabs, Negroes, Persians, Iraqis, Indians, Hindus, Baluchis, and occa-

[9] For information on this mission to Muscat the author is indebted in large part to the writings and comments of Parker Hart, now Director of the Office of Near Eastern Affairs in the Department of State.

sionally a touch of Portuguese. Their houses are built of mats woven from palm leaves, large buildings are of mud, and forts and palaces are of stone. Many of the people are fishermen; sardines are one of the chief catches and are shipped by sailing dhows all over the Persian Gulf and the Indian Ocean. The sharks' fins caught by these fishermen go as far east as China. An important local industry is the manufacture of cotton canvas, much prized by captains of the local dhows for sails. A primitive motor road runs up the coast for more than two hundred miles north of Muscat. Travel on it, or in the interior, is usually by camel, horse, or donkey and is slow, expensive, difficult because of the lack of water, and dangerous because of the unsettled conditions among so many of the tribes.

The main activity of the people in the interior is farming, which has been suffering for many years from an increasing scarcity of water, although in the mountainous interior certain valleys are still well watered and produce dates, limes, peaches, apples, grains, and vegetables. The Muscatel grapes are not indigenous but are said to have been introduced by the Portuguese.

Sweeping south along the Batina, the plane flew over the small Omani seaport of Saham, about 140 miles north of Muscat. Here two American women missionaries operate one of the world's most isolated clinics. The older of these, Dr. Sarah Longworth Hosmon, was for a long time head of the Women's Hospital of the Reformed Church at Muscat. In 1938, however, she decided to organize her own clinic and chose Saham as the site of her labors. After working there alone for more than seven years, she was joined by a youthful assistant. They have done much to bring the benefits of Western medicine to the inhabitants of Saham. In the spring of 1949 this clinic asked help from the American Consulate at Dhahran in the rapid delivery of certain much needed medicines. The supplies were flown to Dhahran, where they were packed for a parachute drop by the air-rescue detachment of the Dhahran air base. A B-29 rescue plane from the base then took off with the package, flew to Saham, and dropped the medicines to the waiting missionaries, saving many weeks compared with the time of delivery by boat.

An hour and a half out of Sharja the plane flew over Sib, the seaside resort of Muscat, to which half the population of the capital moves each summer. Nearby was the town of Matrah, the commercial center of the sultanate, with a population of about ten thousand. Five miles south, in the almost land-locked harbor of Muscat, the partly submerged superstructure of a British steamer lay where it had been torpedoed in World War II by a Japanese U-boat—a reminder of how near the two halves of the German-Japanese axis came to joining forces.

Circling the mountains behind Muscat and Matrah, the pilot finally located the air strip, a short, rough, unpaved gravel runway surrounded by basalt ridges. These hills were not only dangerous in themselves but produced treacherous air currents. In addition, a perpendicular cliff of sheer rock rose up four hundred feet directly at the southern end of the landing field. Under the skillful handling of the Air Transport Command pilot, the C-47 sat down safely, in spite of several concrete rollers that the Arabs had left on the field.

There, the party found a green Ford touring car, out of which sprang forty-two-year-old Dr. William Wells Thoms, American medical missionary and head of the Matrah hospital. He gave them a cordial welcome and took them, in two installments, along a rough road through a narrow pass to Matrah. Driving slowly through the narrow, crowded streets of that city, they came to the high stone wall that enclosed the Knox Memorial Hospital, where they met Mrs. Thoms, looking astoundingly fresh and attractive for a white woman living in so warm and isolated a country. Muscat and Matrah are the hottest towns of the Arabian Peninsula; temperatures of 125 degrees in the shade are not uncommon in the summer noontimes, while the nights are only a little cooler.

A quick trip around the twin cities soon showed the travelers that, although they were in the "air age," Matrah and Muscat were not. The American missionaries and the small British colony lived in an almost unchanged, eighteenth-century Arab world. Apart from the mission, the British Consulate, and the cable office, practically the only signs of the twentieth century were a handful of automobiles, less than a hundred old-style telephones with hand cranks and curved mouthpieces, and a few scattered electric lights.

The following morning Consul Hart, Commander Herring, and their companions proceeded to the palace, where a short, round-faced man came forward to meet them with smiling eyes and outstretched hands. It was His Highness, Said ibn Taimur, the thirty-seven-year-old Sultan. It has been said that Muscat has one foot in Arabia and the other in India. The Sultan's dress bore this out, for he wore an Arab *aba* or robe, while his head was covered by a bright Indian turban.

After introducing the visitors to the only other person in the room, Said Ahmed ibn Ibrahim, the Minister of Internal Affairs, the Sultan

197

sat down in a large chair between two windows with an old-fashioned crank telephone and a push bell beside him. In contrast to most Arabian throne rooms, which are cluttered with as many gilt chairs and overstuffed sofas as can be placed around the walls, this marble-floored chamber contained divans and just enough seats around the "throne" for the visitors and the Minister.

Following a friendly talk with the Sultan which settled most of the problems at hand, the party took their leave and then paid a courtesy call on the British Consulate. It is an impressive establishment, surrounded by a very high stone wall so that it looks like a small fort, dominated by a huge mast with a yardarm and crow's nest. The British consul is the only representative of a Western nation regularly stationed at Muscat. He also bears the British designation "Political Agent." However, unlike the political agents in the Persian Gulf sheikhdoms, he does not handle the foreign affairs of the sultanate. He does enjoy extraterritorial powers over British subjects in Muscat, and his importance is further increased by the advisory role which he sometimes plays in Muscat's internal and external affairs. The best-known British official ever to be stationed at Muscat as adviser to the Sultan was the explorer, Bertram Thomas.

Almost nothing is manufactured locally, so that imports are about twice the value of exports, producing an unfavorable balance of trade which is partly made up by a small British subsidy. A high percentage of the imports is brought in by the two British steamships—one "up" and one "down"—which call at Muscat each month on their run between India and the upper Persian Gulf. The visits of these vessels are great occasions for the foreign colony, for they are the only real source of mail and supplies from the Western world. Most of the Arab imports from Zanzibar, Aden, the sheikhdoms of the Persian Gulf, and the small ports of India are brought in by dhows.

The British keep no troops in Muscat, but a retired British army officer is employed by the Sultan as the commander of his troops. There is a British-operated government hospital as well as an office of the far-flung British communications company, Cable and Wireless, Ltd.

The visitors spent a hot night on the roof of the American mission at Matrah and then took off again by plane. Flying southeast down the wide coastal plain over the city of Sur, a town of about seven thousand inhabitants, they rounded Ras al Hadd, the southeasternmost corner of the Arabian Peninsula, and came, after an hour and a half, to the air strip on the flat and desolate island of Masirah. After a short and very hot inspection, the travelers flew on, following the coast line westward to where the six-thousand-foot mountains came closer to the sea until they formed a high cliff, dazzling white in the sunshine beside the blue water. Beyond lay the broad bay and city of Salalah, capital of the Muscati province of Dhufar and the pleasantest town in the whole country. The Sultan and his court come here during the summer, for the air is fresh and the nights are cool all the year around, in contrast to the terribly hot nights in Muscat and Matrah when the black basalt hills give off the heat which they have absorbed during the day.

Under the guidance of the English-speaking chief of customs, the visitors drove ten miles in the cool of the evening from the airport to the Sultan's newly built palace. They found it surrounded by broad, brick terraces and many acres of flower gardens, fruit groves, and lawns, irrigated by a clear bubbling stream flowing down from the mountains a dozen miles to the north. There the Americans were served refreshing fruit drinks beside a crystal-clear pool. Reclining in easy chairs, they listened to the sound of the running water and understood why the Arabs feel that heaven is a well-watered garden. The palace officials told of hunting trips in the grassy plateaus and green mountains of Dhufar, an area which has been seen by only a few Westerners, including Bertram Thomas and Wendell Phillips, who have reported that it contains some interesting ruins.

The province of Dhufar has been in a state of depression for almost two thousand years, since the collapse of its virtual monopoly of incense production. Furthermore, its isolated position keeps out most visitors and greatly restricts imports and exports. Salalah harbor has little protection against the monsoon winds, so that it is virtually useless for five months of the year. The overland journey from Muscat is impossible for motors and still takes twenty days by camel, while it is even longer and more difficult to get there from Aden. Thus the twenty thousand inhabitants of Dhufar province still live much as they did two thousand years ago, dress their hair in long black braids, wear little more than loincloths, and continue to be suspicious of all strangers, especially those who are non-Moslem.

Because of the air strip at Sharja, the Trucial Coast sees some Europeans come and go. The inhabitants of Yemen are becoming accustomed to meeting jeeps on their rocky trails, and the Arabs themselves are bringing automobiles to the isolated wadies of the Hadhramaut. The twentieth-century, however, has put only one foot inside Muscat and has not penetrated at all into Oman and Dhufar provinces. Unless oil or minerals are discovered there, it seems likely that life in the coastal palm groves and hot mountain valleys of the Sultanate will continue its leisurely pace, much as it did before the good ship "Peacock" dropped anchor under the basalt cliffs of Muscat harbor more than a century ago.

XV

The Colony of Aden:

England's Arabian Gibraltar

FEW ports in the world have a more fearsome reputation for bad climate than Aden. The average traveler spending a few hours ashore there while his ship is being bunkered fills a page in his diary with a doleful description of barren rocks, stone water tanks, and stifling heat. In fact, most people's attitude toward Aden is summed up in the story of the American consul who, after two years' service there, was due to be relieved. One day he received a wire from the State Department in Washington telling him that his relief had been appointed, but the next day there came another wire saying that the man had resigned from the Foreign Service. This happened twice; then at last a relief finally arrived. In a burst of enthusiasm, the consul took him to the club. There was no ice, the fans were not running, and the temperature was over 100 degrees in the shade. After a quick stop at the consular residence where the plumbing had broken down, the consul took the new man up to the top of a hill to show him the panorama of Aden harbor and get a breath of cooler air. Unfortunately, the only air stirring was sultry and powdered with sand. Looking down from the hilltop, the new man said, "What ship is that next to the one I came on?"

"That's our monthly boat from India to the United States," said the consul. "On her way out next month she will bring you all sorts of ice cream and frozen foods."

"No, she won't," said the new appointee. "I'm resigning and going back to the States on her this time."

From May through September Aden is as hot and humid as Washington, D.C., at five o'clock of a sultry August afternoon. May and September are the worst months, for then the monsoon is changing and there are weeks on end of dead, suffocating calm. From October to April, however, when the northeast monsoon is blowing, Aden is comparatively cool, and during November, December, and January the climate is actually pleasant. Now that air conditioning has come, the white man can at last live and work in Aden all year round without losing his health and energy.

In spite of the heat, most Americans who have been stationed there develop a strange fondness of Aden. The hotel is a pleasant-enough gathering place, there are adequate shops and several movie theaters, and the social life of the official, military, and business colonies has much to recommend it. Because of the short hours of work, hardy enthusiasts of golf, tennis, polo, sailing, swimming, fishing, hunting, soccer, and even mountain climbing have a chance to enjoy these sports before the ritualistic "sundowner," which divides the activities of the day from those of the evening. Cocktail parties are frequent and lengthy, and there is an almost constant round of dinners, card parties, and dances. In fact, the strenuous social life is probably as great a menace to health as is the heat. The best proof of the happy mixing of the few Americans in Aden with the large British colony is the fact that two recent American consuls sent there have married British girls.

The Crown Colony of Aden consists of two peninsulas which were formerly two sides of a long-extinct and now drowned volcano crater. The western peninsula, known as Little Aden, is now the bustling site of the new oil refinery. On the eastern arm, Aden proper, is Steamer Point; some of the foreign colony live on the waterfront or on the high ridges here, as well as in a section known as Khormaksar. Old Aden, or Crater as it is usually called, is across the peninsula and east of Steamer Point. The Arab town of Sheikh Othman lies still farther to the north on the mainland.

These peninsulas, topped by Mount Shumshum, which rises to a height of 1,776 feet, give Aden two excellent harbors that explain its importance in world trade. Since the British took possession in 1839, it has become a free port and a vital coal and oiling station, naval base, call junction, and air center for that part of the world.

The population of Aden Colony totals about eighty thousand. It is made up of a mixture of Arabs, Somalis, Hindus, Parsis, Jews, Egyptians, Syrians, Persians, and some Chinese. There are fewer than a dozen Americans and a governing strata of British Army, Navy, and Air Force officers and civil officials.

As early as 1500 B.C., when Aden was probably an island, much of the Indian Ocean spice and silk trade from the Far East passed through it on the way to the south Arab city states of eastern Yemen and the Incense Road to the Mediterranean. Like every other power that has set out to dominate the Red Sea, the Romans early recognized the importance of Aden and captured the seaport about 24 A.D., possibly in connection with the famous expedition to Yemen of Aelius Gallus. The journey from Italy to India in Roman times took four months via Egypt and Aden. Wise travelers left Aden in July for India and returned to it in the early autumn, thus taking advantage of the best winds in each direction.

Christianity first came to Aden in A.D. 356, when the Emperor Constantius II sent a Christian mission there under Theophilus Indus, who built a church. Later Aden was controlled in turn by Abyssinians, Persians, and Yemenis. When Marco Polo visited Aden in 1285, he described it as a prosperous port which dominated the southern coast of Arabia as far east as Muscat and which had a large fleet of armed merchant ships. Di Varthema, an Italian traveler who landed there about 1504, noted that all ships entering Aden harbor had their masts, sails, rudders, and anchors removed by customs officials so they could not depart without paying harbor duty. The first English ship to visit Aden was the "Ascension" in 1609, carrying the merchant and traveler John Jourdain, who had some remarkable adventures in Aden, San'a, and Mocha.

In 1735 the sultanate of Lahej, the largest oasis in the plain north of Aden, threw off the yoke of the Imam of San'a, and Aden remained under Lahej for the next hundred years. During this period it became a sort of international colony for Indian Ocean pirates, who sailed from the base to intercept richly laden ships on their way from India to the Red Sea or the Cape of Good Hope. The well-known American pirate, Captain Kidd, operated out of Aden for a while but did not distinguish himself by any great feats of arms. More successful was another American pirate, Captain Tew, who brought back to America considerable wealth which he had collected in the Gulf of Aden. Returning a second time to the Aden area, Captain Tew was killed trying to capture an English ship in the southern Red Sea. The depredations of these pirates became so annoying to British and American merchant shipping that the British Government of India in 1815 sent an expedition from Bombay. The Arab governor of Aden, acting for the Sultan of Lahej, was undoubtedly making a good thing out of the pirates, for he refused to co-operate with the British in putting down piracy in and around that city.

In 1835 a British ship was wrecked on the shore near Aden, and the crew and passengers were held prisoners by the Sultan of Lahej until the British sent a military expedition to rescue them. After various unsatisfactory dealings with the Arabs, the British took the peninsula by storm in 1839 and set up a garrison there. Captain Haines of the British Indian Marine Service was the first British Resident in Aden.

The British colony in Aden expanded slowly during the early nineteenth century, but its merchants grew rich when the opening of the Suez Canal put the town "on the main street of the world." In World War I Turkish troops advanced as far as the sultanate of Lahej, twenty miles in the interior, but never succeeded in capturing Aden. Italy's Red Sea adventure threatened the trade and security of Aden during the 1930's, and the Italians bombed the town in World War II and their submarines actually sank several ships in Aden harbor.

Commerce is the life of Aden, and the port handles more trade than any other city in Arabia. By virtue of a good harbor, the business acumen of its merchants, and the fact that it is a free port, Aden controls an extensive market, embracing the territories of the Aden Protectorates, Yemen, Ethiopia, and the Somalilands. Furthermore, it is a worldwide entrepôt center on the routes to south Africa and Singapore. Its merchants, acting through local agents in the interior of southwest Arabia and northeast Africa, buy such products as skins, hides, coffee, and mother-of-pearl. These are then resold, principally to the United States, the United Kingdom, India, and Egypt. Thus gaining foreign exchange, the merchants are able to purchase and distribute for sale textiles, kerosene, and other requirements of the area.

Business competition is tough, particularly in the hide and skin trade, where a sizable amount of cash is risked between buying and selling. Since the market has definite limits, a newcomer must have substantial capital and hard-headed business ability in order to compete successfully with the established entrepreneurs who dominate the trade. Two of the large business firms, one headed by a legendary British merchant and the other by a Parsee family, are concerned with undertakings ranging from the printing of church-service programs to coffee monopolies.

The customary garb of Aden's inhabitants requires quantities of highly colored textiles. The women are often covered from head to foot with voluminous-skirted dresses, shawls, and veils, while the men wear either ankle-length gowns or the shorter *loongi* with shawls and turbans. These oriental headdresses each need from three to five yards of material. American exporters had the lion's share of this textile trade after World War I, only to be crowded out in the late twenties by Japanese competition. During the past few years the United States has regained a share of the market, but Japanese cloth is appearing again in the Aden suq. The chief barrier to trade with the United States is the lack of dollars.

Salt is the principal exportable product originating in the Colony. On the side of the harbor opposite the peninsula there stretches an extensive network of acre-size salt pans, overshadowed by picturesque windmills which pump in sea water for evaporation by the brilliant sun. Since the water is particularly salty, it is not long before each pan is a blinding mass of white crystals. On a moonlit evening the whole area appears to be covered with snow, with huge drifts at the water's edge—drifts that disappear in the morning when they are loaded by coolies onto a ship bound for India.

The port is a convenient midway bunkering point for ships bound from Suez to Bombay, Colombo, or South Africa. Fuel oil is brought from the Persian Gulf by the British Petroleum and California-Texas Companies, while one firm maintains stocks of south African coal so that bunkering, Aden's traditional *raison d'être*, continues to net tidy annual profits.

A development which will greatly affect the future of Aden is the construction by the Anglo-Iranian Oil Company Limited of a 100,000-barrel-a-day refinery. This $125,000,000 plant, which is expected to be completed late in 1954, is located sixteen miles from Aden. Some 2,500 American, British, and European technicians and about 10,000 Arab and Indian workers are now engaged on the project. The crude oil which will be processed in the new plant will come largely from Kuwait. One-half the refinery's output will consist of marine fuel oils, and their availability will increase the importance of Aden as a bunkering point on the steamship route from Europe to India and the Far East.

In addition, a not inconsequential source of income results from the spending by ships' passengers, who swarm through the shops during their few hours ashore. Prior to the recent war these unimposing stores put any American bargain basement to shame with fifty-cent silk shirts, twenty-dollar hand-carved camphor chests, fifty-dollar Persian rugs, and innumerable exquisitely worked articles from the Near and Far East. Bargains are fewer now, but they are still to be found if one looks long enough. Aden is within the sterling area, and its trade is restricted accordingly by the government to conserve dollars.

Although trade is the lifeblood of Aden, the British Army, Navy, and Air Force are still in evidence and control a small section of the best residential area. The command, formerly under the jurisdiction of the Army, was transferred before World War II to the Air Force, which could better meet the demands for local and Empire security.

The principal operations base is the Khormaksar airport, situated on the flat, sandy isthmus connecting the peninsula with the mainland. The field is also used regularly by British Overseas Airways on its route between main Red Sea points and Cairo and by the American-operated Ethiopian Airlines. Another aerodrome, equal to Khormaksar in capacity, was built on the boundary of the Colony during the war by the United States Army Transport Command as one of the stopover points on the vital central African route to India. This installation mushroomed into feverish wartime activity, only to be dismantled once its emergency purpose had been fulfilled. Because of the disturbed condition of the Arab world due to the Palestine situation, United States round-the-world military aviation was again temporarily routed through Aden in the summer of 1948.

The internal security of the Colony is maintained by a police force officered by Britishers, while the peace of the Protectorates is kept by two military organizations, the Government Guards and the Hadhrami Bedouin Legion, which are based in the Colony. These two forces are composed of Arab volunteers from the inland tribes who are directed by a handful of British officers. The authorities never have difficulty in obtaining a quota of men from every tribe, since the lure of a warrior's life with pay, food, and clothes attracts more applicants than can be accommodated. So interested are tribesmen in soldiering that, unlike most armies, a standard punishment among these troops is dismissal from ranks during daily drill.

The smaller of the two groups is the Government Guards, which, as the name implies, provides personnel to guard government posts and officials upcountry. A third group, the Aden Levies, is organized into regular army units and trained for combat as infantry, with armored cars and light field pieces. They are used when a rambunctious skeikh in the Protectorates makes war on a neighboring tribe or decides to block the caravan routes and the Guards and Legion prove inadequate.

The average standard of living among the native population of the Colony is low by Western calculations, but is much higher and provides many more opportunities than the simple, primitive life in Yemen and the Protectorates. As the metropolis of the area, Aden attracts a great number of travelers, who arrive daily by foot, camel, dilapidated motor transport, or dhow. The teeming bazaar sections with their innumerable idlers cause any Westerner to wonder how the barren Aden area can support so many people. One explanation lies in the strong family ties of the Adenese. The relatives of a man who has no job feel it their duty to lend him assistance within their means until he is working again, for, by the will of Allah, the lender of today may be the borrower of tomorrow.

Great numbers of the men find employment as laborers on the docks or on construction projects. Others become household servants, office messengers, and small shopkeepers. Those more fortunate have obtained a limited education which enables them to assume clerical positions in business and government. A minority who have had greater opportunities are successful as businessmen, landowners, lawyers, doctors, and educators. Although the Arabs are the largest resident racial group, Somalis, Indians, and Jews also have a chance to earn their livelihood. Owing to the diverse racial, social, and economic elements in the Colony's population, it is difficult to find an appropriate term other than Adenese to identify the entire group.

A majority of the Adenese live in crowded, unkempt brick and plaster houses along the dirt streets of the bazaars. The ground floors of these buildings are usually occupied by small shops, including innumerable cafés which, with the more secluded parlors where the drug *ghat* is chewed, are traditional day-long gathering places and the centers of continual talk. The barber has a unique position in the Aden community. Although he is usually relegated to a humble rung on the social ladder, he plays an important role at weddings and does a lively business in bloodletting, which is, for many of the lower classes, the equivalent to aspirin.

There are numerous mosques in Aden, but for convenience many people gather at appropriate spots in the open to offer their prayers toward Mecca five times a day. From the hills behind the city at dawn, the first words of the call to prayer echo from the minaret of the principal mosque before it is taken up by voices in every corner of the bazaar.

It is the same urgent, commanding cry that follows the sun across two continents, "Allah is great. There is no god but Allah. Mohammed is the prophet of Allah."

In spite of its bleakness, there are a few points of interest which the visitor can see during a drive over Aden's network of hard-surfaced roads. On the side of the peninsula facing the harbor is the fascinating dhow-building yard at Ma'alla. There, Adenese workmen, using a rule-of-thumb virtually unchanged for three thousand years, construct wooden sailing craft which ply the high seas carrying cargo and passengers as far as Basra, Bombay, and Zanzibar. It is said this is the construction site of Noah's Ark and, more probably, of the ship which carried the Queen of Sheba to her meeting with King Solomon, if she went by sea. The legendary part of this dhow yard achieves credibility when one inspects the primitive but nonetheless effective methods of fashioning planks from twisted tree trunks and bending them into place. The product is a dhow of about two hundred tons net weight, with a forward-slanting mast, a lofty poop deck, and the gracefully curved prow widely used in the Red Sea trade.

Behind the dhow yard, on the sheer cliffs facing the mainland extends a serpentine stone wall, a picturesque reminder of days when garrisons defended the settlement against attacks by inland tribes. Near one section of the wall, on a high peak, a visitor will be shown a tomb that is supposed to be the burial place of Cain, for local legend places the Garden of Eden in the Aden area, perhaps on Socotra Island or in the valley of the Hadhramaut.

The old city of Aden, aptly known as Crater since it has been built in the crater of an extinct volcano, contains an ancient system of huge stone reservoirs which were built into the mountainside to catch and conserve rain water. These tanks were discovered and excavated toward the end of the nineteenth century. Archaeologists believe they may go back to the period before Christ when Aden was a port for the cities of the Incense Trail. The size of these tanks, capable of holding twenty million gallons of water, suggests that at one time Aden's rainfall was much greater than today's average of less than an inch per year.

From the day in 1839 when valiant Captain Haines of the Royal Indian Navy successfully planted the Union Jack on the citadel of Aden until 1937, Aden was administered by the India Office of the British Government, a slow and ponderous organization at best. In a situation in which governmental action had to be considered locally, sent to India for clearance, and then referred to London for approval, it is not surprising that change in Aden came slowly. During these one hundred years, the administration of Aden was entrusted to the British military, and a succession of retired army colonels came from Bombay to run the small settlement and to carry on the unchanging Empire traditions of Poona. In 1937, however, Aden was made a Crown Colony and transferred from the Bombay Presidency to the Colonial Office in London. This not only cut out one step in the bureaucracy but tied the newly created colony to the more liberal policies and long-range viewpoints of the Colonial Office.

Postwar Aden has set out to provide itself with the modern necessities and conveniences that have so long been lacking. Shortly after the end of the war, the British Parliament in London granted Aden a sizable sum of money for long-range development projects. An ambitious program of city planning is being undertaken with the hope that the jumble of warehouses, residences, shops, and oil storage tanks will one day be segregated into specific areas, revealing a new and more attractive Aden. Early in 1947 the Colony's first Legislative Council was established, and the members, who are appointed by the Governor, are representative of Aden's various racial groups. Thus the local inhabitants have been given a cautious start toward the day when they will be able to accept their full share of political responsibility.

Early in 1949 a further significant step was taken in the development of a more representative and democratic government for this British Colony when elections were held for members of a Municipal Council, who took their seats in April of that year.

Under the jurisdiction of Aden is the island of Socotra, which lies three hundred miles off the central coast of southern Arabia. It is about eighty miles long and thirty miles wide and has not been visited by more than a dozen Europeans in recent years. Local legend has it that Socotra was the original Garden of Eden. Even if this was not the case, it was undoubtedly a colony of the powerful city states of southern Arabia that flourished along the Incense Trail during the thousand years before the birth of Christ.

A stone ruin in the southwest corner of Socotra is said by local tradition to have been built by the Apostle Thomas.[1] This seems unlikely, but it is known that in the sixth century A.D. a Christian church whose members were Nestorians flourished on Socotra.

The Venetian traveler Marco Polo reported that in his day every ship on its way from India to Aden stopped at Socotra, giving the island

[1] Sir Ernest Bennett, "The Isle of Bliss," *Living Age*, August 1938.

an active trade in spices, gold, and dyes. It was because of this trade that the Portuguese Admiral Albuquerque, who was sent out from Lisbon to take over the trade route between India and Europe, occupied Socotra in 1507 and built a fort there. The island turned out to be too far from the southern end of the Red Sea to dominate that highway of commerce, but the ruins of his fort can still be seen, and the Karshin tribe that occupies the eastern end of the island claims to be descended from these Portuguese invaders. The followers of the admiral made an effort to revive Christianity on Socotra, but a Carmelite priest named Vincenze, who visited the island in the seventeenth century, found the churches neglected and dirty, "while the people marched in procession carrying a cross and a candle and worshipping the moon." [2] So diluted, the remnant of Christianity offered virtually no resistance to the Wahhabi missionaries who came down from the Arabian mainland early in the nineteenth century, carrying their swords and their strict interpretation of Islam.

Although the people of Socotra are Moslem in name, most of them do not understand the principles of that faith and pay it only lip service. They are a primitive, peaceful, and easygoing folk, living on dates, goat's milk, and shark's meat, and doing no more than they have to do to keep alive. [3] There is some fertile land in the north of the island, and the pastures in the center are large enough to maintain herds of cattle which produce ghee, or clarified butter, the only export of importance. Socotra is the home of the dragon's blood tree, whose juice is used by the Arabs for making paints and varnishes. The collection of this juice is a haphazard business, for the intense heat and the high prevalence of malaria and other diseases have long since sapped the inhabitants of whatever energy they may once have had. There are no mules, horses, or dogs on Socotra, but its single-humped camels are famous as hill climbers.

The ruling family of Socotra comes from Ras Farsan, but the island has been a protectorate under Aden since 1886. British rule ended, once and for all, Socotra's long and colorful history of wrecking and piracy. Charles K. Moser, American consul at Aden forty years ago who was the first American official to visit Socotra, records the legend that the women of Socotra were the Lorelei of the Indian Ocean, sitting on the rocks of that island and luring passing mariners to disaster. [4] The high regard for piracy held by the people of Socotra is mentioned by Sir Ernest Bennett who wrote:

[2] *Ibid.*   [3] *Ibid.*
[4] "The Isle of Frankincense," *National Geographic Magazine,* March 1918.

People of this remote Island enjoyed in the Middle Ages an evil reputation not only as pirates but as sorcerers. They took heavy toll from passing merchantmen, and both men and women used magic to control the winds and so bring ships within their power. When an Archbishop rebuked them for their piratical habits, they replied that all their forefathers had been pirates, and they could not violate family tradition.[5]

The chief drawback to the development of the island of Socotra is the absence of a good harbor, for the few exports and imports do not justify spending much money improving roadsteads such as Hadibu. The nineteenth-century coaling station even has been moved to Aden, and Arab dhows are the only regular callers at the island. At present the main reason for Westerners to develop interest in Socotra is archaeological, for its many ruins have had only the most casual study. Scattered about the island are the foundations of buildings whose walls are as much as five feet thick, while many of the fields are enclosed by massive stone walls. Such construction is clearly beyond the energies, or the knowledge, of the approximately ten thousand persons who now inhabit the island and shows a rich past well worth the study of archaeologists. Furthermore, the bedouin of the central plateau, who are said to be descendants of the original inhabitants, speak a language that is believed to have much in common with the language of the ancient south Arabian city states. A study of these primitive people would probably be helpful in increasing our knowledge of Himyaritic days.

Also included in the territory of the Colony of Aden are the Kuria Muria and Kamaran Islands. The small and barren Kuria Muria group, which lie in the bay of the same name off the coast of Dhufar Province of Muscat, are of little interest to any but native fishermen. Kamaran Island, however, off the coast of Yemen, is so situated as to dominate the lower Red Sea. The admirals of Suleiman the Magnificent recognized its importance, and Kamaran was under Turkish control until 1915, when it was captured by the British Navy. In February 1949 the administration of the British Western Protectorate in Aden issued a paper declaring that Yemen had given up its claim to Kamaran and that from now on the island was a British possession.

There are three noteworthy things about Kamaran Island: first, its former quarantine station for pilgrims passing between Mecca and the ports of the Indian Ocean, who were quartered on the eastern side of the island in a well-equipped stone hospital maintained by an international staff; secondly, its airport, which is used regularly by BOAC

[5] Bennett, *op. cit.*, pp. 536–539.

211

planes enroute from Asmara to Aden; and lastly, Major Thompson, the recently retired British colonial officer who for years was known as the uncrowned "king of Kamaran Island." Under his direction, such improvements as an ice-making machine, a water-distillation plant, and a short streetcar line were introduced, and the health and prosperity of the three thousand Kamarani were much improved. He was always most hospitable to such rare Americans as passed through Kamaran on their way in and out of Yemen and was a striking example of that vanishing race of colonial officials who, in spite of heat and loneliness, made it impossible for the sun ever to set on the British Empire.

XVI

The Aden Protectorates:

Lands of Incense and Skyscrapers

FAR larger than the Crown Colony of Aden or its island appendages are the Eastern and Western Aden Protectorates. The Eastern Protectorate covers the picturesque valley and plateau of the Hadhramaut. The Western Protectorate, which lies north of the Colony of Aden, is made up of eighteen small states or confederacies over which rule thirty-two sultans, twenty-four sheikhs, and one amir. Their status is not to be confused with that of British "protected states" of the Persian Gulf, such as Kuwait, Bahrein, Qatar, and the Trucial Coast, which are in theory independent except for the conduct of their foreign affairs. Among these confederacies are Lahej, Haushabi, Audhali, and Dhala—good examples of the English ability to develop forms of government suited to the demands of empire and the needs of local populations as well. Experienced British political officers, some of whom have devoted their lives to the area, move about from capital to capital. Their wisdom, backed up by military force from Aden, is bringing many changes to the Protectorates.

The territory of the Western Protectorate starts behind Aden as a hot, sandy plain some four to forty miles in width. It extends inland over a low range of hills and across a sultry plateau about two thousand feet high to the mountains which form part of the main watershed of southern Arabia. These have a comparatively cool and pleasant climate and are the source of the four rivers and many smaller streams which at times flow through the Protectorate before being lost in the sands. It is a depressing experience to sit on a roof in Aden on a hot evening and watch the big thunderclouds dropping the cool water they have collected over the Indian Ocean upon the mountains of the upper Protectorate in the form of torrential thunderstorms. The possibility of sprinkling these clouds to produce rainfall while they are passing over Aden would seem to be well worth study.

The Protectorate grew to its present size by degrees as the British, wary of attempts on the part of other great powers to outflank the colony, concluded treaties with the Arab tribes in the hinterland. The Pax Britannica is gradually rescuing these tribes from a political state of affairs similar to that of Europe at the bottom of the Dark Ages when no man was safe beyond the walls of his own stone fortress. Ancient blood feuds are dying out, and it is only occasionally that a local ruler tries to extend his domains but, like the Epropean barons of old, he throttles trade routes by imposing transit taxes so exorbitant that he has to be disciplined.

The greatest source of trouble in the area is the fact that the Imam of Yemen still claims that the borders of his country extend all the way south to the Indian Ocean and include the Aden Protectorate and the Colony of Aden as well. He is obviously in no position to threaten Aden Colony, but his restless southern tribesmen not infrequently raid the territory of the northernmost tribes in the Protectorate, who often give back more punishment than they get. When this happens, or when a local chief disturbs the peace, the British political officer tries to settle the case by arbitration. If this proves impossible, the RAF goes into action on a well-worked-out pattern. First, the tribes are told that if they do not mend their ways, they will be bombed. If this threat is not sufficient, they are told just where and when they will be bombed. Smoke bombs are then dropped at the designated place, which has been evacuated by its inhabitants. As a last resort, real but small bombs are used, increasing in size until the chieftains involved come to terms. These raids are not without excitement for the RAF, since warriors of both Yemen and the Protectorate cannot resist shooting their rifles at any low-flying plane. Once the "war" is over, the pilots usually land to look over the results of their bombing, and the tribesmen come out to shake the hands of the pilots and to look over the results of their shooting.[1]

Directly adjoining the Colony of Aden is the Abdali territory, ruled over by the Sultan of Lahej, Amir Ali ibn Abdul Qarim al Abdali,

[1] W. H. Ingrams, *Arabia and the Isles,* pp. 96–100.

whose capital, al Huatah, is a refreshing oasis amid sandy wastes. This settlement, favorably situated between two large wadies, provides much of the food required by the colony. Its lush orchards of limes, dates, guavas, honey, and jackfruit, its vegetable gardens, and its fields of grain are owned for the most part by the Sultan and the local nobles. As might be expected, they live in a manner befitting their superior positions, though protocol never bars even the meanest subject from laying grievances before his sovereign for royal consideration. The people of Lahej, in contrast to those nearer the coast, are tall, strong, pure Arab types, who look down on persons of mixed blood. The national anthem is a medley of marches by the band king, John Philip Sousa, which were adapted by a European adviser of the Sultan. After being destroyed by the Turks in 1915, al Hautah was then rebuilt in comparatively modern style, for the Sultan is impressed with English ways and copies them in many things.

Beyond Lahej a dusty, rutted track winds ten miles through deep sands and across bare wadies to foothills, where boulder-strewn gorges may suddenly become engulfed by devastating flash floods. Along these valleys are villages of straw and stone, whose inhabitants eke out an existence by cultivating irregular patches of rich silt on the floor of the wadies. Although the watercourses provide a means of sustenance for the people, they also are breeding places for malarial mosquitoes, which at one time or another infect every member of these communities. Disease kills a great number of the villagers, but a glance at their cemeteries indicates that violent death is also common. Among every dozen graves, there are usually two or three stone mounds about four feet high where fighting men who have been killed were buried above the ground in accordance with the respect which these people have for their warriors. A man is a fully accepted member of one of these tribes only after he has acquired a rifle and a large ornamental curved knife, known as a *jambiya*.

The unsettled state of affairs in the Aden Protectorates was once again brought out in January 1949 by the murder of Sultan Saleh ibn Omar of Hillin and his son, Omar ibn Saleh. According to the reports that reached Aden, a group of persons had come to visit the Sultan at his ancestral home in the town of Hillin in order to settle a dispute over certain grazing lands. The visitors had dinner with the Sultan and chewed ghat with him until late at night. Then at two in the morning, while the Sultan and his guards were asleep, the guests opened the doors of the palace and allowed ten of their companions to slip in.

The combined group of intruders then rushed to the bedroom of the Sultan and his son, stabbed them both to death, overcame the guards, drove out the women, and occupied the palace.

On hearing of this, young Mohammed ibn Saleh, the second of the Sultan's sons, rallied two thousand tribesmen for an attack on Hillin. On February 22 word reached the outside world that Mohammed and his tribesmen had attacked the fortress, only to find the gates open and the invaders gone, along with the livestock. It may be that their departure had been speeded by leaflets dropped by the British from planes warning the intruders to expect a rain of bombs unless they surrendered.

Each of these mountain villages has its own sheikh, who owes fealty to the regional sultan. In the Haushabi country, a large mountainous tract stretching to the Yemen border, the ruler is Sultan Mohammed ibn Surur, whose capital is the town of Musemir. His palace is a large mud and plaster dwelling, overshadowing the small shacks surrounding it. Visitors drive through a large gate where a group of armed men are lounging and enter the courtyard, which resembles a barnyard, with chickens, goats, and a cow or two moving among groups of soldiers and passing servants. In one corner is the rusted chassis of an old automobile beside a new station wagon, which the Sultan uses for occasional trips to Aden Colony. The Sultan, together with a group of retainers, greets important visitors at the unimposing entrance to the palace and leads them up a dark stairway to the reception room. At the threshold everyone removes his shoes, and the visitors are conducted to a comfortable seat among the cushions and quilts on the floor at the far end of the room. Before the pleasantries are completed, servants begin to pass small cups of bitter coffee and sweet tea. The Sultan is a short, slim man with an extremely volatile personality and is never still. Between giving orders to the men about him, he smokes cigarettes and chews selected bunches of ghat leaves, while his eyes rove about the room. After he half finishes a cigarette, he flips it across the room where a retainer snatches it up for a few puffs. When, after having eaten and rested, the visitors prepare to take their leave, the Sultan presents them with a goat and one or two chickens as a final gesture of hospitality.

As the traveler continues inland, he climbs higher between towering mountains and sheer cliffs. The wadies here are green with ilb, tamarisk, wild fig, *sumr*, gold *mohur*, and *rak*. Troops of baboons which have been raiding the fields can be seen fleeing to the hillsides as they hurl insults at the intruders. During a pause in the journey, one may be fortunate enough to catch a glimpse of a *hoepe*, which is about the size of a pigeon, with brown and white markings. This is the legendary bird which whispered into the ears of the Queen of Sheba and King Solomon and frequently appears in *The Arabian Nights* to warn the leading characters of coming events.

About eighty-five miles from the coast, the Khuraiba Pass marks the beginning of the highest mountains. After driving up this gorge over the narrow road with its frequent hairpin turns overlooking precipitous drops, the traveler welcomes the refreshing sight of the fertile Dhala plateau, whose cool, crisp air presents an almost unbelievable contrast to the oppressive climate of the lowlands.

The town of Dhala, with a population of about four thousand, is a market center and the capital of the Amiri country, which is ruled by the youthful Sheikh Ali ibn Ali Shaif. He leans heavily upon an energetic, Aden-educated Arab who serves as the assistant political officer for that district and the long arm of the British Empire in Dhala. The main problem on which the officer works, apart from improving local medicine and education, is increasing the production of wheat and vegetables and cutting down on the acreage devoted to ghat. This drug, which is widely used in Yemen and the Aden Protectorates, gives its users a kick like benzedrine and has a debilitating effect. Unfortunately it produces most of Dhala's revenue, bringing in Maria Theresa thalers for the local treasury.

One unappetizing delicacy of the region which the Amiris enjoy particularly is a platter of flying ants consumed raw or fried.

There used to be a considerable Jewish population in Dhala and the surrounding villages which earned a living by weaving ornate clothes and making bracelets and necklaces out of silver coins. The Jews of Dhala were easily distinguished by the curls and caps of the men and the bright yellow make-up used by the women, but they have all now emigrated to Israel.

As a result of the new thinking in London in the last few years and the change of authority from the now defunct India Office to the more forward-looking Colonial Office, the pattern of modernization is being speeded up in the states of the Protectorates. The British policy had formerly consisted of little more than stopping wars between the states and ending blood feuds. The policy now is to replace the cash subsidies of from four dollars to two hundred and fifty dollars a month, paid to the tribal leaders, with economic development projects. Thus roads are being improved and a few air strips built to facilitate travel and trade between the states and with Aden. Hospitals are being established in the main centers and clinics in the small towns. A network of schools is springing up, which put much emphasis on better methods of agriculture and the learning of simple trades. Almost all the local rulers now have their own cars, and there are many radios. The leader among them, the Sultan of Lahej, has introduced electric lights, ceiling fans, ice water, and movies into his palace, and their use is spreading to his richer subjects and to his brother rulers in the wealthier states of the Protectorates. There are those who think there may be oil under parts of the Western Protectorate. If this should be true, funds would be available to speed up this program of modernization enormously.

Undoubtedly the most important single improvement would be the proper utilization of the comparatively good supply of water which is available at certain times of the year in the upper Protectorate. After the more torrential rains in the northern mountains, the beds of many of the wadies run six feet deep in water, most of which is wasted. A system of dams, retaining walls, and irrigation ditches would change these floods from a menace into a blessing. During World War II, the British inaugurated a sizable agricultural project to produce vegetables for the military and civilian population of Aden. One farm was established on the Audhali plateau, and another was located at Abyan on the coastal plain where a large wadi cuts across an area of potentially fertile soil and carries destructive seasonal floods down to the sea. Under British guidance the farmers constructed earthernwork dams and irrigation canals, bringing much of the wadi into cultivation. It is hoped that these primitive dams and canals will one day be replaced by permanent structures and the pattern set by them extended to many other parts of the Protectorate. In addition, cotton production is being expanded in this area.

Progress is being made in federating the nineteen chief states of the Western Protectorate into a single political structure. When this is done successfully, real peace may come to the Protectorate. Once they have enough food to eat, reasonable transport facilities, and less ghat to chew, the people of the Protectorate will have taken a long step on the road to becoming useful citizens of the family of nations.

Four hundred and fifty miles east of Aden, a great valley cuts through the coastal plateau to the Indian Ocean. This is the Wadi Hadhramaut, a land as rich in history, archaeology, and romance as any section of the peninsula, and yet one of the places least visited by Europeans. The region was part of the hinterland of Aden for eighty years before the British sent a permanent political officer. Only four State Department officers, several missionaries, a few members of the Air Force, and a handful of American scientists have traveled in the area. This isolation is due not only to the religious attitude of many of the Moslem tribes but also to the fact that the Hadhramaut is shut in east and west by mountains and has no good harbors, while its northern boundary is tightly sealed by the uninhabited Rub al Khali desert.

This Eastern Aden Protectorate has an area of about seventy thousand square miles, and the population is believed to be about three hundred thousand. The coastal climate though hot is better than that of Aden, while on the plateau and in the valley of the Hadhramaut itself the winter weather is cool and refreshing. Some people say that its name, Hadhramaut, comes from the Arabic word *hadir,* meaning a region of cities and cultivated places; others say it springs from the name of the original inhabitants who are called the people of Ad or Had.

The Hadhramaut consists of seven main treaty areas. They are the Qu'aiti state of Shihr and Mukalla, the Kathiri state of Saiun, the two Wahidi sultanates of Bir 'Ali and Balhaf, Qishn, and the sheikhdoms of Irqa and Haura. The most important leader is the Sultan of Shihr and Mukalla, who has the title of Highness and receives a salute of eleven guns; next comes the Sultan of Saiun who rates nine guns.

For a period many thousands of years before Christ, when the deserts of the Arabian Peninsula were fertile plains, the waters from the mountains of eastern Yemen cut the Wadi Hadhramaut on their way to the Indian Ocean. This flow dried up long ago, but at the dawn of history there was still enough rain and subsurface water in the valley to support a considerable population. It may well have been the site of a substantial river valley civilization comparable to the early period on the Nile or the Tigris and Euphrates. Legend, archaeological remains and even present-day Hadhrami architecture tie the early inhabitants of the wadi to Babylon. According to Arab legend, Yoktan, "the father of the Arabs," was born in the Hadhramaut about 2246 B.C. and later moved to Yemen. This legendary date is interesting for it is about the period when early trading between the incense country of the Hadhramaut and Egypt and India attained sufficient proportions to bring prosperity to the wadi.

As the wadi dried out, some of its tribes moved upstream, going eastward to the watershed of the mountains of Yemen, where around 1000 B.C. there sprang up the Minaean, Sabaean, Qatabanean, and Himyaritic kingdoms. At times the towns of the wadi were subject to these early city states, while at other times they threw off their yoke and were independent. In either case, the trade in incense from the Hadhramaut and in spices and silks from India and the East continued to expand from the time of Solomon to the time of Christ, much of it flowing up the Wadi Hadhramaut or its tributaries on its way to the Incense Trail, which led through Mecca to the Mediterranean. When this trade was diverted to ships on the Red Sea and the Persian Gulf, the early trading cities of Yemen collapsed, and hard times came to the Wadi Hadhramaut, hard times which are only just now ending.

The Koran refers to the old Sabaean inhabitants of southwest Arabia as "the people of Ad." It explains the collapse of the eastern Yemen city states and the towns of the upper Hadhramaut as being brought about when the rich men of Ad tried too hard to make a garden paradise by the use of irrigation, a possible reference to the great dam and irrigation system of Marib in Yemen and other towns in the upper Hadhramaut. According to the Koran, Allah was so displeased with the people of Ad that he destroyed them, and their remnants may be seen at Aden (Ad-en) climbing on Mount Shumshum in the form of monkeys, an interesting tale in that it suggests that Aden was an early Yemeni or Hadhrami seaport that continued to exist even after the civilization to the north of it had collapsed.

After years of war and greater and greater stagnation, the Islamic religion came to the valley of the Hadhramaut in A.D. 640. The Hadhrami did not welcome the rule of Mecca, and several revolts had to be put down by force until, in A.D. 757, the ruler of Yemen, who was then subject to the Abbassid Caliphate in Baghdad, forced the inhabitants to wear the distinctive black dress of the Abbassids which is still commonly seen in the Hadhramaut.

For the next twelve hundred years, Hadhramic history is a series of wars and revolts. When the Turks became the caliphs and masters of the Arab world, they did not neglect the Hadhramaut, and Suleiman Pasha equipped seventy galleys and sent out an army of seven thousand Turkish soldiers who took all the seaports along the southern coast of the Arabian Peninsula. The interior of the Hadhramaut, however, paid only lip service to Ottoman rule and never submitted to the spiritual primacy of the Ottoman caliphs. Turkish control of the ports of the Hadhramaut was maintained through the Kathiri family. In 1830 another south Arabian family, the Qu'aiti, who had grown rich in India bought the town of Qatn from one of the Kathiri sultans, and a blood feud began which raged throughout most of the nineteenth century. Gradually the Kathiri lost ground until, in 1888, the British acknowledged the Qu'aiti as the rulers of the Hadhramaut, under British guidance and protection in domestic and foreign matters, thus starting what has grown into the Eastern Aden Protectorate.

The British had been interested in the Hadhramaut since 1835, when a British ship, the "Palmuras," surveyed the coast. The captain noted the following about the Hadhrami port of Mukalla:

> The population of the town may be about 4,500, being a motley collection. . . . The customs duties are 5 per cent. The exports consist in gums, hides, large quantities of senna, . . . and coffee. The imports chiefly of cotton cloth, lead, iron crockery, rice, . . . dates and dried fruit, sheep, and slaves. I have seen 700 Nubian girls exposed in the slave market here for sale. . . . The price varies from £7 to £25 apiece.[2]

While the "Palmuras" was off the Hadhramaut, James R. Wellsted, an Englishman who was on board, went a short way into the interior and obtained a certain number of Himyaritic inscriptions, the first to reach the Western world in modern times.

The first European traveler to write extensively on the Hadhramaut was Adolph von Wrede. In 1843 he traveled in the Hadhramaut disguised as a pilgrim, going up the Wadi Du'an as far as the violently religious town of Khuraiba. His disguise was penetrated, and he was driven out and robbed by the sheikh, nearly losing his life on the way. Von Wrede wrote of his travels and described the high buildings and rich towns he had seen, but he was accused of sensationalism and his stories were not believed. He later emigrated to Texas where he killed himself in 1860, largely because the world doubted his descriptions of the Hadhramaut.[3]

Until 1915 no British official from Aden had visited the Wadi Hadhramaut, although the area was in theory under Adenese control. In order to straighten out the unsettled situation that developed from World War I, the British negotiated a treaty of peace and amity between the Kathiri and Qu'aiti families in 1918. Although not specific regarding boundaries, it has lasted fairly well. Work connected with this treaty opened the eyes of the British in Aden to the possibilities of development in the Hadhramaut, and exploration of the Eastern Protectorate started the following year. During the next twenty years various British

---

[2] R. H. Kiernan, *The Unveiling of Arabia*, p. 200.
[3] D. G. Hogarth, *The Penetration of Arabia*, pp. 148–153.

officials from Aden made periodic trips to the ports of the Protectorate and sometimes went up into the valley. In 1934 the British sent one of their ablest young experts on the Indian Ocean area, W. H. Ingrams, to be Resident Adviser at Mukalla. Ingrams won the confidence and respect of the Arabs and gradually extended his sphere of control inland.

As late as 1936 there was constant fighting between the states, towns, villages, and hamlets. In 1937 Ingrams negotiated a treaty with the Sultan of Shihr and Mukalla under which the British agreed to appoint a resident adviser to the Sultan and the Sultan agreed to accept his advice on all matters except those affecting the Moslem religion and customs. Then Ingrams arranged a general truce, which established a record in having fourteen hundred signatories, probably the greatest number ever to adhere to such a document. The "Ingrams Truce" was extended for ten years in 1940, and by now there is little fighting in the Hadhramaut and it is relatively safe for travel.[4]

Few foreigners have made as many changes in a primitive state as has Ingrams. When he arrived at Mukalla in 1934, the Sultan's government consisted of a wazir, a treasurer, a general, a doctor, and some school teachers. By 1944 this had expanded to a state council or cabinet and twenty organized departments under a state secretary, an Omani Arab who had had experience with the government of Tanganyika. In 1934 the state's revenue was about 600,000 rupees. Ten years later this had risen to 1,500,000 rupees.

In 1944 the slaves owned by the state were freed, and a state hospital was built in Mukalla with a staff of four Arab doctors. When Ingrams arrived there were about three hundred boys in school in the sultanate. Ten years later the number had increased to about 1,700, and some 140 girls were attending school at Mukalla. A group of young Hadhramis was teaching illiterate adults to read and write. All this was done in spite of the loss during the war of substantial remittances from Singapore and Java where many Hadhramis go to work, a seven year's drought, and the death of half the camels in the country.

Ingrams believes that the traditional methods of colonial administration are not the best ways of teaching a primitive area to govern itself. He feels that interference in the internal affairs of states of the Arabian Peninsula should be kept to a minimum and that, once law and order are established, the emphasis should be on advice and medical and economic assistance. He found that best results were obtained when the

[4] W. H. Ingrams, "Political Development in the Hadhramaut," *International Affairs*, 1945.

people were given full responsibility and when the foreign adviser worked and lived as one of the people and looked at things from their point of view.

There is still enough water flowing through or under the Wadi Hadhramaut to make possible considerable farming. The chief crops are wheat, maize, millet, indigo, tobacco, sesame, dates, coconuts, and cotton. Honey is also an important product, the total production being about a hundred thousand pounds a year. The best grade, which comes from the Wadi Du'an, is exported to Aden and to Europe. An excellent brand of leaf tobacco, known as *hummoni,* is grown on the coast between the towns of Shihr and Mukalla. This used to be smoked in hubble-bubble water pipes by the richer Arabs up and down the Red Sea and in southern Arabia, but the younger Arabs now prefer British or American cigarettes. Some of this hummoni tobacco is watered by a complicated system of underground viaducts, much like the Persian kanats, to which they may be related. A small amount of frankincense is still produced, going to India and the Mediterranean world as it has for the last three thousand years. After the date palm, the ilb is the most important and useful tree in the Hadhramaut. It needs no irrigation, provides food for man from its apple-colored berries, fodder for goats from its leaves, and wood for building.

The primitive industries of the Hadhramaut include the production of yarn and the weaving of cloth, the tanning of hides, the making of lime for plaster, and the preparation of indigo. Along the coast boat-building and catching and selling fish occupy many of the natives.

There are two phenomena worth noting about the people of the Hadhramaut. One is the division of the population into seven classes or castes. The other is the curious practice of many in the merchant class of spending fifteen or twenty years abroad, making their fortunes before returning home. The castes are, in order of their importance:

1. Sayyids. These are aristocratic descendants of Fatima and Ali, who claim to have the purest pedigrees of all Arabian sayyids. They are descended from a sayyid from Basra, Ahmed al Muhajir, who came to the Hadhramaut about the year 900, and they are recognized as the spiritual leaders of the area. There are about eight authentic sayyid families, which, until recently, held a position in the Hadhramaut rather like that of medieval churchmen in Europe, having complete sway in the field of religion, law, and learning—a position in which temporal rulers, such as sultans and sheikhs, did not interfere. The sayyids do not carry arms or have bodyguards but rely for safety en-

tirely on the reverence of the people. Most of them are well educated by Arab standards.[5] The sayyids are aware of the ancient glories of the Hadhramaut and would like to see its greatness restored, but are afraid that modernization will undermine their position. In this they are right, for many of the younger men are jealous of their privileges and consider them too reactionary. In the parts of the Hadhramaut dominated by the Qu'aiti family, the influence of the sayyids is almost gone, but in the Kathiri areas of the country they are more progressive and are holding their own.

2. Sheikhs. Although rating below the sayyids, the sheikhs are respected leaders who are often well educated. Because of their exalted positions, they seldom bear arms except for war or hunting, in contrast to the rest of the population who are always armed.

3. Yafa'is. These are a sort of Janizary corps, who are the actual rulers of the Qu'aiti part of the Protectorate. They were originally brought in as mercenaries but have now taken over much power for themselves.

4. Tribesmen. Three of the tribes found in the Hadhramaut are Sabini (Subeihi), Nuwah, and Humumi. The latter are prognathous dwarfs, probably a neolithic survival pushed out of the valleys long ago. Each of these tribes has a single leader but is divided into clans, sections, and subsections. The tribesmen are nomadic, and the carrying trade of the Hadhramaut is in their hands, each tribe traveling only along certain designated routes. They often go about armed and carry on blood feuds, but are noted for keeping their word once it has been given.

5. Townsmen. The inhabitants of the main towns in the wadi are for the most part descended from the eighty families of Iraqi immigrants who came to the Hadhramaut with Sayyid Ahmed al Muhajir. They are divided into four subclasses of merchants, artificers, laborers, and servants. They pay most of the taxes and include many wealthy merchants who are prominent in the government of the towns. It is this group that provides the chief link with the outside world.

6. Slaves. There are still slaves to be found in the Hadhramaut although most of them are owned by the sultanates rather than by private persons. They are usually well treated, often comparatively well educated, and some hold important government positions. The flow of slaves from Africa has been much reduced by the tight British naval

[5] D. van der Meulen, *Aden to the Hadhramaut*, p. 70.

24. Aden harbor, with Steamer Point in the distance. Legend claims that Cain was buried near the tree. (Picture by Wide World Photo.)

25. Colonel William A. Eddy signing the agreement of commerce and friendship with Yemen in the guesthouse in San'a, April 1946. (Courtesy of *Foreign Service Journal*.)

26. The entrance to the Moon Temple at Marib being excavated by the Expedition of the American Foundation for the Study of Man. (Photo by American Foundation for the Study of Man.)

blockade. Slaves are not permitted to take Arabic names, they must marry among themselves, and their women do not wear veils.

7. Akhdam. This group, somewhat similar to the "untouchables" of India, does most of the menial labor of the Hadhramaut, acting as sweepers and unskilled agricultural workers. They are said to be the descendants of the Abyssinian invaders who came in during the wars of the third to the sixth centuries and cannot take part in blood feuds. Incidentally, not only manual labor but the playing of music is considered an occupation for lower-class persons in the Hadhramaut.

With the collapse of the world market for frankincense and myrrh, the towns of the Hadhramaut went into a depression which lasted almost a thousand years. Steadily increasing dryness limited farm produce for export, except in very small quantities to Yemen, and the lack of good harbors kept the people along the coast from developing seafaring qualities. Little by little the unusual custom sprang up of having the young men in the merchant families leave the Hadhramaut, after they were married and had children, and go abroad for fifteen or twenty years to make their fortunes. Some went to east Africa, the Somalilands, and Egypt, where they became petty merchants. Others went to India, particularly Hyderabad, where they made up an important part of the bodyguard of the Nizam.

For over a hundred years, however, the most successful group has gone to the Malay states and Indonesia. There they have become prosperous traders, businessmen, and hotelkeepers. Ninety-five per cent of the Arabs in the Straits Settlements are Hadhrami, and whole streets of shops are owned by them in Singapore. According to W. H. Ingrams, 20 to 30 per cent of Hadhrami men leave the country and go abroad to make their fortune.

Although the men of the Hadhramaut may stay abroad for over twenty years and may marry and raise a family during this time, they almost always come home once they have made their fortunes. On their return they live in luxury. The richer ones have built a series of mosques, palaces, and summer residences that have no equal anywhere in Arabia except for the new homes of the Saudi princes. Local blood feuds are not forgotten during the stay overseas, and up to the last ten years hardheaded businessmen who had made millions of dollars in such centers as Singapore returned to the Hadhramaut and started shooting at their neighbors just as if they had never been out of the country.

This economic pattern contributed in large part to the terrible depression which overtook the Hadhramaut during the two World Wars. In World War II crops failed for several successive seasons, and the financial structure collapsed when remittances from the Indies were cut off by the Japanese occupation. In the midst of starvation the weaknesses of the caste system became tragically evident, and great numbers of sayyids, who, like generations of their forebears, had never done a stroke of manual labor, refused to work. The darkest days came when the camels, the traditional means of transport, began to die for want of food. The British Government took such emergency measures as flying in grain by RAF planes, shipping army trucks to Mukalla to remedy the breakdown in transportation, and setting up soup kitchens. Outside assistance, like the Egyptian Government's donation of several thousand pounds, was also given to the Hadhramis. Hasty agricultural reforms were introduced which proved successful when the area was finally blessed with a good harvest.

During early 1949 another serious famine was reported in some sections of the Hadhramaut due to lack of rain. Furthermore, grain from the coast could not be transported into the interior because the camels had neither their usual supply of grass nor the dried sardines on which they are often fed. The government of Aden tried to provide motor transport in place of the camels in order to move grain into the valley, but the camel drivers objected. The RAF, therefore, on February 4 began a food lift based on Riyan, a town about four hundred miles east of Aden, using Dakota airplanes to drop more than seven hundred tons of food to the starving Hadhramis. So helpful was this that forty of the leading citizens of the valley wrote a letter of thanks to the British resident adviser at Mukalla.

An example of this curious Hadhrami practice of working abroad is the Al Kaf family, the richest and most powerful in the Eastern Protectorate, who are very influential in the Hadhramaut. Although they have extensive local holdings, most of the money with which they have built palaces at Mukalla or Saiun or Tarim has come from their activities in Singapore and Java.

Thanks partly to the British and partly to rich Hadhramis like the Al Kafs, life in the wadi of the Hadhramaut is beginning to be modernized. Although the camel and the ass still remain the chief means of communication along the three-thousand-year-old caravan routes, the days of the camel are numbered. Beginning in the 1920's wealthy Hadhramis returning from abroad had automobiles taken apart and packed into the wadi on camels. At their destination the parts were reassembled by mechanics especially trained for the job. Now, however, there is a hard-surfaced road from the port of Shihr to the city of Tarim, and even before World War II Freya Stark reported as many as eighty automobiles in the Hadhramaut. In addition to improved roads, the RAF has built several air strips in the interior, thus making possible rapid transportation, which before long will grow into a regular air line.

The center of this modernization is the town of Tarim, which is also the spiritual and intellectual center of the Hadhramaut. It is the headquarters of several brothers of the Al Kaf family, wealthy, learned, and modern-minded men. Thanks to their initiative, Tarim now has telephones, radios, electric lights, and even motion-picture showings. More and more of the houses now have plumbing; buildings in the modern European style are springing up outside the walls of the city; and the camels, donkeys, and women who formerly worked the pumps are being replaced by gasoline and Diesel motors. The architecture of its mud-brick houses reflects Malayan influence. Exteriors are frequently painted blue, gray, yellow, or pink. Some interiors are quite Western, and there is some form of bath with each room.

The most impressive city in the Hadhramaut is the towering fortress of Shibam, the "New York of the Hadhramaut," which has six hundred many-storied houses, some as much as eight stories in height. Most travelers, however, rate Saiun, which is set in a belt of palm groves, as the most beautiful city of the Hadhramaut. It is the Kathiri capital and has a population of perhaps fifteen thousand. The Sultan's palace is one of the most beautiful buildings in Arabia, comparable to the Palace of Joy at San'a or King Ibn Saud's great palace at Riyadh. The houses of Saiun are decorated with delicate lacework and tracery done in whitewashed stucco, and the drains, in contrast to most south Arabian cities, are all covered and run into roofed cisterns of mud, so that one can walk about without fear of stepping in a sewer.

Throughout the Hadhramaut one sees wide doors, heavy and ornamented with iron nails whose heads are polished brightly. But the most striking feature of the towns of the Hadhramaut is the height of the buildings, which run up to eight or more stories, exceeding even the skyscrapers of San'a. At Shibam, for instance, Ingrams reports that the height of a house facing the outside of the city wall must be 105 feet at a minimum. One of the indications that the early Hadhramis may have come from Babylon is the similarity between their present architecture and ruins in that ancient city.

The first floor of most Hadhrami houses is used for storage. The second is for slaves and servants, the third is for guests, and the floors above that—and there may be seven or eight in all—are for the harem and general family use, including one or more large sitting rooms. The wealth of the owner can be judged by the amount of whitewash on the outside of the house.

Intercity peace has come so recently to the Hadhramaut that the basic motive of construction up to the last ten years was defense. Although the early Arabs apparently built entirely of stone, masonry is now used only for foundations, and most building is done with adobe bricks and the wood of the ilb trees. Cement is just beginning to come into use in and around Tarim. Glass is almost unknown, and door keys are of wood. Hadhrami architecture was great and still continues so, although Western influence is beginning to hurt it, for the Hadhramis are copying late Victorian hotel architecture.

The suqs in the towns of the Hadhramaut are not impressive. There are few permanent shops, and most of the trade is done by peddlars who take their wares directly into the wealthier homes. The chief items carried by shopkeepers are sugar, ginger, coffee, rice, salt, palm-leaf mats for floor coverings, and baskets.

An interesting currency used in the area is silver Maria Theresa thalers. Their value depends upon the price of silver, and they are frequently melted down to make smaller coins or silver bracelets, necklaces, and other ornaments. From time to time such silver is collected by the merchants and sent to Aden, whence it goes back to Europe and is once more minted into Maria Theresa thalers, carrying the old pattern and dated A.D. 1786, for newer issues are considered inferior. In spite of the Moslem opposition to interest, money can be had at 10 per cent on mortgages.

Most of the townspeople are strict Moslems, but little formal religion is practiced outside the towns; a high standard of honor and a great sense of fatalism seem to suffice for the bedouin.

Legal practices are very reminiscent of Anglo-Saxon law, including the ordeal by fire and by eating dry bread—if the person being tried is burned by the fire or chokes over the bread, it is a sign that he is guilty. All crimes have their price, and there is a complicated tariff for repayment of each kind of bodily injury.

Various local dialects are to be found in the different wadies of the Eastern Protectorate, including one called Mahari, which comes from ancient south Arabic. The close ties between the Hadhramaut and

228

Malaya, parts of Africa, and India are shown by the fact that Malay, Swahili, and Hindustani are all used in trade throughout the area. A tremendous amount of work remains to be done in studying not only the early history and archaeology of the Hadhramaut, but also local dialects and the Himyaritic and other early inscriptions and tablets which are found there and which make it, along with eastern Yemen, one of the world's most promising fields for research.

Like those of Yemen and other remote parts of the Arabian Peninsula, the streets of most cities of the Hadhramaut are dirty. Once one leaves the street, however, everything is surprisingly clean. Dishes and glasses are frequently fumigated with frankincense, which gives a sweet, sickening flavor to everything put in them. The people of the Hadhramaut think that soap is dangerous, producing illness and spoiling the skin.

Medicine in the Hadhramaut is extremely primitive, except in Tarim and one or two other centers where rich merchants have brought back with them from the outside world a few Western ideas about health. Hadhrami medicine men or women usually diagnose illness by smelling the hair of the sick person. In order to heal a wound, the nostrils are first plugged, for the Hadhramis believe that smells from sores are harmful; then a bit of iron, tin, copper, or lead is tied directly on the wound. Shock treatment, such as burning with a hot iron, is a favorite remedy for hysteria and similar ailments, which are said to be caused by worms sent by jinn, or evil spirits. The Hadhrami have a childlike faith that any European can cure any disease. When a European does not cure him or herself, then the local doctors try a hand, as they did with Freya Stark when she lay sick of the measles at Du'an.

They were anxious to try a hot iron on me at the back of my neck. . . . I avoided this, but I was not so lucky with an old witch of a woman who came in one day from Hajarain, all decorated with little coloured patches, and with her elderly horsey face still painted yellow. . . . When she saw me lying helpless, she pounced upon me; she uttered invocations, and whirled her indigo fingers and skinny arms like windmills about my head . . . and then she suddenly bent over me and spat. It was meant kindly.[6]

Like all primitive peoples, the Hadhramis are very superstitious and live in great fear of spirits or jinn. They think that many evil jinn inhabit ancient ruins or caves, but there are good jinn such as those who live in ilb trees and who enjoy combing and beautifying the hair of

6 Freya Stark, *The Southern Gates of Arabia*, p. 140.

those who fall asleep in the shadow of their branches. To them the fox is a particularly unlucky animal.

Women of the upper classes in the Eastern Protectorate are even more secluded than those in Saudi Arabia, but there is almost no veiling among the lower classes. For the most part women receive virtually no education after they are nine years old. Not so the overeducated widow of Saiun, one of whose "salons" Freya Stark attended. According to Miss Stark:

> The widow was young, plumpish and bright-eyed with a gay little curl on either side of her face. . . . She punctuated her periods with pretty little hennaed fingers, quoting the Prophet, the Koran and the poets, for she was a poetess herself and had entered open competitions and once won a complete tea-set as a prize. Every day, she said, the ladies gathered here and listened to one of the five books—the Quran, Bokhari, Muslim, and two other traditionists which I have forgotten.[7]

Most upperclass women marry by the time they are fourteen and then have a good many children, although the infant mortality rate is very high. Divorce is common in spite of the fact that wealthy Hadhramis have more than one wife. The lot of women in the merchant and town families is particularly hard, for after they have had two or three children their husbands go abroad often for as long as twenty years, seeking their fortune and raising another family while leaving the first wife at home to bring up the first set of children.

Near the coast the women wear dark blue or black clothes; at Shibam and Saiun they dress in sky blue; and at Tarim their clothes are either brown or red. All wear a great deal of what we would call costume jewelry, usually made out of silver coins, decorated with semiprecious stones. Children are dressed just like their parents in miniature. Upperclass women paint their faces heavily. Girls put green on their forehead, nose, cheek, and chin, while adults add yellow to this coloring.

Oftentimes a bride does not know that she is going to be married until her hair is washed for the event. Her face is then varnished yellow, and her hands and feet are covered with a pattern. A great feast is held, and on the third day of the wedding she sits under a red veil, which her husband finally lifts from her face at night. The next morning he is expected to leave ten Maria Theresa thalers on the pillow. After the second night, he leaves a tray with handkerchiefs, ten thalers, a pile of clothes, scent, and incense. The bride wears her wedding

[7] *Ibid.*, p. 201.

finery for forty days, and the mother stays with the bride for two weeks after the marriage.[8]

Throughout the whole length of the Wadi Du'an, none of the women Miss Stark met could read, and she wondered how they passed their days since they did little sewing or cooking. Long formal calls seemed to take up most of their time. Almost none of the women, other than the bedouin, ever come up out of the wadies in which their towns are located to have a look at the *jol* or plateau above.

Six years of free education are available to all boys in theory, but except in the richer families parents do not let their children attend school for more than four years as the additional learning does not increase their earning powers. Education is, of course, built largely around the Koran and related religious books, which provide grammar, reading, diction, composition, and law. More advanced students study drawing, arithmetic, geometry, and history. Because certain of the Hadhramis travel widely, their geography is better than that taught in most Arabian Peninsula schools. Some of the children of the sayyids are now being sent to Islamic schools and universities in Baghdad and Cairo, and more of the children of the merchants are attending schools in Aden, India, Singapore, and Indonesia. A strange example of the impact of the West on Hadhrami education is the fact that in the Qu'aiti territory signaling with flags is frequently considered the culmination of a boy's education.

One of the most remarkable things about the Hadhramaut is its history as a center of incense production. The plateau and mountains of the Hadhramaut and Dhufar were undoubtedly the Maratha Mountains, mentioned by Ptolemy, and the Mons Excelsis, referred to by Pliny as the incense country of southern Arabia. The first recorded Egyptian expedition into the Hadhramaut for incense was in the twenty-eighth century B.C., and the trade continued to expand for about three thousand years thereafter. Pliny described the incense traffic as follows:

The incense, after being collected, is carried on camels' backs to Sabota [Shabwa], of which place a single gate is left open for its admission. To deviate from the high road while carrying it, the laws have made a capital offense. At this place the priests take, by measure and not by weight, a tenth part in honor of their god, whom they call Sabia; indeed it is not allowable to dispose of it before this has been done; out of this tenth the public expenses are defrayed for the divinity generously entertains all those

[8] *Ibid.*, p. 120.

strangers who have made a certain number of days journey in coming thither. The incense can only be exported through the country of the Gebanitae and for this reason it is that a certain tax is paid to their King as well. . . . The whole trade is an immense machine, delicately adjusted. . . . There are certain portions also of frankincense which are given to the priests and king's secretaries and in addition to these, the keepers of it, as well as the soldiers, who guard it, the gatekeepers and various other employees, have their share as well. And then besides all along the route there is at one place water to pay for, at another fodder, lodging of the stations, and various taxes and imposts besides; the consequence of which is, that the expense for each camel before it arrives at the shore of our sea [Mediterranean] is 688 denarii.

Pliny also reported that the collection of frankincense was considered a religious rite, and only Sabaeans and Minaeans were allowed to witness the tapping of the trees, which were owned by some three thousand families. Strabo tells of the conduct of the Sabaeans on the Incense Road. They "receive in continuous succession the loads of aromatics and deliver them to their next neighbors [the Debae living in the vicinity of present-day Mecca], as far as Syria and Mesopotamia; and when they are made drowsy by the sweet odours they overcome the drowsiness by inhaling the incense of asphalt, goats' beard, and chicory."

The marbles of Nineveh furnish frequent illustrations of the offering of incense to the sun god and his consort. The kings of Assyria united in themselves the royal and priestly offices, and on the monuments they erected they are generally represented as offering incense and pouring out wine to the Tree of Life. According to Herodotus, frankincense to the amount of one thousand talents' weight was offered every year, during the feast of Bel, on the great altar of his temple in Babylon. And the monuments of Persepolis and the coins of the Sassanians show that the religious use of incense was as common in ancient Persia as in Babylonia and Assyria. Herodotus states that every year the Arabs brought one thousand talents of frankincense to Darius as tribute. The Parsis in western India still preserve the pure tradition of the ritual of incense as followed by their race from the most ancient times. The commonest incense in ancient India was probably frankincense. It is likely that the sweet-smelling gums and resins of the countries of the Indian Ocean began to be introduced into Greece about the sixth century B.C.

Among the Romans, the use of frankincense became very common in religious ceremonials, on various state occasions such as in triumphs, and in connection with certain occurrences of domestic life. In private it was daily offered by the devout to the *lar familiaris;* and in public sacrifices it was not only sprinkled on the head of the victim before its slaughter and afterward mingled with its blood, but also thrown upon the flames over which it was roasted.

Along with the age-old Hadhrami trade in frankincense went that in myrrh, another gum-resin esteemed by the people of ancient times for use in their temples and also for embalming. One of the gifts offered to the infant Jesus by the Magi was myrrh.

After incense had ceased to be carried by land up the Incense Trail, it went out to ports such as Cana. The port of Shihr near Ras al Kalp was mentioned by Marco Polo, who said that the profits of the local prince on incense were 800 per cent. Gradually through the Middle Ages, however, intertribal warfare resulted in the destruction of most of the frankincense trees.

A few of the trees still grow in the Hadhramaut, and a little of their whitish gum goes to India and the Mediterranean world. South Arabian frankincense trees are tapped during the rainy season, and the transparent gum is collected into balls and dried before shipment. Trees are no longer carefully cared for, as was once the case when their treatment was somewhat comparable to that of plantation rubber trees. The best frankincense is that grown in Dhufar, four days by mule inland from Marbat east of Salalah. The value is determined by color, purity, and size of the ball and varies from $40 to $320 a ton.

The historic trail between the Dhufar and Hadhrami incense areas, which was well known to the ancient world, is virtually unexplored by Westerners, except for the part of it covered late in 1946 by Major T. Altounyan.[9] Taking with him only the barest necessities, he rode from Mukalla by car and camel to Saihut, the largest and most important town in the Mahra area with about three thousand inhabitants. From there he went by rowboat to the town of Qishn, located along a beautiful beach on a large bay, the residence of the sultans of Qishn who are also the sultans of the island of Socotra. Since the death in 1953 of Ahmed ibn Afrar, Sultan Khalifah, his cousin, runs the country. The young Sultan, a forceful man of twenty-five, lives very simply and walks about barefooted, carrying his own rifle.

From Qishn the major proceeded eastward along the coast to Ghaidha, at which point he turned west along the caravan trail that led 260 miles across the mountains and down into the valley of the Hadhra-

[9] T. Altounyan, "The Land of the Mahra," *Royal Central Asian Journal,* July 1947.

maut at Tarim. There was constant watch for raiders but no actual incident. The primitiveness and poverty of the people showed the need for work such as that done by Ingrams at Mukalla.

The Hadhramaut has had a magnificent past, the uncovering of which offers a great challenge to historians and archaeologists. Because of the money which is coming into the Protectorate from the outside, the possibility of there being oil or other mineral resources, and the modern spirit possessed by some of its men, it seems likely that the medieval face of the Hadhramaut will be lifted during the next generation.

XVII

Land of the Imam

YEMEN is the least-known member of the United Nations. Ask ten people in the street what is the capital of Tibet, and half of them will tell you it is Lhasa. Ask the same ten the name of the capital of Yemen, and most of them will say, "Where is Yemen?" This is the more surprising because Tibet is hidden away at the back of India, while Yemen's shore line runs for more than three hundred miles along the southeastern coast of the Red Sea opposite Eritrea, and its former capital, San'a, is an hour inland by plane. Nor is Yemen a strip of empty desert. Whereas Saudi Arabia, with an area of about 927,000 square miles, has a population of about 5,500,000, mountainous but fertile Yemen, with 75,000 square miles, has a population of almost 4,000,000.

Part of the explanation for Yemen's isolation lies in its geography. The coastal waters of the Red Sea are shallow and full of treacherous reefs. Yemen's most famous port is Mocha, about seventy-five miles north of the straits of Bab el Mandeb. For years the high-grade coffee that is grown in southern Arabia reached the outer world through Mocha, giving the product its name. Now this trade has been diverted to Hodeida and Aden, and most of the houses in Mocha are in ruin and the harbor is filled with silt. The other two Yemeni ports, Hodeida and Luhaiya, are just gravel beaches sheltered by reefs.

A strip of hot, malarial, and sandy desert, known as the Tihama, runs inland from the coast for twenty to fifty miles. Behind rise foothills and range after range of rugged mountains which run up to ten thousand feet in altitude and whose lowest passes are over seven thousand feet above sea level. East of them, running north and south for about two hundred miles, lies a central valley which varies in width from ten to forty miles and is blocked by mountains at both ends. Beyond rise still more mountains that fall away gradually to the east until they are lost in the sands of the Rub al Khali. Thus there is no easy route into Yemen, nor any easy travel within its borders, for it has no railroads or good roads, only winding trails that can easily be blocked by a few riflemen.

This leads to the second and more basic reason why Yemen has been visited by only a handful of Europeans. The Arabs who live in the fertile valley of the High Yemen and the smaller valleys which run off it are well aware that they own the most desirable part of the Arabian Peninsula. They are strong, active men, quick with a knife, accurate with a gun, and ready at all times to keep intruders from entering their country. In addition, they are devout Shi'a Moslems who have a low regard for Sunni Moslems and little regard for Christians. The combination of rugged terrain and its fanatical Moslem protectors makes traveling in Yemen impossible without the approval of the imam or king of the country. And the imams of Yemen, recalling the repeated invasions of their country, have been isolationists.

In spite of geography and present isolationist feelings, the "Main Street" of the world once ran through Yemen's back yard, and around it centers one of the most fascinating chapters of history. Because the story of the south Arabian city states is so interesting and yet so little known, it is presented here at some length.

When the curtain of antiquity rose on the burning sands of Arabia, the peninsula was already occupying the role of a bridge between the East and West.[1] The temples of Karnak and Luxor, of Babylon and Nineveh needed much incense, a product which came, in part, from the frankincense trees that grew in the mountains of southern Arabia. Egyptian records tell of trips for incense as early as 2800 B.C., and by about one thousand years before Christ a trade route had developed down the western coast of the Arabian Peninsula to these mysterious mountains. Traders from India felt their way west from harbor to harbor until they also reached the frankincense country of southern Arabia. These rival groups undoubtedly fought each other at first; then they realized that each had products the other could use.

In addition to incense, the growing Mediterranean cities were clamor-

---

[1] For some of the material in the next two chapters, the author is indebted to Professor Philip K. Hitti's excellent book, *History of the Arabs*.

ing for cinnamon and pepper from India, pearls from the Persian Gulf, silks, ointments, and dyes from China. Moreover, the ancients were heavy meat eaters and, having no refrigerators, they needed spices from the islands of the Eastern seas. India and China, for their part, wanted Mediterranean gold, metalwork, and leather. And both East and West were willing to pay high prices for African slaves, ivory, ostrich feathers, and monkeys. All of these were goods of little bulk, and trade in them developed rapidly. Because the Red Sea was infested by pirates, these products did not go north by ship but moved along an inland Incense Trail. This started at ports such as Aden and Mukalla, skirted the eastern slopes of the mountains of Yemen, and went north through Najran, Mecca, and Medina.

The most active merchants along this trail were the inhabitants of eastern Yemen. They probably started out as robbers, preying on the few caravans that passed their way. Then robbery changed to organized toll. Before long the Yemenis were sending out their own caravans and so had to protect them from the tolls of others. Thus forts were built, the road was improved, and water and resting places were provided, until the Yemenis, some nine centuries before Christ, found themselves with a virtual monopoly on one of the chief trade routes between the Mediterranean world and Africa, India, and China. Thanks to this monopoly, the struggling settlements of eastern Yemen grew into five rich and powerful kingdoms.

The earliest of these was the town of Ma'in, the capital of what is called the Minaean kingdom, which flourished from about 950 to 650 B.C. It was located where the mountains of northeastern Yemen flatten out into the Rub al Khali desert. At the height of its power, it controlled most of southern Arabia. The names of twenty-six Minaean kings have been deciphered, along with enough ruins and inscriptions to indicate that Ma'in was a city of considerable size and prosperity.

Almost as old as Ma'in was the town of Timna, the capital of another kingdom called Qataban. Qataban was located in what is now the northeast corner of the Western Aden Protectorate, south of Ma'in on the Incense Trail. Only recently did the British antiquities officer discover the ruins of Timna in the Wadi Beihan.[2] According to Robert Ferris, American vice consul at Aden who visited the ruins in June 1949:

The sands of the desert are gradually covering this site, but one can easily trace the outline of houses and large buildings in the central part of the vil-

[2] Careful study of the Timna area was made by the Wendell Phillips expedition in 1950–1952. For details, see p. 241.

lage. There are large cut and shaped stones everywhere, of many different colors and beautifully polished, the use of which by the natives the British have stopped until such time as they might persuade an expedition to excavate there. In the very center of the city square there stands an obelisk, completely inscribed, but now nearly covered with sand. The sand had once been removed down to a depth of about fifteen feet and the base of the obelisk had not then been uncovered. One side of the wall and part of the terrace of the old temple of Amm is still standing, a large structure of huge hewn stones.[3]

Of somewhat later date was the kingdom of Hadhramaut in the valley of that name, whose capital was the incense-collecting point of Shabwa. The location of that town has long been known, although very few Europeans, other than Philby, have studied the site with any care.

Although the Ethiopians claim that the Queen of Sheba was an Abyssinian princess, while others, such as Philby, claim she came from northern Arabia, there is reason to believe that she came either from the ancient town of Saba (Sheba) or from Shabwa in the Hadhramaut. Jerusalem in Solomon's time was importing growing quantities of incense, gold, spices, silks, and other products that moved through Sheba and Shabwa, and it is not unlikely that a princess of those lands might have traveled north to look over this new market and to meet the "wisest man in the world." If the legend is true that her husband was dead and that the elders told her she also would be killed if she did not have a son, there was ample reason for the Queen of Sheba to consult Solomon.

About 650 B.C., Ma'in, Timna, and Shabwa were overshadowed by the rise of the town of Marib, the capital of the Sabaean kingdom which was located on the Incense Trail about fifty miles north of Timna. The few Westerners who have visited Marib report ruins of extensive temples, public buildings, walls, and gates. Marib's greatest claim to fame, however, was the series of dams with which its inhabitants caught the waters from the mountains of Yemen. The largest of these, the Great Dam of Marib, is reported to have been over a mile long and fifty feet high. It is believed to date from about 500 B.C., and its ruins can still be seen, evidence of one of the most useful engineering projects in ancient history.

The Sabaean city state flourished between 650 and 115 B.C. and produced the highest level of trade, prosperity, and culture that the Ara-

---

[3] Unclassified report to the State Department.

bian Peninsula saw until the eighth century. For five hundred years it sat astride one of the main highways of the world, and its citizens grew rich on the camel loads moving between the East and the West. Then the seat of power shifted once again, this time going into the highlands of Yemen to the town of Zofar, near the present Yemeni city of Yarim. The fifth of the great south Arabian city states is known as the Himyarite kingdom. At the peak of its power, about the time of Christ, it extended for hundreds of miles north and south along the Incense Trail and east across the frankincense country of the Hadhramaut as far as the Persian Gulf.

During that period what is now Yemen was called the "land of castles." The most famous of these was the Ghumdan in the city of San'a. This citadel, reportedly built of granite, porphyry, and marble, is said to have been twenty stories high. Its roof was covered by alabaster, so transparent that birds could be distinguished through it. The four outer walls were each faced in different-colored stones, while the metal lions that guarded each corner of the roof roared when the wind blew through them. Of this building the Arab historian, Al Hamadani, wrote, "It had clouds for a turban and marble for a belt." Such research as has been given the Himyaritic state makes it possible to piece together a picture of a feudal aristocracy living in castles and ruling over primitive peasants in a civilization quite similar to that of Yemen today. The relative wealth of modern Yemen, however, cannot compare with that of the kingdom of Zofar, with its virtual monopoly on one of the great East-West trade routes of the world.

The control exercised by the south Arabians over this trade route for about a thousand years weakened shortly before the time of Christ. The change came in the first century B.C., when Roman galleys made their appearance for the first time on the reef-torn waters of the Red Sea and swept the pirates before them.

The high price of incense and of so many other African, Indian, and Far Eastern products was blamed by the Romans on the exorbitant profits made by the merchants of Yemen. The sons of Romulus were not a people to sit idly by and allow another nation to grow rich at their expense. Once they became familiar with the geography of the Red Sea, the Romans decided to send an expedition into Arabia to break the Yemeni monopoly. In the year 24 B.C. ten thousand soldiers under the leadership of the Roman general Aelius Gallus crossed the Red Sea from Egypt, landed in Arabia north of the old port of Yanbu, and marched southward along the Incense Trail toward Yemen. For six months these well-disciplined legions struggled on through desert and mountain, harassed by hostile tribes, plagued by lack of food and water, and misdirected by a treacherous guide from Petra. At last, with its supplies exhausted and its numbers decimated by battle and disease, the Roman army reached the little town of Mariaba, near Marib on the Yemen border. Roman courage could go no farther in the face of organized resistance and rugged terrain. Brokenhearted, Gallus led his troops back to the Red Sea and thence north by boat to Egypt. He had not reached the Himyaritic capital nor penetrated the frankincense country. But it was sixteen hundred years before an outside power again attempted a major military campaign in the Arabian Peninsula, and even then the Turks met with little more success than did the Romans.

The soldiers of Rome did not destroy the Himyaritic civilization, but the sailors of Rome did when they learned the secret of the Indian Ocean—the fact that the monsoon blows from the east for part of the year, then turns around and blows steadily the other way. By A.D. 60 the Himyaritic monopoly of Mediterranean–Indian Ocean commerce had been broken, and the great days of south Arabian culture were over.

In an effort to regain their share of world trade, a series of energetic Yemeni kings expanded their control southward over the valley of the Hadhramaut and along the coast of the Red Sea. This brought them into closer contact with the Abyssinians, but before long the conflict changed to alliance. Christianity had been strengthened in south Arabia by a mission sent there by the Roman Emperor Constantius II, and it spread widely in northern Yemen. Judaism also came down from the north at this time and became so powerful that the last Himyaritic king, Dhu Nuwas, was a Jew. When he wiped out the Christians in what was then the northeastern Yemeni city of Najran [4] in 523, the remaining Christians of Yemen asked help from the Christian ruler of Abyssinia. The Ethiopians sent some seventy thousand men to Yemen who swept all before them until Dhu Nuwas fled on horseback across the sands of the coastal plain, "plunged into the waves of the sea and was never seen again." With his death in A.D. 525 the Himyarite kingdom came to an end, bringing to a close the most glorious period of south Arabian culture.

Once they had gained control of Yemen, the Abyssinian Christians moved the capital north from Zofar to San'a, where about A.D. 550 they built a magnificent cathedral out of stones taken from the ruins of Marib. Some of the Christian bishops of San'a, such as Mar Petrus

---

[4] It is now in Saudi Arabia.

(A.D. 840), were famous throughout Christendom. In Arab history, however, the chief event of this period in southern Arabia was the bursting
of the Great Dam at Marib about the middle of the sixth century. Fewer
caravans meant less wealth, while internal strife and unsuccessful wars
with the Abyssinians had led to the neglect and eventual collapse of
the extensive irrigation system on which eastern Yemeni civilization
had relied. These economic and political changes were hard to describe,
so the Arab writers centered their attention upon the bursting of the
dam, which they explained as being caused by the work of a huge rat;
an interesting example of man's effort to explain the rise and fall of
empires in terms the average mind can understand. It has been suggested that the foundation of the dam may, in fact, have been undermined by a species of gopher that is known to exist in that part of Arabia.

After about A.D. 600 knowledge of this south Arabian civilization was
lost to the Western world for over a thousand years. Then in 1772 a
Dane by the name of Carsten Niebuhr first informed Europe of the
existence of the south Arabic inscriptions. In 1835 an English naval
officer, James R. Wellsted, penetrated a little way into that historic
area, to be followed six years later by a Frenchman, Thomas S. Arnaud,
who discovered the ruins of Marib. In 1870 European knowledge of
the south Arabian kingdoms was expanded further by another Frenchman, Joseph Halévy, a brilliant orientalist who was the first European
to visit the country northeast of Marib since Aelius Gallus. The most
extensive work on this area was done by an Austrian, Edward Glaser,
who made four scientific expeditions to Marib in the 1880's. Many years
later an American plane carrying Yemeni dignitaries and several
Americans circled the ruins in 1947.

From 1950 into 1952 the American Foundation for the Study of
Man under the presidency of the brilliant California organizer of
expeditions, Wendell Phillips, conducted two archaeological campaigns
in the Aden Protectorate and one in Yemen. These expeditions were
elaborately organized in both personnel and equipment with the well-
known scholar Dr. W. F. Albright of Johns Hopkins University acting
as chief archaeologist. Among their results was the first archaeological
survey of southeast Yemen and parts of the Western Aden Protectorate.
A detailed study was made of the irrigation systems of the ancient
south Arabian kingdom of Qataban. A five-month excavation of the
mound of Hajar Ibn Humeid was carried on, bringing to light pottery
and artifacts covering some two thousand years. Several palaces and

temples were excavated in Timna, the old capital of Qataban, producing many archaeological finds which made it possible to date the last destruction of Timna at about 25 B.C. Part of the ancient cemetery of Timna was also excavated and many inscriptions were copied and photographed.

The Foundation's Yemen expedition was the first American group to penetrate to Marib, where the ruins of the seventh-century B.C. Temple of the Moon God and the Great Dam of Marib were excavated. Numerous bronze and alabaster works of art and many new Sabaean inscriptions were discovered. Despite difficulties with the local government, which brought the expedition to a sudden and dramatic end, considerable new light was shed on the Sabaean civilization of south Arabia. But Europeans have only just scratched the surface of this long-lost south Arabian culture. Once the Yemenis open their country so that further archaeological research can be carried out, scholars may well accord the civilization of the south Arabian city states almost equal importance with that of Egypt and Mesopotamia.

With the near disappearance of the traffic in Arabian incense and the diversion of the spice and silk trade from the Far East to other routes, the world left Yemen to itself and to the Turks, who moved in about 1500. Only eight Americans penetrated the Tibet of the Red Sea before 1946. One of these was an American missionary, Charles F. Camp, who went to Yemen in 1905 with his wife, the first American woman to visit Yemen. Traveling inland from Hodeida, the couple visited San'a and then returned to settle in Manakha, where Camp established himself as a carpenter. Unfortunately, Camp's zeal was greater than his discretion, and over the next few years he antagonized both the Arabs and their Turkish rulers. Early in 1910 word reached Charles K. Moser, the American consul at Aden, that Camp had been killed, and Moser was authorized by the Department of State to investigate the circumstances.

Taking a small pilgrim's steamer which was on its way to Jidda, he landed on the beach at Hodeida in May 1910. Moser obtained horses from the local Turkish governor and rode across the hot sands to the walled town of Bajil. Thence his route led through the foothills to Obal and up over the mountains to Manakha and San'a, where he was put up at a private house. The young Zaidi Imam Yahya welcomed him and helped his investigations, which led Moser to the conclusion that Camp had been taken prisoner and killed by the Turks. As he was mounting his horse to leave San'a, his saddle turned and Moser was thrown and broke his leg. There was no medical assistance worthy of the name nearer than Aden, and no carriages or carts in Yemen. Moser himself set the bone and by a series of forced rides, often at a gallop, he reached Hodeida in five days. By this time the bone had worked through his skin, but he was able to get on board a small coastal steamer which took him to Aden, where he literally crawled on his knee down the gangplank and was rushed to the British hospital. In spite of this experience, which would have killed most men, Moser recovered and had a long career in government service, retiring from the Department of Commerce in 1947.

There was no contact between the United States and Yemen for eight years after Moser's visit. Then in a letter to the "President of the United States the Great," the Imam Yahya wrote, "In the name of humanity I ask your Excellency to exert your influence with your government's endorsement to establish the rights of Imamship in the Yemen and the independence of the Arabs." After stating that President Wilson had brought peace to the world, the Imam went on to request "confirmation of the known boundaries of the Yemen and its full independence under the rulership of El-Imam El-Mutuwakel Al Allah, Yahya ibn Mohammed Hamid ad Din, whose ancestors governed the Yemen unceasingly for 1,000 years as well history proves." President Wilson took no action on this request of the Imam, but during the next few years the Imam was able to overcome opposition and extend his authority over all of High Yemen, the adjoining valleys, and the coastal plain of the Tihama.

The next traveler from the United States to visit Yemen was Ameen Rihani, an American of Arab descent, who spent some time there in the early 1920's.

After World War I Charles Moser was transferred to China, where he served with distinction at various posts. During one of these tours of duty Moser was snowbound in Mukden with the American Minister to China, Charles R. Crane. Crane had lived much of his youth in Egypt, where he had developed an interest in Arab affairs. He had been a member of the King–Crane Commission that made a study of the Palestine problem for President Wilson. Moser expounded at length upon his adventures in Yemen and gave a graphic account of the wild grandeur and historic interest of that country. Crane was so interested that, when his duties in China were finished, he got in touch with the Imam Yahya and visited San'a in the winter of 1926–1927. The two became fast friends; they drank tea in the gardens of the palace, rode horseback together around the city, and talked at great length. Crane explained that the geology of Yemen was such that it undoubtedly contained many worth-while minerals, while its agriculture and transport could be much improved. After thinking this over, the Imam said that he would like to hire an American engineer. Crane, who was a man of large heart and ample pocketbook, told the Imam that he would be happy to provide the services of such an engineer as a gift to Yemen, an offer which the Imam gratefully accepted.

Later that spring an American engineer, Karl S. Twitchell, passed through Aden, and the young consul told him that Crane was looking for an engineer to work in Yemen. Thus did Twitchell, the father of economic development in the peninsula, enter the Arabian scene.

Between 1927 and 1932 Twitchell made six trips to Yemen, one of them with Crane's grandson, Charles Bradley. The charming and fragile-looking Mrs. Twitchell accompanied her husband on horseback on several of these trips over some of the roughest mountain passes in Yemen and came out none the worse for her experiences, although the Yemini were amazed to see a woman riding astride and unveiled.

On these various expeditions Twitchell and his associates studied the possibility of developing Yemen's minerals. They also surveyed and laid out several roads and helped the Yemeni organize some model farms, complete with hand-operated and animal-operated farm implements, pumps, and windmills. But Twitchell's most unusual accomplishment was the erection of the only steel truss bridge in the Arabian Peninsula, which was a gift from Charles Crane. He built the bridge over the Wadi Laa, where for many months of the year a raging stream cuts across the main trail from Hodeida to San'a not far from Haja.

Crane and Twitchell were effective in building up admiration and friendship for the United States in Yemen. When Crane left San'a in 1927, he carried with him the Arabic draft of a proposed treaty with the United States, the chief feature of which was to be the extension by the United States of full recognition to Yemen. The Department of State was not then disposed to conclude formal treaty relations with Yemen but approved in principle Crane's activities in developing friendly relations. In this connection James Loder Park, the United States vice consul at Aden, was given permission to make an informal visit to Yemen. Thus, eighteen years after Charles Moser had made the trip, the second American official rode over the high mountain passes to the cloud-wrapped city of San'a. Except for the passing of the Turks and the erection of a telegraph line connecting San'a with

Hodeida, Ta'izz, and Aden, he found Yemen virtually unchanged since Moser's visit. The Imam, now a matured ruler secure on his throne, was as hospitable as ever.

In addition to the activities of Crane, Twitchell, and Park, the late 1920's were marked by other signs of budding American economic interest. Two American geologists made a hurried survey of the coastal plain for an American oil company, but, except for traces of oil in the neighborhood of Mocha and somewhat larger seepage on the Farasan Islands, nothing was discovered. A New York corporation tried to obtain a kerosene monopoly. Nothing came of this because the company was unable to deliver surplus American military uniforms which the Imam wanted in exchange. A Turkish concession had mined substantial amounts of salt near Salif, north of Hodeida, and an American syndicate sought a concession for this salt. In spite of the high favor in which Americans were held, the Imam refused on the ground that he could not permit any of the natural resources of his country to be placed in the hands of foreign interests. He did, however, allow an American anthropologist, Carlton Coon, to go to the Yemen in 1933 but did not permit him to visit Marib.

As is so frequently the case on the Arabian Peninsula, the northern frontier of Yemen was not marked by a clear-cut line, but was fixed by the "southern grazing limit of the Najran tribes." This group of semi-nomadic Arabs moves north and south many miles each year seeking green pastures for their flocks. A long-standing dispute over Asir between the Imam and King Ibn Saud came to a head in 1933 and eventually led to war. Ibn Saud's troops under the leadership of Prince Faisal, moving in part by motorcar and truck, rode down the Tihama past Hodeida as far as Zabeid, while another column under the present King, who was then the Crown Prince, defeated Prince Ahmed of Yemen near Najran and almost arrived at Saada. King Ibn Saud did not want to push his advantage further, so the short war ended with the Imam still on his throne but agreeing in the future to close consultation with King Ibn Saud on many matters of policy.

Charles R. Crane tells an interesting story about this dispute. According to Crane, the Imam Yahya was dissatisfied with the boundary set by Saudi Arabia. He approached King Ibn Saud and asked that the matter be negotiated. The King agreed and suggested that the Imam name a single arbitrator whose judgment would be final. The Imam thereupon named King Ibn Saud as the arbitrator, and the King, after studying the matter, decreed that the boundary as set was unjust and that the Imam's line was the one to be followed, a rare example of courtesy between nations.

Sixteen more years passed following young Park's visit, with United States–Yemeni relations continuing on an informal basis. Then in May 1944 an agent of the Imam, Sayyid Hussein al Kibsi, approached the American Legation in Cairo with a request for United States intervention in a dispute that had developed between the government of Yemen and the British over the location of the southern border of Yemen. It was decided that the point was one to be settled by negotiations between the government of Aden and the Imam. However, a firsthand survey of the situation in Yemen by a United States official appeared desirable.

With instructions from the Department of State, Harlan B. Clark, newly appointed consul at Aden, sent a note to senior Prince Ahmed of Yemen asking whether it would be acceptable to His Majesty if a small American mission visited Yemen. In a letter dated February 3, 1945, to "Our dearest friend, the Consul for the United States," Prince Ahmed replied:

We have received Your Excellency's letter and found it to be the most amiable letter we ever received from a European man. In both phraseology and content it was full of courtesy. We therefore esteem it as a model of politeness and high literature. We could immediately sense that with your courteous expressions and modesty you will prosper much in the service of your Government and of your country and will shortly succeed to the highest official rank. You will receive this success the more . . . by firming and strengthening the close friendship between your honorable Government and the Government of His Majesty, the Imam Yahya. . . . You are welcome.

Clark left Aden, accompanied by Lieutenant Commander Alfred W. Palmer, a United States Naval Reserve doctor. With him also were his interpreter, a skillful driver, a Yemeni guide, and an escort, Sheikh Ali Jahdery, whom the Imam had sent personally to Aden. Taking the consulate jeep and a light truck, they went northwest across the Aden Protectorate to the sultanate of Lahej. Beyond that oasis the "yellow desert" gave way to "black desert" of volcanic rock, a barren world dotted with clumps of camel thorn and filled with the silence of the desert. They spent the first night in Ta'izz, capital of southern Yemen headquarters of Prince Ahmed, the present Imam.

After meeting with Prince Ahmed, Clark and his party drove west through the mountains and across the flat, unfertile country of the

246

southern Tihama to the high mud walls and citadel of the ancient university town of Zabeid. There the Americans enjoyed meeting Arab scholars and would have liked to linger in its peaceful, well-watered gardens filled with bananas, grapes, papayas, lemons, coconuts, and figs.

From Zabeid the trail crossed low sandy hills interspersed occasionally with fertile valleys whose sides were lined with irrigated terraces. The next stop was forty miles to the north at the flourishing market town of Beit al Faqih, which means "house of the jurist." The travelers ate the watermelons for which the district is famous and noted that the complexions of the people were darkening from an intermingling of African blood. At Beit al Faqih, as in every town in Yemen visited by Dr. Palmer, he was called upon to treat officials and their families, who were found to be suffering from everything from malaria to trachoma.

The sandy desert of the Tihama began in earnest north of Beit al Faqih. Often there was no visible road, and the trail was so deep in sand that even the jeep and truck, with their four-wheel drives, bogged down. Just as night was setting in, Clark was surprised to come upon a Ford station wagon standing in the sand. In it was the amil, or mayor, of Hodeida, who had driven fifteen miles out of town to make sure that the visiting Americans did not get lost. A half-hour later the party reached Hodeida, where they were greeted by a crowd of curious citizens and, according to Arab custom, were put up for the night on the third floor of the government guesthouse, looking out over the Red Sea.

Clark's party spent two nights and a day in the humid atmosphere of Hodeida. Then they proceeded north and east along a sand-blown desert track to Bajil and thence up a broad valley that leads into the mountains. The trail to San'a on which Charles Crane's bridge was situated had proved too long to be used as the main auto road. The Yemenis, therefore, had improved a shorter and more southerly route up a series of valleys and over three mountain ranges.

The party slept that night on cots set up in the open, high enough in the foothills for the air to be cool and moderately free of malaria. The next day they crossed the eight-thousand-foot pass that led to the town of Ma'bar, and after a night's rest went on to San'a. The group spent a week in the Yemeni capital, where they found the Imam an old man, though his welcome was as warm as ever. Once again the Imam raised the question of recognition of Yemen by the United States and asked for help in developing his country. Clark returned to Aden and wired this information to Washington.

247

This brought about a review of United States–Yemeni relations, for many changes in the American position in the Near East had occurred since the Imam's earlier communications. The United States now had a direct interest in the Arabian Peninsula, and it was decided that the time had come to recognize Yemen. This was not something that could be carried out by letter. It meant the sending of a representative of the President to San'a as envoy extraordinary and minister plenipotentiary, a mission which in this case called for oganizing and equipping a complete expedition. After considering various candidates, William A. Eddy, the American Minister to Saudi Arabia, was chosen to head the mission. The author, representing the Department of State, and Harlan Clark, the consul at Aden who had made the preliminary survey, were the other diplomatic members.

It had been a long time since an American diplomatic mission had had to worry about providing its own food, clothing, tents, radio telegraph, and medicines, but experience had shown that it was not wise to rely on the Yemenis for these items. The United States Army supplied the transport in the form of jeeps and a baggage truck, while one of the first postwar Fords was obtained for Colonel Eddy. In view of the Arab custom of giving gifts when visiting, it was decided to leave the big radio set in San'a as a present to the Imam. Several smaller sets were taken as gifts for other officials, plus a supply of flashlights and a dozen of the new ball-point fountain pens.

Colonel Eddy's party had to go down the Red Sea to Hodeida. As there were no regular steamers on this run, the United States Navy was kind enough to put a new destroyer, the "Ernest G. Small," at its disposal. Dawn of April 8 found the "Small" at anchor off the coast of Yemen, where field glasses showed the white buildings of Hodeida topped by the spires of three minarets and flanked by Turkish forts half hidden among clumps of palm trees. At a signal from Captain McGrath, the five-inch guns of the destroyer fired a twenty-one-gun salute. Soon a puff of white smoke billowed up from the largest fort as the Yemeni returned the American salute. This turned out to be a lengthy process, for the old Turkish muzzle loaders could fire only once every six minutes and took over two hours to complete the twenty-one shots, by which time Hodeida had been blanketed in smoke.

When several hours passed without further notice from the town, a reconnaissance party was sent shoreward in the "Small's" largest launch. Two miles from the city it met an ocean-going dhow with an ornate blue hull and a huge lateen sail, full-bellied by the morning wind. Four blacks in loincloths stood before the mast, and half a dozen turbaned Arabs, each wearing flowing robes and a dagger, sat amidship. Under the red and white Yemeni flag with its scimitar and five stars, which flew at the stern, sat a regal figure in a white turban and spotless white robes. A green embroidered scarf was thrown over one shoulder, and a large curved dagger hung from a broad belt of golden embroidery. It was Clark's friend, Qadi Fadl ibn Ali al Akwah, Yemeni landowner, scholar, government official, and personal representative of the Imam Yahya, who had traveled all the way from San'a to greet the mission. Once on board the destroyer and strengthened by coffee and ice cream in the wardroom, Qadi Fadl gave Colonel Eddy the Imam's greeting and extended a hearty welcome to the Americans.

The hot, dusty town of Hodeida stretches for a mile along the coast, between the sand of the Tihama and the sand of the beach. Its northern half resembles Jidda, although the houses are not so tall or tired-looking and most of them lack the carved wooden balconies for which that town is justly famous. The southern part is a jumble of grass huts inhabited by Negroes. The tide was low when the mission arrived at the dilapidated stone jetty about fifty yards long that ran out from the central square. A dozen Negroes in loincloths waded out to guide the launch to a pair of rowboats moored at the end of the jetty. Colonel Eddy and the rest jumped into the first rowboat, which was half full of water, clambered over the second boat, and were helped up a rusty iron stairway to the pier. There they were greeted by the adjutant of the governor of Hodeida, whose dark skin showed the colored touch so often seen in the lower Yemen. Beside him was Harlan Clark, who had just arrived by jeep from Aden.

The national dress which the adjutant wore was not like the flowing robe, coils, and headpiece of the Saudi Arab, a costume designed for comfort in the hot and sandy desert. The rulers of Yemen are mountaineers who need not worry about blowing sands and are more interested in keeping warm than in keeping cool. Their headdress is a white silk turban wound over an embroidered skullcap. Their robe, which among better-class Yemeni is always spotlessly white, stops six inches above the ground, frequently showing well-shined, European-type shoes. This robe is gathered at the waist by a wide leather belt covered with gold and black embroidery, and edged in red. A curved dagger with a bone handle in a gold-washed metal sheath is always worn directly over the stomach. The ornateness of this dagger is an indication of the wearer's rank, and those belonging to important officials are museum pieces. Yemeni boys wear a sheath only until they have proved their manhood, when they are given the dagger at a ceremony. The costume of the Yemeni aristocrat is topped off by a green woolen scarf, which is carefully folded over the shoulders with the long end hanging down to the left knee. Some of these scarves are made locally, but others are imported from Iran and India.

A guard of two hundred Yemeni riflemen was lined up on either side of the jetty, wearing the traditional yellow turbans that indicate the service of the Imam. Voluminous white robes were gathered at their waists by cartridge belts, and their rifles were mostly Turkish models, dating from World War I. As the mission moved shoreward along the jetty, a barefooted band burst into the haunting martial music of Yemen. It is not oriental, or Arab, or Turkish, but a little of all three. The band was composed of brass instruments with curved trumpets, such as David used when he played before Solomon, along with a mixture of discarded Turkish bugles, cymbals, and drums. The musicians threw themselves wholeheartedly into their work, and the effect was quite overwhelming, for Yemeni music is an acquired taste and should be heard first at a distance.

Leaving the jetty, the mission crossed the main square between lines of riflemen, who saluted with more zeal than precision. Behind them the square was packed solid with curious onlookers, a few dressed like the adjutant, but most of them in brown or gray robes. Some were mountaineers in sheepskin jackets which must have been unbearable, since the temperature was close to 100 degrees in the shade. The most striking feature of the crowd was the variety of its headgear, which varied according to whether the wearer came from the High Yemen, from coffee-rich Mocha, the Crown Colony of Aden, the wadi of the Hadhramaut, the rock-bound harbor of Muscat, the docks of Karachi, or the suqs of Zanzibar. Scattered among the crowd were unveiled peasant girls, servants, and slaves, most of them Negro women, with a sprinkling of veiled Arab ladies. Men and women alike watched in open-mouthed curiosity as Colonel Eddy led his party to the governor's palace, a masterpiece of unbalanced architecture whose arched doorway was off-center, its three projecting balconies of unrelated design, and its roof topped on one side by a white dome and on the other by a glassed-in roof garden that looked like an abandoned greenhouse.

Leaving the glaring Red Sea sunlight, the party climbed a rickety wooden stairway and was shown into a room whose bare walls were lined with stiff chairs. A cool breeze blew in off the ocean through

half a dozen open windows, carrying with it the blare of the band and
the pounding of the surf on the beach. Sitting at a small table with his
back to the windows was the governor of Hodeida, Qadi Abdul Rahman
ibn Ahmed al Sayyaghi. He was a dark-skinned man of middle height,
about forty-five years old, dressed in the traditional white robe, gold
belt, and green shoulder scarf of an upper-class Yemeni. He came forward to greet Colonel Eddy, and the mission members were soon seated
for a discussion of the Imam's health, the governor's health, Colonel
Eddy's health, and plans for the mission. Qadi al Sayyaghi was courteous but gave the impression that he thought Yemen was doing all
right the way it was and that any changes brought about by Westerners
would be for the worse.

After half an hour of talk, coffee, and lukewarm bottled orange pop,
the Americans took their leave and were escorted across the main square
to the three-story Hodeida guesthouse. The ground floor of that building looked like the inside of a deserted warehouse. From it a stone stairway wound up to a large hall on the top floor, flanked by a series of
bedrooms on the ocean side which were furnished with simple chairs,
European-type beds, mosquito nets, and ornate mirrors, hung at odd
angles over an assorted collection of wash basins. The bathroom was
on the other side of the hall, equipped with several buckets of water
and a slot in the floor through which slops ran out and down the side
of the building.

Venturing out onto the paved streets of Hodeida in the cool of the
early evening, the party wandered about, looking at the weather-beaten,
unpainted houses, much of whose plaster was cracked and whose doors
and windows needed repair. The most interesting architectural features were the elaborate carvings and Arab scripts intricately done in
wood over the doorways of the better houses. A friendly crowd of men,
boys, and unveiled women followed the Americans on their tour. The
visitors walked through the market place, several blocks of narrow
streets lined with small stores or tiny stalls and sheltered from the sun
by lattice hangings. Some of the shops sold rice, maize, and durrah,
and there was an abundance of watermelons, limes, and vegetables,
along with piles of freshly caught fish and mutton buried under swarms
of black flies. Other stores were stocked with textiles, mostly colored
prints from India. More food was evident than in Jidda, but the market
looked dirtier and the people were more diseased, maimed, or blinded
than in the Saudi Arabian seaport.

A visit to a warehouse showed piles of fragrant Yemeni coffee being put in bags by women squatting on the ground. Hodeida coffee is rated among the world's best. It sells in Aden for the top international market price and is used as a blend with other coffees, such as Java. The Yemeni, however, do not make the most of their coffee-growing possibilities, and modern methods of production, transportation, sorting, packaging, and shipping could greatly increase the wealth they derive from it.

The party spent next afternoon looking over Hodeida Bay, an almost landlocked body of water just north of the town. More than twenty years ago a Greek syndicate was given a hundred thousand pounds to build a dock here, but the officials disappeared after the first ten thousand pounds were spent. All that remains of their efforts is a short stone pier and a rusty, narrow-gauge railroad with a dozen dump cars and a locomotive encased in straw and in a hopeless state of disrepair.

Dinner at the guesthouse was followed by a night tour of Hodeida. The moonlight seemed to kill the smells and bathe the dusty shabbiness of the tall buildings in mystery and beauty. From the rooftops and windows the people stared down at the strangers, while from the shadow-draped streets came the shouts of the watchmen who guard every building and keep awake by calling to each other through the hours of the night, as Yemeni guards have done since the Arab world was young.

XVIII

Mission to Yemen

THE road inland from Hodeida was a desert track which followed the coast north for a while, winding among clumps of green shrubs and small sand dunes. At one point it provided a clear view of the heavily wooded island off which young Prince Mohammed of Yemen was drowned in 1923 while trying to save the life of two friends. He was reported to have been one of the ablest royal princes, and his death was a great blow to the Imam. As the caravan bumped along, it passed lines of mangy, supercilious camels, loaded with textiles, kerosene, hardware, and salt, starting on the long trip to the High Yemen. Flocks of black sheep and herds of fat, hump-backed Indian cattle grazed near scattered groups of thatched huts with pointed, African-looking roofs. Here and there a whitewashed building on the top of a low hill marked the tomb of a holy man.[1]

The coastal plain was fertile enough so that the inhabitants could live as farmers rather than as nomads. Many of the fields had been plowed recently, and there was water in the irrigation ditches that crossed the road at frequent intervals. These ditches, which must be forded, are a great drawback to motoring in Yemen, sometimes cutting the trail every thirty or forty yards. When the Yemenis decide to replace these ditches with culverts, the speed of motor travel in the country will be doubled. The unwatered parts of the plain were dry, and as the wind rose with the sun the Americans could see as many as five brown

[1] Part of the material used in this chapter has already appeared in an article by the author in the *Foreign Service Journal*.

columns of dust, some of them 150 feet high, swirling one behind the other across the plain.

Shortly before noon the caravan left the sandy Tihama and entered the broad mouth of a valley whose graveled floor ran between low hills to the walled town of Bajil. This little city is noted for the beauty of its women and for the fact that a British political mission, heading for San'a under Lieutenant Colonel H. F. Jacobs, was held prisoner here for three months in the autumn of 1919. With this incident in mind, Colonel Eddy was none too happy on entering Bajil to find a line of Yemeni soldiers drawn up across the central square of the town completely blocking the road to the east. It soon appeared that he was not being taken prisoner but merely stopped by the hospitable amil, who begged Colonel Eddy to mount with him to the second floor of the guesthouse for a little refreshment. There the party reclined on high benches and sipped Yemeni coffee while strains of music from the Bajil band drifted in through the open windows, and the cool shade of the low-ceilinged room afforded welcome relief from the noonday glare. After complimenting the amil on the decorative brick designs which were the distinguishing feature of the town's architecture, the Americans were on their way, creeping along streets crowded with farmers in town for the weekly market.

The going became rougher beyond Bajil. Sometimes the caravan bumped along stony river bottoms; at other times it wound over dry hills. Occasionally, on short stretches where the big stones had been rolled aside, speed reached thirty miles an hour. This was possible because as soon as the Imam had heard that Colonel Eddy was coming he had put six thousand men to work on the road. Several gangs of these road workers were passed—bearded men in dark turbans who leaned on their primitive hoes and waved cheerfully.

Not far beyond Bajil the caravan stopped for lunch at Bahah, a dozen grass huts surrounded by a stockade of thorns. Beds of rope stretched between wooden frames were waiting here in the shade of a thatched hut, and the Americans lay down gratefully and ate bananas and *battickh,* a delicious native melon that tastes like papaya. The "rest house" was run by a toothless old woman who bustled about bringing food and tried to lay the dust by sprinkling the floor under the beds with water from a hand-painted water jug, a process that disturbed several chickens, two sheep, and a goat. After lunch the hostess produced an ornate silver hubble-bubble that stood three feet high, and Colonel Eddy puffed away contentedly at the end of the hose.

Near Bahah the road passed under the telegraph line from Hodeida to San'a, a single wire stretched on rickety poles, propped on little piles of mud. Then, after several sharp ups and downs, it came to Rirbar, the first village with houses made of stone. Beyond lay a beautiful little valley full of pink blossoms like lilacs, where flocks of yellow birds flew up from the thorn trees. Coveys of quail fluttered overhead, and troops of long-tailed baboons scampered over the black rocks of the hillsides as the jeeps passed, looking back over their shoulders and chattering angrily.

From here on the route was a constant succession of ups and downs, and as the valleys grew smaller they became more fertile, and the stone terraces for which Yemen is famous began to appear. Some of the fields made by these terraces were two or three acres in extent, while others were no more than fifty feet across, but all were covered with rich soil and carefully cultivated. The retaining walls of these terraces were made without mortar and varied from two to ten feet in height. The streams which originally flowed down the center of the wadies had been diverted into canals that ran along the hillsides, with ditches fanning out, so that each terraced field was well supplied with water, and the black earth and green vegetables contrasted sharply with the parched hills above.

At kilometer 118 from Hodeida the first hilltop village was passed— a group of square stone houses perched on an inaccessible-looking crag. This was the real entrance to the High Yemen, whose Zaidi rulers prefer such locations, both for safety and in an effort to escape malaria. The Zaidis are a subdivision of the Shi'a sect of Moslems. Power in mountainous Yemen rests with them and with the big landowning and merchant families. On the coast most of the population belongs to the Sunni sect of Moslems, and the dominant families are traders or men of the sea. There are almost no nomads in Yemen. It was said that the women and children who lived in these hilltop homes spent as long as six months at a time without coming down onto the flat.

The hot moist air of the Red Sea piled up huge masses of black clouds that hung low above these valleys, giving them a feeling of unreality and bringing drenching white downpours that blotted out the ranges and turned the stream beds into rushing torrents. During a halt to change a tire, the peasants who flocked around the jeeps were full of tales of unwary travelers who had been drowned in these flash floods.

With the mountain ranges now rising on all sides, the sun dropped out of sight by five-thirty in the afternoon. Rather than sleep in the bug-infested interior of some local guesthouse, the Americans camped on a little plateau under the shadow of two abandoned Turkish forts. The sky cleared at sunset, the stars came out as the quick tropical twilight fell across the valley, and a pale moon wrapped the barren mountains in hazy light. Farmers from the low stone huts of Gana brought a supply of firewood, pieces of flat native bread two feet across, a roast lamb, and some rice. The air was fresher here than on the dusty Tihama, appetites were good, and spirits rose. Then, wrapped in blankets for the first time in many months, the travelers lay down and slept soundly while fleecy clouds chased each other across the moon, and the only sound that disturbed the quiet of the mountain gorge was the distant barking of a village dog.

The soldiers who escorted the mission were early risers, and the crackle of a fire and the pungent smell of Yemeni coffee awoke the travelers as the first early light began to spread over the valley. The trail wound up and east from Gana, passing terraced fields in which the men wore goatskin jackets and the women, dressed in long black trousers and loose coats held in by broad belts, wore pointed straw hats that gave a Chinese appearance to the scene. At Medinat al Abid, "town of slaves," the first coffee bushes appeared, about twelve feet high, growing in the shade of taller eucalyptus trees. A grove of banana trees waved their wind-whipped leaves below the whitewashed castle of the local amil, perched on top of a perpendicular cliff.

The next point of note was Hammam Ali, the most famous hot springs in Yemen. Rich people come from all over the country to bathe in the water and sleep in the primitive stone cabins that give the hill to the north of the springs the appearance of a Stone Age village. Hammam Ali had become so popular during the last two years that a sizable building had been constructed over the springs, complete with dressing rooms, steam rooms, and several pools of clear, blue, sulphur-smelling water bubbling constantly over the rocks. If malaria, so prevalent in this valley, could be wiped out and a modest hotel built there, Hammam Ali might become the watering place for the whole southern Red Sea.

East of the springs a forbidding-looking mountain rose into the thinning air, five thousand feet above the floor of the valley and ten thousand feet above the Red Sea. This was Jebel Masna‘a, the last great barrier to the High Yemen. Compared to it, previous mountains seemed like hills. The newly improved auto road, winding in switchbacks up

256

27. Wood market in the central square in San'a, Yemen.

28. A house in the residential section of San'a, showing ancient stone foundations, stained-glass windows, whitewashed brick decoration, and outside drainage system.

the face of the mountain, was too steep for anything but low gear, forcing frequent stops for water and cooling the motor. The rains had loosened rocks that occasionally came bounding past or stopped in the middle of the road and had to be pushed aside. Even the new jeeps were laboring, and the old Dodge which the amil of Hodeida had lent Colonel Eddy when his Ford broke down stopped so often that the party got out and walked part of the way. At last the summit was reached, and the panting Americans stopped to put on sweaters and look down into the distant valley from which they had come. The scene was suggestive of our own Grand Canyon, for from the summit it was possible to see that the nearer mountains were flat on top, with cliffs that fell perpendicularly for two or three thousand feet. Beyond were the ragged summits of the coastal range, cutting off any view of the distant Tihama. Hodeida, the Red Sea, and the outside world seemed very far away.

On the eastern side of the pass a drop of a few hundred feet brought the road to the flat plain of the High Yemen, which at this point was about ten miles wide, with a low range of mountains shutting in the eastern horizon. Most of the land was stony, but about ten miles north of the pass the unwalled town of Ma'bar stood in the center of a rich farming district. Thanks to the telegraph line from Hodeida, the amil was well posted about the mission and came out to greet its members at the huge wooden gate of the guesthouse. After much handshaking the visitors were led up a stone stairway to a heavily carpeted suite consisting of sitting room, bedroom, and dining room, all furnished alike with piles of pillows ranged around the walls. The keeper of this establishment turned out to be a local Oscar of the Waldorf, redecorating the table for every meal with sticks two feet long to which roses were tied. His chef d'oeuvre, however, was his arrangement of white napkins into accordionlike folds rising out of the glass at each place.

Thanks to plentiful applications of DDT, the party slept well in the bracing mountain air and were on the road again early the next day, going north along the valley of the High Yemen. There was more traffic now—long camel caravans on their way from Aden or Hodeida, groups of donkeys trotting patiently under piles of firewood or mounds of hay as big as themselves, and parties of men in red and yellow turbans, white tunics, and broad belts with curved daggers. Occasionally a family would pass with the man riding on a small donkey, his sons walking beside him, and several women in black robes bringing up the rear.

Less than an hour north of Ma'bar, the road climbed over the Geslah hills that run east and west, cutting the valley in half. After two more hours of easy going, the dark bulk of Jebel Nuqum rose two thousand feet above the plain on the east, with the graceful minarets of the city of San'a, then the capital of Yemen, rising at its feet.

A stone building stood by the roadside three miles south of the town, where travelers were expected to wash and change into fresh clothes before entering the city. Here a crowd of curious onlookers had assembled to get a first view of the strangers from the outside world. In front of them, resplendent in a freshly washed, white silk robe stood the palace chamberlain, ready with a greeting from the Imam and an invitation to his guesthouse. A detachment of cavalry was on hand to escort the party into the city, led by a colorful officer, on a white horse, whose beard was dyed henna red. With this Kip- lingesque figure in the lead, the caravan moved on, surrounded by cavalrymen moving at a trot between two solid lines of spectators. Soon several of the younger princes joined the procession, dressed in white turbans and square-shouldered coats of blue and white silk and beautifully mounted on small Arab horses. The day was cloud- less, the horses pranced, the crowd shouted, and the whole scene was something out of *The Arabian Nights*.

The road led across the treeless plain, past the "workshop," a com- bination foundry and factory where, under the direction of a Polish engineer named Danziger, the motors of San'a were kept running and rifles made for the Imam's troops. Beyond it was the main gate of San'a, the Bab al Yemen, whose stone columns, about thirty feet high, flanked a simple arch topped with a marble plaque. On either side round brick towers separated the gate from the weather-beaten mud walls that completely surrounded the city. The guards of this gate, some two hundred strong, supported by a brassy Yemeni band, lined up to welcome the visitors to the city and escort them to the guest- house.

This was the most modern building in San'a, a square, two-story, gray stone structure with large European-style windows arched at the top. It was built around a central courtyard where an ornate foun- tain played day and night, and was equipped with tables, chairs, beds, electric lights, and some plumbing, which required a certain amount of installation before it functioned properly. For the next three weeks this guesthouse was the comfortable home of the mission, who were assigned to separate rooms opening on a covered cloister that ran around the second story of the patio. Colonel Eddy had a sitting room, overfurnished with elaborately brocaded chairs, that became a general meeting place when it was not being used for conferences. Meals were served in a cool dining room on the western side of the building, and were so similar to those at Hodeida and Ma'bar as to suggest that they had been prepared by the same kitchen staff, which turned out to be the case. The best meal of all was breakfast, of delicious Yemeni coffee, oranges, sweet lemons, apples, and eggs done in all possible styles. At first these were eaten with flat Yemeni bread; then by chance it was discovered that one of the waiters had worked in a restaurant in Detroit, and he was persuaded to make toast.

The early mornings were cloudless, and the bright sunshine that filled the patio soon drove away the cool of the night. Even at noon it was not too hot, however, for San'a is located seventy-two hundred feet above the Red Sea. In midafternoon black clouds piled up around Jebel Nuqum, and a cold rain fell for several hours. Then the clouds blew away as fast as they had come, producing beautiful, clear sunsets but leaving the streets of the city deep in mud, while the freshly planted fields outside turned greener daily.

The more energetic members of the mission usually went riding after breakfast, when the air was still cool and washed by the rain of the previous afternoon. The horses they were given were small Arab thoroughbreds, high spirited and eager to leave the crowded streets of the city behind. Sometimes the riders circled the high mud walls of the city, a ride which took about two hours, or cantered out to the nearby plains where the Imam's cavalry and camel corps held daily maneuvers. Rides through the city were interesting, but the streets were too narrow and crowded for anything faster than a walk.

These rides and frequent tours by jeep showed that the city of San'a was divided into three separate towns, all enclosed by the same outer wall but shut off from each other by inner barriers. To the east was the Arab city, possibly the finest example of a medieval Arab town to be found anywhere in the world today. The streets were narrow, crooked, and unpaved. Most of the houses had lower floors of large stone blocks, while the upper stories were of dried brick. The average height of the buildings was three stories, but some of them went up to seven or eight floors. Entering through a heavy wooden gate, one found the bottom floor a storeroom. Above were rooms for servants, then the women's quarters, and on the top floor one or more large sitting rooms with views out across the rooftops of the city.

Windows were divided into two parts, the lower section of clear glass closed with shutters at night. The upper half was made either of stained glass or of a single slab of translucent alabaster which let in the light but not the glare of the sun. At night the darkness hid the fact that sewage ran in troughs down the outside of these buildings. The moonlight lit up the projecting bricks, which were freshly whitewashed and set in decorative patterns around the windows, and the lamplight, shining through the colored glass and alabaster, turned the town into a virtual fairyland in which the windows seemed like "magic casements opening on the dome of San'a Mosque in Yemen forlorn." Some of the houses in this part of San'a were fortresslike buildings that dated from the eleventh century. The Arab city also contained more than a dozen beautiful mosques. The oldest was said to have been built in the time of Mohammed on the ruins of a cathedral which, like it, was built with stones taken in part from the Great Dam of Marib. Some of the most graceful minarets in Arabia rise above these mosques, tall and elaborately decorated with designs worked out in whitewashed brick.

The heart of the old Arab city was the suq or market place, a hodgepodge of winding lanes, some of them less than six feet wide. These little streets were lined with booths whose open fronts were protected from sun and rain by flimsy wooden awnings. Some sold grains, vegetables, fruits, and fly-covered meats, while others carried textiles or finished robes, capes, and skullcaps. Many were stocked with broken lamps, scraps of leather, parts of old hoes, opened tin cans, and homemade pitchers and candlesticks beaten out of kerosene tins. To Western travelers the most interesting were the stalls of the silversmiths who, on being pressed, produced beautifully wrought necklaces, bracelets, boxes, and trays. Some of this jewelry came from India or other parts of the Arabian Peninsula and was of great age. Most of the modern silver pieces were made by the members of the former Jewish colony of San'a, who melted down silver Maria Theresa thalers and produced intricate filigree work that was particularly effective in cigarette cases.

Throughout the daylight hours the streets of the Arab city were crowded with men, boys, and a few heavily veiled women, who went about completely covered by a brightly ornamented scarf through which they could see with great difficulty. Some of these scarves were decorated with white circles which the women wore over their faces, making them look like large-eyed owls. The streets, for the most part, were deserted after sunset, and all the gates of the city were shut and barred.

The central section of San'a where the guesthouse stood was the Turkish quarter, laid out with broader streets and well-watered gardens around many of the houses. Here were located San'a's nine schools, some of them attended by boys from all over Yemen. The subjects dealt largely with the Koran, although a few schools gave courses in history and geography and, under the guidance of instructors who had been in other parts of the Arab world, encouraged setting-up exercises and soccer among the boy students. An unusual feature of Yemeni schooling was the practice of fastening leg irons and chains on boys who did poorly or who needed punishing. These were left on from five minutes to three months, as the offense warranted.

Also in the Turkish quarter was the post office, where things moved at so leisurely a pace that it took the gray-bearded postmaster half an hour to open his archaic safe and sell a dozen postage stamps. Yemeni stamps are much in demand by collectors and have been a great help to the pocketbooks of the royal family.

At that time, before the recent emigration of a large number of Jews to Israel by plane, via Aden, there were about fifty thousand Jews in Yemen, most of whom lived in the Jewish quarter at the western side of San'a. Many of these Jewish families traced their lineage back to the time of dispersion in the first century A.D., while others went back to the time, about A.D. 500, when the king of Yemen was a Jew. The men always wore long gray robes and had black curls hanging down each cheek from their skullcaps. The women were often unveiled and frequently wore elaborate silver decorations on their headdresses. The Jews of Yemen paid special taxes and were excused from military service, from veiling their women, and from the prohibition against making or drinking wine. But they were restricted to their quarter of the city after dark and were not allowed to own land, ride on a horse or in an automobile, or carry a weapon. Until recently their houses had been limited to two stories in height, but this rule was no longer enforced. In addition to being the most skillful silverworkers in Yemen, they also made wine out of the grapes for which the country is justly famous.

One day the members of the mission were invited to the summer palace of the Imam at Wadi Dhahar. This valley, located about ten miles north of the city, was a canyon whose vertical walls dropped five hundred feet below the level of the San'a plain. The wadi was first settled in Himyaritic times, and near the head of the canyon were ruins of an old dam. A seasonal stream ran down the center of the valley, whose floor was green with walled gardens filled with lemons and limes. The valley was dotted with four- and five-storied houses, but these were dwarfed by the summer palace, an eight-story building perched on top of a high rock in the center of town, where the Imam went during the hot summer months.

Another outing was to the town of Al Roda, a garden suburb five miles north of San'a where several of the princes had summer houses. The occasion was a luncheon given for Colonel Eddy by Prince Hussein. The sons of the Imam are called Seif al Islam, "The Sword of Islam," and the name indicates the theocratic nature of the Yemeni state. For more than an hour the slim, Malayan-looking Prince and his jovial, heavy-set brother Mutahhar led the Americans through the paths of their well-watered garden, pointing with particular pride to the huge muscatel grapes growing on hand-cut stone poles. The water table was about ninety feet below San'a, and the artificial watering of such gardens kept a small army of men and animals busy, while the wooden water wheels squeaked all the time. Lunch was served in a summer house that overlooked the garden and a pool of water into which fountains played. The meal was an eight-course affair with chicken, rice, beans, and one roast lamb cooked whole for every four guests. The service was, as usual, handled by the familiar waiters, who brought not only the dishes but even the tables and chairs from the dining room of the guesthouse. Prince Hussein was a charming host, full of stories of his travels in Japan and England. His brother, Prince Mutahhar, one of the great eaters of Yemen, carved the lambs with gusto and ate two huge helpings of everything.

After the meal ghat was served to everyone. Ghat is a shrub, not unlike a coffee tree, which grows in some parts of the Yemeni highland, where it is cultivated to the virtual exclusion of other plants. When mature, the tenderest stalks are cut, wrapped in wet cloths and rushed to market, where they are quickly sold. Then every afternoon the men of Yemen gather in groups, strip off the ghat leaves, and roll them into a ball which is chewed for an hour or two. As the taste begins to fade, fresh leaves are added until the chewers' cheeks bulge with the quid. The leaves are then spat out and several glasses of water drunk, producing an effect on the ghat chewer somewhat like that of benzedrine or marihuana. The pupils of the eyes contract and the addict becomes excited and happy. He talks volubly, often not making complete sense but convinced of the brilliance of his own remarks and feeling a great sense of elation and superiority.

An example of this was shown in the case of one of the mission's drivers, who was called out of a ghat session to drive to the palace. Usually a cautious man, he raced across the city and, on coming to a hole in the road, drove directly at it pulling up on the stearing gear, apparently in the delusion that he could lift the car over the hole. After two or three hours of elation, a reaction sets in which leaves the ghat user tired, irritable, and unhappy until he can get more ghat. It is estimated that three out of every four of the men of Yemen chew ghat, often enough to interfere with other activities, while perhaps a quarter of the women also use this stimulant.

Ghat has an unpleasant taste, somewhat like the leaf of the sumac tree, and the members of the mission who tried it got no kick out of it whatsoever, probably because it must be chewed for several weeks in order to build up a sufficient supply of the stimulant in the system to produce any effect. The widespread use of this unusual drug in Yemen not only cuts down the food which might otherwise be grown, but renders a high percentage of the men of the country comparatively useless for most of each afternoon. It has been a contributing factor in keeping Yemen retarded. As one of the few traveled Yemeni put it, "What we need is a CocaCola factory."

Colonel Eddy's mission had two purposes: to recognize the Kingdom of Yemen and to conclude a simple agreement of commerce and friendship that would open the way for closer business relations. The first of these had actually been accomplished by the twenty-one gun salute at Hodeida. Then, on Sunday, April 14, the second got under way when word came from the palace that the Imam would receive the mission that morning. The civilian members promptly changed into black trousers and white dinner jackets, a costume which had been decided upon as most suitable for formal dress. It seemed as though half the population of San'a were packed into the Sharara square in front of the guesthouse that morning. Without the waving saber of the red-bearded commander on his white steed and the prancing hoofs of his cavalrymen, the two cars carrying the mission could never have got through. The last block of the route from the royal mosque to the palace gates was lined with turbaned riflemen, and the members of the mission held their hats over their hearts in salute to the many red Yemeni flags that fluttered in the morning breeze. The party dismounted at the outer gate, where the royal band, thirty strong, was filling the air with haunting discords.

Crossing the courtyard of the palace between lines of soldiers, the visitors were met at the door of the Palace of Thanks by the venerable Foreign Minister, the seventy-year-old Raghib Bey, one of the most extraordinary figures in Near Eastern diplomacy. He was born in Constantinople about 1874 of well-to-do Turkish parents. Upon graduation from school he entered the Turkish diplomatic service and was stationed in Bucharest, Petrograd, Paris, and Morocco. During the Turkish occupation of Yemen, he became governor of Hodeida and Ta'izz and stayed on in Yemen after the Turks were driven out in World War I. One of his daughters married Prince Ahmed and another married Prince Hussein, and he was also closely related by marriage to the Prime Minister. Thanks to these high connections and to his diplomatic skill, he accomplished the incredible feat of changing from governor of a conquered country to being its foreign minister after it obtained its freedom.

Raghib Bey was tall, good-looking, and possessed of an imposing presence. His white beard and spotless turban framed a firm but friendly countenance, and his blue eyes had lost little of their youthful fire. In addition to Turkish and Arabic, he spoke fluent French, which he liked to use with foreigners. The stone house in which he lived near the guesthouse was furnished in European style, and its walls were hung with many pictures showing the high lights of his career, which he said had been spent backward, the first twenty years in the brilliant diplomatic capitals of Europe and the last thirty in forgotten San'a. On informal occasions his eyes would light up as he told of the great balls he had attended in Vienna under the Hapsburgs and the brilliant scenes in which he had played a part, such as the coronation of the last czar of all the Russias. Raghib Bey had cultivated the friendship of the Imam and pursued a policy of balance of power in southwestern Arabia with such skill that he dominated Yemen's comparatively few dealings with foreign powers for almost thirty years.

Escorted by this remarkable diplomat, the mission climbed a curving, stone, outside staircase to the second-story entrance to the palace. The way led through a whitewashed hall, low ceilinged and plainly furnished, to the throne room. Its floor was soft with Persian rugs, and the many windows were hung with blue satin curtains, while a row of gilt chairs with blue silk backs lined the walls. The throne stood behind a small table at the eastern end of the room, a high-backed wooden chair upholstered in blue silk and decorated with five stars and two crossed scimitars.

Raghib Bey talked to Colonel Eddy for a few minutes, asking about life at the guesthouse and suggesting that the squeaking of the wooden water wheels in the garden of the palace, a sound which also rose from wells all over the city, was "the native music of San'a." Suddenly and unannounced, the palace chamberlain appeared, followed by a short, stocky, white-bearded Yemeni in spotless silk robes. The jeweled skullcap on his head was almost hidden by a white silk turban with the end hanging down at one side, and his unusually broad and richly embroidered belt carried an ornate gold dagger. It was the Imam Yahya, the eighty-year-old absolute ruler of Yemen. For religious reasons the Imam did not allow any picture to be taken or painted of himself, and the only known sketch, which is the frontispiece of Ameen Rihani's book, bears little resemblance to him. That drawing gave him a thin face, a long narrow nose, and a cruel mouth, while actually he had a round face, a broad nose, and a genial expression. The Imam Yahya did not give the sense of power imparted by the late King Ibn Saud, but he did strike visitors as a redoubtable mountain chieftain, a strong but local man. Furthermore, like many other Zaidi leaders, he was a Koranic scholar of note and the possessor of a library filled with rare religious and historical manuscripts.

The Imam welcomed Colonel Eddy warmly in Arabic and asked about his trip and his comfort at the guesthouse. Colonel Eddy, who had the finest command of Arabic of any senior American diplomat, thanked the Imam for his kindness and said that the trip had been quick and the guesthouse comfortable. When asked about the state of his health, the Imam said he had consulted many foreign doctors, but that none had done him any good except Dr. Palmer, who had accompanied Consul Clark the year before, and Dr. Hedley, the American physician whom Colonel Eddy had brought with him, who had already given him new hope.

The Imam apologized for the appearance of his countrymen, who, he said, were so badly in need of textiles that many had to stay indoors on holidays because they had no good clothes. Changing the conversation to the field of international affairs, the Imam said that, since World War I, his chief Western contact had been with the Italians, but that they had turned out to be personally antagonistic toward him. Hitler had courted him and sent him presents, but he had refused to sign a treaty or deal with such a man. He was glad to welcome the

Americans, with whom he had had several happy contacts, including the generous Charles R. Crane and his energetic engineer, Karl Twitchell, who he hoped was in good health.

Colonel Eddy thereupon presented a letter from President Truman to the Imam recognizing the absolute independence of the Kingdom of Yemen and an autographed photograph of the American President. Colonel Eddy then indicated the desire of the United States to conclude an agreement of commerce and friendship with Yemen along the lines of the agreements and treaties which the United States had with more than sixty nations of the world. The Imam expressed approval and designated the Foreign Minister and his spade-bearded assistant, Qadi Abdul Karim Mutahhar, as the Yemeni negotiators.

About eleven o'clock each morning for the next two weeks the clatter of a horse's hoofs resounded on the hard-packed earth of the street outside the guesthouse, heralding the approach of the Yemeni officials in the old-fashioned black carriage of the Foreign Minister. The riflemen at the door would snap to attention, and the steep stone stairs would click with the sound of Raghib Bey's cane as he climbed to the elaborately furnished sitting room where the negotiations were held. The proposed draft of the agreement had been carefully worked out, but as the talks progressed the Yemenis suggested certain minor changes that had to be referred to Washington, via the portable radio station the mission had brought along. Under the direction of Colonel Nahas and Corporal McClure, this transmitter gave excellent service, contacting Asmara in Eritrea across the Red Sea, which in turn talked directly with Washington. More than once McClure, who was laid low by dysentery, dragged himself out of bed when he had a high fever to send urgent messages.

Seventeen busy days passed quickly, and it seemed that a meeting of the minds would soon be reached with the Yemenis on the wording of the agreement. Then suddenly the negotiations took a turn for the worse. Raghib Bey and his assistant, Qadi Mutahhar, dropped out of the picture and their place was taken by small, wiry Prince Hussein, the third son of the Imam. Although he had traveled more than any of his brothers and had a sharp mind and a beaming personality when he wished to exert it, all progress came to an end as soon as he entered the negotiations. In the long and difficult discussion that began this new phase, Prince Hussein said that he had worked on several such matters, and none had ever ended successfully. With this melancholy start, he proceeded to go through the text of the proposed agreement, paragraph by paragraph, raising a multitude of objections. Long hours and many telegrams to Washington smoothed out most of them, but one all-important point could not be reconciled. The American mission insisted that the agreement should contain the phrase "subjects of his Majesty the King of Yemen in the United States, and nationals of the United States of America in the Kingdom of Yemen shall be received and treated in accordance with the requirements and practices of generally recognized international law." This sentence in virtually the same form is to be found in all United States agreements and treaties. Without it, American citizens could be thrown into jail without due process, kept there indefinitely, and subjected to inhuman punishments under the harsh legal practices of Moslem law.

Prince Hussein, on the other hand, took the position that the law of Yemen should be paramount in that country, where it was impossible to separate religious teaching and common law. He felt that any recognition of Western law in Yemen would be the first step in breaking down the religious and social pattern of his country. Each succeeding talk became more difficult and produced nothing like a solution. Indirect approaches were made by both sides, but the stalemate was complete. The mission packed quietly at first and then ostentatiously, but the Yemenis did not yield. At last Colonel Eddy sent word to the Imam that the talks had broken down and requested a final interview in which to say good-bye.

On the morning of April 23 the cavalry escort again formed outside the guesthouse, and the entire mission was escorted between lines of spectators across the Sharara square and past the white domes of the royal mosque to the palace gates. Doctors Hedley and Lapenta had made good progress with the Imam's health, and he strode into the blue throne room that morning with far more vigor than he had shown before. After the usual politenesses, the Imam asked what was the matter and was told that the American position had been made clear in a letter sent to him two days before. The Imam said he had seen nothing of such a letter and asked his plump son, Qasim, to get a copy. It became evident that Prince Hussein had centered all lines of communication in his own hands. All messengers from the American mission to the Foreign Office, from the mission to the palace, and from the Foreign Office to the Imam had been intercepted by Hussein's men. Apparently Prince Hussein was waiting just outside the throne room, for Prince Qasim came back in less than a minute with the original of Colonel Eddy's letter. The Imam read it carefully, thought a moment, and said, "There is nothing in here that cannot be worked out with a little patience on both sides. Please do not leave until you have talked further on this matter. I wish for Qadi Raghib Bey to take over the discussions once again."

There then occurred one of the most extraordinary incidents in the history of modern American diplomacy in the Arabian Peninsula—a scene which, had it been shown in a movie, would have seemed to out-Hollywood Hollywood. At the Imam's command, seventy-year-old Raghib Bey walked forward till he stood at the table directly in front of the silver throne, erect in his purple robe and white turban. With a voice that trembled with emotion, he burst forth in a torrent of Arabic oratory. He said that he had served the Imam faithfully for thirty-one years, that during much of that time he had acted as Foreign Minister, and that he had successfully guided the international relations of the Kingdom of Yemen through many difficult crises. Now he was getting old and he would soon die, but before he died he wished to be sure that the foreign policy of Yemen was headed in the right direction.

As he had so often told the Imam, the twentieth century was a troubled period with strife between the great powers. Now that Germany, Italy, and Japan were reduced in importance, there remained England, Russia, and the United States as the major powers in world affairs. Every small nation in the world, if it was to survive, must join with one or the other of these powers. As every true Moslem was agreed, the godlessness of Russia and the ruthlessness of its policies toward small nations made any alliance with the USSR out of the question. Great Britain was a strong nation, but unfortunately Yemen and Great Britain had not been able to agree for many years over the southern boundary of Yemen. There remained only the United States, a nation which had shown that it had no imperialist designs. Yemeni contacts with American citizens had been of the most pleasant, including a remarkable friendship with Charles Crane, who had given a bridge and much machinery to Yemen. Now the government of the United States was ready to conclude an agreement of commerce and friendship with Yemen. Raghib Bey felt that this agreement would be the crowning achievement of his career; it did not mean that Yemen was being handed over to the United States; it merely meant that Yemen had a great and good friend with whom she could deal in the future.

By this time Raghib Bey was bending over the little table in front of the throne. Tears came to his eyes, and he leaned forward and waved a hand under the very beard of the Imam as he continued approximately as follows:

"Just as I was about to conclude this international masterpiece, the work was taken out of my hands, and I was kicked out of your palace like a dog. In my place your unskilled son, Hussein, took over the negotiations. He dropped the masterpiece that I had made upon the floor of the guesthouse, where it was broken into a thousand pieces. All progress came to a halt. When it is clear that something must be done, you call me back like a sweeper to pick up the broken pieces and reconstruct something worth while from the wreck which your son has made. I will not be pushed about like a slave of the palace; I resign as Your Majesty's Foreign Minister. I can no longer stay in Yemen; I ask permission to leave, to go back to my native land of Turkey to die."

Beneath his swelling purple robe, Raghib Bey's frame was shaken with sobs, and the hand that he waved before the Imam's face was trembling with emotion. The American mission, sitting on the edge of their chairs on either side of the throne room, leaned forward in amazement; and the two doctors felt that such emotion in the rarefied air of San'a might well lead to Raghib Bey's death.

Another spectator had even more alarming thoughts. Qadi Kolala, the Imam's personal bodyguard, had watched the start of Raghib Bey's oration from the door of the throne room. As the old man's emotion became greater, Kolala apparently feared that the Foreign Minister might actually do physical violence to the eighty-year-old ruler. Tiptoeing up behind Raghib Bey, Kolala put his right hand on his curved jambiya, or dagger, in the ornate sheath at his belt, while with his left hand he signaled to the Imam. The slightest nod from the ruler was all that Kolala needed to put an end to the long career of the Turkishborn Foreign Minister. But the Imam never nodded.

He waited patiently until Raghib Bey's oratory died away into sobs, then smiled like a tolerant father and said, "Do not upset yourself, Raghib Bey; things will come out all right. Rest and you will feel better soon."

The Foreign Minister went back panting to his chair in the far corner of the throne room, and the Imam asked Colonel Eddy if he would be willing to continue the negotiations.

"We will be at the guesthouse for one hour more," the American diplomat replied. "If you have any messages to send to me or my government, I shall receive them there."

Again the Imam asked Raghib Bey to take over the talks, but the venerable Turk merely reminded the Imam that he was no longer the Foreign Minister. The ruler thereupon designated Qadi Mutahhar to act in his place and asked Colonel Eddy to leave his interpreter, Mohammed Effendi, at the palace. The young Saudi not only had pleasing ways and an excellent mind but had a firsthand familiarity with the way King Ibn Saud had dealt with Americans, and the Imam wished his judgment in such a matter involving the Moslem religion and Western ways. Colonel Eddy and the members of his mission thereupon took their leave of the Imam, who grasped each tightly by the hand and wished him a safe return to America.

Back at the guesthouse the time dragged on interminably. After half an hour one of the palace guards appeared, bringing Mohammed Effendi. He reported that as soon as the Americans had left, Prince Hussein and various other advisers had crowded into the throne room for a spirited discussion. Hussein protested that the agreement, as desired by the Americans, was the beginning of the end of Moslem life in Yemen. He was overruled by the Imam, and the young Saudi Arab and Qadi Mutahhar had started out for the guesthouse by motor. Halfway across the Sharara square the car had been stopped by a detachment of cavalry that forced Qadi Mutahhar to get out and walk back to the palace. Things looked worse than ever, and the mission sat down to lunch in a most dejected mood.

Just before the end of the hour, a guard came running into the dining room to say that Qadi Mutahhar was coming up the stairs. Once settled in the living room of the guesthouse, he said that he had been empowered by the Imam to sign the agreement and that the American wording in regard to "the requirements and practices of generally recognized international law" would be acceptable. In a few minutes the battered text of the draft had been changed to everyone's satisfaction. While it was being typed in final form, a messenger appeared from Prince Hussein, and it was feared that once again the agreement had been blocked. But instead he asked that certain letters the Prince had written during the past four days, letters that had raised many obstacles to the agreement, be returned. This was gladly done, and the messenger departed. Then, in the presence of the entire American mission and a small group of Yemeni officials, the agreement of commerce and friendship between the United States and the Kingdom of Yemen was finally signed by Colonel Eddy for the United States and Qadi Mutahhar for Yemen. There was much handshaking and taking of pictures. Wreathed in smiles, Qadi Mutahhar tucked the Yemeni copies under his voluminous robes and walked off on foot toward the palace.

By four-thirty Colonel Eddy, who was overdue in Saudi Arabia, had left by jeep for an all-night ride that took him down the valley to Ma'bar, over the pass, and through the foothills to the sands of the Tihama and Hodeida. The following day he and his party went by jeep to a point where they could be carried on straw bedsteads on the heads of Yemini to a launch that took them to Kamaran Island, where they caught a BOAC plane for Jidda. Most of the mission left soon afterward, going overland down the High Yemen.

Two of the mission members, however, stayed on to instruct the Yemenis in operating the radio set which was presented to the Imam as a gift. All speed records for construction in Yemen were broken in the building of a small house on the grounds of the palace to shelter this set. There, in mid-July, the Imam's radio station was officially opened in the presence of a large gathering of Yemeni officials. And, strangely enough, it was the isolationist Prince Hussein who made the opening address over Radio San'a.

XIX

Revolt in San'a

THE next official contact between the United States and Yemen occurred in September 1946, when the newly appointed American Minister to Saudi Arabia and Yemen, J. Rives Childs, went to San'a to present his credentials. With him went Harlan Clark, the State Department's Yemen expert who had been made second secretary at Jidda, and the interpreter, Mohammed Effendi Massoud, by now almost indispensable. The Imam Yahya had recently suffered a stroke but rose from his sickbed to receive Childs, remarking, "If I had the heart of a camel and had suffered this stroke, it would have melted as if in a fiery furnace."

The most interesting entertainment offered Childs during his stay in the Yemeni capital was a luncheon given for him in a pavilion in one of the vineyards of Al Roda. Except for senior Prince Ahmed, who had not visited San'a for some years, and Prince Abdullah, the Yemeni "ambassador to all the world," who was then in London, this gathering included all the important Yemeni princes. There were Prince Hussein, who had proved so difficult during Colonel Eddy's negotiations; the large and energetic Prince Qasim, Minister of Communications; and Prince Ali, former Minister of Economic Affairs, an irresponsible prince with a broad sense of humor. Once, when asked how many of the Imam's sons were living, he replied, "None are alive." Also at the luncheon were Prince Hassan, Minister of Education; Prince Ismail; Prince Ibrahim, who was destined soon to escape to Aden; Prince Abdul Rahman, and others rarely seen by Westerners.

Before leaving San'a Childs called upon Dr. Adnan Tarsisi, the head of the Lebanese mission that had just come to Yemen to assist in the development of the country, an example of an Arab state looking elsewhere in the Near East for help in its first steps toward modernization.

Childs did not follow the usual route to Hodeida and Kamaran Island, but took the difficult horseback trail directly south through the cities of Yarim and Ibb to Ta'izz. At Yarim he visited the ruins of the ancient Himyaritic capital of Zofar, where he was conducted through a series of subterranean vaults held up by massive stone columns and decorated with carved figures.

In May 1947 Seif al Islam Abdullah, who was in Cairo, began negotiating a surplus property agreement with the United States Government and was invited by the Department of State to come to Washington. He agreed but said he should first talk with his father. In order to facilitate his quick return, the Imam put five thousand Yemeni to work leveling an air strip near the capital. As soon as word was flashed to Cairo that the irrigation ditches had been filled and the plowed fields packed down, Prince Abdullah left in the airplane of Colonel William McKnown, the American military attaché, en route to Aden.

Early next morning the Americans in the party took off from the airport at Aden and headed north over the mountains that guard the southern frontier of Yemen, leaving Prince Abdullah in Aden because of the dangers of a pioneer flight. Many of the lower summits were topped with villages built in characteristic skyscraper style, and the stone castles of the Zaidi nobles could be seen on some of the more inaccessable peaks.

Once over the broad fertile valley of the High Yemen, the fliers picked up the mounds which support the telegraph line to the capital. Fifteen minutes later they spotted the bulk of Jebel Nuqum and the city of San'a spread out on the plain below. The new air strip was on the gravel plain west of the city, and a low sweep over the field showed that all irrigation ditches had been filled in and that, as directed, the Yemenis had whitewashed a circle in its center and built a smoky fire on one side. Colonel McKnown sideslipped in from the southwest, making a perfect landing on the rough runway, the first American aircraft to land in Yemen.

A tent had been set up at the north end of the runway where the party was greeted by Prime Minister Qadi Abdullah al Amri, the old amil of San'a, and the Imam's personal bodyguard, Kolala, who had played so dramatic a role during Colonel Eddy's last interview with the Imam. These dignitaries were shown around the plane, and all stared in wide-eyed amazement at the comfort of its interior fittings and the complicated nature of its controls. Soft drinks were served on board while the party waited for Prince Hassan, who was to go to Aden in order to accompany his brother back to the capital. Much difficulty was then encountered in clearing the runway for the take off, and it was learned that the last airplane to visit San'a, an Italian ship carrying Seif al Islam Hussein, had injured several people with its propellers.

Colonel Eddy's trucks had taken eleven days to come from Aden, and four days were considered good time for a person traveling light. But three hours after Colonel McKnown's plane took off from San'a it had been to Aden and was back again. By then the airfield was surrounded by lines of infantrymen, cavalry, camel corps, and the royal San'a band as Colonel McKnown made another perfect landing, and Prince Abdullah and his party stepped out.

The return of Seif al Islam Abdullah was a great personal triumph for that popular prince. Dense crowds lined the streets and cheered him loudly as he drove to the palace to greet his father. His reception at the palace was favorable also, and a celebration was staged that night in his honor. Flares made from camel dung dipped in kerosene were burned on the tops of most of San'a's skyscrapers, and the sound of rifle shots and the boom of cannon echoed over the city, whose sleepless population milled through the usually deserted streets. As their part in the celebration, the Americans collected a Very pistol from the plane and shot colored flares from the roof of the guesthouse, a sign of friendship which was greeted by cheers from the neighboring rooftops. Long after the lights in the palace had been turned out, the crowds were still marching. San'a had not seen such a night since the departure of the Turks in World War I.

In view of the resignation of the venerable Turkish-born Foreign Minister, Raghib Bey, at the close of Colonel Eddy's mission, the Americans were interested to find that he was not only in good health but was once again Foreign Minister. Even the Imam appeared to be better than at the time of Minister Childs' visit the previous September, having recently ridden from the palace to the royal mosque on the back of a white mule.

Among others, the visitors called on Madame Audizio, the wife of an Italian doctor and one of three European women in Yemen, who introduced them to an Egyptian archaeologist, Ahmed Fakhry Bey. He turned out to be curator of the Cairo Historical Museum and surprised the visitors by saying that he had recently returned from a twenty-four-day trip to the northeast corner of Yemen, an area unvisited by foreigners since Glaser was there in 1888.

Fakhry Bey, who of course was familiar with the archaeological ruins of Egypt, said he had seen few more beautiful or more important than those of eastern Yemen. He had examined the ruins of the Great Dam and some of the palaces at Marib, which he found of particular interest because of the many inscriptions and carvings still visible on them, including bas-reliefs of dancing girls. He said he had found Egyptian influence in the Marib ruins, which he believed dated from about 800 B.C. The finest remains of all that he saw were in the Jauf area north of Marib, where whole temples of the Minaean period still stand intact, decorated by graceful carvings of indigenous design worked on solid granite blocks, some of which he estimated to weigh as much as twenty-five tons. Tall, sixteen-sided columns contributed an unusual motif to some of the Jauf buildings.

When the party took off again by plane, they were able to obtain permission to make the first known flight over northeastern Yemen. Flying from San'a, they passed out of the valley of the High Yemen and followed a wadi until it broadened into the dry but potentially fertile land between the mountains of Yemen and the Rub al Khali desert of Saudi Arabia. Karl Twitchell, who was on board, noted several extinct volcanic craters and dried lava flows. One larger crater did not look particularly volcanic and may have been caused by a falling meteor, possibly made at the same time as the meteor craters found by Philby in the center of the Rub al Khali. Fakhry Bey was on the plane and proved invaluable in guiding the fliers to the valley of Marib, where they could see irrigation ditches. The main portion of the dam was invisible from the air, having been either swept away by floods or buried in sand, but the fliers could make out huge stone blocks standing at each end of the damsite. Not far away were the ruins of an ancient city, marked by tall granite columns, and a circular wall enclosing a courtyard with five square columns standing at its entrance, which the Egyptian archaeologist called the arch of Queen Balkis (Sheba). Other places in this part of the valley were dotted with massive stone ruins.

From Marib the plane continued northward over unmapped territory, crossing a cultivated plain on which were villages and large pools of water. After flying for an hour, Twitchell recognized the Saudi Arabian town of Najran, which he had last visited in 1942. Here the amazed inhabitants flocked onto the streets and rooftops. The plane then turned west across the mountains of the Asir province of Saudi Arabia to the coast, which was followed to Jidda. As one of the Americans noted, the flight had been over country where the inhabitants did not live in the present or even in the time of Mohammed, but rather in the time of Abraham and Isaac. Once the Yemenis can be convinced that important finds will not be taken out of their country, the area which was seen from the air for the first time that day offers what is probably the greatest archaeological prize in the Near East.

Thanks to the time saved by Colonel McKnown's plane, Seif al Islam Abdullah was able to keep his appointment with President Truman and make a tour of the United States. During his visit he emphasized the desire of his country to join the United Nations. The matter was carefully considered, and the United States Government decided to support the Yemeni membership. The Arab states gave the Yemeni delegation strong support, and on September 25, 1947, Prince Abdullah took his place in the General Assembly of the United Nations, representing the fifty-sixth nation to join that body.

For the next few months Prince Abdullah set up his headquarters in a suite on the thirtieth floor of the towers of the Sherry Netherlands Hotel in New York, which for all practical purposes became the Yemeni Legation in the United States. There he held frequent conversations with American financial and business groups, talking much about Yemen's need for harbors, roads, hospitals, and dams. But while his much-traveled son sat looking out across Central Park, the Imam in San'a became the center of a dark and bloody plot. Although all the details are not known, the following summary is believed to cover the more important aspects of the Wazir revolt.

To understand the events of the first five months of 1948 in San'a, one must realize that for many generations two powerful families have dominated Yemen. These are the Hamid ad Din clan, to which the Imam belongs, and the Al Wazir family, another powerful clan of landowning Zaidi aristocrats, which has also supplied Yemen with imams and other important government officials. The leader of the Al Wazir clan at that time was Abdullah al Wazir, a white-bearded patriarch of sixty, who had held many offices and was chief negotiator in the Yemeni-Saudi peace talks of 1933.

Although Imam Yahya had freed the country from the Turks and brought law and order to most of the land, his rule was stern, and he and his older sons had made enemies. These centered in two places. The first group was known as the "Free Yemenis," or Greater Yemeni Society, which had its headquarters in Aden, where some fifteen thousand Yemenis had gone to make a living. Like almost all Yemenis who leave their country, this group realized the need for modernization at home and for some years had carried on a campaign aimed at liberalizing the government.

The other center of opposition was in the Al Wazir family, a huge clan with numerous subdivisions, which was related by marriage to the Imam and a great number of important landowners. It should be borne in mind that succession to the throne in Yemen is not hereditary. On the death of an imam, the Council of Religious Elders elects, as the new imam, the man they feel best qualified for the post. In some cases this turns out to be the oldest living son of the former imam, but this is not always so. Thus, although Imam Yahya had favored his oldest living son, Prince Ahmed, as the next imam, there was opposition to the idea of his succession. Ahmed had lived for many years in the southern city of Ta'izz. Although he had carried on certain modernization projects under the supervision of a young German engineer named Hansen, he had taxed the people heavily. As a result, a move had sprung up in High Yemeni circles to win the votes of the Council of Elders for Abdullah al Wazir.

An interesting link between the two groups opposed to Prince Ahmed was Seif al Islam Ibrahim, one of the Imam's sons who was in his early twenties. Because of his interest in reform, this prince fell into the bad graces of the Imam. In 1947 Ibrahim announced that he was sick and persuaded his father to let him travel to Addis Ababa to see a specialist. Instead of returning to San'a, Prince Ibrahim settled in Aden, where he became the titular head of the Free Yemenis. It is not known what part Prince Ibrahim played in writing them, but a series of manifestoes was issued in his name, deploring the backwardness of conditions in Yemen and urging the establishment of a more limited monarchy whose goal would be the modernization of the country. Although they did not say so openly, the candidate of the Free Yemenis for the next imam was Abdullah al Wazir.

Also secretly working against Prince Ahmed as the next imam was his brother, Prince Hussein, who pretended to support Al Wazir but had personal ambitions of his own. Lastly, the Prime Minister, Qadi Abdullah al Amri, although an old friend of the Imam, was opposed to the succession of Prince Ahmed and apparently wanted the imamate for a relative in order that it might come into his family. Thus, at the beginning of 1948 there were, in addition to the Free Yemenis group, three main plotters who pretended to be working together but each of whom was actually out for himself. There is a possibility that influences from other Arab states were also at work.

Under normal circumstances the Wazirites would have waited until the Imam, who was already over eighty, died, and then would have pushed their claim to the imamate. But there is no such thing as a normal political situation in Yemen, unless it be a condition of plot and counter-plot. Someone betrayed the plan of the two Wazirites to the old Imam, who sent for Prince Ahmed to come to San'a. When, in mid-February, the senior Prince's baggage began to arrive in the capital, the plotters felt they must act. On the morning of February 17, Qadi al Amri went to the Imam and told him that a spring of water had been found on a royal farm not far from San'a. The Imam and the Prime Minister there-upon set out in the Imam's 1940 red Buick limousine to look over this property. On the way they were stopped by a truck which barred the road. Out of it came tribesmen armed with machine guns, who called to the Prime Minister to get out of the car. The old Imam seized Qadi al Amri's wrist, preventing him from moving, and the tribesmen opened fire, killing the Prime Minister, but by accident not wounding the Imam. The monarch, who by now thought it was an attack against Qadi al Amri alone, called, "Stop—he is dead," but the assassins shot again, riddling him with bullets.

Prince Hussein, who had been watching from the palace, immedi-ately set out for the arsenal in order to take control of the city for him-self. Just outside the palace, he was blocked by soldiers who were loyal to Al Wazir. When he ordered them out of the way, he was shot down. This left the field clear for Al Wazir, who took over the arsenal and the national treasure in the vaults under Jebel Nuqum and was promptly appointed Imam by the Elders of San'a. Prince Mutahhar, who was known to be loyal to Prince Ahmed, was imprisoned, while Prince Ibrahim and a group of Free Yemenis flew up from Aden in a chartered plane.

The Wazirite cause looked bright for a while as several other impor-tant cities fell in behind the new Imam. After losing several battles, Prince Ahmed continued along the coast to the northern provinces, which he believed were favorable to him. On the way he stopped at the port of Hodeida, whose governor was part of the Wazir plot and was expected to kill him. Instead, the governor sided with Prince Ahmed and helped him reach the town of Hajja in northern Yemen.

There Prince Ahmed began rallying his supporters, including a group in San'a who prepared a counter *coup d'état*. Striking unexpectedly, they freed Prince Mutahhar, locked Al Wazir in the same cell, and took control of the city. The captured Wazirites were taken to the town of Hajja for trial, and the Elders of San'a took stock of the changed situation and voted senior Prince Ahmed the new Imam. After a prolonged trial, Abdullah al Wazir and thirty of his chief supporters were beheaded. Prince Ibrahim, the intellectual leader of the Free Yemenis, died in prison of a "heart attack."

It has been reported that Abdullah al Wazir, after his appointment as Imam, sent word to King Ibn Saud asking for recognition but received a stern negative reply. In addition, notice was sent by the King from Riyadh to Seif al Islam Ahmed urging him to fight to gain his father's throne and implying that help would come to him from Saudi Arabia.

Imam Ahmed made Ta'izz his capital rather than San'a. The loyal governor of Hodeida was made chamberlain for a while as a reward for betraying the Wazirite plot, and the new Imam selected as Prime Minister Prince Hassan, who exerts a strong conservative influence on his older brother. The venerable Turk, Raghib Bey, who had sided with Prince Ahmed, was also rewarded for a time by getting back his old post of Foreign Minister but has been supplanted by Prince Abdullah, who is the man best qualified for the post if he will return to Yemen and take it over.

Meanwhile, the pattern of life and government within Yemen appears unchanged. It would seem that Yemen opened one window, took a quick look at the modern world, and then closed the shutters. But it is unlikely they will remain shut for long. Yemen Legations have been opened in Washington, Cairo, and London, and Yemen's contacts with the outside world, especially Germany, are increasing. Not even the Imam of Yemen can keep out the twentieth century much longer. In Yemen, as in the rest of the Arabian Peninsula, the forces of change are too strong to be stopped. It is the challenge of Arabia to the Arabs, and to the Western world, that those changes be for the good of all.

Acknowledgments

THIS book would never have been completed without the assistance and guidance of many persons who are intimately familiar with various aspects of the Arabian Peninsula. Among them the author wishes to thank particularly the Honorable J. Rives Childs and Raymond A. Hare, former American Ambassadors to Saudi Arabia; Edwin Wright, Harold Glidden, and Robert Sethian, of the Department of State; and Foreign Service officers James Moose, Gordon Mattison, Parker T. Hart, Harlan Clark, Francis Meloy, Rodger Davies, Robert Stein, Max Bishop, and Hermann Eilts.

In addition, the author has been greatly helped by Colonel William Eddy, former U.S. Minister to Saudi Arabia, Terry Duce, Floyd Ohliger, Roy Lebkicher, Harry Synder, and other officials of the Arabian American Oil Company; C. W. Hamilton and Nils Lind of the Gulf Oil Company; Charles Rayner and Herbert Lebesny of the American Independent Oil Company; Thomas Borman of International Bechtel Corporation; Colonel Kavanaugh of the Bahrein Petroleum Company; Richard F. Goodwin of the Saudi Arabian Mining Syndicate, and Karl Twitchell of the American Eastern Corporation. Both David Rogers and John Edwards were most helpful in regard to the agricultural developments in Al Kharj.

Thanks also go to President Stephen Penrose and Professor Nabih Faris of the American University of Beirut for their constructive criticism.

The author is further indebted to various Saudi Arabs who lent

280

valuable assistance in the preparation of this book, including His Excellency, Sheikh Asad al Faqih, the Saudi Arabian Ambassador to the United States, and Sheikhs Ahmed Abdul Jabbar and Mohammad Mutasib of the Saudi Arabian Embassy in Washington.

Particularly useful items of research were contributed by Homer C. Miller, T. L. Jones, and Harry F. Hopper, who are responsible for parts of the bibliography. The author wishes to thank the secretaries who worked nights, week-ends, and holidays helping to type this book. They include Gloria Hamilton, Mary Jane Bradley, Rutherford Lowry, Meda Stidham, Betty Cullers, Sybil Cooper, Ellen Ardinger, Ethelyn Nelson, Mariam Sabbagh, Rida Nasr, Linda Salamoun, and Patricia Hammond.

The writer is deeply indebted to the many authors to whose works on Arabia he has turned for valuable background information and whose names are noted in various footnotes throughout the book.

He thanks the Arabian American Oil Company, the California Texas Oil Company, the Gulf Oil Company, Karl Twitchell, Harold Green, Wendell Phillips, and Wide World Photos for making available the prints of photographs.

Lastly he wishes to thank Mrs. Parker T. Hart, the wife of the former Consul General at Dhahran, for her detailed and constructive editing of this manuscript, Mrs. Harold Voorhees for preparing the index, and his wife for her patient help.

Bibliography

THE following is a selected list of books and periodicals in English chosen for the value and wealth of their material, their readability, and their availability. Documents, pamphlets, rare travel and history books, and specific magazine articles have for the most part not been listed. For these and additional titles, see:

The Arabian Peninsula: A Selected, Annotated List of Periodicals, Books and Articles in English. Washington: Library of Congress, 1951.

A Selected and Annotated Bibliography of Books and Periodicals in Western Languages Dealing with the Near and Middle East with Special Emphasis on Medieval and Modern Times. Ed. by Richard Ettinghausen. Washington: Middle East Institute, 1952.

"Bibliography of Periodical Literature," prepared by Sidney Glazer. A regular feature in the *Middle East Journal*, Washington, 1947–.

BOOKS

Survey and General Reference

Antonius, George. *The Arab Awakening: The Story of the Arab National Movement.* London: H. Hamilton, 1938.

Brockelmann, Carl. *History of the Islamic Peoples.* Trans. by Joel Carmichael and Moshe Perlmann. New York: Putnam, 1947.

Bullard, Sir Reader. *Britain and the Middle East.* London: Hutchinson's University Library, 1951.

Handbook of Arabia, A. Vol. I, General. Compiled by the Geographical Section, Naval Intelligence Division, Naval Staff, Admiralty of Great Britain. London: H.M. Stationery Office, 1920.

Hitti, Philip K. *History of the Arabs*. 5th ed. New York: Macmillan, 1950.

Hogarth, David G. *Arabia*. Oxford: Clarendon Press, 1922.

Hogarth, David G. *The Nearer East*. New York: D. Appleton, 1902.

Huart, Clemént. *A History of Arabic Literature*. New York: D. Appleton, 1903.

Kirk, George E. *A Short History of the Middle East from the Rise of Islam to Modern Times*. Washington: Public Affairs Press, 1949.

Kohn, Hans. *Nationalism and Imperialism in the Hither East*. London: G. Routledge, 1932.

Lane-Poole, Stanley. *The Mohammedan Dynasties*. London: Constable, 1894.

Magie, David. *Roman Rule in Asia Minor to the End of the Third Century after Christ*. Princeton, N.J.: Princeton University Press, 1950. 2 vols.

Middle East, The: A Political and Economic Survey. London, New York: Royal Institute for International Affairs, 1950.

Montgomery, James A. *Arabia and the Bible*. Philadelphia: University of Pennsylvania, 1934.

Nicholson, R. A. *A Literary History of the Arabs*. 2nd ed. Cambridge, Eng.: Cambridge University Press, 1930.

Philby, H. St. J. B. *Arabia*. New York: Scribner, 1930.

Roosevelt, Kermit. *Arabs, Oil and History: The Story of the Middle East*. New York: Harper, 1949.

Security of the Middle East, The: A Problem Paper. Washington: Brookings Institution, 1950.

Warriner, Doreen. *Land and Poverty in the Middle East*. London, New York: Royal Institute of International Affairs, 1945.

Zwemer, S. M. *Arabia, The Cradle of Islam*. New York: Fleming H. Revell, 1900.

Islam

Andrae, Tor. *Mohammed, the Man and His Faith*. Trans. by Theophil W. Menzel. New York: Scribner, 1936.

Arnold, Sir Thomas, and Guillaume, Alfred, eds. *The Legacy of Islam*. Oxford: Clarendon Press, 1931.

Burckhardt, J. L. *Arabic Proverbs*. 2nd ed. London: B. Quaritch, 1875.

Encyclopaedia of Islam, The. Leyden: E. J. Brill, 1913–1938. 4 vols. and Supplement. Published in English, French, and German.

Gibb, H. A. R. *Modern Trends in Islam*. Chicago: University of Chicago Press, 1945.

——. *Mohammedanism: An Historical Survey*. London: Oxford University Press, 1949.

Guillaume, Alfred. *The Traditions of Islam*. Oxford: Clarendon Press, 1924.

Hazard, W. W., and Cook, H. L., Jr. *Atlas of Islamic History*. Princeton, N.J.: Princeton University Press, 1952.

Hughes, Thomas P. *A Dictionary of Islam*. London: W. H. Allen, 1935.

Kor'an, El-, or, *The Koran*. Trans. with surahs in chronological order by J. M. Rodwell. London: Everyman, 1918.

Levy, Reuben. *Sociology of Islam*. London: Williams & Norgate, 1930–1933. 2 vols.

MacDonald, Duncan B. *The Development of Muslim Theology, Jurisprudence, and Constitutional Theory*. New York: Scribner, 1903.

Qur'an, The. Trans. with a critical rearrangement of the surahs by Richard Bell. Edinburgh: T. and T. Clark, 1937–1939. 2 vols.

Schacht, Joseph. *The Origins of Muhammadan Jurisprudence*. Oxford: Clarendon Press, 1950.

Wilson, J. Christy. *Introducing Islam*. New York: Friendship Press, 1950.

Pilgrimage

Blunt, Lady Anne. *A Pilgrimage to Nejd, the Cradle of the Arab Race*. London: John Murray, 1881. 2 vols.

Burckhardt, J. L. *Travels in Arabia*. London: H. Colburn, 1829. 2 vols.

Burton, Sir Richard Francis. *Personal Narrative of a Pilgrimage to Al-Madinah and Meccah*. Ed. by Isabel Burton. London: G. Bell & Son, 1898. 2 vols.

Hurgronje, Christiaan Snouck. *Mekka in the Latter Part of the 19th Century; Daily Life, Customs and Learning, the Moslems of the East-Indian Archipelago*. Trans. by J. H. Monahan. London: Luzac, 1931.

Philby, H. St. J. B. *A Pilgrim in Arabia*. London: Robert Hale, 1943.

Rutter, Eldon. *The Holy Cities of Arabia*. London, New York: Putnam, 1928. 2 vols.

Saudi Arabia and Its Antecedents

Armstrong, H. C. *Lord of Arabia, Ibn Saud*. Harmondsworth, Eng.: Penguin, 1938.

Burckhardt, J. L. *Notes on the Bedouins and Wahábys*. Vols. I and II. London: H. Colburn & R. Bentley, 1831.

Cheesman, R. E. *In Unknown Arabia*. London: Macmillan, 1926.

Carruthers, Alexander D. M. *Arabian Adventure*. London: H. F. & G. Witherby, 1935.

de Gaury, Gerald. *Arabia Phoenix*. London: G. G. Harrap, 1946.

——. *Rulers of Mecca*. London: G. G. Harrap. 1951.

Dickson, H. R. P. *The Arab of the Desert*. New York: Macmillan, 1949.

Doughty, Charles Montagu. *Travels in Arabia Deserta*. New York: Random House, 1937. 2 vols.

Graves, Robert. *Lawrence and the Arabian Adventure*. New York: Doubleday, 1928.

BIBLIOGRAPHY

Guarmani, C. *Northern Nejd*. Trans. from Italian by Lady Capel Cure. Ed. by D. Carruthers. London: Argonaut Press, 1938.

Hogarth, D. G. *The Penetration of Arabia: A Record of the Development of Western Knowledge Concerning the Arabian Peninsula*. New York: F. A. Stokes, 1904.

Kheirallah, George. *Arabia Reborn*. Albuquerque: University of New Mexico Press, 1952.

Kiernan, Reginald Hugh. *The Unveiling of Arabia: The Story of Arabian Travel and Discovery*. London: G. G. Harrap, 1937.

Lawrence, Thomas E. *Seven Pillars of Wisdom*. Garden City: Doubleday, Doran, 1936.

Lebkicher, Roy; Rentz, George; and Steineke, Max. *The Arabia of Ibn Saud*. New York: Russell F. Moore, 1952.

——. *Saudi Arabia*. New York: Russell F. Moore, 1952.

Musil, Alois. *Arabia Deserta*. New York: American Geographical Society, 1927.

——. *The Manners and Customs of the Rwala Bedouins*. New York: American Geographical Society, 1928.

——. *The Northern Hegaz: A Topographical Itinerary*. New York: American Geographical Society, 1926.

——. *Northern Negd. A Topographical Itinerary*. New York: American Geographical Society, 1928.

Palgrave, W. G. *Personal Narrative of a Year's Journey through Central and Eastern Arabia (1862–1863)*. London: Macmillan, 1866. 2 vols.

Philby, H. St. J. B. *Arabian Highlands*. Ithaca, N.Y.: Cornell University Press, for The Middle East Institute, 1952.

——. *Arabian Jubilee*. London: Robert Hale, 1951.

——. *The Heart of Arabia*. New York, London: Putnam, 1922–1923. 2 vols.

——. *Arabia of the Wahhabis*. London: Constable, 1928.

——. *The Empty Quarter*. New York: Henry Holt, 1933.

Raswan, Carl R. *Black Tents of Arabia (My Life Among the Bedouins)*. Boston: Little Brown, 1935.

Rihani, Ameen F. *Around the Coasts of Arabia*. Boston, New York: Houghton Mifflin, 1930.

——. *Ibn Sa'oud of Arabia, His People and His Land*. London: Constable, 1928.

——. *Maker of Modern Arabia*. New York, Boston: Houghton Mifflin, 1928.

Thomas, Bertram. *Arabia Felix: Across the Empty Quarter of Arabia*. New York: Scribner, 1932.

Twitchell, K. S. *Saudi Arabia; With an Account of the Development of Its Natural Resources*. Princeton, N.J.: Princeton University Press, 1947.

Williams, Kenneth. *Ibn Sa'ud, the Puritan King of Arabia*. London: Jonathan Cape, 1933.

Eastern Arabia: Oman, Trucial Coast, Persian Gulf

Buckingham, James S., *Travels in Assyria, Media and Persia*. London: Henry Colburn & Richard Bentley, 1830.

Coupland, Reginald. *East Africa and Its Invaders, from the Earliest Times to the Death of Seyyid Said in 1856*. Oxford: Clarendon Press, 1938.

Faroughy, Abbas. *The Bahrein Islands*. New York: Verry, Fisher, 1951.

Harrison, Paul W. *The Arab at Home*. New York: Thomas Y. Crowell, 1924.

——. *Doctor in Arabia*. London: Robert Hale, 1943.

Miles, Samuel Barrett. *The Countries and Tribes of the Persian Gulf*. London: Harrison, 1919. 2 vols.

Rogers, Edmund. *Embassy to the Eastern Courts of Kochin-China, Siam and Muscat in the Sloop of War "Peacock" during the Years of 1832, 1833, 1834*. New York: Harper, 1937.

Ruschenberger, W. S. *A Voyage Around the World*. Philadelphia: Carey, Lea and Blanchard, 1838.

Said-Ruete, Rudolph. *Said bin Sultan (1791–1856) Ruler of Oman and Zanzibar: His Place in the History of Arabia and East Africa*. London: Alexander-Ouseley, 1929.

Salil ibn Ruzaik. *History of the Imams and Seyyids of Oman from A.D. 661–1856*. Trans. and suppl. by George P. Badger. London: Hakluyt Society, 1871.

Schoff, W. H., tr. *Periplus of the Erythraean Sea*. London: Longmans Green and Co., 1912.

Thomas, Bertram. *Alarms and Excursions in Arabia*. Indianapolis: Bobbs-Merrill, 1931.

Trew, Cecil G. *From Dawn to Eclipse, the Story of the Horse*. London: Methuen, 1939.

Villiers, Alan John. *Sons of Sinbad*. New York: Scribner, 1940.

Wellsted, J. R. *Travels in Arabia*. Vol. I. London: John Murray, 1838.

Wilson, Sir Arnold. *The Persian Gulf*. Oxford: Clarendon Press, 1928.

Southern Arabia: Aden, Hadhramaut

Aden Blue Book, 1937. London: H.M. Stationery Office, 1939.

Annual Report on Aden and Aden Protectorate. London: H.M. Stationery Office, 1946–.

Bent, James T. and Mabel. *Southern Arabia*. London: Smith, Elder, 1900.[1]

Caton-Thompson, Gertrude. *The Tombs and Moon Temple of Hureidha* [Hadhramaut]. London: Oxford University Press, 1944.

Coon, Carleton S. *Southern Arabia, a Problem for the Future*. Cambridge, Mass.: Harvard University, 1943. Peabody Museum Papers, vol. XX.

Hamilton, R. A. B. *The Kingdom of Melchior, Adventure in South West Arabia*. London: John Murray, 1949.

[1] Material on Bahrein and Oman also included.

BIBLIOGRAPHY

Hunter, Frederick Mercer. *An Account of the British Settlement of Aden in Arabia.* London: Trübner, 1877.

Ingrams, W. H. *Arabia and the Isles.* London: John Murray, 1942.

——. "House Building in the Hadhramaut," *Geographical Journal,* LXXXV (April, 1935), 370–372.

——. *A Report on the Social, Economic, and Political Condition of the Hadhramaut.* London: H.M. Stationery Office, 1936. Colonial No. 123.

Meulen, D. van der. *Aden to the Hadhramaut: A Journey in South Arabia.* London: John Murray, 1947.

—— and Wissmann, H. von. *Hadhramaut: Some of Its Mysteries Unveiled.* Leyden: E. J. Brill, 1932.

Pearn, Norman Stone, and Barlow, Vernon. *Quest for Sheba.* London: I. Nicholson and Watson, 1937.

Philby, H. St. J. B. *Sheba's Daughters.* London: Methuen, 1939.

Stark, Freya. *Seen in the Hadhramaut.* New York: E. P. Dutton, 1939.

——. *The Southern Gates of Arabia.* New York: E. P. Dutton, 1945.

——. *A Winter in Arabia.* London: John Murray, 1940.

Yemen

Bury, G. Wyman. *Arabia Infelix, or the Turks in Yamen.* London: Macmillan, 1915.

——. (*Pseud.* Abdullah Mansur). *The Land of Uz.* London: Macmillan, 1911.

Faroughy, Abbas. *Introducing Yemen.* New York: Orientalia, 1947.

Harris, Walter Burton. *A Journey through the Yemen and Some General Remarks upon That Country.* Edinburgh, London: W. Blackwood, 1893.

Niebuhr, Carsten. *Travels through Arabia and Other Countries in the East, Performed by M. Niebuhr.* Trans. from German by Robert Heron. Edinburgh: R. Morison, 1792, 2 vols.

Rihani, Ameen F. *Arabian Peak and Desert.* Boston, New York: Houghton, Mifflin, 1930.

Scott, Hugh. *In the High Yemen.* London: John Murray, 1942.

Tritton, Arthur S. *The Rise of the Imams of Sanaa.* London, New York: Oxford University Press, 1925.

Oil

Arabian American Oil Company. *Summary of Middle East Oil Developments.* New York, 1952.

Caroe, Olaf. *Wells of Power: The Oilfields of South-western Asia; a Regional and Global Study.* London: Macmillan, 1951.

Hoskins, H. L. *Middle East Oil in United States Foreign Policy.* Washington: Public Affairs Bulletin No. 89, 1950.

Lebkicher, Roy. *Aramco and World Oil.* New York: Russell F. Moore, 1952.

287

Mikesell, R. F., and Chenery, H. B. *Arabian Oil, America's Stake in the Middle East.* Chapel Hill: University of North Carolina Press, 1949.

Pratt, Wallace E., and Good, Dorothy. eds. *World Geography of Petroleum.* Princeton, N.J., Princeton University Press, for American Geographical Society, 1950.

PERIODICALS

Geographical Journal. London, 1893–. Monthly.

Geographical Magazine. London, 1935–. Monthly.

Geographical Review. New York, 1911–. Quarterly.

Middle East Journal. Washington, 1947–. Quarterly.

Middle Eastern Affairs. New York, 1950–. Monthly.

Newsletter. Washington, 1949–. Monthly.

Muslem World. Hartford, Conn., 1948–. Quarterly.

National Geographic Magazine. Washington, 1889–. Monthly.

Neglected Arabia. New York, 1892–.

Oil and Gas Journal. Tulsa, 1902–. Weekly.

Oil Forum. New York, 1947–. Monthly.

Petroleum Press Service. London, 1934–. Monthly.

Petroleum Times. London, 1919–. Fortnightly.

Royal Central Asian Journal. London, 1914–. Quarterly.

World Oil. Houston, Texas, 1947–. Weekly.

World Petroleum. New York, 1930–. Monthly.

Index

Abdali, Amir Ali ibn Abdul Qarim al (Sultan of Lahej), 214, 215
Abdul Aziz ibn Saud, 5, 28-40, 55-56, 62, 67-69, 101, 110, 151-152, 245, 279
Abdul Rahman al Saud (father of Ibn Saud), 31
Abdullah al Hamid ad Din (Prince of Yemen), 272-274, 276, 279
Abha, 31
Abqaiq, 89-90, 103, 113, 116, 119
Abu Bahr, 136
Abu Dhabi, 173, 175
Abu Hadriya, 103, 116, 165
Abyan, 218
Abyssinians, 240
Aden, 201-234; government, 208-209; history, 203-204, 208-211; population, 203-204
Aden Levies, 206
Aden Protectorates, 213-234; government, 222-223; history, 215, 219-222; population, 223-225
Afif, 42
Afrar, Khalifah al (Sultan of Qishn and Socotra), 233
Agreement of San'a, 270
Agriculture, 66-67, 196, 218, 255; see also Al Kharj and Crops
Ahmadi, 166-167
Ahmed al Hamid ad Din (Imam of Yemen), 246, 277-279
Ain Dar, 113, 116
Airlift, 115-116

Airports, 2, 44, 114, 147, 176-177, 206, 211-212, 273
Ajman, 179
Akhdam, 225
Akwah, Qadi Fadl ibn Ali al, 249
Al Hamriya, 179
Al Hani, 89
Al Kharj, 58-72
Al Khobar, 102-103, 140-141
Al Khobar Power Company, 117
Al Roda, 262
Albright, Dr. W. F., 241
Albuquerque, Admiral, 209-210
Alireza family, 12
Altounyan, Major T., 233
American Eastern Trading Corporation, 7
American Foundation for the Study of Man, 241-242
American Independent Oil Company, 165
Amri, Qadi Abdullah al, 273, 276-278
Amusements, 14-15, 24, 105-106, 179, 202
Anglo-Iranian Oil Company, 99, 163
Antonius, George, 33
Arabdar, see Tribes
Arabian American Oil Company (Aramco), 3, 63, 99-112, 164-165; commissary, 107; history, 99-105; housing, 104-105, 109; wages, 106, 108
Aradh, 138

289

Archaeology, 25-26, 126, 139, 141, 180, 208-209, 211, 241, 273, 275
Architecture, 2, 6, 8, 10, 44, 93, 178, 227-228, 239, 250, 258-259
Arnaud, Thomas S., 241
Asir, 30, 158
Audhali, 218
Audizio, Madame, 274-275
Aviation, 4-5, 113-114, 194-195, 206, 273
Awali, 147-148

Badia palace, see Guesthouses
Bahah, 254
Bahr al Safi, 138
Bahrein Islands, 140-149; history, 141-142; government, 142-143; oil, 100, 147-148; population, 140-141
Bahrein Petroleum Company, Ltd. (Bapco), 100, 147-149
Bajil, 242, 247, 254
Baluchis, 174, 195
Banajan, 129
Bandar Abbas, 192
Banque de l'Indochine, 10
Batina Plain, 195
Bazam Channel, 176
Bechtel, see International Bechtel Corporation
Bedouin, 48, 80-88, 181
Beit al Faqih, 247
Belgrave, Sir Charles D., 143
Bible, 96
Birka, 22
Blunt, Lady, 26, 143
Bolton, Mrs. Frances, 38-39
Boundaries, 122-123, 152, 214, 245-246
Brett, Homer, 191
British East India Company, 170
British Government, 29-30, 142, 171-173, 206, 208-209, 211, 213, 217, 221, 246
British Indian Survey, 147
British Mesopotamian Expeditionary Force, 30
British military mission, 15
British Overseas Airways, 177
Brookshier, Frank, 63
Buchanan, Dean R. E., 63
Buraida, 77
Buraimi, see Oases
Burghan field, 163, 165
Burton, Sir Richard, 11
Busaid, Said ibn Taimur al (Sultan of Muscat), 193, 194, 197

Cable and Wireless, Ltd., 198
Calverly, Dr. E. E., 167

Camels, 75-77, 134, 161
Camp, Charles F., 242
Caroe, Sir Olaf, 169
Cattle, 176, 210, 253
Childs, J. Rives, 5, 110, 272-274
Chinese, 202-203
Christianity, 203, 240
Clark, Harlan B., 246-249, 272
Climate, 21, 60, 87-88, 90, 128-129, 140, 173, 195, 197, 201-202, 213, 259
Coffee, 88, 235, 251-252, 256
Communications, 33, 197-198, 244-245, 255, 266, 271
Communism, 56
Consulates, 4, 6, 198
Coon, Carlton, 245
Cornwall, P. B., 141
Cox, Sir Percy, 30, 152
Crane, Charles R., 16, 194, 243
Crops, 69, 146-147, 196, 217, 223
Currency, 8-9, 228

DDT, 67, 93, 130, 257
Dahna sands, 43, 73-74
Dalma, 173
Dame, Dr. L. P., 17
Dame, Mrs. L. P., 38
Dammam, 100-101, 105-107, 117
Dances, 159
D'Arcy, William Knox, 99
Dates, 64, 86, 97-98, 155
Davies, Fred A., 100
Davies, Ralph K., 165
Deserts, 21-22, 42-43, 73-74, 246; see also Rub al Khali
Dhahran, 102-106, 113-114
Dhala, 217
Dhows, 143-144, 153-163
Dhufar Province, 126-127, 199
Dibai, 173, 176-177
Diplomacy, 4, 32-33, 186-195, 244, 263, 266
Divorce, 81, 94, 230
Dockweiler, T. A. J., 165-166
Dogs, 85
Doha, 123
Donkeys, 146
Dress, 14, 160, 205, 220, 230, 249
Dukhan, 123-124
Durham, O. R., 22
Dutch Reformed Church Mission, 17, 190
Duwadami, 42
Dykstra, Dr. Dirk, 191, 193, 197

East Africans, 141
Eddy, William A., 5, 248-271
Eddy, Mrs. William A., 38

Education, 53, 110, 149, 167, 217, 222, 231, 261
Edwards, Kenneth J., 63, 68-69
Egyptians, 167, 172, 202-203, 226
Embassies, 2, 6
Eve's tomb, 13
Exports, 25, 145, 150, 185, 204-205, 223, 235

Faisal al Saud (Crown Prince of Saudi Arabia), 12, 30-33, 36, 47, 55-56
Fakhry, Ahmed, 275
Falconry, 79-80
Famine, 226
Farasan Islands, 245
Farhaja, 128
Ferris, Robert, 237-238
Feuds, 176, 181-182, 214-215, 225
Fillmore, Millard, 189-190
Finance Minister (of Saudi Arabia), see Suleiman, Sheikh Abdullah
Fish, Bert, 4
Fishing, 176, 196
Foods, 9, 86-88, 90-91, 127, 156, 159, 217, 251, 259
Foreign Economic Administration, 60-61
Frankincense and myrrh, 126, 223, 225, 229, 232-233, 236; see also Incense
Free Yemenis, 277
Furnishings, 46, 93, 259, 264

Gallus, Aelius, 203, 239
Game, 128, 131, 255
Gana, 256
Garden of Eden, 208
Gellatly Hankey, 7
Geology, 16-17, 244-245
Getty, J. P., 165-166
Ghaidha, 233
Ghat, 207, 216-217, 262
Glaser, Edward, 241
Gold, 17, 20
Guesthouses, 45, 89, 168, 175, 251, 257-258
Gulf Oil Company, 163

Hadbar, see Tribes
Hadhramaut, 213, 218-234
Hadhrami Bedouin Legion, 206
Haifun, 157
Hajj, 96-97
Hajja, 279
Halévy, Joseph, 241
Hamadani, Al, 239
Hamilton, J. G., 5, 59
Hamilton, Lloyd, 100
Hammam Ali, 256
Handicrafts, 9, 76, 146, 223

Haradh, 116
Hare, Raymond A., 6
Harem, 14, 94
Harra Desert, 21-22
Harris, Dr. Franklin Stewart, 63
Hart, Parker T., 195
Harun al Rashid (Caliph of Baghdad), 20, 22
Hasa Province, 29, 106-107
Hashimites, 31-32
Hassan al Hamid ad Din (Prince of Yemen), 279
Haushabi, 216
Hedley, Dr. Oswald F., 265, 267
Hejaz Railway, 30, 82, 117-118
Henry, Krug, 100-101
Hera, 179
Himyarite Kingdom, 239-240
Hitti, Dr. Philip K., 51
Hodeida, 10, 235, 247, 249, 251, 253
Hofuf, see Oases
Holmes, Major Frank, 100
Horses, 77-78, 150, 178
Hosmon, Dr. Sarah Longworth, 196
Hotels, 105, 202
Housing, 65, 148, 164, 176, 207; see also Al Kharj and Aramco
Hukra, see Tribes
Humeid, Rashid ibn (Sheikh of Ajman), 178
Hunting, 78-79
Hussein, Abdullah al (late King of Jordan), 7, 30-31
Hussein al Hamid ad Din (Prince of Yemen), 262, 266-272, 277-278

Ibn Majid, 159
Ibn Saud, see Abdul Aziz ibn Saud
Ibrahim al Hamid ad Din (Prince of Yemen), 277, 279
Ikhwan, 29, 33-34, 151; see also Religion
Imam of Yemen (late), see Yahya ibn Mohammed al Hamid ad Din; (present), see Ahmed al Hamid ad Din
Imports, 9, 12, 65, 161-162, 164-165, 177, 204
Incense, 199, 220, 231-233, 236-237; see also Frankincense and myrrh
Indians, 141, 174, 195, 202-203, 207
Ingrams, W. H., 222, 225
International Bechtel Corporation, 3, 7, 104, 121
Iraq Neutral Zone, 152
Iraq Petroleum Company, 99-100, 123
Iraqis, 195
Irrigation, 58-59, 61, 65, 218, 223, 253

Islam, *see* Religion
Italians, 107, 265

Jabir, Rahmah ibn, 171
Jaluwi, Abdullah ibn, 28, 91, 129
Jaluwi, Amir Saud ibn, 69, 91-92
Jarab, 30
Jawasmis, 171-173, 180
Jebel Masna'a, 256
Jebel Nuqum, 258
Jews, 141, 202-203, 207, 217, 261
Jidda, 2-15
Jidda Agreement, 110-111
Jiddawis, 13
Jubaila, 43, 101
Judaism, 240

KLM (Royal Dutch Airlines), 114
Kaaba, 96-97
Kamaran Island, 11, 211
Kanats, 130
Khalifah, Sir Salman ibn Hamad al
    (Sheikh of Bahrein), 100, 122, 149
Khor al Batin Channel, 173-174
Khormaksar, 202, 206
Khuraiba, 221
Kibsi, Sayyid Hussein al, 246
Kidd, Captain, 170, 203
King Saud, *see* Saud al Saud
Knabenshue, Paul, 192
Koran, 95-96
Kuria Muria Islands, 211
Kuwait, 150-169; government, 150-151,
    168-169; history, 150-152, 159-160;
    oil, 163-166; population, 150, 164
Kuwait Neutral Zone, 152-153, 165
Kuwait Oil Company, Ltd., 163, 168

Labor, 65; *see also* Workers
Lahej, 213-215
Languages, 228-229
Lapenta, Dr. Rocco G., 267
Law, 35, 55-56, 71, 228, 267
Lawrence, T. E., 6, 30, 78
Legations, 6, 34
Lermitte, Basil, 177
Lith, 10
Locusts, 61, 87
Luheiya, 235

Ma'alla, 208
Ma'bar, 247, 257
McClure, Cpl. William P., 266
McKnown, Col. William, 273-274
Madriga, 22
Magwa, 164
Mahad Dhahab, 20, 23-25
Ma'in, 237

Maktum, Said ibn (Sheikh of Dibai),
    175-176
Manakha, 242
Manama, 140
Manners and customs, 15, 25, 46, 84-
    88, 90-92, 155-156, 178, 193, 207,
    216, 229, 258
Manwakh, 137
Maqainama, 131
Marbat, 233
Marib, 220, 238, 240-241, 245, 275
Marrat, 43
Marriage, 94, 230-231
Masirah, 187
Masjid-I-Suleiman, 99
Massoud, Mohammed Effendi, 270, 272
Matrah, 162, 196
Mecca, 4, 11, 38, 95, 220
Medical facilities, 9, 107-109, 148-149,
    167, 191, 193, 197, 211, 218, 222, 229
Medina, 21, 95
Medinat al Abid, 256
Military, 44, 206-207, 250
Milk, 86
Miller, Bert, 100-101
Mina al Ahmadi, 164, 166
Minaean Kingdom, 232, 237
Minerals, 16
Mining, 24-25
Minor, Harold, 115-116
Mirages, 73, 180
Missionaries, 190, 196
Miteb, Abdul Aziz ibn, 83
Mocha, 235
Mohammed (the Prophet), 11, 13, 21,
    26, 38, 77, 95
Mombasa, 158-159
Moose, James S., Jr., 4-5, 192
Moser, Charles K., 210, 242-243
Moslems: Shi'a and Sunni, 141, 236,
    255
Motion pictures, 14-15, 24
Motor vehicles, 12, 14, 20, 101, 103,
    121, 174, 226
Mount Shumshum, 202
Muhajir, Ahmed al, 223-224
Muhammad, Saqr ibn (Sheikh of Ras al
    Khaima), 180
Muharraq, 140-141
Mukalla, 156, 222
Muscat, 184-200; history, 184-191; pop-
    ulation, 195-196
Music, 6-7, 215, 250, 254
Mutahhar, Qadi Abdul Karim, 266, 270-
    271
Mutahhar al Hamid ad Din (Prince of
    Yemen), 262, 278, 279
Muwaih, 41

Nafud, 42-43, 74
Nafud al Sirr, 42-43
Nahas, Col. Jack N., 266
Naifa, 132, 135
Najran, 138, 276
Nakhodas, 143-146, 153-163
Near East Development Company, 123
Negroes, 144, 174, 182, 195, 249
Neibuhr, Carsten, 241
Nejd, 42
Netherlands Trading Society (Dutch Bank), 10
Noah's Ark, 208
Numaila, 131

Oases: Asfan, 21; Buraimi, 182; Hofuf, 29, 58, 69, 90; Jabrin, 130; Khurma, 30-31; Qatif, 69, 109; Sulaiyil, 137-138; Turaba, 32; Wadi Fatima, 7
Oil, 89-90, 99-124; exploration, 100-101, 116, 163, 166; off-shore, 121-122; production, 110-111, 116-124, 147-148, 165; refineries, 104, 116, 148, 205; royalties, 101-103, 110-111, 149, 165-166, 169
Oman, 170, 181, 191
Omar, Saleh ibn (Sultan of Hillin), 215
Oqair, 152
Ostrich, 131, 136
Owen, Garry, 6

Pacific Western Oil Company, 165-166, 168
Pakistanis, 141
Palaces, 13, 44-45, 67, 199, 216, 227, 264
Palestinians, 107
Palmer, Dr. Alfred W., 246-247
Park, James Loder, 244-245
Pearling, 143-150, 174-175
Persian Gulf, 155, 170
Persians, 141, 150, 174-175, 180, 195, 202-203
Petroleum Concessions, Ltd., 177
Petroleum Development Qatar, 123
Philby, H. St. John B., 8, 30, 100, 129-137, 241
Phillips, Wendell, 241
Piers, 102, 117, 120-121
Pilgrims and pilgrimage, 7, 10-11, 96-97, 115, 211
Pipe lines, 116, 119-120
Pirates, 170-173, 203-204
Pliny, 170, 231
Polo, Marco, 170, 203, 209-210
Port Sudan, 10
Ports, 10, 140, 164, 180, 202, 235
Portuguese, 4, 209-210

Princes: Saudi Arabian, 39; Yemeni, 262, 272

Qariya, 138-139
Qasim, Saqr ibn Sultan al (Sheikh of Sharja), 178
Qataban, 237, 241
Qatar Peninsula, 123, 129
Qishn, 233
Quarantine, see Tor and Kamaran
Queen of Sheba, 208, 238

Raghib Bey, Qadi, 264-266, 268-269, 274
Railroad, 39, 117-119
Ramadan, 96
Ramlat al Shuait, 133
Ranatl Bani Maaradh, 138
Randolph, John, 192
Ras al Hadd, 162, 198
Ras al Khaima, 172, 180
Ras al Masandam, 171
Ras al Mish'ab, 102, 120
Ras Baraka, 173
Ras Kantor, 174
Ras Tanura, 102, 104-105, 107, 113, 117
Rashidis, 28, 31, 151
Raswan, Carl, 76
Red-Line Agreement, 163
Religion, 13, 24, 29, 32-33, 37-38, 95, 96, 110, 207-208
Rice, 86
Rihani, Ameen, 243, 265
Riqji, 34
Rirbar, 255
Riyadh, 12, 44-45, 57
Roads, 22, 41, 116, 139, 164, 174, 227, 254, 256-257
Roberts, Edmund, 185-188
Rogers, David, 53, 60-63
Roosevelt, Franklin D., 5, 59, 118, 194
Rub al Khali, 43, 74, 125-139
Rugs, 9
Russia, 151
Ryan, Sir Andrew, 34

Sabaean Kingdom, 232, 237-238
Sabah, Abdullah ibn Salim al (Sheikh of Kuwait), 169
Sabah, Sir Ahmed al Jabir al (late Sheikh of Kuwait), 152, 165, 169
Sabah, Mubarak ibn, 151
Sabkha Matti, 173
Saham, 196
Saihut, 233
Sailors, 154-163
Saiun, 227
Salalah, 199

Salt, 129, 205, 245
Samam, 128
San'a, 235, 240, 242, 258-265, 277- 279
Saud al Saud (King of Saudi Arabia), 2, 46-57, 66; tour of United States, 48-54
Saudi Arabia, 1-139; foreign policy, 56; government, 35-36; history, 4, 27-32, 34-35; population, 80, 235
Saudi Arabian Airlines, 14, 114-115
Saudi Arabian Mining Syndicate (Sams), 2, 15, 20, 23-25
Sayyaghi, Qadi Abdul Rahman ibn Ahmad al, 251
Sayyids, 223-224
Seer Beni Yas, 173
Seiynn, Sultan of, 219
Servants, 10, 45, 91, 94
Shabwa, 238
Shaif, Ali ibn Ali (Sheikh of Dhala), 217
Shakespear, Captain W. H. I., 30
Shamailiya Mountains, 180-181
Shanna well, 127, 133
Sharia, see Law
Sharif, see Tribes
Sharja, 177-179
Sheikh of Abu Dhabi, see Sultan, Shakbut ibn
Sheikh of Ajman, see Humeid, Rashid ibn
Sheikh of Bahrein, see Khalifah, Sir Salman ibn Hamad al
Sheikh of Dhala, see Shaif, Ali ibn Ali
Sheikh of Dibai, see Maktum, Said ibn
Sheikh of Kuwait, see Sabah, Abdullah ibn Salim al; see also Sabah, Sir Ahmed al Jabir al; Sabah, Mubarak ibn
Sheikh of Oman, see Taimur, Suleiman ibn
Sheikh of Qatar, see Thani, Ali ibn Abdullah al
Sheikh of Ras al Khaima, see Muhammad, Saqr ibn
Sheikh of Sharja, see Qasim, Saqr ibn Sultan al
Sheikh Othman, 202
Sheikhs, 224
Shibam, 227
Shihr, 227
Shinana, 29
Shipbuilding, 153-154, 208
Sib, 196
Sidon, 106, 120
Singing sands, 127, 132-133
Sitrah, 140
Skinner, E. A., 100
Skyhook, 121
Slaves, 157-158, 182, 224

Smuggling, 154, 157-158
Snyder, Harry, 110
Socony-Vacuum Oil Company, 101, 124
Socotra Island, 208-211, 233
Solomon, King, 17, 208; mines, 16-26
Somalis, 157, 202-203, 207
Standard Oil Company of California, 100, 147-148
Standard Oil Company of New Jersey, 101, 123-124
Stark, Freya, 227, 231
Storrs, Ronald, 6
Sulaiyil, 134-135; see also Oases
Suleiman, Sheikh Abdullah, 3, 11-12, 36, 59, 67, 69-70, 90
Sultan of Haushabi, see Surur, Mohammed ibn
Sultan of Hillin, see Omar, Saleh ibn
Sultan of Lahej, see Abdali, Amir Ali ibn Abdul Qarim al
Sultan of Muscat, see Busaid, Said ibn Taimur al
Sultan of Qishn and Socotra, see Afrar, Khalifah al
Sultan, Said ibn (early Sultan of Muscat), 184-185, 188, 193
Sultan, Shakbut ibn (Sheikh of Abu Dhabi), 175-176
Suqs, 8, 10, 93, 147, 175, 178, 186, 205-206, 228, 251, 260
Surur, Mohammed ibn (Sultan of Haushabi), 216
Syrians, 202-203

Taif, 15, 21, 55-60, 69
Taimur, Suleiman ibn (Sheikh of Oman), 192
Ta'izz, 246, 279
Tannous, Dr. Afif, 63
Tarim, 227, 233-234
Tarsisi, Dr. Adnan, 273
Tarut Bay, 116-117
Tea, 25; see also Manners and customs
Technical training, 24, 37, 53-54, 106, 110, 114, 149
Tents, 82, 85
Texas Company, 100, 148
Textiles, 9
Thani, Abdullah ibn Qasim al (former Sheikh of Qatar), 124
Thani, Ali ibn Abdullah al (Sheikh of Qatar), 122, 124
Thesiger, Wilfred, 125, 137-139
Thievery, see Law
Thomas, Apostle, 209
Thomas, Bertram, 125-129, 198
Thompson, Major, 212
Thoms, Dr. William Wells, 197

Thubs, 23, 87
Tihama, 235
Timna, 237-238
Tor, 11
Trade, 156-157, 175, 204; *see also* Imports *and* Exports
Trans-Arabian Pipe Line Company (Tapline), 119-120
Trans World Airways, 114
Transportation, 11, 34, 41, 44, 73, 77-78, 101, 257
Treaties, 33, 142, 172-173, 184-186, 219, 221-222
Treaty of Jidda, 33
Trees, 64, 195, 216, 223, 256
Tribes: Ajman, 83, 130, 182; Anizah, 81-82; Arabdar, 80; Beni Hajir, 173; Beni Qitab, 174; Beni Yas, 173, 176; Buhaih, 130; Duwasir, 173; Hadbar, 81; Harb, 82; Hukra, 81; Humumi, 224; Jawasmi, 171-173; Karshin, 210; Manasir, 83-84, 129, 173, 181-182; Manshil, 129; Murra, 127-129; 173; Mutair, 83; Nizar, 181; Nuwah, 224; Ruwala, 82; Sa'ar, 129; Sabini, 224; Shammar, 28, 83; Sharif, 80; Utubi, 150; Yaman, 181
Trucial Coast, 170-183; government, 173, 178; history, 170-173; population, 173-174
Tumuli, *see* Archaeology
Turks, 27-29, 151, 202-203, 220
Tuwaiq Mountains, 43, 58
Twitchell, Karl, 5, 16, 59, 100, 244-245
Twitchell, Mrs. Karl, 16, 38

Ubar, 126, 132
Ulema, 33-35
Umm al Qaiwain, 179-180
Umrah, 96
United Nations, 12, 276
United States agricultural missions, 5, 59, 62-63
United States diplomatic missions to Yemen, 246-247, 247-271, 272-276
United States Government, 122
Uthmaniyah, 113

Wabar, *see* Ubar
Wadi Dawasir, 136, 138
Wadi Dhahar, 261
Wadi Du'an, 221, 223, 231
Wadi Fatima, 69
Wadi Hadhramaut, *see* Hadhramaut
Wadi Hamma, 22
Wadi Sahba, 130
Wadsworth, George, 6
Wahhab, Mohammed ibn Abdul, 27
Wahhabis, 27-29, 32, 38, 129, 151, 172
Walking stone, 131
Warfare, 29-32, 34, 78; *see also* Feuds
Water, 7, 20, 58-59, 65, 68, 86, 92, 128, 133, 140, 164, 175, 208; *see also* Irrigation
Wathen, A. L., 5, 59
Wazir, Abdullah al, 276-277, 279
Wazir revolt, 277-279
Weather station, 67
Wedj, 10
Wellsted, James R., 221, 241
Women, 13-15, 68-69, 71, 85-86, 93-94, 153, 156, 188, 230-231, 255
Workers, 62, 64, 107-109, 111-112, 148, 207
World War I, 2, 4, 29-30, 192, 204
World War II, 103-104, 197, 204
Wrede, Adolph von, 221

Yafa'is, 224
Yahya ibn Mohammed al Hamid ad Din (late Imam of Yemen), 16, 214, 242-243, 245-246, 265-272
Yanbu, 10, 239
Yarab, 80
Yarim, 239
Yemen, 235-279; government, 277; history, 236-242; industry, 258; population, 235

Zabeid, 247
Zaidi, 255
Zanzibar, 159-162
Zofar, 239, 273
Zwemer, Rev. Peter J., 190